D1625796

C334303637

JOHN CONNOR is Senior Lecturer and Head of the Humanities Research Group at the University of New South Wales, Canberra. He is one of Australia's leading military historians and has published widely on World War I. His previous books include *The Australian Frontier Wars, 1788–1838*.

'John Connor's accessible and illuminating reinterpretation of World War I presents that conflict as a fundamentally imperial phenomenon. This was a war fought and ultimately won not only in France, Belgium and Palestine, but in East Africa and New Guinea; in the Indian and Pacific Oceans as well as the Dardanelles and the North Sea; and on the farms of the Canadian prairie, the cattle ranches of Argentina and the sheep stations of Australia, as surely as in the munitions works of Britain. *Someone Else's War* is a capacious global history of a crisis poorly understood if viewed through a Eurocentric lens.'

Frank Bongiorno, Professor of History,
The Australian National University

SOMEONE ELSE'S WAR

FIGHTING FOR THE BRITISH EMPIRE IN WORLD WAR I

JOHN CONNOR

I.B. TAURIS
LONDON · NEW YORK

Published in 2019 by
I.B.Tauris & Co. Ltd
London • New York
www.ibtauris.com

ISBN: 978 1 78453 270 3
eISBN: 978 1 78672 543 1
ePDF: 978 1 78673 543 0

A full CIP record for this book is available from the British Library
A full CIP record is available from the Library of Congress

Library of Congress Catalog Card Number: available

Typeset by Initial Typesetting Services, Edinburgh
Printed and bound in Great Britain by TJ International Ltd.

Dedicated to my partner in life, Karen Costello,
without whose continued love and support this book
could not have been written.

In memory of my grandfather, William Boyles, Sydney tram mechanic.
Demoted for taking industrial action in the Australian Great Strike
of August–September 1917, he would not regain his original position
until the Labor Party was returned to government in the
New South Wales state election of June 1925.

Contents

List of Illustrations   ix

List of Tables   xiii

Acknowledgements   xv

Map   xix

Introduction – The British Empire and World War I   1

1   1914: The *Emden* in the Indian Ocean   9

2   Shipping, Trade and Rationing   29

3   1915: The Three Battles of Aubers Ridge, France   53

4   Making Munitions   79

5   1916: The East African Campaign   113

6   Dissent   131

7   1917: The Battle of Messines   154

 8   Volunteers and Conscripts   176

 9   1918: The Battles of Amiens and Megiddo   201

10   Farmers and Agriculture   227

     World War I Timeline   249

     Notes   269

     Select Bibliography   317

     Index   331

List of Illustrations

Map   Map of the world with modern state boundaries, showing   xix
      the extent of the British Empire in 1914

Chapter 1
1914: The *Emden* in the Indian Ocean

1.1   Pre-war postcard of Seiner Majestät Schiff (His Majesty's   10
      Ship) *Emden*, one of the warships of the German East
      Asian Squadron based at Tsingtao in northern China. From
      September to November 1914, Captain Karl von Müller's
      cruiser captured 24 merchant ships in the Indian Ocean,
      shutting down trade with disastrous effects for the Indian
      economy. Image: Sea Power Centre – Australia.

1.2   His Majesty's Australian Ship *Sydney*, commanded by   28
      Captain John Glossop, defeated the *Emden* at the Cocos
      (Keeling) Islands on 9 November 1914. Glossop told the
      naval authorities in Ceylon (modern Sri Lanka) that his ship
      should not be cheered when it entered Colombo harbour
      out of respect for the surviving German sailors. Image: Sea
      Power Centre – Australia.

Chapter 2
Shipping, Trade and Rationing

2.1   The Aberdeen Line's *Themistocles* in Cape Town harbour. In   40
      1916, the UK government closed the Mediterranean Sea to
      transiting shipping due to the success of German submarine
      operations. The return voyage from Britain to Australia via
      South Africa now took six months. Image: Academy Library,
      UNSW Canberra, Papers of the Doug Robertson Maritime
      and Naval History Collection MS 126, Robertson Box 235,
      5, *Themistocles*.

2.2   The *Clan Macewen* of the Cayzer, Irvine Line survived   49
      the war, but the company lost 28 ships to U-boats. Image:
      Academy Library, UNSW Canberra, Papers of the Doug
      Robertson Maritime and Naval History Collection MS 126,
      Robertson Box 151, 1 Clan Macewen.

Chapter 3
1915: The Three Battles of Aubers Ridge

3.1   Indian soldiers, including these men of the 2nd Rajput Light   69
      Infantry armed with a French Benét–Mercié machine gun,
      played a significant role in the 1915 battles around Aubers
      Ridge. Image: UK Ministry of Defence 103991.

3.2   French troops putting on an early version of a gas mask.   78
      Chemical weapons were used by both sides in 1915. Image:
      UK Ministry of Defence 104053.

Chapter 4
Making Munitions

4.1   Women and men worked long hours in Canadian munitions   88
      factories to make artillery shells. Dorothy Stevens, *Munitions
      – Heavy Shells*, etching, *c.*1918. Image: Beaverbrook
      Collection of War Art, Canadian War Museum, Musée
      Canadien de la Guerre 19710261-0686.

4.2   Canadian soldiers searching ruins following the Halifax   110
       explosion. Image: Library and Archives Canada/Biblio-
       thèque et Archives Canada PA-000704.

Chapter 5
1916: The East African Campaign

5.1   Nigerian troops with ambulance, German East Africa.   119
       Image: Imperial War Museum Q 15614.

5.2   German askari prisoners of war, Llembule, German East   130
       Africa. Image: Imperial War Museum Q 34474.

Chapter 6
Dissent

6.1   Captured Irish Republican with British Army guard in the   140
       aftermath of the Easter Rising, April 1916. Image: Imperial
       War Museum HU 55529.

6.2   Workers in the blast furnace of the Steel Company of   144
       Canada, Hamilton, Ontario, 1918. Image: Library &
       Archives Canada/Bibliothèque et Archives Canada MIKAN
       227609 A024645.

Chapter 7
1917: The Battle of Messines

7.1   British Royal Engineers mining and counter-mining   167
       beneath Messines. General Sir Herbert Plumer ordered
       the excavation of 21 deep mines at Messines. Some were
       completed and filled with explosives more than a year before
       the battle took place. Image: UK Ministry of Defence
       110689.

7.2   New Zealand troops' rehearsal for the assault on   169
       Messines Ridge on 7 June 1917. The success of the attack
       demonstrated the increasing expertise of British Empire
       troops with accurate artillery support in capturing German

positions. Image: Alexander Turnbull Library, Wellington, New Zealand 1/2-012752-G.

Chapter 8
Volunteers and Conscripts

8.1   The domineering General Sam Hughes arriving in France   180
       to visit Canadian troops, 1916. Image: Library and Archives
       Canada/Bibliothèque et Archives Canada PA-022744.

8.2   Australian anti-conscription flyer 1917: 'The Death Ballot.   192
       Polling Day, December 20. Vote "No"'. Image: Museums Victo-
       ria, https://collections.museumvictoria.com.au/items/ 1769514.

Chapter 9
1918: The Battles of Amiens and Megiddo

9.1   German soldiers killed in the Allied offensive at Amiens,   216
       9–11 August 1918. Image: UK Ministry of Defence 103636.

9.2   Indian troops played a significant role in the final stages of   220
       the Middle East campaign. Image: Tom Baker Collection,
       Australian Army History Unit, 11.24.50.

9.3   Canadian soldiers with German prisoners of war, August   225
       1918. By September, the German Army was disintegrating.
       Image: UK Ministry of Defence 104566.

Chapter 10
Farmers and Agriculture

10.1   Victorian Farmers Union Conference, Melbourne University   231
       Hall, 26 September 1915. By November 1917, the VFU
       had become a major political force in state politics. Image:
       Museums Victoria, https://collections.museumvictoria.com.
       au/items/768315.

10.2   Canadian farmer parties gained strength in the period   235
       immediately after World War I. Canadian wheat harvest, 20
       August 1918. Image: Library & Archives Canada/Biblio-
       thèque et Archives Canada MIKAN 3337605, a046043-v8.

List of Tables

2.1	United Kingdom Food Supply, 1917	30
2.2	British Empire Shipping Losses, 1914–18	46
3.1	First British Army Ammunition Stocks and Usage, 10 March 1915	65
3.2	British Empire Casualties, Neuve Chapelle, 10–12 March 1915	66
3.3	British Empire Casualties, Festubert, 15–25 May 1915	73
4.1	UK Female Employment, 1914–18	86
4.2	Irish National Factories Munitions Production, 1915–18	90
4.3	Canadian Artillery Shells Exports, 1914–18	107
5.1	East African Force, November 1918	126
6.1	British Empire Military Executions 1914–22	148

6.2   Courts Martial as a Percentage of Total Number of   148
       Troops, 1914–20

7.1   British Empire Casualties Messines, 1–12 June 1917   172

8.1   British Empire Total Enlistments, 1914–18   177

9.1   German Offensives 1918   207

9.2   Ottoman Army, September 1918   222

9.3   Egyptian Expeditionary Force, November 1918   223

10.1   Irish Wheat, Oats and Potato Production in Acres,   237
       1914–16

Acknowledgements

This book could not have been written without the assistance of many people. At Bloomsbury Publishing, Jo Godfrey, Sophie Campbell and Carolann Young patiently and painstakingly brought the idea of the book into a reality. I thank the Canberra campus of the University of New South Wales for providing me with a UNSW Canberra Academic Startup Research Grant in 2007, a UNSW Early Career Researcher Grant in 2008, and a Special Studies Program in 2012 which enabled me to conduct the bulk of the United Kingdom archival research. This research trip was abruptly truncated for the happiest of reasons when my eldest daughter Claudia was joined by her little sister Claire, who was born in Canberra four weeks premature on 25 October.

I express my gratitude to the expert and helpful staff at a wide range of archives, libraries and museums. In Australia, the UNSW Canberra Library was always my first port of call, and revealed many hidden gems, including a small cache of letters and papers by George McMunn, author of *The Armies of India,* and the vast photographic collection of the Doug Robertson Maritime and Naval History Collection. To this must be added the other great national institutions in Canberra: the Australian War Memorial, the National Archives of Australia, and the National Library of Australia, including its magnificent collection of private papers and digitised newspapers. I thank the Western Australian Branch of the Australian Labor Party for granting me access to their papers held at the J.S. Battye Library of West Australian History in Perth.

In the United Kingdom, research took me to the British Library, the Cayzer Archives, the Imperial War Museum – where accessing the private papers of Sir Henry Wilson was made easy, thanks to the detailed catalogue of the General's correspondence compiled by the late Professor Keith Jeffery of Queen's University, Belfast – the Liddell Hart Centre for Military Archives at King's College London, The National Archives and the National Maritime Museum in London. I also visited the Bodleian Library in Oxford, the Churchill Archives Centre in Cambridge and the Wiltshire and Swindon History Centre in Chippenham. I must thank Kate Lamb and Gareth Mitchell for all their generous hospitality over many years.

In Ottawa, I researched at Library and Archives Canada/Bibliothèque et Archives Canada, and Canadian War Museum/Musée Canadien de la Guerre; in Wellington, Archives New Zealand/Te Rua Mahara o te Kāwanatanga, and in Dublin, the National Library of Ireland/Leabharlann Náisiúnta na hÉireann.

I thank the following institutions and individuals for generously providing images without charge: Dr Andrew Richardson of the Australian Army History Unit, Greg Swinden of the Sea Power Centre – Australia, and the National Library of New Zealand/Te Puna Mātauranga o Aotearoa. Susan Ross and Dr Tim Cook at the Canadian War Museum/ Musée Canadien de la Guerre helpfully guided me through their image ordering process.

Many of the ideas and arguments incorporated in this book originated and were developed in seminar and conference papers at a diverse range of venues. These include 'Australia, empire and the Great War' presented at the Menzies Centre for Australian Studies, King's College London in October 2012, 'World War I, farmers and elections' presented at UNSW Canberra in May 2013, 'The British Empire and the Great War: Colonial Societies/Cultural Responses' conference at Nanyang Technological University, Singapore, in February 2014, the 'Conscription Conflict and the First World War' workshop, funded by the Academy of Social Sciences in Australia, at the University of Melbourne in April 2015, and the 'Military Education and Empire 1854–1918' conference at the Royal Military College of Canada, Kingston, Ontario, in November 2015.

In 2016 and 2017, I was fortunate to be the Australian team leader of an Australia–Germany Joint Research Cooperation Scheme/Deutscher

Akademischer Austauschdienst (DAAD) grant entitled 'The First World War, 100 Years on: Transnational cultures of remembrance in interdisciplinary comparison'. This project brought together my UNSW Canberra colleague Dr Christina Spittel and doctoral candidate Tom Sear in collaboration with Prof. Oliver Janz, Dr Andrey Zamoisky, Dr Michael Elm, Martin Bayer and Nicolai Burbass of Freie Universität Berlin. Hosting our German colleagues in Canberra, where they encountered the uncritical commemorative culture of the Anzac Day dawn service at the Australian War Memorial, and then having the opportunity to contrast this interpretation with the brutal reality of conflict in the exhibits of the Militärhistorisches Museum der Bundeswehr in Dresden was an education in itself. Working with Professor Janz and his colleagues and students broadened my understanding of the Great War and its aftermath and influenced the writing of this book.

I must thank the community of scholars with whom I discussed various aspects of the book. These include Dr Robin Archer (London School of Economics), Dr Kate Ariotti (University of Newcastle Australia), Prof. Ian Beckett (University of Kent), Prof. Frank Bongiorno (Australian National University), Prof. Carl Bridge (King's College London), Prof. Joy Damousi (University of Melbourne), Prof. Brian Farrell (National University of Singapore), Prof. Richard Grayson (Goldsmiths, University of London), Dr Ian Henderson (King's College London), Dr Spencer Jones (University of Wolverhampton), Prof. Jennifer Keene (Chapman University, California), Dr Jenny Macleod (University of Hull), Assistant Prof. John Mitcham (Duquesne University, Pennsylvania), Dr David Monger (University of Canterbury, New Zealand), Dr William Mulligan (University College, Dublin), Prof. William Philpott (King's College London), Prof. Jan Rüger (Birkbeck, University of London), Prof. Gary Sheffield (University of Wolverhampton), Dr Richard Smith (Goldsmiths, University of London), Prof. Ian van der Waag (Stellenbosch University) and Dr Peter Yule (University of Melbourne). Before his sudden death on 26 July 2016, I had many insightful discussions with Prof. Jeffrey Grey – the first non-American to become President of the Society for Military History – in the morning tea-room chats in the School of Humanities and Social Sciences which doubled as an unfailing and thought-provoking history seminar.

Finally, I must thank all my colleagues at UNSW Canberra. Prof. Shirley Scott has been a supportive Head of School. I need to acknowledge the constant assistance of Bernadette McDermott, Marg McGee, Shirley Ramsay and Eric Zhang, without whom the School of Humanities and Social Sciences could not function. I thank Ricardo Banos of the UNSW Canberra Creative Media Unit for creating the map of the British Empire in 1914. In particular, I must express my deepest admiration to the indomitable members of the History Discipline: Emeritus Prof. Peter Dennis, Dr Richard Dunley, Dr Elizabeth Greenhalgh, Associate Prof. Eleanor Hancock, Dr Debbie Lackerstein, Dr Tom Richardson, Dr David Stahel, Prof. Peter Stanley and Prof. Craig Stockings, currently at the Australian War Memorial as the Official Historian of Australian Operations in Iraq, Afghanistan and East Timor. Over the last three years, the History Discipline has faced the challenge of maintaining the teaching programme as historians who left or retired were not replaced. Through all of this, it remained united and maintained collegiality. My colleagues even enabled me to take internal release from teaching in the second half of 2017 in order to complete the writing of this book, an act of generosity for which I will be eternally grateful. To perhaps steal a phrase from Dr Richard Dunley, our new naval historian, we have endured stormy seas and now look forward to calmer waters.

BRITISH EMPIRE IN 1914

UNITED KINGDOM

Gibraltar

NEWFOUNDLAND

CANADA

BR. HONDURAS

Bermuda

Bahamas

Jamaica

St Lucia
Barbados
Tobago
Trinidad

BRITISH GUIANA

Falkland Is

Malta

Cyprus

Aden

GAMBIA

SIERRA LEONE

GOLD COAST

NIGERIA

Ascension

St Helena

EGYPT

SUDAN

UGANDA

BR. SOMALILAND

KENYA

Laccadives

Seychelles

Zanzibar

NYASALAND

Mauritius

RHODESIA

BECHUANALAND

Walvis Bay

BASUTOLAND

SOUTH AFRICA

INDIA

BURMA

Wei Hai Wei

Hong Kong

Ceylon

Maldives

Chagos

Singapore

Cocos Is

FED. MALAY STATES

BR. BORNEO

NEW GUINEA

AUSTRALIA

Gilbert Is

Ellice Is

Solomon Is

Fiji Is

Tonga

Norfolk Is

NEW ZEALAND

Map of the world with modern state boundaries, showing the extent of the British Empire in 1914

Introduction –
The British Empire and World War I

From Aden to Zanzibar, World War I affected the lives of almost every person across the British Empire. More than 8.5 million men would volunteer or be conscripted to fight the Central Powers of Austria–Hungary, Bulgaria, Germany and the Ottoman Empire in bloody campaigns that spanned the globe. Of these, 2.8 million British Empire soldiers would be killed or wounded.[1]

When the war began in August 1914, recruiting was initially limited to mostly – but not entirely – white soldiers from Britain and Ireland, the self-governing Dominions of New Zealand, South Africa, Newfoundland, Canada and Australia and the 'martial races' of the Indian Army. However, following the unprecedented losses of British Empire lives on the Western Front during 1915, Andrew Bonar Law, the United Kingdom Colonial Secretary, called in October of that year for 'raising troops in large numbers in our Colonies and Protectorates for Imperial service'. Recruiting was broadened to include an increasing number of non-white troops from Africa, the Caribbean, New Zealand Maori, Canadian First Nations and Indigenous Australians. From December 1916, most British Empire troops employed in the East African campaign were black Africans. By the time of the Ottoman surrender in October 1918, four-fifths of the divisions in the Egyptian Expeditionary Force included Indian units.[2]

The soldiers who made the longest journey to take part in the war were 500 Polynesian volunteers from Niue and the Cook Islands in the South Pacific who served with the New Zealand Expeditionary Force (NZEF). However, when they arrived on the Western Front in early 1916, their exposure to the bitter northern European winter weather resulted in over half the Niue contingent being admitted to hospital. By May, they were being repatriated to their tropical home.[3]

Across the Empire, supporters of the war contended with those opposed to involvement in the conflict, the continuation of the colonial connection, and individuals enduring harsh wartime economic conditions. In April 1916, the withdrawal of troops from Bongo in the West African colony of Gold Coast led to a local revolt that was quashed by a military punitive expedition that killed almost 60 people. At the beginning of August 1917, tram mechanics in Sydney went on strike to oppose the introduction of time cards that would calculate how many hours each employee worked. The tram mechanics' cause struck a chord with workers across the country and led to what economic historian Peter Yule described as 'the most serious and prolonged industrial action [. . .] in Australian history'. Seventy-six thousand workers across three of the six Australian states walked out in sympathy. The depressed economy forced other men to take jobs as non-union strike breakers, one of whom was killed. By the time the strike ended in September, 2.5 million man-days and 1.7 million pounds in workers' wages had been lost. The New South Wales government, having defeated the workers, installed their time clocks in the Sydney tramway workshops.[4]

The British Empire was the greatest political entity the world had ever seen, and it would expand even further at the end of the war with the annexation of German colonies and Ottoman Empire territory. The 1911 census calculated that the British Empire had a population of 424,133,076. This exact number offered a comforting façade of scientific accuracy that, like many other aspects of the Empire, did not reflect a more ramshackle reality. The inhabitants of Sarawak in Borneo went uncounted, the population of British Somaliland was an estimate, and the Gold Coast census figure was subsequently admitted to be an undercount.[5]

The British Empire was a complex collection of political entities that ranged in scale from India, with a population over 250 million inhabitants, which King George V ruled as a separate realm with the title of Emperor of India, to the tiny, storm-tossed Ascension Island in the South Atlantic, administered by the Admiralty and inhabited by a scattering of Royal Marines and sailors.[6]

The monarchy was identified as the central foundation of Empire. George V was crowned on 22 June 1911, following the death the previous year of his father, Edward VII. The mystical aura that surrounded the monarchy at this time was reflected in British journalist Philip Gibbs' dreamlike vision of the coronation; he wrote of the new monarch:

> He is the central, lonely figure of the great drama which has been a year in preparation. He is the most powerful King on earth, who in a little while has to receive the symbols of his power, to be anointed in the pretty office of kingship, to be consecrated to the people. His people!

During the anointing ceremony, Gibbs imagined the King hearing the whispered advice of previous kings crowned in Westminster Abbey: Edward the Confessor, William the Conqueror and Charles I. After the ceremony, he heard 'the tumult of a nation's enthusiasm, and in his heart the fire of great love for all the people of whom he is the Chief'.[7]

The coronation was celebrated in various ways across the ethnically diverse Empire. In the Straits Settlements, made up of the ports of Malacca, Penang and Singapore in Southeast Asia, the population of 714,069 consisted mostly of Malays, Chinese and Indians. Colonies generally lacked fully democratic institutions. The Straits Settlements' government consisted of a governor, Sir Arthur Young, appointed by the Colonial Office, an unelected executive council of senior officials and a legislative council of appointed members with two men nominated by the Singapore and Penang Chambers of Commerce.[8]

In the week leading up to the coronation, prayers for the King were offered in churches, temples and mosques. The Singapore *Straits Times* patriotically proclaimed:

> We speak in many languages, follow many creeds, represent various types of civilisation, and possibly also, a few degrees of barbarity. But we are all loyal to the Flag that waves over us, because we know that

it represents as near an approach to the perfect theory of equality and justice as any human institution of our time can reach.[9]

An anonymous *Straits Times* journalist described the Singaporean coronation parade:

> Afterwards came the long, weird procession, formed by the Chinese, Malay and Indian communities [. . .] Those who have never witnessed such a display of native rejoicing must have marvelled greatly at the quaint costumes and mannerisms of the actors in the performance. Here were bold warriors with their sundangs and tombaks; there were flashes of light from grotesque lanterns; elsewhere rumbled along a decorated car carrying little girls and a big silver crown. There, the jumpy Chinese dragon would shamble along, followed by illuminated paper fish resting contentedly on poles held by youngsters who took a pride in their special clan. Further along one would me[e]t an electrically illuminated Singhalese bungalow with live inhabitants pummelling away on drums, or instruments resembling drums [. . .] But everything appeared to harmonise or should have done so in view of the strangeness of it all.

However, it was clear that the journalist was oblivious to the significance of the dances and the music he had observed. He concluded: 'If only one knew what it meant there would be an interesting story to tell.'[10]

The self-governing Dominions – Australia, Canada, Newfoundland, New Zealand and South Africa – sent their prime ministers to London to witness the coronation and attend the Imperial Conference. The Dominions determined their own internal governance, but the United Kingdom government conducted foreign policy on behalf of the entire Empire. This meant that if Britain went to war, the Dominions were at war, though they could – and would – determine the extent of their contribution in time of conflict.[11]

As part of the conference, Sir Edward Grey, the British Foreign Secretary, briefed the Dominion ministers on foreign policy in a closed meeting of the Committee of Imperial Defence on 26 May 1911. Grey outlined to his audience the decline in British–German relations. He stated that it was now 'apparent that our relations with Russia and France were better than our relations with Germany'.[12]

The Foreign Secretary's comments marked a significant shift in the United Kingdom's external relations. Britain and France had come close to war over colonial claims in Africa in 1898, but London and Paris had ended their territorial disputes with the signing of the 'Entente Cordiale' or 'friendly agreement' on 8 April 1904. Berlin objected to the increasing French influence in Morocco and threatened to go to war with France. The most significant outcome of what became known as the First Moroccan Crisis was that the French and British armies began discussing in early 1906 how they might work together in the event of a war with Germany.[13]

The Second Moroccan Crisis arose at the beginning of July 1911, about a month after the Imperial Conference. Like the first, it was a dispute between Germany and France over control of Morocco. David Lloyd George, Chancellor of the Exchequer in H.H. Asquith's Liberal government, publicly stated on 21 July that the United Kingdom would not stand aside in the event of a war between the two continental powers. He asserted:

> I would make great sacrifices to preserve peace. I conceive that nothing would justify a disturbance of international good will except questions of the greatest national moment. But if a situation were to be forced upon us in which peace could only be preserved by the surrender of the great and beneficent position Britain has won by centuries of heroism and achievement, by allowing Britain to be treated where her interests were vitally affected as if she were of no account in the Cabinet of nations, then I say emphatically that peace at that price would be a humiliation intolerable for a great country like ours to endure.

Once more war was averted, but in August Brigadier Henry Wilson, the Director of Military Operations, told Home Secretary Winston Churchill:

> In my opinion a war between ourselves and Germany is as certain as anything human can be. If it does not come today it will tomorrow or the next day, and in all probability it will come at a time which suits Germany and not us.[14]

From 8 to 12 July, King George and Queen Mary visited Dublin, 'the second city in the Empire'. Ireland was a divided society with two communities. The first was the Catholic majority that was mostly – but not entirely – demanding Home Rule with the creation of a separate parliament in Dublin. The second was the Protestant minority that was mostly – but not entirely – demanding to remain part of the United Kingdom. Irish nationalists protested and distributed leaflets, but the royal visit was not disrupted. The King visited St Patrick's College, the Catholic seminary and degree-granting college of the National University of Ireland, at Maynooth, west of Dublin, where he was hosted by Daniel Mannix, the College President and future Archbishop of Melbourne who would become a strident opponent of conscription in Australia. This would be the only time a reigning British monarch visited Ireland while the entire island was completely part of the United Kingdom.[15]

On 11 November, the King and Queen began their last major task of the coronation year: sailing to India to take part in the Durbar (royal court) in Delhi. They arrived at Bombay on 2 December, and travelled by train to Delhi. Here the royal couple met men and women of the Indian elite. The Durbar took place on a plain near the Jumna (Yamuna) river. At its heart was a dais with a marble platform with two thrones made of solid silver covered in gold. There was an inner circular amphitheatre for princes and dignitaries, and a larger outer amphitheatre that could seat 10,000 people. George wore the Crown of India – the £60,000 cost having been borne by Indian taxpayers – which, having been worn once, was returned to London and placed in the Tower of London.[16]

The King announced at the Durbar on 12 December that the province of Bengal – controversially partitioned on religious lines in 1903 by the then-Viceroy, Lord Curzon – would be reunited, and that the Indian capital would be moved from Calcutta to Delhi. The Maharaja Gaekwar of Baroda, second in rank among Indian rulers, turned his back on the King-Emperor and Queen Empress when departing the pavilion. This apparently deliberate snub caused outrage in Britain and led to demands for the Maharaja's removal.[17]

The Indian Army was considered one of Britain's 'great strategical assets', due to its large size and military competence. Following the great mutiny of 1857, recruiting for the Indian Army shifted to take considerably fewer men from the Hindu majority and more from non-Hindu ethnic minorities, particularly Punjabi Muslims and Sikhs, in the belief they would be less likely to revolt. A pseudoscience of 'martial race theory' was developed to justify this new recruiting practice. George MacMunn argued that, unlike in Europe, where all males can become soldiers, 'in the East, with certain exceptions, only certain clans and classes can bear arms; the others have not the physical courage necessary for the warrior'. This assertion would be proved false when the Indian Army expanded without declining in military effectiveness during World War I.[18]

The United Kingdom general election of December 1910 had resulted in Prime Minister Herbert Asquith retaining power with the support of John Redmond's Irish Parliamentary Party. As part of the parties' agreement, the government introduced an Irish Home Rule Bill to Parliament in spring 1912. Tragically, Home Rule supporters did not offer concessions that might have eased the concerns of Ulster Unionists. Instead, the Ulster Volunteer Force was created in January 1913 to oppose Home Rule, and Nationalists established the National Volunteers in November. It has been argued that the outbreak of World War I prevented the outbreak of an Irish civil war in 1914. When Asquith gave a speech in Dublin on 26 September, the London *Times* reported the 'spectacle of Irishmen of both parties fighting shoulder to shoulder will gladden the whole Empire and smooth the way, we trust, for a better understanding afterwards'. But, as Keith Jeffery points out, the intervention of conflict actually prevented the finding of 'an accommodation in Ireland' in 1914, and resulted in extremism and decades of conflict.[19]

On 28 June 1914, Archduke Franz Ferdinand, heir to the throne of Austria–Hungary, was assassinated in Sarajevo by Gavrilo Princip. Many senior political and military figures in Austria–Hungary feared the rise of nationalist movements that would lead to the break-up of the multi-ethnic empire. General Franz Conrad von Hötzendorf, the army chief, had called for a pre-emptive war with Serbia on several occasions, but had been denied by Franz Ferdinand. Ironically, the Archduke's death opened the way for the Serbian invasion he had always opposed.[20]

On 5 July, Count Alexander Hoyos of the Austro-Hungarian Foreign Ministry visited Berlin and gained Kaiser Wilhelm's support for a punitive war on Serbia, once the army returned at the end of the month from their annual leave to bring in the harvest. The Kaiser told Ladislaus de Szögyény-Marich, the Austro-Hungarian ambassador to Germany, that if Vienna 'really recognised the necessity of warlike action against Serbia, then he would regret if we did not make use of the present moment, which was so favourable for us'.[21]

The ultimatum was presented in Belgrade on 23 July. Although the Serbian government accepted almost all of the demands, Austria–Hungary declared war on Serbia on 28 July. Gunboats in the Danube began the bombardment of Belgrade the following day. On 31 July, on the order of President Raymond Poincaré, French troops withdrew ten kilometres from the border 'to show the public, and the English Government, that France will not, under any circumstances, be the aggressor'. Elsewhere, the situation swiftly deteriorated. Tsar Nicholas II ordered the general mobilisation of the Russian Army – the largest military force in Europe. Germany responded on 1 August by declaring war on Russia.[22]

Berlin's strategy, known as the Schlieffen or Moltke Plan, put most of the German Army in the west with the aim of advancing through Belgium to quickly defeat France and then transfer the troops to the east to defeat Russia. On the evening of 3 August, the British sent an ultimatum to Germany warning Berlin not to invade Belgium. They did so the following day. When a second ultimatum expired at 11.00 pm on 4 August, the British Empire was at war. That night, the English writer John Galsworthy wrote in his diary: 'Belgium's neutrality violated by Germany. *We are in . . .* The horror of the thing keeps coming over one in waves; and all happiness has gone out of life.'[23]

Important Note

Regarding the term 'coloured': in South Africa in the early twentieth century, 'coloured' denoted a multiracial ethnic group, with mixed ancestry, who identified as neither 'white' nor 'black'. This definition was based not only on physical characteristics but also on family history and cultural practices. The term is retained in this book in its historical context.

1

1914: *The* Emden *in the Indian Ocean*

The Great War came to India on the balmy tropical night of
22 September 1914, when the German cruiser *Emden* sailed undetected
into the harbour of Madras (modern Chennai). D.S. Bremner, a journalist
with the *Madras Mail*, was travelling to his newspaper office to prepare the
next day's edition when, around 9.30 pm, the *Emden* suddenly announced
its presence by illuminating the night sky with its four searchlights.
Bremner told his Indian driver to halt his horse-drawn carriage, jumped
out and made for the esplanade. He had not travelled far when the *Emden*,
having located the Burmah Oil Company's facility north of the city, began
firing its starboard broadside of five 4.1-inch (105-millimetre) guns at the
six enormous white fuel tanks. Almost immediately, a 'column of flame
sprang into the sky' as two tanks containing kerosene exploded. Bremner
ran to the beach alongside three soldiers of the Royal Dublin Fusiliers, two
on foot and a third in a rickshaw pulled by an Indian man. Here they saw
the German cruiser, made visible by the glow of its searchlights, sailing
at full steam in the harbour. The *Emden* had fired about 130 shells at the
fuel tanks when the guns of Fort St George began their tardy reply around
10.00 pm. At this, the *Emden* extinguished its searchlights, silenced its
guns and, shielded by darkness, slipped out of the harbour and escaped
unscathed to the open sea.[1]

When Bremner finally made his way back from the beach towards
the *Madras Mail* office, he came across a man who 'was explaining the

situation' in Tamil to a gathering crowd. The journalist did not detail how this man was making sense of the unexpected and unprecedented event, but we do know why Karl von Müller, the *Emden*'s 41-year-old captain, carried out the attack.[2]

Von Müller reported that he bombarded Madras 'as a demonstration to arouse interest among the Indian population, to disturb English commerce, to diminish English prestige'. His aim was to destroy British property but spare Indian lives. He decided to target the Burmah Oil Company tanks because the *Emden*'s gunners could fire at them while minimising injury to civilians in a city of half a million inhabitants. The German raid destroyed two fuel tanks holding 346,000 gallons (some 1.5 million litres) of kerosene worth 180,700 rupees, but killed only five men – a Burmah Oil security guard, three Indian policemen, and a British merchant sailor in the *Chupra* moored in the harbour – and wounded only 12 people: Indian women and men and British men.[3]

Fig. 1.1 Pre-war postcard of Seiner Majestät Schiff (His Majesty's Ship) *Emden*, one of the warships of the German East Asian Squadron based at Tsingtao in northern China. From September to November 1914, Captain Karl von Müller's cruiser captured 24 merchant ships in the Indian Ocean, shutting down trade with disastrous effects for the Indian economy.
Image: Sea Power Centre – Australia.

The success of the raid on Madras led the German Foreign Office to propose that the *Emden*'s next exploit should be to liberate two radical Indian nationalists, Vinayak Damodar Savarkar and Hemchandra Kanungo Das, imprisoned in an isolated penal colony for violent acts against British authority, and secretly return them to India to lead an armed revolt. However, the difficulties in successfully carrying out such an elaborate scheme meant it was soon abandoned.[4]

There would be no rebellion in India in 1914, but the *Emden*'s raid was certainly seen by many Indians as a blow to British prestige. The day following the attack on Madras, thousands of the city's inhabitants went to the shoreline to observe the flames rising from the burning fuel tanks and spent the day looking out to sea in the hope of seeing the *Emden*, an indication they did not fear the German warship's return. In the Province of Bihar and Orissa, just to the west of Bengal, it was pointed out that '[t]he little cruiser's raid [. . .] did not pass unnoticed even among the classes which might not be supposed ordinarily to regard the war as a personal affair'. The Calcutta *Statesman* warned of 'quite unnecessary but mischievous panic' unless the Government of India was 'able to reassure the public and are aided in their efforts by the leaders of Indian opinion'. In the inland Bengali town of Purulia the *Emden*'s attack led to a run on the local savings bank. In Rangoon (now Yangon, Myanmar), W.H. Barton, proprietor and publisher of the *Times of Burma*, believed that the attitude towards the British 'among the native residents in the quarter where his office was situated' had declined so much that he deemed it necessary to break censorship regulations – for which he would face court and plead guilty – and 'published information regarding the dispositions of one of His Majesty's ships and also with reference to the pursuit of the Emden' in an attempt to salvage the reputation of the British administration.[5]

The *Emden*'s presence in the Bay of Bengal had a disastrous effect on the Indian economy. Within hours of the attack on Madras, British authorities closed the Bay of Bengal to merchant traffic. Indian trade in September 1914 was 44 per cent lower than September 1913; in October, trade would be 61 per cent down on the same month the previous year. Ships clogged the ports. In Colombo in Ceylon (modern Sri Lanka), the harbour filled to capacity and 15 merchant ships had to be anchored outside the breakwater. Marwari financiers, who provided short-term loans to Indian importers, had no business. They abandoned the eastern ports of Calcutta and Madras (Kolkata and Chennai) to wait out 'the slack time' at their homes in the western princely states of Rajputana.[6]

The halt to shipping in the Bay of Bengal had a devastating effect on trade of all kinds. Most serious was the effect on jute, India's highest-earning export. Mostly grown in Bengal, 90 per cent of the crop was exported either as raw jute or as fabric – called gunny – for bags and sacks to hold wheat and other commodities. In the 1913/14 financial year there were 64 jute mills, mostly in Calcutta, with over 36,000 looms and employing a daily average of 216,000 workers. Jute exports to the United Kingdom alone were worth £10 million.[7]

The war began just as the jute harvest commenced in Bengal. Australian wheat farmers needed gunny to arrive in Australia in September for wheat bags to be manufactured in Sydney, Melbourne and other cities in time for the harvest at the end of the year. However, the merchant ships allocated for this cargo had been requisitioned in August by the Government of India to transport Indian soldiers westwards to Europe and other locations. In early September, the Calcutta *Capital* noted that jute bags were 'accumulating to an enormous extent' in the city and warned:

> If this condition continues much longer it means curtailing pro-duction, as it will be absurd to manufacture goods which cannot be delivered. The attendant evils, such as short time, which would reduce the consumption of jute, and the possible closure of mills, which would throw labour out of employment and make for discontent and distress.[8]

When the *Emden*'s raid shut down shipping in the Bay of Bengal in late September, Calcutta jute mill owners did not cut production and lay off workers. Instead, they increased production, keeping their factories working six days a week rather than the usual five. The Calcutta *Capital* commented on 8 October: '[e]ven to the man in the street it seems a suicidal policy for mills here to increase their production when the bulk of it is going into their goods godowns'. No reason for keeping jute manufacture at such high levels was provided. There had been industrial disputes in the jute mills in August, and it may have been that the mill owners feared that sacking large numbers of workers in the atmosphere created by the *Emden*'s incursion would lead to protests and riots.[9]

The shipment of jute fabric from India to Australia, having been postponed in August because of the Indian Expeditionary Force convoys, was again delayed in September due to the *Emden*. Australian buyers invoked the clauses in their contracts to cancel their purchases. Lord Hardinge, the Viceroy of India, sent a telegram on 14 October to Sir Ronald Munro Ferguson, the Australian governor-general, pointing out the 'present stagnation of trade at Calcutta and shipping crisis caused by raids of Emden' and pleading to Australian businessmen to keep to their contracts and wait for shipping to be resumed. W. Freeman Nott, Secretary of the Melbourne Chamber of Commerce, replied that wheat farmers required that the 'bags shall be to hand at a certain season of the year, and unless they are promptly received, the season itself is lost'. Frederick Winchcombe, his equivalent in Sydney, simply stated 'it will be impossible' to meet the viceroy's request.[10]

Why was there a German warship off the coast of India in the second month of World War I? It must be remembered that in 1914 Germany had a small colonial empire scattered across Africa, the Pacific Ocean and China (it would lose all these colonies at the end of the war). This empire consisted of Togo and Kamerun (Cameroon) in West Africa, South West Africa (Namibia) and German East Africa (Rwanda, Burundi and mainland Tanzania); German New Guinea (Papua New Guinea), Samoa and Nauru in the South Pacific; the Karolinen (Caroline), Marshall and Marianen (Marianas) Islands in the North Pacific; and the northern China enclave of Kiautchou (Jiaochow).[11]

The *Emden* was based in Tsingtao (Qingdao), the main city in Kiautchou, and home port of the German Navy's East Asian Squadron. This consisted of the light cruisers *Emden*, *Leipzig* and *Nürnberg* and the large armoured cruisers *Scharnhorst* and *Gneisenau*. When the United Kingdom declared war on Germany on 4 August, the *Emden* was the only German cruiser at Tsingtao. It departed the next day to join the rest of the squadron, which had been undertaking its annual tour of the German Pacific island colonies, and arrived eight days later at Pagan in the Marianen Islands. On 13 August, Vice Admiral Maximilian von Spee, the squadron commander, held a conference of his captains to decide on a strategy for their wartime operations. German naval planning for a war with the British Empire had envisaged that the East Asian Squadron would conduct a campaign of economic warfare by attacking merchant ships carrying Australian exports to the United Kingdom, such as wool – necessary for making military uniforms – and wheat – vital to sustain a British population reliant on imported food.[12]

Von Spee decided that his cruisers could not implement this plan. This was because eight months previously, in October 1913, the battlecruiser *Australia*, flagship of the newly created Royal Australian Navy, with its brand new supporting cruisers and destroyers, had arrived in Sydney. The *Australia* was newer, faster and had larger guns than the *Scharnhorst* and *Gneisenau*. As von Spee wrote in a letter to his wife Margareta on 18 August: 'The English Australian Squadron has as flagship the "Australia", which alone for the Cruiser Squadron is such a superior opponent that it must be avoided.' Von Spee was also anxious to distance himself from the Japanese Navy, which had two modern battlecruisers, the *Ibuki* and *Kurama*. Japan had a treaty of alliance with Britain, and would declare war on Germany on 23 August. The German admiral therefore decided the entire squadron should sail eastwards across the Pacific Ocean, away from Australia and Japan, and operate off South America, where his ships could be resupplied with coal from neutral Chile.

Von Müller disagreed with von Spee's plan. He conceded that it would be impossible to operate all the German ships off East Asia, Australia or India, but argued that deploying one light cruiser in the Indian Ocean would have economic effects on shipping and political effects in India. The other captains and officers supported the idea, and von Spee directed von Müller to sail the *Emden* and the collier *Markomannia* to the Indian Ocean to attack merchant shipping 'as best you can'. That evening all the German ships departed Pagan. The next morning, *Emden* and *Markomannia* left the convoy and headed for the Indian Ocean. The East Asian Cruiser Squadron sailed towards the coast of Chile, where, on 1 November, it fought and defeated some obsolete British cruisers at the Battle of Coronel. Von Spee then sailed around Cape Horn into the South Atlantic where, on 8 December, he and his ships confronted two modern British battlecruisers, the *Invincible* and the *Inflexible*, and six smaller warships in the Battle of the Falkland Islands. The *Scharnhorst*, *Gneisenau*, *Leipzig* and

Nürnberg were outgunned and outnumbered and all were sunk (the cruiser *Dresden*, which had joined the squadron from deployment off Mexico, was the only German ship to survive the battle). Von Spee and hundreds of his sailors were killed in the battle.[13]

As the East Asian Squadron headed towards South America, the *Emden* and its collier journeyed unnoticed across the Pacific Ocean, and threaded their way through the islands of the neutral Netherlands East Indies (modern Indonesia). On 5 September, the two German ships entered the Indian Ocean north of Sumatra. Von Müller set a course to intersect the major Colombo–Calcutta shipping route in the Bay of Bengal just south of Madras. On 9 September, the German light cruiser began a six-week campaign which would result in the capture of 24 merchant ships with a combined gross tonnage of over 100,000, carrying cargoes worth £2.2 million.[14]

Why was the *Emden* able to cause so much physical damage and economic dislocation in India and its adjacent waters? Across the British Empire, people were at a loss to explain the German cruiser's string of successes. The London *Times'* naval correspondent speculated that Grand Admiral Alfred von Tirpitz was using the new technology of radio to directly control the movements of the *Emden* half a world away:

> The notion of Berlin being able to direct operations at such a distance is almost uncanny. If they do so, no more striking exhibition of the use of wireless in naval war could well be imagined. We may picture Von Tirpitz in his office in Berlin. He receives news of the situation in the Bay of Bengal and realizes the opportunity for a little *coup*. There is a cruiser a few miles away which has been carefully hidden until some such chance presented itself. He calls her up and gives information and orders. The raider does the rest.[15]

It is true that Germany did have a worldwide network of radio stations in 1914, but the secret of the *Emden*'s success was much simpler. It was based on three factors. First, there were at this time few Royal Navy warships in the Bay of Bengal and eastern Indian Ocean to trouble the German light cruiser: they were mostly in the western Indian Ocean escorting troopships from Bombay (modern Mumbai) towards Europe, Egypt and East Africa.

Second, the Indian Ocean's geography aided the *Emden* in finding prey: ships sailing towards the Bay of Bengal or Southeast and East Asia had to converge to the west of India at either the Eight Degree or Nine Degree channels, above and below Minikoi (Minicoy) Island, and at Dondra Head, on the southern tip of Ceylon. The Admiralty did warn merchant ship captains to keep away from the normal route where it was possible to do so, but most captains kept their ships on the usual track, or within a few miles of it, in order to save fuel and time. Third, most merchant ships in this period were coal-powered and their funnels belched big black clouds of smoke that were visible at some distance. All von Müller had to do to capture British ships was put a man in the *Emden*'s crow's nest, where, in clear weather, he could see for 30 miles (some 50 kilometres), sail in a zigzag pattern to 30 miles each side of the shipping route, and head towards smoke whenever it was seen on the horizon.[16]

The *Emden* began its campaign against British shipping in the Indian Ocean on the night of 9 September when it stopped the Greek steamer *Pontoporos* in the Bay of Bengal. Greece was at this time neutral, but the *Pontoporos* was carrying 6,600 tons of Bengal coal on a British government contract, so its cargo was a legitimate target for the German warship. Von Müller put an officer and some sailors aboard to supervise the Greek crew and had the ship follow the *Emden* and *Markomannia*. On 10 and 11 September, the *Emden* captured the *Indus* and then the *Lovat*. Both ships were sailing in ballast (without passengers or cargo) from Calcutta to Bombay, where they were to join a convoy carrying Indian soldiers and horses to the war. The master of the *Indus*, H.S. Smaridge, became the first, but not the last, British merchant ship captain who assumed the *Emden* was a British warship right up to the moment that he realised the sailors boarding his ship were wearing German uniforms. The crews of the *Indus* and the *Lovat* were transferred to the *Markomannia* and both ships were sunk.[17]

On 12 September, von Müller halted the *Kabinga*, but on finding its cargo was bound for the neutral United States, he could not sink the ship. Instead, he ordered it to accompany the *Emden* for the moment. On 13 September the Germans came across the *Killin*, carrying 6,000 tons of Bengal coal, the *Diplomat*, carrying 10,000 tons of tea, worth £250,000, and the *Trabboch*, sailing in ballast. All three ships were sunk.[18]

The *Emden* also stopped the neutral Italian merchant ship *Loredano*. Von Müller asked Captain Giacopolo to accept the crews and passengers of the ships he had captured and take them to Calcutta. The Italian captain refused and continued his journey. Von Müller then transferred all his temporary captives to the *Kabinga* and ordered the captain to sail to Calcutta. When the *Loredano* approached Calcutta, Captain Giacopolo sighted the *City of Rangoon* sailing towards him, at the commencement of its voyage, and sent a message by semaphore that there was a German cruiser in the Bay of Bengal. The *City of Rangoon* had a radio – still a rarity for merchant ships at this time – and broadcast the Italian captain's information. On receiving this alarming news, the Royal Navy immediately shut down all shipping in the Bay of Bengal.[19]

Ships that had left port were still in danger from the *Emden*'s depredations. Just before midnight on 14 September, Arthur Bray, Third Officer on the *Clan Matheson*, sailing from Madras to Calcutta, heard the sound of two warning shots aimed behind the stern of the ship. A radio message in Morse code ordered the captain, William Harris, to stop the ship. Harris had been informed in Madras that the Bay of Bengal was safe and the *Clan Matheson* was sailing with full lights.[20] A second Morse message told the captain to receive a boat from the warship. As Bray later wrote in a letter to his mother:

> we never thought for an instant that she was anything but British so we got a ladder & cluster light over side for the boat, which presently came alongside with some 20 men & 3 officers all armed to the teeth. As soon as I saw the sailors caps I knew they were Germans, so I shouted down & told the skipper who was on the lower bridge. All he said was 'My God'.[21]

The *Emden*'s sailors ordered the *Clan Matheson*'s crew to collect their personal possessions and depart the ship for the *Markomannia*. The *Clan Matheson* was carrying a cargo worth £8,725 including locomotives, cars and a racehorse. A German sailor euthanised the unfortunate creature with a single shot to the head before the ship was sunk in the early hours of 15 September.[22]

Bray found the Germans did as much as was possible to make him and his shipmates comfortable during their confinement on the *Markomannia*. Von Müller sailed his flotilla to the vicinity of Rangoon, where the *Emden* took on coal from the *Pontoporos*, the Greek ship carrying Bengal coal on a British contract, which had been the *Emden*'s first prize. Von Müller paid Indian sailors from the *Clan Matheson* to assist with the dirty and exhausting task of re-coaling at sea. He then ordered the *Pontoporos* to head for a certain point off Sumatra in the neutral Netherlands East Indies for a future rendezvous. On 17 September, the *Emden* came across the neutral Norwegian ship *Dovre* and put the *Clan Matheson*'s crew aboard it. They reached Rangoon on 19 September.[23] Bray was enraged by the *Emden*'s audacity. He wrote:

> It is a disgrace that a light cruiser like she is should be allowed to do what she did 20 miles off the Indian coast & right up at the head of the Bay of Bengal & then drop us off 20 miles off the mouth of the Rangoon River & get off scot free.[24]

On 22 September British authorities reopened the Calcutta–Colombo route because the *Emden* had not been sighted for some days. That evening von Müller bombarded Madras, and the Bay of Bengal was once more shut down for shipping.[25]

The *Emden* sailed southwards to Ceylon to resume attacks on British shipping in a new location. On 25 September the *Emden* sank the *King Lud*, sailing in ballast off Galle, the *Tymeric*, carrying £60,000 worth of sugar from Java for Britain off Colombo, and on 26 September stopped and retained the *Gryfevale*, sailing in ballast, where the Bombay and Aden routes to Colombo converged, to hold the two ships' crews detained the previous day.[26] On 27 September, the *Emden* captured three ships near Minikoi Island, on the route to and from the Suez Canal. Two ships, the *Ribera* and *Foyle*, were sailing in ballast and were sunk. The third was carrying what would be the *Emden*'s most mundane, but most important prize. This was the *Buresk*, a Burdick & Cook collier chartered by the Admiralty to carry 6,600 tons of South Wales coal for the Royal Navy at Singapore.[27] As Colonel Hubert Foster, the Director of Military Science at Sydney University, explained:

'Cardiff coal' [. . .] is superior in steam production and smokelessness
to any other. It thus gives warships using it the advantages of greater
speed and secrecy of movement, with less work on board, as it is hard,
clean, free-burning, and leaves little ash or clinker.[28]

The significance for the *Emden*'s crew was that the Bengal coal from the
Pontoporos they had previously been using was 35 per cent less efficient
than the South Wales coal they had just acquired.[29]

Von Müller placed the captured merchant seamen on the *Gryfevale*,
which set a course for Colombo. The *Emden*, accompanied by the
Markomannia and the *Buresk*, headed south to the Maldive Islands. On
29 September the *Emden* was coaled at a secluded atoll for the last time
from the *Markomannia*, whose supplies were almost expended. The faithful
collier was then sent to join the *Pontoporos* off Sumatra, with orders to take
as much of the Bengal coal as it could from this ship, and then allow the
Greek ship and its crew to go free. On 12 October this coaling was taking
place when the British light cruiser *Yarmouth* came across the two ships.
The *Markomannia* was captured and sunk, the 60 German sailors became
prisoners of war and the men of the *Pontoporos*, once more at liberty, sailed
for Singapore.

After bidding farewell to the *Markomannia*, von Müller sailed south
from the Maldives to the Chagos Archipelago. These islands lay across
a straight line drawn between Australia and Aden. The German captain
expected to find ships carrying refrigerated Australian meat to Britain, and
troopships that, having conveyed Indian Army units, would now be sailing
to Australia and New Zealand to embark their expeditionary forces. What
von Müller did not realise was that the main Australian shipping route
did not go direct to Aden, but via Colombo, and therefore the track he
was seeking was further to the north. After several fruitless days, in which
he did not see a single ship, von Müller continued southwards to Diego
Garcia, the main island of the Chagos Archipelago, a dependency of the
British colony of Mauritius.[30]

On 9 October the *Emden* and the *Buresk* arrived at Diego Garcia,
described in the *Colonial Office List* as a coral atoll 'nowhere over ten feet
high, but forming a spacious bay, roomy enough for large vessels to enter'.
The only regular shipping service to the island was a schooner that came

every three months: the last time the ship had visited was in late July. This meant that the 500 islanders did not know that Britain and Germany were at war. Von Müller naturally ensured that the locals remained in ignorance of this fact.[31]

The life of a sailor on the *Emden*, or any other Great War warship, consisted of an endless cycle of physical labour in an austere environment. The *Emden* was coal-powered, so one of the main tasks for the crew during their brief stay in Diego Garcia was to shift 475 tons of the *Buresk*'s precious South Wales coal to the *Emden*. The other major job was to scour the ship's hull of the marine plants and animals that had accumulated over the previous eight weeks. If not removed, these growths would reduce the *Emden*'s maximum speed by one knot.[32]

The German sailors also had to endure shortages of a wide range of items. Fresh water, as Dan van der Vat put it, 'was treated like gold'. The *Emden* had salt-water showers on deck for relief from the tropical heat, but sailors longed to wash in fresh water. This meant:

> Whenever a rain-squall was sighted and circumstances allowed, the officers of the watch would step up speed and steer for it while all those free to do so would strip naked and wash themselves in the rainfall; if the ship ran out of the squall or the rain simply stopped too soon, men would be caught covered in soap.[33]

When the *Emden* left Tsingtao after receiving news of the British declaration of war, soap was one important item that had been forgotten in the rush to prepare the ship for departure. Fortunately for the sailors, this deficiency was rectified on 10 September when the German cruiser captured the *Indus* carrying 150 cases of soap.[34]

Fresh food was another treasured item on ships lacking refrigeration. Many of the vessels the *Emden* captured had chickens, ducks, geese, cattle, sheep or pigs on board to provide fresh eggs, or to be slaughtered for fresh meat. In 1914 one third of the German population was engaged in agriculture, so enough of the *Emden*'s crew knew how to tend livestock and keep fowl. While at Diego Garcia, the crew caught fish in the atoll, while the local residents gave the visitors fruit, vegetables, and a live pig.[35]

The next day, the *Emden* and the *Buresk* departed from Diego Garcia, the sailors having made the most of their brief opportunity to be on dry land for the first time in two months. The two ships headed north; the *Emden* took more coal from the *Buresk* in the Maldive Islands, and returned to the major shipping route near Minikoi Island.[36]

In the early morning darkness of 16 October the *Emden* stopped the *Clan Grant*, sailing from Glasgow and Liverpool to Madras and Calcutta. This was followed through the day by the *Ponrabbel*, a dredger going to Australia to take up duties in the port of Launceston in northern Tasmania, and the *Benmohr*, travelling from Leith to Yokohama. The crews were moved to the *Buresk* and the ships were sunk. Two days later the *Emden* captured the Blue Funnel Line *Troilus* on its maiden voyage carrying 1,000 tons of Malayan tin as well as rubber and copper with an insured value of £130,000. Later that day came the *St Egbert* with a cargo for the neutral United States. On 19 October the *Emden* captured the *Exford*, carrying South Wales coal to Hong Kong under Admiralty contract for the Royal Navy, and the *Chilkana* bound for Calcutta. The nearly 600 captured crew and passengers from the seven ships were transferred to the *St Egbert*, except for 12 Chinese sailors who accepted a German offer to continue working in the *Exford* for their existing pay rate. The *St Egbert* set sail for Cochin in India, von Müller retained the *Exford* and its Welsh coal, and sank the *Troilus* and the *Chilkana*.[37]

The *Emden* now sailed to Penang on the west coast of Malaya. Von Müller had learned that warships of the various allied navies were using the port. There were no large guns or forts defending Penang, which made it possible for him to plan an audacious raid. The *Emden*, which had been painted dark grey and had a dummy fourth funnel made of wood and canvas erected so it would resemble a Royal Navy cruiser, entered the port on 28 October at 5.00 am. The Germans began firing their guns and launched a torpedo at the old Russian light cruiser *Zhemchug*. The Russian sailors had only a handful of shells on deck and barely fired a shot at the German cruiser. A British merchant seaman, W.M. Meager was in the *Nigaristan*, one of a row of merchant ships moored near the *Zhemchug*, when he was awoken by the gunfire and raced up on deck. He wrote: 'For the next 15 minutes we saw an actual Hell on Earth, in which were embodied the extremes of many emotions – desperate bravery, exaltation, hate, despair and terror. Of mercy there was none.' After sailing past the merchant ships and turning to head out of the harbour, at 5.28 am von Müller ordered a second torpedo to be fired at the *Zhemchug*.[38]

Meager witnessed the result:

> When the 'Emden' was nearly abeam of her victim, the final catastrophe happened. Suddenly from the forepart of the Russian an intensely riven column of light spurted up to a great height, spreading out towards the top. It vanished in a second, and was followed by a dull muffled report. (Not a bit loud, as one would imagine). Immediately a great cloud of dense smoke mercifully covered the horror from our sight. For a brief space there was an awesome silence followed by wild cheering on the German ship. It was terrible to listen to the Germans cheering at the death cries of their fellow men – for which they were responsible.[39]

Of the 340 Russian sailors and officers of the *Zhemchug*, 86 were killed and 114 were wounded – five of whom would subsequently die of their injuries. The Penang General Hospital was overwhelmed by the large number of casualties. Seven local doctors and 27 female volunteers worked desperately to dress the wounds of every wounded Russian sailor.[40]

The *Emden*, as it left Penang, stopped the merchant ship *Glenturret* carrying a cargo of ammunition with the intention of capturing it. The German plan was aborted by the approach of the French destroyer *Mousquet*. The larger guns of the German cruiser sank the smaller French destroyer within seven minutes. Von Müller sent out two boats that rescued 36 sailors from the *Mousquet*. These remained on the *Emden* until 30 October, when von Müller halted the British merchant ship *Newburn*, found it was carrying a neutral cargo, and transferred the French sailors to the ship so they could be taken to nearby Sabang in Sumatra to receive full medical treatment.[41]

On 31 October the *Emden* met with the *Buresk* off Sumatra and took on more coal. Von Müller decided that his next foray would be to attack merchant shipping in the western Indian Ocean near Aden and the Red Sea entry to the Suez Canal. Before doing so, he would first go to the Cocos (Keeling) Islands to destroy the radio station and cut the telegraph cable linking Australia to Britain. Severing these vital communication links would seriously affect the British Empire war effort. The *Nürnberg*, one of the *Emden*'s sister ships in the East Asian Squadron, had cut the telegraph cable connecting Australia to Canada at Fanning Island in the Pacific Ocean on 7 September 1914, and the link would not be restored until 1 November. Von Müller also believed the *Emden*'s appearance at the Cocos Islands would lead the British to assume the cruiser was intending to attack shipping in Australian waters and force them to spread their resources by deploying warships in this region. The German captain had already ordered the *Exford*, captured on 19 October and carrying South Wales coal, to wait for him just north of the Cocos Islands.[42]

So far, von Müller had been able to avoid British warships because the Royal Navy's East Indian Squadron was fully occupied in the western Indian Ocean escorting convoys carrying over 100,000 Indian troops to Europe, Egypt, East Africa and Basra in Mesopotamia (Iraq). The *Emden*'s sister ship *Königsberg*, based in German East Africa, posed a threat to the safe passage of all these convoys, as it demonstrated on 20 September, when it made a sortie to the nearby British protectorate of Zanzibar and sank the old British cruiser *Pegasus*. Each convoy therefore required an escort of warships, at least one of which had to be capable of defeating the *Königsberg*.[43]

The Government of India's inept actions had also assisted the *Emden*'s campaign. The Bay of Bengal had been closed to shipping after the raid on Madras, but authorities reopened all routes in the Bay of Bengal and to Colombo, Bombay and Karachi on 2 October even though they did not know the cruiser's location. The immediate outpouring of shipping from Calcutta and Colombo was immediately followed by the *Emden*'s capturing seven ships in three days off Ceylon. According to the *Times of India*, merchants complained, 'not because the Emden has not been captured but because the shippers have been misled into believing the routes safe'. When the cruiser *Hampshire* was transferred from the China Station to operate in Indian waters, its commander, Captain Henry Grant, had to tell the Government of India to stop sending him uncoded radio messages because the *Emden* could also hear them and use the information to avoid Grant's ship.[44]

The exploits of the *Emden* affected individuals across the British Empire beyond India. In Canada, New Zealand and Australia, von Müller's cruiser evoked fears for the safety of the convoys carrying their soldiers to war. Two days before the departure of the Canadian Expeditionary Force (CEF), Joseph Pope, the senior civil servant in the Department of External Affairs, expressed his concern to his son that 'a number of German Cruisers [. . .] would scour the North Atlantic and attack Canada as the Emden is at present attacking our possessions, ships and Commerce in the far East'. Canadian Prime Minister Robert Borden made a last-minute request to the British government to provide a larger naval escort for the CEF convoy that sailed on 3 October. When German submarines were sighted off the English south coast, the Canadian troopships had to be diverted on 14 October to the closest port of Plymouth.[45]

The New Zealand Expeditionary Force (NZEF) convoy of ten ships was originally to have sailed in late September from Wellington to the Western Australian port of Albany escorted by three obsolete *Pelorus*-class cruisers. However, when von Spee's Cruiser Squadron appeared in the South Pacific off Samoa on 14 September and bombarded Papeete in the French colony of Tahiti on 22 September, the New Zealand government became justifiably concerned for the convoy's security. On 2 October, Prime Minister William Massey wrote to his Australian counterpart, Andrew Fisher, that he and his Cabinet 'have felt a great deal of anxiety here with regard to the escort of the ships'. The Admiralty decided that the risk of the German squadron attacking the convoy meant that the NZEF transports required the escort of two modern cruisers, the British *Minotaur* and the Japanese *Ibuki*. When this decision was made, these ships were in the Indian Ocean searching for the *Emden*, and it would take them some time to sail to New Zealand. Lord Liverpool, the New Zealand Governor-General, believed the seriousness of the war situation meant the convoy needed to depart immediately. On 4 October, Liverpool made the extraordinary proposal to the government that he should – in his (ceremonial) role as Commander-in-Chief of the New Zealand military forces – take responsibility for making the decision for the convoy to sail before the British and Japanese cruisers arrived. Massey was aghast at the idea and threatened to resign as prime minister. Liverpool backed down. It was not until 16 October that the NZEF convoy, escorted by the *Ibuki* and *Minotaur*, left Wellington.[46]

The departure of the Australian Imperial Force (AIF) convoy led to a dispute between the Australian government and the AIF commander, Brigadier General William Bridges. Following the recommendations of a

1910 Committee of Imperial Defence report on the wartime transport of troops, which assumed British command of the sea, Bridges rejected the use of convoys and planned to send each ship individually, beginning with the slow-moving horse transports. Senator George Pearce, the Australian Defence Minister, however, took Admiralty advice and gained Cabinet agreement to delay the ships' departure until the *Ibuki* and *Minotaur* arrived with the NZEF convoy. Bridges told Pearce on 26 September that his decision was wrong, that there was little chance of German warships attacking the transports and that 'delay is in this, as in most, military operations, more dangerous than action'. The fear of the German cruisers was endemic among Australian decision-makers. Arthur Jose, Australian correspondent for the London *Times*, later wrote that Prime Minister Fisher 'had conjured up a picture of thirty thousand young untried men afloat, of enemy cruisers dashing in to sink them, of Australia, unused to war, shocked and angered'. Rear Admiral Sir William Creswell, the senior officer of the Royal Australian Navy, wrote on 26 October of the 'terrible damage' the *Emden* could do 'diving into a mass of 40 transports on a dark night'. It was therefore with some trepidation that the ten New Zealand and 28 Australian transports escorted by the British *Minotaur*, Japanese *Ibuki* and Australian *Sydney* and *Melbourne* sailed from Albany on 1 November.[47]

By the time the Australian and New Zealand convoy departed, Admiral Sir Martyn Jerram, Commander-in-Chief of the China Station, had far more naval resources at his disposal than when the *Emden* had commenced its campaign in early September. With the Japanese declaration of war, the *Ibuki* and *Chikuma* had been deployed to Singapore. After the *Emden*'s raid on Penang, Jerram was able to request more Japanese warships to search for the German cruiser in the Netherlands East Indies. Once the task of escorting the Indian Army convoys had been completed, British warships returned to the Bay of Bengal. In addition, four passenger ships in Hong Kong, the *Empress of Asia*, *Empress of Japan*, *Empress of Russia* and *Himalaya* had been taken over by the Admiralty on the outbreak of war and converted into Armed Merchant Cruisers. On 27 October, Admiral Sir Henry Jackson, Chief of Staff to Winston Churchill, the First Lord of the Admiralty, told his minister 'we are now starting a systematic hunt' for the *Emden* 'which will either bring her to destruction or more probably drive her into some other less dangerous theatre of operations'.[48]

The Canadian Pacific Steamships' *Empress of Asia*, which in peacetime sailed the Hong Kong–Vancouver route, was now armed with eight 4.7-inch (120-millimetre) guns manned by 20 artillerymen, including 22-year-old Gunner Edgar Mole who was stationed in Hong Kong with the Royal Garrison Artillery. Twenty-five sepoys from the 40th Pathans Regiment were also embarked to carry the ammunition to the guns. In August and September, the *Empress of Asia* patrolled between Hong Kong and Singapore. In October the ship sailed to Ceylon to operate in the Indian Ocean. Here, the Chinese stokers suffered an astonishing death rate: six died in ten days. On 8 October the *Empress of Asia* left Colombo, rendezvoused with the *Hampshire* and 'went scouting for the Emden'. The two ships sailed south and arrived at Diego Garcia on 15 October. Mole was a member of the party sent ashore. They questioned one of the islanders who told them of the *Emden*'s recent visit. Mole noted in his diary: 'They did not even know there was a war on and they only laughed at us when we told them.'[49]

On 8 November the *Emden* and the *Buresk* rendezvoused with the collier *Exford* just north of the Cocos Islands. The following morning the staff at the radio and cable station on Direction Island saw a ship sailing towards them. Realising that the *Emden*'s canvas fourth funnel was a fake and that it was a German warship, they immediately sent out a radio message that was received by the *Melbourne*, which was escorting the Australian and New Zealand convoy and was only 50 miles (80 kilometres) away. Captain Mortimer Silver in the *Melbourne* ordered Captain John Glossop in the *Sydney* to go to the islands to investigate, while the other warships remained to protect the convoy in case the *Emden* was accompanied by the *Königsberg*.[50]

As soon as von Müller realised there was a cruiser approaching, he took the *Emden* out to sea, abandoning the landing party who had brought down the radio mast and cut the telegraph cable to Australia. (These men would escape the islands on the schooner *Ayesha* and return to Germany by way of the Ottoman Empire.) Then began what the British naval historian Julian Corbett described as the 'unequal' battle between the *Sydney* and the *Emden*. The *Sydney* was newer, larger and faster than the *Emden*. The Australian cruiser's 6-inch (152-millimetre) guns with shells weighing 100 pounds (45 kilograms) had longer range and more destructive effect than the German cruiser's 4.1-inch (105 millimetre) guns with shells weighing 38 pounds (16 kilograms).

The *Emden*'s only chance for survival was to get in close to the *Sydney*, inflict early damage to slow down its foe and launch a torpedo to sink the Australian cruiser. Von Müller fired his guns first at 9.40 am, catching Glossop by surprise. The first salvo had the range of the *Sydney*; the second salvo hit its target. Fifteen German shells hit the *Sydney*, but only half exploded and none did major damage. Glossop manoeuvred the *Sydney* beyond the range of the *Emden*'s guns. Once the *Sydney*'s gunners found the range of the German cruiser at 9.50 am, they systematically wreaked destruction on the *Emden* and its men: at 11.20 von Müller ran the *Emden* onto a coral reef to save his crew. By this stage, the *Emden* was, as Able Seaman Richard Broome in the *Sydney* wrote in his diary, 'a total wreck, on fire from the bridge to the stern, all three funnels, foremast & bridge gone, all her guns silent'.

Of the 316 men aboard the *Emden*, 134 were killed in the encounter or subsequently died of wounds and 65 were wounded. The *Sydney*'s casualties were four killed or died of wounds and 11 wounded. Von Müller survived the battle unharmed. Glossop next went in pursuit of the *Buresk*: the German crew scuttled the collier and were then brought aboard the *Sydney*. That evening, Jerram ordered the *Empress of Asia* to depart from Colombo and sail at full steam and with no lights to the Cocos Islands. Mole wrote in his diary that the ship's engineers 'were standing over the Chinese stokers with loaded revolvers so as to keep them at work'. When the *Empress of Asia* reached the islands, Mole and the other British and Indian soldiers were sent ashore in a vain search for any fugitive German sailors.[51]

The battle between the *Emden* and the *Sydney* had been brutal and lethal. Its aftermath, however, was more in accordance with peacetime ideas of gentlemanly behaviour. Von Müller had gained the respect of the British because of his impeccable behaviour towards captured sailors and passengers. When Mole had gone on leave in Colombo in October, he 'met several seamen whose vessels had been sunk by the *Emden*. They were treated well and gave the captain a good name.'[52]

Glossop sent a radio message to Ceylon stating that the *Sydney* should not be cheered went it sailed into Colombo out of respect to the wounded German sailors now on board the Australian cruiser. When King George V

Fig. 1.2 His Majesty's Australian Ship *Sydney*, commanded by
Captain John Glossop, defeated the *Emden* at the Cocos (Keeling) Islands on
9 November 1914. Glossop told the naval authorities in Ceylon that his ship
should not be cheered when it entered Colombo harbour out of respect for the
surviving German sailors. Image: Sea Power Centre – Australia.

was informed of the defeat of the *Emden*, his immediate response was to
enquire whether von Müller and Prince Franz Joseph von Hohenzollern,
an officer on the *Emden* and distant relative to the British royal family,
had survived the battle. Churchill instructed that the *Emden* survivors were
'entitled to all the honours of war', and all officers 'should be permitted to
retain swords'.[53]

The *Times of India* commented on 14 November that the destruction
of the *Emden* 'has caused wide-spread satisfaction' and predicted a revival
in Indian business confidence. Large parts of the Indian economy would
continue to be adversely affected by the war. However, jute overcame
the difficulties of 1914 to become a commodity that remained in high
demand until the armistice in 1918. On the Western Front, the end of
1914 marked the beginning of trench warfare. Sandbags became essential
for constructing trench systems: Indian jute mills would manufacture
1.4 billion sandbags over the next four years.[54]

Shipping, Trade and Rationing

The *Emden* had demonstrated how vulnerable the British Empire's trade and shipping was in wartime. One small German cruiser had shut down all trade in the Bay of Bengal, resulting in economic distress across India and panic in the New Zealand, Canadian and Australian governments, in dread that enemy warships would attack their troop convoys.

The economies of every part of the British Empire relied, to a lesser or greater extent, on exporting and importing raw materials and manufactured goods. Most of this trade was carried by sea. The British merchant fleet was the largest in the world in 1914, and was four times larger than its nearest rival Germany's. Each year British trade required the carrying of over 150 million tons of cargo. There were 287,000 British merchant seamen in 1913: 209,000 white British subjects, 31,000 white non-British subjects and 47,000 non-white sailors of Chinese, Indian and other backgrounds. Racial prejudice determined sailors' wages: in April 1917 white sailors' monthly wages ranged from 170 to 200 shillings, but Chinese sailors were paid only 120 to 130 shillings.[1]

The British tradition of free trade meant the United Kingdom and the various components of the British Empire were as likely to trade with foreign states as they were to trade with other parts of the Empire. In 1913, only one quarter of British and Irish imports came from India, the dominions and colonies, and only one third of British and Irish exports stayed within the Empire.[2]

The 46 million people of the United Kingdom depended on food from overseas for 64 per cent of their calories.[3] The extent of the reliance on imports is shown in Table 2.1.

TABLE 2.1

UNITED KINGDOM FOOD SUPPLY, 1917[4]

	IMPORTED (%)	LOCALLY PRODUCED (%)
CEREALS	79	21
MEAT	40	60
BUTTER	64.5	35.5
CHEESE	80	20
EGGS	50	50
MARGARINE	49.5	50.5
VEGETABLES (NOT POTATOES)	36	64
FRUIT	73	27
SUGAR, COCOA, CHOCOLATE	100	0

This table understates the British reliance on imports, as a quarter of the fodder for British meat and dairy animals was imported. Equally significant was the trade in commodities. All cotton, silk, oil, rubber, jute and hemp was imported; three quarters of the annual consumption of wool was imported; and around two million tons of timber was shipped each year to provide props for Welsh and English coalmines.[5]

The United Kingdom traded with Europe where possible because it was closer and therefore quicker and cheaper to transport. Russian wheat shipped through the Black Sea and the Mediterranean was more convenient than wheat from Canada or Australia. Three quarters of British sugar imports in 1913 came from Austria–Hungary and Germany rather than the West Indies and Fiji.[6]

As J.A. Salter would write in 1921, World War I was, for Britain and Germany, 'a war of competing blockades, the surface and the submarine'. The Germans would implement unrestricted submarine campaigns in an attempt to sink sufficient merchant ships sailing for the United Kingdom that the population would be starved into submission. The Royal Navy established a cordon, enforced by armed merchant ships rather than warships as they were more stable in the often-stormy North Sea, to strangle German imports. British civilians would suffer occasional food shortages, especially in 1917, but hundreds of thousands of German civilians would die from the effects of long-term food scarcity. British Prime Minister David Lloyd George recognised the vital importance of wartime trade soon after he became prime minister in late 1916 when he stated that shipping 'has never been so vital to the life of the country as it is at present, during the war. It is the jugular vein, which, if severed, will destroy the life of the nation'.[7]

The war begins: rationing in British North Borneo

North Borneo was a territory of mostly tropical rainforest that the sultans of Brunei and Sulu had granted to the British North Borneo Company in 1881. Its estimated area of 31,000 square miles (80,300 square kilometres) was equivalent to that of Scotland. The United Kingdom government declared the territory (now the Malaysian state of Sabah) a British Protectorate in 1889, and took control of its external relations. Its internal administration, however, remained the responsibility of the seven-member Court of Directors of the British North Borneo Company, based in London. It was the Court of Directors who, with the Colonial Secretary's approval, appointed the governor. According to the 1911 census, the colony's population consisted of about 180,000 indigenous people, who mostly practised subsistence nomadic agriculture in the rainforests, and about 30,000 Chinese and 400 Europeans who mostly worked on tobacco and rubber plantations, mined coal at Cowie Harbour and were engaged in a growing trade in exporting timber to northern China.[8]

Norddeutscher Lloyd, a German shipping company, ran the weekly service from Singapore to British North Borneo that supplied all the food for the European community and half of the rice required by the Chinese community. When the war began, the German ships stopped sailing, and there was an immediate food shortage. Governor Cecil Parr introduced rationing and set a maximum price for rice to prevent profiteering.[9]

On 5 August 1914, J. West Ridgeway, Chairman of the British North Borneo Court of Directors, warned Sir John Anderson, the senior civil servant in the Colonial Office:

> North Borneo is in a precarious position as regards food [. . .] The prospect is appalling if the supplies for the Chinese Coolies – all 12000 – is entirely cut off and indeed apart from humanity the consequent catastrophe would [. . .] injure the prestige of the Empire in the East.

Anderson had an intimate knowledge of this part of the world as he had served in Singapore as governor of the Straits Settlements from 1904 to 1911. Ridgeway asked for the Colonial Office to 'instruct' Sir Arthur Young, the current governor, 'to do his utmost' to remedy the situation.[10]

The outbreak of war had caused a financial crisis in London, and the British government had imposed controls on the movement of funds outside the United Kingdom. This made it impossible for the British North Borneo Company to purchase food in Singapore and hire a vessel to transport it to North Borneo. Lord Harcourt, the Colonial Secretary, had to provide his personal approval for the Singapore branch of the Chartered Bank of India, Australia and China to pay £6,000 to the British North Borneo Company 'in order to meet the food requirements of the inhabitants of British North Borneo'. With this authorisation, the funds were made available and a few days later a ship arrived in North Borneo carrying rice and other foodstuffs to alleviate the shortages.[11]

A permanent solution was then devised. The North Borneo government's shipping agents in Singapore, Messrs. Guthrie & Co, and the Straits Settlements government worked together to enable the Straits Steamship Company to take over the Singapore–Borneo run. On 10 September, Sir Edward Grey, the British Foreign Secretary, agreed to requisition three German ships interned in Singapore so the Straits Steamship Company could charter them to service North Borneo.[12]

Nigeria: palm kernels and shipping cartels

It had been relatively simple to solve the shipping problem in the small colony of North Borneo. It would be far more difficult to overcome the effects of the wartime disruption to shipping and trade in Nigeria. This was for three reasons. First, Nigeria was the most populous British colony in Africa with about 17.5 million inhabitants. Second, a significant proportion of the African population, particularly in the south, grew crops such as cotton and cocoa for export to Europe. Third, much of this produce went to Germany on German ships.[13]

The most important export was the 'monarch of the Nigerian forest', the palm kernel that could be crushed to extract palm oil to make a high-quality margarine. About 80 per cent of Nigerian kernels – 131,886 tons, worth £2.4 million in 1913 – went to Hamburg, mostly carried in the ships of the Woermann-Linie group. Only Germany had sufficient specialised crushing plants to process such a large amount of kernels. With the outbreak of war, the market for Nigerian palm kernels collapsed: those landed in Liverpool from August to October 1914 were literally unsaleable.[14]

R.E. Dennett, Deputy Chief Conservator in the Nigerian Forestry Department, presented a lecture to the Royal Colonial Institute in London on 26 October 1914 entitled 'The war: British and German trade in Nigeria' that outlined the three requirements that Nigerian palm kernel producers would need to secure their future. These were: 'a line of steamers [. . .] to take the place of the German line which had run from Hamburg'; a new 'great seed-crushing centre [. . .] capable of taking and treating Nigeria's exports of palm kernels'; and the creation of a British market for 'palm kernel meal and cake' – the by-product of the oil extraction process that was used as animal feed.[15]

The British government immediately recognised that Nigeria's 'palm kernel difficulty is a serious one', and worked with British manufacturers to ensure that Dennett's second and third propositions were brought into reality. Lord Islington of the Colonial Office met with soap-makers Lever Brothers and the Liverpool and London Chambers of Commerce in August 1914 and discovered that there were only three small mills capable of crushing palm kernels in the entire United Kingdom. Fortunately, soap and margarine manufacturers expressed their willingness to order new machinery and construct large crushing mills. By 1915 Nigerian palm kernels that had previously gone to Germany were now being processed in factories in Liverpool, Hull and London.[16]

The West African Section of the London Chamber of Commerce issued a report in March 1915 on 'the question of the Palm Kernel Industry as affected by the War' which argued that the high cost of establishing new crushing plants meant that markets would need to be found for both palm oil and for crushed palm kernel cake as animal feed. German manufacturers had established a large market for palm kernel cake among European farmers. The small crushing mills in operation in Liverpool in 1914 had sold a small amount of palm kernel cake to Irish farmers, but their main market had been Germany and Scandinavia.[17]

The campaign to persuade British farmers to purchase palm kernel cake for their stock animals was carried out on two fronts. Professor Wyndham Dunstan, Director of the Imperial Institute in London, successfully lobbied the Board of Agriculture and Fisheries to produce a leaflet on palm kernel cakes that was issued in January 1915. This explained that the product was 'being brought prominently to the notice of stock holders as a result of the war' because 'hitherto practically all the palmnut kernels produced in Nigeria and other British Colonies [which] have been exported to Germany [. . .] have now been diverted to the United Kingdom'. Owen Phillips, Chairman of the London Chamber of Commerce, contacted the principals of British agricultural colleges in October 1914, for advice in 'getting farmers to take an interest in this matter'. Phillips found a general appreciation of 'the Imperial aspect of the question' and that 14 colleges had commenced trials to provide information to agriculturalists. He accurately predicted that 'Palm Kernel Cake will be welcomed by farmers as a new and useful feeding material, as soon as it is made known to them, and is commercially "pushed"'.[18]

By 1915, Nigerian palm kernels that had been exported to Germany were now being processed in Britain to make margarine, and British farmers were buying palm kernel cake for animal feed. But what of the third of R.E. Dennett's recommendations for extra British ships to be put on the West African route to make up for the withdrawal of German hulls?

This was never achieved. Nigerians suffered shipping shortages for the duration of the war. At the end of 1915 there were over 300 railway wagons clogging Nigerian railway yards loaded with palm kernels awaiting shipment. It is true that this occurred in many parts of the Empire. When Governor-General Sir Frederick Lugard informed Colonial Secretary Andrew Bonar Law of 'the absence of adequate shipping' in Nigeria, he acknowledged that his 'description no doubt does not differ materially from that which reaches you from many, if not most, of the Colonies at the present time'. What made the situation in Nigeria worse, however, was that the removal of the Woermann-Linie group's ships gave the British Elder Dempster group a virtual monopoly on the West African route. As well as this, the shutting down of German business in Nigeria meant that British trading companies and the French Compagnie Française de l'Afrique Occidentale now controlled the colony's export trade and formed cartels to use this power to their advantage.[19]

The colonial administration in Nigeria recognised that indigenous producers and traders had real grievances. Edward Harding in the Colonial Office commented on 1 January 1916:

> The position is very unsatisfactory, but it is difficult to see what can be done to improve matters. With the disappearance of German firms, there is, it would seem, a real danger of Nigerian trade falling into the hands of a ring of firms powerful enough to crush out opposition and to exploit Nigeria for their own personal profit.[20]

Both Elder Dempster and the cartel trading companies made huge profits from Nigerian exports during the war. Elder Dempster used its monopoly position to force a 40 per cent increase in the cost of transporting palm kernels between August 1914 and December 1915. The cartel companies retained their profit despite Elder Dempster's freight rises because they combined to force down the price that Nigerian producers received for palm kernels and other produce. The pre-war difference between the Lagos price and Liverpool price for palm kernels was between £4 and £5 per ton: in 1916 the difference in prices between Lagos and Liverpool had widened to £13. Palm kernels could be purchased in Nigeria for less than half the British selling price.[21]

Elder Dempster and the cartel companies colluded to prevent independent traders gaining access to shipping space. Archibald Cooper,

General Manager of Nigerian Railways, calculated in October 1916 that the cartel companies received 63 per cent of the available shipping. The remaining 37 per cent was divided between three groups of non-cartel traders: the British Cotton Growing Association (10.5 per cent), European companies (13.5 per cent) and African traders (13 per cent).[22]

In districts where the independent traders operated alongside the cartel companies, farmers received better prices as there was competition for their produce, but the independent traders found it difficult to get their goods exported. African merchants including Karimu Kotun, T.B. Dawodu and Moses Coker presented a petition to Lugard in July 1916, complaining that Elder Dempster allocated them only 350 tons of the 9,000 tons of available shipping space. In October, Samuel W. Duncan, Managing Director of the newly formed Association of Native Merchants told the governor-general: 'If we are unable to obtain the tonnage in the only steamers trading with Lagos, it means we are to become the slaves of the Combine or retire from business.'[23]

While Elder Dempster and the cartel companies amassed their profits, the Nigerian people suffered. The shipping shortage did lead to the development of local industries such as the manufacture of roofing tiles, and the establishment of a furniture factory in Lagos and a coal mine at Udi. However, it also meant the price of imports such as salt, kerosene and textiles increased by between 150 and 300 per cent. Harding in London noted in May 1916 that Nigerian revenue from import duties had fallen due to the 'reduction of the purchasing power of natives owing to the low prices paid by the ring merchants'. Export duties had to be introduced to raise funds, large infrastructure projects, such as the railway to the inland town of Kaduna, were cancelled, and, as Ayodeji Olukoju has argued, Elder Dempster's exorbitant freight rates were 'detrimental' to Nigerians' 'economic interests'.[24]

Ireland: stained glass windows revival

The loss of the Hamburg trade had been economically disastrous for Nigeria. In Ireland, however, the halt in German imports enabled the rebirth of the local manufacture of stained glass windows. As the poet William Butler Yeats, as a member of the Irish Free State Senate, would later point out, German mass-produced 'inferior stained-glass' dominated the Irish market in 1914. The outbreak of war, however, meant that 'our Irish stained-glass had not to face that competition', and Yeats argued that Irish artists demonstrated their ability to create 'beautiful glass' that 'found an exceedingly fine market at home'.[25]

This artistic renaissance was centred on Sarah Purser's Dublin studio named, in the Irish language, An Túr Gloine ('The Tower of Glass'). The artists included in this circle included Purser, Catherine O'Brien, Ethel Rhind, Wilhelmina Geddes, Alfred Ernest Child, Michael Healy and Harry Clarke. In the absence of imported German stained glass, Irish exponents in this craft gained commissions for churches, public buildings and private houses. In February 1916, An Túr Gloine exhibited stained glass windows by Rhind, O'Brien and Healy that the *Irish Times* praised for their 'brilliancy and originality', and the *Irish Builder and Engineer* published an article outlining the work of the main Irish glass artists. Four months later, Harry Clarke displayed windows of Irish saints that were installed, alongside windows by O'Brien, Rhind and Child, at the Honan Chapel built adjacent to University College, Cork.[26]

One project that confirmed the reputation of Irish stained glass artists occurred when the Duke of Connaught, Governor-General of Canada and Queen Victoria's son, commissioned Geddes in 1915 to create a stained glass window to commemorate ten men of his personal staff who died on the Western Front while serving with the British Army or the Canadian Expeditionary Force. The Duke of Connaught had been Commander-in-Chief of the British Army garrison in Ireland from 1901 to 1904, and probably used the Irish connections that he had established during this period to identify Geddes as the suitable artist for this project. The dramatic window, showing a deceased soldier being carried by angels to eternal life in Heaven, was unveiled in St Bartholomew's Church in Ottawa on 9 November 1919.[27]

Argentina and Uruguay: beef contracts and ship requisitions

After the North American and Oriental routes, the next most important for British shipping was the track from South America. A large part of this traffic consisted of refrigerated ships loaded with beef from Argentina and Uruguay, sailing to Britain from the River Plate. Large and small shipping companies plied this profitable route. One of the smallest was the Argentine Cargo Line, owned by the British and Argentine Steam Navigation Company. Established in 1908, this company owned two refrigerated ships, *La Blanca* and *El Argentino*.[28]

On the outbreak of war, shipping from South America ceased. Contracts were suspended and shipowners and businesses could not insure their ships or cargo. The UK government intervened to establish a state insurance scheme to cover 'War Risks', but the industry took some time to recover. *El Argentino* resumed sailing from the River Plate to Liverpool, but no work could be found on this route for *La Blanca*. At this time the Australian and New Zealand governments had requisitioned a number of refrigerated ships to transport their expeditionary forces to Egypt, and the combination of the time required to complete this voyage and to reconfigure the refrigerated ships afterwards for commercial use created a shortage of this type of vessel on the Australia/New Zealand route. *La Blanca* was chartered to an Australian firm, the Federal Steam Navigation Company. Between September 1914 and August 1915 this ship made a return voyage from England to Australia and a return voyage from England to New Zealand. Following this, *La Blanca* was chartered by Messrs Armour & Co. Ltd and returned to the South American route.[29]

Certainty returned to the South American route before the end of 1914 when the Board of Trade appointed Sir Thomas Robinson, businessman and Queensland Agent-General in London, to negotiate contracts for Argentina to provide 15,000 tons of frozen meat per month for the British Army. Charles Evans, the Queensland Railway Commissioner, who was visiting London at this time, commented that Robinson worked 'almost continuously in his own office, or at the War Office, night and day' to complete these agreements. The newly created Royal Commission on Sugar Supplies negotiated a similar contract in 1914 with a single shipping company, Messrs Alfred Holt & Co., to import sugar from Java in the Netherlands East Indies to make up for the wartime loss of European sugar. In January 1915, the British and French governments agreed to Robinson's proposal that he should jointly negotiate on their behalf the purchase of refrigerated beef from the main meat-producing nations of Argentina, Uruguay, Australia and New Zealand 'so as to avoid clashing' and 'secure the regular delivery of all Government supplies' without relying on a single source of supply.[30]

The need to secure meat imports for the United Kingdom led the Board of Trade on 13 April 1915 to requisition all insulated space on British Empire merchant ships sailing from New Zealand and Australia. By the end of the month, insulated space on British ships sailing from the River Plate came under similar government control. The Argentine Cargo Line initially estimated that the government's payment for the insulated space was the same as that previously received from meat companies, though the company would complain in 1916 that freight rates had not kept pace with the 'very substantial increase in operating expenses' since the imposition of requisition. The Board of Trade did not requisition the shipowners' vessels, but by taking over the refrigerated areas, the British government now controlled where, and with what cargo, the ships sailed.[31]

Shipping control

During 1915 the British Empire's shipping difficulties increased. The short pre-war voyages from Europe to Britain had been replaced by longer journeys from North America and Australia with the result that ships spent longer in transit and were therefore delivering less cargo. British wheat imports declined in the second half of 1915 for two reasons. The first was the failure of the Gallipoli campaign to reopen the Dardanelles and restore the export of Russian grain. The second was drought in Australia that resulted in a poor wheat harvest. In October 1915 the Board of Trade encouraged shipowners to put their vessels on the North American route to import Canadian wheat. In November, the Board of Trade was granted the power to requisition ships to carry food, and the newly created Requisitioning (Carriage of Foodstuffs) Committee prohibited British merchant ships over 500 tons gross from sailing to ports outside the British Empire without the Committee's permission.[32]

On 27 January 1916 the increasing wartime authority of the UK government over British shipping was seen on three fronts. Prime Minister Asquith appointed the Shipping Control Committee, chaired by Lord Curzon, the former Viceroy of India. In the House of Commons Walter Runciman, President of the Board of Trade, announced restrictions on the import of paper goods, the first of a series of measures to reduce the transport of non-essential items. F.P. Robinson of the Requisitioning (Carriage of Foodstuffs) Committee told Runciman that the Board of Trade should avoid purchasing Australian wheat and 'confine their operations to sources of supply nearer to this country than Australia' because the 'diversion of tonnage East of Suez to Australia would of necessity hamper' more vital imports to Britain from India, Ceylon and Burma such as rice and manganese.[33]

The Commonwealth of Australia was badly affected by the British government's shipping controls. German submarines had begun operating in the Mediterranean Sea, and due to the increased risks, the British government announced on 7 March 1916 that no British Empire shipping was to enter this body of water unless they were discharging cargo in a Mediterranean port. The route from Australia, New Zealand and the Far East to Britain was therefore altered to travel via South Africa. A return voyage from Australia to the United Kingdom would now take six months,

Fig. 2.1 The Aberdeen Line's *Themistocles* in Cape Town harbour.
In 1916, the UK government closed the Mediterranean Sea to transiting shipping due to the success of German submarine operations. The return voyage from Britain to Australia via South Africa now took six months. Image: Academy Library, UNSW Canberra, Papers of the Doug Robertson Maritime and Naval History Collection MS 126, Robertson Box 235, 5, *Themistocles*.

making the route a much less attractive destination in comparison to Argentina, India and North America, where the round trips were four months, three and a half months and two months respectively.[34]

When Billy Hughes, the Australian Labor prime minister, visited Britain in the first half of 1916, one of his major tasks was to secure markets and shipping for Australian commodities. He clashed with Curzon, the chairman of the Shipping Control Committee, who refused to put ships on the Australian route to carry wheat. Not to be deterred, Hughes secretly obtained a line of credit for £3 million from the state-owned Commonwealth Bank of Australia and covertly bought 15 small tramp merchant ships. On 21 June, Curzon and Hughes were both invited to attend the Cabinet War Committee, where Hughes announced his nautical purchases – which would become the Commonwealth Shipping Line. Curzon blustered that his Shipping Control Committee could requisition Hughes' ships, but Bonar Law, the Conservative Colonial Secretary, supported Hughes by pointing out that unless Australia could export and earn income, it could not contribute to the Empire's war effort. Prime Minister Asquith had to adjudicate, and as economic historian Peter Yule puts it, 'he characteristically took a middle course between the two positions', recommending that the Australian government should keep control of their 15 ships, but should not make any further purchases.[35]

The U-boat campaign (1): 1914–16

German submarines had been attacking British merchant ships since the beginning of the war. The first victim was the *Glitra*, a small vessel sunk off the coast of Norway by *U.17* on 20 October 1914. The U-boat commander, Captain Johannes Feldkirchner, surfaced his submarine beside the *Glitra*, determined that the ship's cargo of coal, iron and oil could be used for military purposes, which meant it could be sunk under existing international naval law. He ordered the crew to go to their lifeboats. The Germans sank the ship by opening the sea valves: U-boats in this period were small, carried few torpedoes, and where possible sank merchant ships by the method used here, by explosive charges or the submarine's deck gun. Feldkirchner then attached lines to the British lifeboats and towed them in the direction of the nearest land for 15 minutes before releasing them, an action comparable to Captain Karl von Müller's gentlemanly treatment of merchant sailors at the same time in the Indian Ocean.[36]

On 4 February 1915, in response to the British blockade, the German government declared the waters around Britain and Ireland to be a war zone where merchant ships were liable to be attacked. During the first two months of the U-boat campaign, the Germans targeted Entente ships and neutral ships carrying cargo to Entente ports. When U-boats attacked neutral ships carrying cargo to neutral ports, the German government apologised for their error and paid compensation to the shipowners.[37]

The British passenger liner *Lusitania* was torpedoed by *U.20* off the south coast of Ireland on 7 May 1915 with the loss of 1,198 lives, including 128 neutral American citizens. So as not to inflame the situation further and to prevent the United States entering the war, German Chancellor Theobald von Bethmann Hollweg gained Kaiser Wilhelm's agreement on 5 June to halt attacks on large passenger ships. On 18 September, the new German Chief of Naval Staff, Admiral Henning von Holtzendorff ordered a moratorium on unrestricted attacks – where merchant ships were sunk without first being stopped and their cargo identified – west of the United Kingdom, in the English Channel and the North Sea. The Admiral then sent his U-boats to the Mediterranean, where they were less likely to sink a ship carrying American passengers.[38]

The German Navy continued a restricted U-boat campaign until March 1916, when the German Army's Chief of General Staff, General Erich von Falkenhayn, then fighting the French in the titanic Battle of Verdun, called for the resumption of unrestricted submarine warfare to force the British to surrender. This campaign was soon halted on 24 April, after a U-boat attacked a French ferry in the English Channel carrying American citizens.[39]

From September 1916, Germany conducted a de facto unrestricted submarine campaign. U-boats continued to avoid targeting United States vessels to ensure American neutrality, but attacked all ships from other neutral states and the Entente.[40]

Ministry of Shipping

H.H. Asquith resigned as prime minister of the coalition government on 4 December 1916. Wholesale food prices in the United Kingdom were

now 90 per cent higher than they had been in July 1914. The new prime
minister, David Lloyd George, had to confront the looming shipping crisis.
On 22 December, Lloyd George created the Ministry of Shipping with
Sir Joseph Maclay, from the Glasgow shipping firm Maclay & McIntyre,
as its Controller (Maclay was not a minister as he was not a member of
either the House of Lords or House of Commons). The appointment
was not universally welcomed. Sir Hubert Llewellyn Smith, Secretary
to the Board of Trade, did not believe 'Maclay would be suitable for this
particular purpose', and attributed his elevation to his connections to fellow
Glaswegian and Conservative Leader, Andrew Bonar Law. On taking the
position, Maclay ordered that all his company's ships be requisitioned by
the government to avoid accusations of conflict of interest.[41] Maclay's role
was described as having responsibility for

> everything to do with the employment of mercantile shipping, whether
> for the Navy, Army, or the commerce of the country, and also the
> means by shipbuilding, chartering from neutrals or any other source,
> of maintaining the supply of ships adequate for the requirements of
> the Nation and the Allies.[42]

The British government response to the shipping shortage took two
forms: the first was to eliminate unnecessary imports; the second was to
make efficient use of ships by allocating them only to the shortest and
most vital routes. At the same time as the creation of the Ministry of
Shipping, Lloyd George had appointed Curzon to chair a committee on
import restriction. Thirty thousand tons were freed up for alternative uses
by halting the import of luxury food and drinks such as mineral water
and sweets. Further savings were made by limiting the import of coffee
and tea, due to there being large stocks of these products in the United
Kingdom, and limiting the import of fresh fruit on the grounds that its
nutritional value was not proportional to the volume and weight required to
transport it.[43]

The Ministry of Shipping concentrated merchant vessels on the North
American route to Canada and the United States and the South American
route to Uruguay and Argentina. In 1917 the Tonnage Priority Committee
gave precedence to importing grain from North America. Australia had

harvested an abundant wheat crop, but as Ernest Fayle wrote, 'there was no intention of allocating British tonnage to lift wheat from so distant a source'. In May 1917, refrigerated ships were transferred from sailing to New Zealand, Australia and the Far East to carry meat from the River Plate. In 1917 there were approximately 2,000 return voyages on the North Atlantic route, but only around 150 to 200 voyages to Australia and New Zealand. Those few ships sailing to the Antipodes were limited to visiting one Australia port and two or three New Zealand ports to ensure a quick turnaround.[44]

Shipping shortages became common across large parts of the British Empire. British shipping to the Caribbean was shifted to other routes, and, while North American imports filled part of this gap, West Indian colonies suffered food shortages from 1917 to 1919. Laws were passed requiring landowners to cultivate vegetables and corn, Food Controllers were appointed, and meatless days were introduced in the Jamaican capital of Kingston.[45]

India experienced shortages in particular products, making it difficult for the Government of India to provide logistical support to the campaigns in Mesopotamia, East Africa and Salonika. Shipping shortages led Colonel G. Sanders, Purchasing Officer for Indian Army Supplies to visit Australia in the first part of 1917 and negotiate contracts with companies to provide tinned oatmeal, jam and other products for the Indian Army.[46] The Indian Munitions Board similarly sourced and purchased steel plate in Shanghai, locomotives in Singapore, and acetone, a chemical used in the production of cordite, from Australia.[47]

The inhabitants of the Seychelles Islands suffered the worst effects of the wartime shipping shortages. An island group in the Indian Ocean, just south of the Equator, and about 1,000 miles (1,600 kilometres) east of Africa, in 1911 the Seychelles had a population of 22,691 of African, Chinese, Indian and European backgrounds. Before the outbreak of war, three shipping companies regularly visited the main island of Mahé: a Messageries Maritimes steamer sailed every four weeks from Marseilles to Mauritius and docked on its outward and return voyage, as did the Deutsche Ost-Afrika-Linie which travelled every six weeks from Zanzibar to Bombay, while the British India Company came once a month on its route from Bombay to the East African ports. This regular traffic enabled the Seychelles to import rice, flour and other foodstuffs from India, and export copra, guano, vanilla, cinnamon, tortoise shell and other items worth just over 1,750,000 rupees in 1912.[48]

The outbreak of war severely reduced shipping to the Seychelles. The German shipping line stopped sailing, the British India Company reduced their service to one ship from India every three months and sailed to India even less frequently, taking 'very little cargo out of the Colony'. The Messageries Maritimes was given a subsidy to continue calling at Mahé, but ended this service when the payments ended in April 1918.

The lack of shipping devastated the Seychelles. J. Louis Devaux's 1919 report on the colony recorded that the steep decline in food imports from India meant the price of locally produced food increased 25 per cent, imported rice and flour went up 100 per cent, and imported tinned meat and processed foods doubled in price. In 1914, the colonial government imposed controls on the price and supply of food; in 1918 a Labour Bureau was created with the power to force landowners and labourers to cultivate staple crops on designated lands. Even with these attempts at amelioration, labourers and their families suffered more than wealthier islanders. As Devaux wrote:

> For them there has been much less employment and wages have hardly increased. The consequence is that poverty and crime have been on the increase. Many of the children of this class have been underfed and more easily fell a prey to disease.[49]

The U-boat campaign (2): 1917–18

In August 1916 General Paul von Hindenburg became Chief of the German General Staff, and, with General Erich Ludendorff as Quartermaster General, became responsible for directing the German war effort. Hindenburg and Ludendorff worked with the Chief of the German Naval Staff, Admiral Holtzendorff, to devise a new German strategy. Holtzendorff had previously been sceptical of the effectiveness of submarines, but in December 1916 he sent the generals a proposal to use U-boats in order to win the war. This argued that an unrestricted submarine campaign against the United Kingdom commencing in February would sink 600,000 tons of shipping per month and would force the British to surrender in five months. Kaiser Wilhelm agreed to the strategy in January, and the operation began on 1 February 1917.[50]

When the U-boat campaign began, the German Navy had 69 operational submarines based in Belgium or with the High Seas Fleet at Kiel, and 23 operational submarines in the Mediterranean Sea. The German strategy had early success. From 1 February to 30 April 1917, 470 ocean-going vessels constituting 1.2 million tons of shipping had been sunk, the equivalent of the annual output of all British shipyards. As J.A. Salter commented: 'the submarine campaign became a greater danger to the Allies than the surface blockade was to Germany'. Nor did the United States' declaring war on Germany on 6 April, a direct result of U-boats sinking American merchant ships, relieve the shipping crisis, as the British now needed to allocate British vessels to transport American troops and supplies across the Atlantic.[51]

As Table 2.2 demonstrates, 1917 saw the greatest British shipping losses of the entire war.

TABLE 2.2

BRITISH EMPIRE SHIPPING LOSSES, 1914–18[52]

YEAR	TONS OF SHIPPING
1914	241,000
1915	856,000
1916	1,238,000
1917	3,730,000
1918	1,695,000

The unrestricted submarine campaign was also effective in limiting neutral shipping to the United Kingdom for fear of being sunk. The British government forced neutral Dutch and Scandinavian ships to continue to sail to British ports by refusing to allow neutral ships that had unloaded their cargo to leave port until another ship from that nation arrived.[53]

Merchant sailors of all nationalities experienced the perils of U-boat attacks. On 19 March 1917, the *Alnwick Castle* was torpedoed and sunk in the Atlantic more than 300 miles (480 kilometres) west of Cornwall. 139 men boarded the lifeboats. Benjamin Chave, the *Alnwick Castle*'s captain, compiled a harrowing account of the crew's ordeal. After four days with little water, they spent the night in rough seas, constantly baling to keep the boats afloat. Some men collapsed, weak with hunger and exertion, others became delirious. Chave wrote: 'The horrors of that night, together with the physical suffering are beyond my power of description'. When they were rescued, nine days later, by the French merchant ship *Venezia*, there were only 24 survivors. The men were so weak they had to be hoisted by ropes onto the ship.[54]

Ah Yee, quartermaster on the Cunard Company *Volodia*, demonstrated great leadership when his ship was torpedoed off Brittany on 21 August 1917. Ten men were killed in the torpedo explosion and the survivors took to the lifeboats. Ah Yee steered one of the boats for three and a half days in heavy seas, gale force winds, rain and hail, sailing 300 miles to reach the south coast of England.[55]

The German submarine campaign would result in the loss of both the *El Argentino* and *La Blanca* and the end of the Argentine Cargo Line. *El Argentino* had been sunk on 26 May 1916 by a mine laid by U-boat off Lowestoft on the east coast of England. All 100 crew members survived the attack and reached shore safely.[56]

The sinking of *La Blanca* on 23 November 1917 was more controversial. The ships had sailed from the River Plate carrying 3,910 tons of refrigerated meat and 400 tons of other commodities. *La Blanca* developed engine trouble and came into Plymouth, but it was unable to unload its precious cargo of beef because there were no cold storage facilities in the port. The ship left port as part of a convoy on 23 November when it was hit by a torpedo at 10.15 pm on the same night and began to list. John Clark, the Chief Refrigerating Officer, was in his cabin when the attack occurred and had to struggle against wreckage and the ship's incline to get up on deck. After a second torpedo hit the ship at 10.50 pm, the crew went to the lifeboats and *La Blanca* sank along with its cargo.[57]

La Blanca's Master, R. Smiles, blamed the ship's loss on 'the inefficient escort' at Plymouth. The Royal Navy enquiry made a similar finding. On 4 December, questions were asked in both the House of Commons and the House of Lords to confirm that *La Blanca* had reached an English port but could not discharge its cargo before it was sunk. A retired admiral, Lord Beresford, described the event as 'unpardonable', and stated that 'if the Admiralty had not got enough ships to act as escorts, the boats should be kept in port until escorts were available'.[58]

The Argentine Cargo Line was now a shipping company without ships. At its final annual general meeting on 12 March 1918, it appointed a liquidator to wind up the company.[59]

The British gradually overcame the U-boat threat during 1917. The two main contributing factors were the arming of merchant ships and the introduction of convoys. The first ships fitted with naval guns were refrigerated ships carrying meat from Argentina, Australia and New Zealand in the middle of 1915. The aim of the armament was to defend the vessel and its cargo: the gun was mounted at the rear of the ship and was to be fired while sailing away from submarines. Later, guns were installed on other types of merchant ships at all the main British ports as well as Gibraltar, Port Said, Marseilles, Dakar, Cape Town and Kingston. From February 1917, 'submarine menace' courses were offered to merchant sailors in the United Kingdom, the Mediterranean, Bombay and Halifax in Canada. By the end of the war, 5,887 merchant ships had been armed, of which 1,684 were lost due to enemy action or other causes.[60]

Convoys were initially opposed by the Royal Navy in the belief that merchant seamen would be unable to keep to convoy formation. However, the heavy shipping losses in early 1917 meant action was needed to reduce such losses. The first convoys were established in February for colliers sailing to France. Shipowners soon demanded convoys to protect shipping, and after trials in May demonstrated that this method was practicable, convoys from North America to the United Kingdom began in July 1917. Convoys saved shipping because ships sailing in formation were concentrated in a smaller area of the ocean than ships sailing singly; this meant U-boats patrolling the Atlantic Ocean were less likely to find a merchant ship to attack. Before the introduction of convoys, the Germans sank one in ten Allied or neutral ships. Once convoys commenced, the loss rate reduced to one in a hundred. By November 1918, 90 per cent of Allied shipping was sailing in convoys. From the end of June 1918 onwards, there were few successful German submarine attacks on shipping.[61]

Fig. 2.2 The *Clan Macewen* of the Cayzer, Irvine Line survived the war,
but the company lost 28 ships to U-boats. Image: Academy Library,
UNSW Canberra, Papers of the Doug Robertson Maritime and Naval History
Collection MS 126, Robertson Box 151, 1 Clan Macewen.

The war at sea was costly in lives and ships: 14,661 merchant sailors
died due to military action by the Central Powers, and the number of
British ocean-going vessels declined by a quarter. To consider the wartime
experience of one shipping company as an example, Elder Dempster,
which sailed the West African route, began the war with 101 merchant
ships, ended the war with 58, and lost 487 men at sea.[62]

The war ends: rationing in Britain

Food shortages became common in Britain during 1917. This was mainly
the result of the success of the German submarine campaign in sinking
merchant ships, but was also caused by local factors, such as a poor potato
crop in the first part of the year. The Ministry of Food Control had been
created with Lord Devonport as Minister in December 1916. A War
Cabinet meeting with the Minister of Food Control on 7 May 1917 raised
concerns that the 'the poor in the East of London' were running short of
some food items because 'these were being bought up by the wealthier

classes as economical substitutes'. In a number of cities, including Birmingham, rationing for some foods was imposed at a municipal level. The situation worsened as Christmas approached, as shoppers waited in long queues for declining quantities of meat and tea. On 12 December, a deputation told Lloyd George that some districts were without butter, lard, margarine and bacon.[63]

Lord Rhondda, who replaced Devonport as Food Controller in June 1917, asked the War Cabinet on 28 November for permission to devise detailed plans for a 'comprehensive system' of rationing. On 25 February 1918, compulsory rationing was introduced in London and the surrounding Home Counties for meats and fats (butter and margarine). Sugar soon joined the list of rationed commodities, but other items such as bread and potatoes did not. On 7 April, meat rationing was extended to the rest of England, Wales and Scotland. A week later, compulsory rationing was imposed on all of Britain, but it was not necessary to apply the measure to Ireland. The amount of food allocated to each individual depended on their type of employment: women and men employed in 'heavy' industrial or agricultural work received more calories than sedentary workers. Young children were given 'a prior claim to milk' and the ration scales took account of vegetarians. Rationing meant that people ate less of the foodstuffs in limited supply due to U-boat attacks and shipping shortages, but it attempted to ensure that scarce items would be fairly distributed across British society.[64]

During the final two years of the war, the United Kingdom government had to take unusual measures to make up shortfalls resulting from the shipping crisis. The first occurred in August 1917 during the Third Battle of Ypres. Artillery shells required cordite for propellant; the production of cordite, as already mentioned, required a chemical called acetone, and acetone was manufactured from imported grain.

The Director of Propellant Supplies in the Ministry of Munitions decided to make acetone by replacing imported grain with British horse chestnuts, which, as the London *Times* commented, had been occasionally used to feed goats and deer, but were otherwise 'a waste crop'. Every two tons of horse chestnuts would allow one ton of imported grain to be freed for human consumption. Schoolchildren in Wales, Scotland and England were mobilised to beat horse chestnut trees with sticks and collect the seeds as they fell, harvesting about 3,000 tons that were dried and sent to explosives factories in Norfolk and Dorset. Horse chestnut collection was not extended to Ireland because it would require the allocation of scarce shipping space to transport the bulky cargo across the Irish Sea.[65]

The government called upon child labour for a second time in July 1918. The 'comparative failure' of the British and Irish soft fruit crop raised fears that they would face an 'extreme difficulty to provide enough Jam to meet the requirements of the Forces and the civilian population'. To make up this shortfall, Labour Party MP John Clynes, who had become the Minister of Food Control on 9 July, declared that 'the systematic collection of Blackberries throughout the entire Country has become a matter of paramount importance'. With a 'serious shortage of ordinary labour', Clynes called on the Board of Education to assist by 'enlisting the services of School children and Teachers'.[66]

When children had harvested inedible horse chestnuts in 1917, they were unpaid, though some headmasters had offered a prize to the child who collected the largest number. Picking blackberries, however, required students to be granted special school holidays and to be paid – two or three pence a pound – to ensure the crop survived the harvesting process uneaten, to be made into jam. The Ministry of Food established 100 receiving depots, mostly in schools, and 11 pulping stations in towns in Cambridgeshire, Gloucestershire, Kent, Worcestershire and Yorkshire.[67]

As with the collection of horse chestnuts, shipping costs meant that Ireland was not included in the Ministry's scheme. Nonetheless, the *Irish Times* reported that 400 tons of crab apples, whorts and blackberries from Clonmel in County Tipperary had been sent to Irish and English jam factories, and the prosperous linen manufacturers in Belfast paid schoolchildren to pick blackberries and bore the cost of packaging and transporting the fruit to Britain. In the Essex town of Chelmsford, A.S. Duffield, a former member of the local Rural Food Control Commission warned that 'farmers might object if the picking was entrusted to children on the ground of hedges being broken down'. The *Essex County Chronicle* stoutly responded:

> Essex farmers would be adding to their already great reputation
> for patriotism, if they, like Nelson of old, turned their blind eye to

the matter of broken fences, the extent of which it is quite easy to exaggerate.[68]

The United Kingdom's ability to maintain its shipping lanes with crucial markets such as Argentina, Canada and the United States was key to the Allied victory in 1918. The concentration of merchant ships on the North Atlantic and South American routes, however, resulted in shortages and economic stagnation across much of the rest of the Empire from New Zealand to Nigeria. For the Seychelles, the lack of shipping was so severe it resulted in a tragic rise in child mortality. The war began with the loss of shipping and the imposition of rationing in British North Borneo, a small colony on the periphery of the British Empire. By the time the war ended, the German submarine campaign and shipping shortages had resulted in the introduction of rationing in Britain itself.

1915: The Three Battles of Aubers Ridge, France

The 'air seemed to be one long scream'. This was how J.W. Barnett, the 34th Sikh Pioneers' Medical Officer, described the artillery bombardment of 10 March 1915 that tore the sky above the village of Neuve Chapelle in the Artois region of northern France. Commencing at 7.30 am, 340 British artillery pieces hurled 3,000 shells in 35 minutes on a 2,000-yard (1.8-kilometre) section of the German front lines held by men of the 13th and 16th Infantry Regiments and the 11th Jäger Battalion. This was not random gunfire. Each artillery unit had been allocated a particular location as their target. During the preceding weeks, the gunners – alongside their regular shelling of the enemy emplacements – had covertly fired shells to ascertain the exact range to the positions they would target on the day of the attack. At 8.05 am, the guns shifted their aim 300 yards to the east, just beyond Neuve Chapelle. It was then that the Garhwal Brigade of the Indian Army's Meerut Division and the 23rd and 25th Brigades of the British 8th Division began their assault across the 200 yards of no-man's-land.

The water table in this part of France was so high that it was impossible to dig trenches without them flooding, so the German positions were above-ground breastworks constructed of piles of sandbags. These were less than six feet six inches (two metres) in width, and they could not protect the soldiers from the artillery storm. The Indian and British soldiers overwhelmed the outnumbered German troops, still stunned by the surprise and strength of the 'hurricane' bombardment, and broke through the front line. By 8.50 am, several battalions of the 39th Garhwal Rifles, alongside the 1st Battalion Royal Irish Rifles and 2nd Battalion Rifle Brigade had reached the initial goal of Neuve Chapelle. Rifleman Gane Gurung of the 2nd Battalion 3rd Gurkha Rifles entered a house in the village on his own and captured eight German soldiers. When he emerged with his prisoners, nearby British soldiers erupted with a spontaneous cheer for the Indian Army soldier. By the end of the day, the British Empire force had breached the German line on a 4,000-yard (3.7-kilometre) front to a maximum depth of 1,200 yards. Six miles to the east loomed Aubers Ridge, which, although it rose only 40 feet (12 metres) above the flat plains, dominated the surrounding landscape. An advance of seven more miles (11.2 kilometres) from Aubers Ridge would reach their final objective of Lille, the industrial city and railway centre that had been under German occupation since October 1914.[1]

That this chapter's title refers to three separate battles of Aubers Ridge indicates that the initial triumph in breaking into the German lines at Neuve Chapelle on 10 March would not be followed by a swift advance and the capture of Aubers Ridge and Lille. For the British Empire soldiers on the Western Front, 1915 would be, as James Edmonds and Graeme Wynne wrote in the British Official History, a period of 'education and instruction' in which officers and men would have 'to discover by bitter experience the methods of the new warfare'. It would also be a year of few successes and bloody losses: the total British Empire casualties on the Western Front in 1915 numbered 285,107.[2]

The failures of the attacks at Neuve Chapelle, Aubers Ridge and Festubert would demonstrate in stark terms the three main requirements for military success on the Western Front in World War I. The first was that an effective artillery bombardment would be vital to protect soldiers if they were to advance and capture ground on the increasingly lethal battlefield. The second was that the British Empire's ammunition output would have to be greatly increased to ensure there would be sufficient shells to protect advancing troops. The third was that a long 'learning process' would be required to develop and perfect techniques that would eventually end the stalemate of the trenches and enable the return to mobile warfare by 1918.

The British Expeditionary Force (BEF) had begun embarking to France on 9 August 1914, five days after the United Kingdom government declared war on Germany. As mentioned in the Introduction, Brigadier General Henry Wilson, the Director of Military Operations, had devised a plan in July 1911 to enable the deployment of an expeditionary force to Europe in the event of a German invasion of France. On 5 August, Field Marshal Sir John French – who had been Chief of the Imperial General Staff until his sacking in March 1914 for stating that the army would not be used to enforce Irish Home Rule on Ulster Unionists – was confirmed as BEF commander. Cabinet decided to initially deploy 150,000 of its precious professional soldiers, organised into four infantry divisions and one cavalry division.[3]

The BEF began its advance towards Belgium on the left side of the French Fifth Army on 21 August. On the morning of the second day of the march, the three divisions of the II British Corps collided near Mons with the five divisions of the IX German Corps, part of General Alexander von Kluck's First Army. The outnumbered Irish and British regulars held their ground during the day, as their constant, rapid and accurate rifle fire ripped apart the massed formations of German conscripts, but were forced to abandon Mons at dusk. The British suffered about 1,600 casualties in the battle: about 5,000 Germans were killed or wounded. On 26 August, Kluck's troops inflicted a brutal defeat on the BEF at Le Cateau. II Corps lost 8,000 men: a casualty rate of 15 per cent. Sir John French was unnerved by the lethality of modern combat. Instead of an orderly withdrawal maintaining contact with the Fifth Army, French broke contact with both his enemies and allies on 29 August and fled southwards with the aim of reaching the safety of the far bank of the Oise River to rest and re-equip his troops.[4]

The following day, Wilson and General Charles Lanrezac, the Fifth Army commander, convinced Sir John French to halt his retreat, halfway between the Aisne and Oise Rivers. A late-night cabinet meeting in London on 31 August directed the BEF commander to cooperate 'closely and continuously' with General Joseph Joffre, the French Army's Commander-in-Chief. On 1 September, War Secretary Field Marshal Lord Kitchener travelled to Paris to directly convey the government's message. John Spencer comments that the relationship between the two field marshals shattered 'under the stresses of modern warfare'. The meeting became a shouting match, but the BEF re-joined the battle.[5]

By the beginning of September, the advantage had begun to shift away from the Germans, and towards the French and British armies. An unexpected Russian victory at Gumbinnen (Gusev) in Prussia on 20 August had led a panicked Moltke to transfer two infantry corps to the Eastern Front. In the west, the First Army had marched some 300 miles (500 kilometres) from the German–Belgian border to within 60 kilometres of Paris, but the units were mostly at half strength, having suffered almost 11,000 battle casualties, and over 9,000 cases of illness mostly caused by heat exhaustion, lack of food and foot ailments. On Moltke's orders, Kluck shifted the First Army's line of advance to the east of Paris, to protect the vulnerable flank of the Second Army. In doing so, Kluck placed his own troops in danger of being attacked by French troops from Paris.[6]

The military governor of Paris, General Joseph-Simon Galliéni, received fresh troops including marines, reservists and Arab soldiers of the 45th Algerian Division. Kitchener sent reinforcements to the existing units of the BEF and added the 4th and 6th Divisions. In the next battle, for the first time, French and British troops would outnumber the Germans.[7]

Kluck and his soldiers were travelling blind through the French countryside. In contrast, French soldiers captured a map showing the First Army's change of direction when they ambushed a German officer's car, French intelligence had broken the German radio code, and French and British aircraft were observing the enemy advance.[8]

On 3 September, Wilson, Galliéni, Joffre and the new commander of the Fifth Army, General Louis Franchet d'Espèrey, all arrived at the same conclusion, that the Germans were vulnerable to a joint French–British attack. The remaining obstacle to enacting this combined operation was Sir John French. Joffre travelled around 120 miles (200 kilometres) to see the field marshal at the BEF headquarters at Château Vaux-le-Pénil. Fearful that French would not deploy his men, Joffre declared that 'the honour of England is at stake'. Sir John French attempted to reply in French, but the emotion of the moment and his inability in the language failed him. Instead, he told one of his staff officers: 'Damn it, I can't explain. Tell him that all that men can do our fellows will do.'[9]

The Battle of the Marne began on 5 September when the French Sixth Army advanced from Paris and attacked the flank of the German First Army. Kluck decided to counter-attack, but in redirecting his troops towards Paris, he created a 30-mile (50-kilometre) gap between the First Army and General Karl von Bülow's Second Army. The next morning, the main offensive commenced with 980,000 French and 100,000 British troops with 3,000 artillery pieces attacking 750,000 German soldiers with 3,300 guns. The BEF and the left arm of the Fifth Army marched into the gap between the two German armies. Their only opposition was some German cavalry. Four days later, French and British soldiers crossed the Marne River. The German armies withdrew to the safer high ground on the north bank of the Aisne River. Moltke's strategy for a swift victory over France had failed. On 14 September, Kaiser Wilhelm dismissed Moltke and appointed Erich von Falkenhayn, the Prussian War Minister, as the new Chief of the General Staff.[10]

Northern France and Belgium offered the one remaining open flank in which the German, French and British armies could manoeuvre around the enemy's divisions and attack their supply lines. Sir John French returned the BEF to its original position on the left of the French Army and moved northwards towards the French and Belgian Channel ports. This would simplify supplying his troops from the United Kingdom and enable the British to contribute to the defence of the main Belgian port of Antwerp. However, the Germans captured Antwerp on 10 October, and took Lille – where the BEF was to deploy – two days later.[11]

The fighting in Belgium for the remainder of 1914 focused on Ypres, a town with 17,000 inhabitants in the kingdom's south-west. German cavalry had passed through the town on 7 October, but had not remained. This allowed General Sir Henry Rawlinson's troops, who were retreating southwards from Ghent, to occupy Ypres on 14 October. The United Kingdom force in Belgium became a British Empire army on 20 October, when Indian soldiers arrived by train at the northern French town of Hazebrouck, about 20 miles (30 kilometres) south of Ypres.[12]

The Cabinet in London had agreed on 6 August to commit Indian troops to the conflict. Initially the Indian Expeditionary Force A (IEF A) was to garrison Egypt, but following the British defeat at Le Cateau on 26 August, Asquith determined the contingent was required to fight on the Western Front. This was the first time that Indian soldiers had served in Europe since 1878, when they had temporarily garrisoned the British Mediterranean colonies of Malta and Cyprus as a precaution during the Russo-Turkish War. Lord Hardinge, the Viceroy of India, praised the decision to end the race-based restriction that Indians should not fight European soldiers, while the India Secretary, the Marquess of Crewe, declared that a significant Indian military contribution was a necessity to ensure Indian public support for the war.[13]

The *Emden*'s presence in the Indian Ocean delayed the sailing of some of the troopships, but IEF A disembarked in Marseilles on 26 September. The force of 24,000 men consisted of two infantry divisions – the 3rd and the 7th – and the 9th Cavalry Brigade. These were renamed the Lahore Division, Meerut Divisions and the Secunderabad Cavalry Brigade respectively to acknowledge their Indian origin and to avoid confusion with the numbered British divisions and brigades. More Indian cavalry brigades would be sent to Europe to eventually enable the creation of two Indian cavalry divisions. As mentioned in the introduction, the fear that Indian soldiers would mutiny against their colonial overlords meant that Indian regiments were always issued with weapons that were less advanced than their British counterparts. This policy was abandoned when IEF A arrived on the Western Front: Indian soldiers exchanged their Lee–Enfield Mark II rifles for the latest Mark III version used by the BEF.[14]

On 20 October, the same day Indian soldiers detrained at Hazebrouck, Falkenhayn ordered the German Fourth and Sixth Armies to attack north and south of Ypres to encircle and defeat the BEF and IEF. The German force included a large number of reserve regiments. A quarter of these soldiers were trained reservists, but the remainder were volunteers or underage and overage men with minimal training. On 22 August, these reserve regiments attacked the British north of Ypres at Bixschoote, in what the Germans named the Battle of Langemarck. The offensive was a disastrous failure. Some units suffered 70 per cent casualties.[15]

The First Battle of Ypres continued until 24 November, by which time the soldiers were fighting as snow fell. The Allies retained Ypres, but the town was now in a salient, surrounded on three sides by German troops and vulnerable to constant artillery bombardment. The loss of life between 15 October and 24 November revealed the new nature of war.

The Germans suffered 134,300 casualties, including about 19,600 deaths. Belgian troops, 52,683 of whom had escaped from Antwerp, suffered 33 per cent casualties in 12 days. French casualties at Ypres numbered between 50,000 and 85,000. British, Indian and Irish troops had 58,155 casualties, of whom 7,960 were killed. As Beckett put it, the First Battle of Ypres marked the end of 'mobile warfare' and 'the onset of the deadlock that was to characterize the Western Front for the next four years'.[16]

Germany had been unable to achieve victory on the Western Front with Moltke's defeat on the Marne and Falkenhayn's failure to capture Ypres. It had lost almost half its field army between the German declaration of war and the middle of November: 800,000 casualties including 116,000 dead. Falkenhayn realised he needed to devise a new strategy if he was to win the war.[17]

On 18 November, the general met with the German Chancellor, Theobald von Bethmann Hollweg, and asked the government to take a diplomatic approach and conclude a negotiated peace with one of Germany's surrounding foes. Russia appeared to be more vulnerable than France and the United Kingdom, and the expanses of the Eastern Front offered the German army more opportunity for manoeuvre warfare. Falkenhayn began shifting troops to the east from late November 1914 in preparation for a major offensive against the Russians in Spring 1915. At the same time, he ordered a second line of defensive positions be prepared on the Western Front about 1,000 yards (one kilometre) behind the existing front line.[18]

As Spencer Jones has written, the BEF 'had been effectively destroyed by the end of 1914'. A quarter of all British Army officers had become casualties by the end of the First Battle of Ypres. The main task during the winter would be 'expanding' and 'regenerating' the British and Indian forces. James Edmonds, who edited the British Official History of the Great War and wrote several of its volumes, criticised Kitchener for clumping together the surviving regulars in five divisions. Edmonds argued that these experienced officers and soldiers should have been dispersed 'to train and leaven' the many 'New Army' divisions that were being created from the mass of Irish and British volunteers who had little or no previous military experience.[19]

Rebuilding the IEF was similarly difficult due to the Indian Army's enlistment restrictions. Soldiers could be recruited only from the restricted number of 'martial races'. Officers had to be British, but many of those commissioned from the Indian Army Reserve lacked proficiency in South Asian languages, requiring the establishment of a language school in Marseilles offering intensive courses in Urdu.[20]

Nonetheless, the BEF, which had comprised only two infantry corps and one cavalry division in August 1914, expanded during the winter to become a force of six infantry corps and two cavalry corps. On 26 December, the BEF was organised into two armies: the Second British Army at Ypres, commanded by General Sir Horace Smith-Dorrien, and the First British Army in northern France, under the control of Lieutenant General Sir Douglas Haig. During 1915, the British and Indian Army regulars on the Western Front were augmented by other forces. The first British volunteer reservists of the Territorial Army to arrive was the 46th (North Midland) Division in March, followed by the first New Army formation, the 9th (Scottish) Division, in May. Other British Empire contingents began to appear on the Western Front. In February 1915, the 1st Canadian Division joined the Second Army in Belgium. In April, the Canadians suffered 5,592 casualties when it fought alongside African, French and British troops in the Second Battle of Ypres where the Germans used chlorine gas as a weapon. The first group of Australian soldiers arrived in northern France in July. These were the mechanics and drivers of two motorised transport companies, who had been sent to England when the rest of the Australian Imperial Force was disembarked in Egypt in December 1914. These transport units were assigned to the British 17th (Northern) Division.[21]

Despite these additions to the BEF, the French Army remained the largest Allied force on the Western Front, and it must be remembered that the British offensives in 1915 were always 'an adjunct to much larger French attacks'.[22]

French and British military leaders spent November and December 1914 struggling to come to terms with the unprecedented military environment that had emerged on the Western Front. As Callwell despondently told Wilson on 19 December:

> what with the flat sodden ground and the barbed wire and machine
> guns and you are in reality up against an entirely new war problem

[...] I am afraid it will be a slow business clearing the German out of the occupied territory.[23]

Despite these obstacles, there was considerable optimism that the offensives planned for 1915 would succeed due to the reduced number of German troops on the Western Front. Joffre's focus was to eliminate the German position at Noyon, only 60 miles (100 kilometres) from Paris, with plans for major offensives on the salient by the Tenth French Army in Artois in the north and by the Fourth French Army at Champagne in the south, with five supporting attacks intended to prevent the enemy from concentrating their forces.[24]

On 30 December, Haig met with his three corps commanders, Lieutenant General Sir Charles Monro of I Corps, Major General Sir Henry Rawlinson of IV Corps and Lieutenant General Sir James Willcocks of the Indian Corps, to discuss a proposal for the BEF's first offensive in the new trench warfare environment: an attack on the Germans at Neuve Chapelle. Haig remains a controversial figure in the history of World War I. He had many flaws, but he was not a technophobe. The battles of 1914 had demonstrated the importance of artillery on the modern battlefield, and Haig realised that the infantry's ability to advance would depend on the effectiveness of the artillery bombardment. The British Army's *Infantry Training* pamphlet of 1914 called for infantry and artillery to work together on the battlefield. However, as Timothy Bowman and Mark Connolly have noted, the document 'gave no instruction on how it should be achieved'.[25]

In early February, Haig met with both Sir John French's artillery adviser at BEF General Headquarters (GHQ), Major General John Du Cane, and the senior artillery officer in the First Army, Major General H.F. Mercer. Haig presented GHQ with three offensive options on 12 February, and gained approval for his preferred operation at Neuve Chapelle. Optimism prevailed in the early stages of planning. The First Army commander stressed that the battle 'is not a minor operation', but 'a serious offensive with the object of breaking the German line' and advancing beyond Neuve Chapelle to reach Aubers Ridge. If Haig's infantry advanced this far, Indian and British cavalry – the fastest moving troops in any Great War army – would be sent forward to gallop along the ridge 'into the open country behind the German lines'. As the day of the battle approached, however, it became clear that the number of troops and the available stocks of artillery ammunition would limit the duration of the battle to three days.[26]

The planning for the assault at Neuve Chapelle exhibited some strengths but many weaknesses. Royal Flying Corps aircraft had photographed the enemy positions at Neuve Chapelle to a depth of between 700 and 1,500 yards (640 and 1,300 metres). These images were used to produce maps of the enemy-held terrain: each of the three corps taking part in the operation was issued with 1,500 maps. Unfortunately, British intelligence officers and cartographers did not identify from the photographs that the Germans had constructed a line of concrete machine-gun positions some 1,100 yards behind the frontline.[27]

British gunners had conducted tests in January 1915 on replicas of German barbed-wire positions in order to calculate how many shells were required to cut the wire. The result of these trials resulted in the 35-minute bombardment that opened the battle on 10 March. The method used to surreptitiously register the German targets to be shelled was mostly effective, but the British artillery plan had two significant shortcomings that would retard the advance.

First, the artillery plan placed a low priority on counter-battery fire. Initially only eight heavy artillery pieces were tasked to fire on the German artillery units. The British quickly recognised their error. When the Battle of Neuve Chapelle concluded on 12 March, all but seven of the British guns were targeting the German artillery. As will be seen in the chapters on the battles of Messines in 1917 and Amiens in 1918, developing the techniques to enable accurate counter-battery fire on the Western Front would make it increasingly difficult for German gunners to bombard the advancing Allied troops. The successful implementation of counter-battery fire would play a significant role in the British Empire's part in the defeat of Germany.[28]

The second failing at Neuve Chapelle was that two 6-inch (150-millimetre) howitzers did not arrive until the afternoon before the battle, and there was no time for the gunners to register their targets or devise their bombardment plan. This meant that a 400-yard section of the German line, where the left side of the 23rd Brigade of the British 8th Division was to advance, was not thoroughly shelled.[29]

The two battalions that attacked this part of the German line were the 2nd Middlesex and the 2nd Cameronians (Scottish Rifles). Just before the artillery bombardment commenced, each soldier in IV Corps was handed a piece of paper bearing a message from the corps commander, Henry Rawlinson. The concluding sentence stated:

> The Army and the Nation are watching the result and Sir John French is confident that every individual in the 4th Corps will do his duty and inflict a crushing defeat on the German 7th Corps which is opposed to us.[30]

British Army officer John Baynes, who served with the Cameronians after World War II, described in his classic 1967 study *Morale: A Study of Men and Courage* what the Scottish soldiers at Neuve Chapelle confronted when the bombardment ceased and the advance began:

> As the guns stopped firing there was a moment of silence. Then the guns started firing again, firing behind the German lines on to the village of Neuve Chapelle. Almost at the same moment came another noise; the whip and crack of the enemy machine-guns opening up with deadly effect. From the intensity of their fire, and its accuracy, it was clear that the shelling had not been as effective as expected. Worse than its lack of effect on the enemy was the fact that it had scarcely touched the wire. Instead of being broken up, the wire and the thick hedge looked just the same as they had before the bombardment.[31]

The 2nd Battalion Cameronians were cut down by German fire. Working from accounts by survivors, Baynes attempted to describe the hellish scene: 'But four hundred human beings lying dead or wounded in a space little more than 200 yards by 100 is almost too terrible to consider.' On the morning of the attack, the battalion had about 700 personnel: at day's end only 145 men had survived. The one surviving officer was a second lieutenant, the most junior commissioned officer rank in the British Army. A week after the battle, Lieutenant Robin Money, of the 1st Battalion Cameronians, sister regiment of the destroyed battalion, was informed – with some understatement – 'that the 2nd Battalion had had a baddish knock', and was ordered to accompany Major Richard Oakley to Neuve Chapelle to rebuild the unit.[32]

On 10 March, the Indian and British soldiers achieved what Lieutenant John Smyth of the 15th Ludhiana Sikhs described as 'absolute surprise'. The British Empire assault force outnumbered the defenders by a factor of more than four to one. Almost all the 1,400 German soldiers in the front line were killed or captured. Only a few escaped to the German second line.[33]

Having captured Neuve Chapelle, however, the attack lost momentum. German machine-gun fire halted the advance. Communication broke down between the British headquarters and the front line. Rawlinson kept his IV Corps troops waiting in the village for the Indian Corps to arrive before ordering a joint advance by the two corps. This halt gave the Germans five hours to prepare a new defensive line, call for reinforcements and commence counter-attacks. The British did not resume the attack until 5.30 pm. They did advance a further 500 yards, but were forced to halt when night fell.[34]

At 11.30 pm, Haig issued orders for the 7th and 8th Divisions to continue the attack at 7.00 am on 11 March. The gains of the first day would not be repeated on the second and third days of the battle. What the senior BEF commanders had not anticipated was the effectiveness of the German defensive system, which allocated small numbers of troops to hold the forward lines until reinforcements arrived to counter-attack and regain the lost ground.[35]

Four infantry battalions of the 14th Bavarian Reserve Brigade had arrived by train on the evening of 10 March and entered the line. A further 16 battalions were deployed to Aubers Ridge in anticipation of a counter-offensive. German troops laboured through the night to dig a new continuous trench line. British First Army Headquarters were not aware of either the arrival of German reinforcements or the construction of the new trench.[36]

The British resumed the battle on 11 March at 6.45 am with an artillery bombardment that was both brief – only 15 minutes, as a large proportion of the ammunition stocks had been expended the previous day (see Table 3.1) – and inaccurate. The assault launched at 7.00 am by three brigades from the 7th and 8th Divisions was halted by the reinforced German force and was an utter failure. The Germans then commenced a three-hour artillery bombardment that blasted the entire BEF line. This cut telephone lines and forced the British to rely on slow moving runners to carry messages. The 7th Division attempted a second attack in the afternoon and was equally unsuccessful.[37]

TABLE 3.1

FIRST BRITISH ARMY AMMUNITION STOCKS AND USAGE,
10 MARCH 1915[38]

Artillery type & quantity	Shell stocks	Shell fired	Percentage fired
13-pounder gun (60)	36,000	9,052	25%
18-pounder gun (324)	132,840	41,810	31%
4.5-inch howitzer (54)	11,500	6,040	52%
60-pounder gun (12)	5,400	523	10%
4.7-inch gun (32)	14,000	n/a	n/a
6-inch howitzer (28)	8,000	3,364	42%
6-inch gun (4)	1,600	175	2%
9.2-inch howitzer (3)	1,000	243	24%
2.75-inch pack gun (12)	6,000	n/a	n/a
15-inch howitzer (1)	35–40	12	33% (approx)

Haig ordered the British artillery to be brought forward to support a third attack the following day. However, before this could take place, six German infantry battalions were brought into the front line on the evening of 11 March for a counter-attack. At 4.30 am on 12 March, the Germans bombarded the line held by the Indian Corps and IV Corps. The artillery fire missed the British Empire front line, but it hit the troops waiting in the reserve areas. The German attack began at 5.00 am. The morning mist shrouded the advancing soldiers until they were 60 yards from the British lines. Despite these advantages, the attack failed. The Indian and British forces did not immediately take the initiative and advance. By the time they did attack in the afternoon, only a small area of ground was captured, and that evening Haig and Rawlinson decided to halt the advance. Sir John French ordered a formal end to the operation on 15 March.[39]

The three days of the Battle of Neuve Chapelle had resulted in 12,892 Irish, Indian and British casualties, mostly in the four assaulting infantry divisions, and approximately 12,000 German casualties, including 1,687 prisoners of war. The German Army studied Neuve Chapelle and made changes to their defensive tactics and strengthened their positions. Edmonds and Wynne described the operation in the British Official History as 'an important landmark in trench warfare' because it demonstrated that it was possible to 'break-in' the German lines, though it would remain difficult to maintain the momentum following the initial 'set piece' attack. Niall Barr argues that the lessons gleaned from this battle would become 'the model for most of the British attacks for the rest of the war'. Haig saw Neuve Chapelle as significant in establishing the BEF's military credentials. In 1925, he told Edmonds:

> In judging our attitude at Neuve Chappelle, it should always be remembered that until that action was fought, the French were of opinion that the British might be helpful to hold on & act defensively [. . .] but that they w[oul]d be of little help to *drive* the Germans from France.[40]

TABLE 3.2

BRITISH EMPIRE CASUALTIES, NEUVE CHAPELLE, 10–12 MARCH 1915[41]

Lahore Division	1,694
Meerut Division	2,353
7th Division	2,791
8th Division	4,814
Other units	1,330
TOTAL	12,892

The second British Empire Western Front offensive in 1915, called the Battle of Aubers Ridge, took place on 9 May, as a minor operation within the French Tenth Army's offensive known as the Second Battle of Artois. The operation was instigated in response to events on the Eastern Front. As mentioned earlier, Erich von Falkenhayn, on becoming Chief of the General Staff, had devised a strategy to gain a negotiated peace with Russia in the east so as to concentrate all Germany's resources to defeat France and the United Kingdom in the west. Following discussions with the Austro-Hungarian Chief of General Staff, Franz Conrad von Hötzendorf, a joint German and Austro-Hungarian Army Group of 352,000 troops attacked 219,000 soldiers of the Third Russian Army on 2 May between the towns of Gorlice and Tarnow in Austria–Hungary. The Russians were defeated and forced into what became known as the 'great retreat'. Germany sent peace proposals to Russia through third parties, but the Tsar refused to negotiate.[42]

The failure to knock Russia out of the war led Falkenhayn to invade Serbia on 7 October in a combined offensive by German, Austro-Hungarian and Bulgarian troops. The Serbian Army was outnumbered, overwhelmed and forced to make a winter retreat through the Albanian mountains. Half the soldiers died from cold and disease. The survivors who reached the Adriatic Sea were embarked on Allied ships and transported to Salonika (Thessaloniki) to open a new front in Macedonia. With the Central Powers dominating the Balkans, the direct train route from Berlin to Constantinople would be revived in January 1916.[43]

Following the Battle of Gorlice–Tarnow, the French continued their attacks in Artois from 9 May to 18 June to demonstrate their commitment to their Russian ally and to prevent Germany transferring more troops to the Eastern Front. In contrast, the British battle at Aubers Ridge was abandoned after only one day.[44]

The British believed that the assault on Aubers Ridge would be 'Neuve Chapelle [all] over again'. Haig's aim was for I, IV and the Indian Corps to break through the German front line and quickly advance 3,000 yards (some 2.7 kilometres) to reach Aubers Ridge before the enemy could recover. The preliminary artillery bombardment would be 40 minutes in duration with an 'intense' final 10 minutes. As at Neuve Chapelle, the Germans did not realise an attack was imminent, though as part of the learning process following the March battle they had strengthened their positions and deployed more troops in the forward trenches.[45]

The British artillery barrage began at 5.00 am on 9 May. On IV Corps' sector, 4.7-inch (119-millimetre) guns had been tasked to conduct counter-battery fire on the German artillery units. Many of the British gun barrels were worn and in need of replacement. Many shells fell short of their target. Nonetheless, enough munitions reached the German positions to wreak destruction. Otto Bestle of the 16th Bavarian Reserve Infantry Regiment wrote: 'It seemed as though the earth itself was on fire'. He saw a comrade named Meisl torn in two when he was struck by a shell in his midriff. At 5.30, the bombardment increased tempo, but as Sanders Marble points out, all this did was give the German soldiers 'a final warning Zero Hour was a few minutes away and they should be ready to leave their dugouts'.[46]

At 5.40 am, the artillery shifted their range 600 yards to the rear and the infantry began their attack. Edmonds wrote in the British Official History that when the 1st, 2nd and 47th (2nd London) Divisions 'left the shelter of the trenches heavy machine-gun fire was opened on them [. . . and m]any fell dead on the ladders and on the parapets', though others did manage to scramble into no-man's-land. The Meerut Division 'found it impossible to advance more than a few yards from the front parapet'. Their advance stalled in the middle of no-man's-land and the Indian trenches 'were quickly blocked with dead and wounded'. The British lacked large-calibre howitzers, and the lighter field artillery had not destroyed the augmented barbed wire entanglements protecting the German line. The British attempted a second attack later in the morning. A third artillery bombardment at 4.35 pm was not followed by an attack as the two brigade commanders decided an assault would have no chance of success.[47]

Hauptmann Karl Windhorst of the 58th Field Artillery Regiment described the lethal German response to the British attacks:

> Because the weather was clear, observation was good. Even if the enemy assault waves could not be fired on directly, the batteries sent a hail of iron into the reserve positions and the strong points behind the front line trenches. This helped to hinder the activities and destroy the concentrations of enemy troops. Troops moving forward to relieve, ammunition columns, batteries closing up and even mounted cavalry

were spotted by the observation posts and brought under immediate fire. In the gun lines, the reports of the observation officers were received with glee. 'Shells on target. The enemy is retreating with huge casualties!'[48]

The one fleeting success occurred on the 8th Division's front, where 2nd Battalion, Rifle Brigade, 1st Battalion, Royal Irish Rifles and 1/13th London Regiment (Kensington Battalion) – a Territorial unit – captured the German front line and advanced a few hundred yards. Haig considered ordering a second attack to commence at 8.00 pm, but, on being told that fresh troops could not be brought forward in time, he decided to end the battle. The 21st Bavarian Reserve Infantry Regiment reported that the British battalions who had broken into the German lines held firm against relentless counter-attacks until dusk. Around 3.00 am, some of the

Fig. 3.1 Indian soldiers, including these men of the 2nd Rajput Light Infantry armed with a French Benét–Mercié machine gun, played a significant role in the 1915 battles around Aubers Ridge. Image: UK Ministry of Defence 103991.

exhausted surviving soldiers withdrew under the cover of darkness to the British lines: the rest were killed or captured.[49]

Haig met his corps commanders at 9.00 am on 10 May when he was informed that the First British Army had expended most of its ammunition and therefore could not continue the operation. The Battle of Aubers Ridge concluded with 11,161 Irish, British and Indian casualties and no ground gained. Edmonds described the operation as a 'serious disappointment' because the German forces had defeated every attack without being required to bring up any reserves.[50]

The third and final British offensive at Aubers Ridge in 1915 was fought around the village of Festubert, south of Neuve Chapelle. The Battle of Festubert began on 15 May and continued for ten days, making it the longest offensive battle the BEF had fought since the war had commenced.[51]

The planning for this attack had commenced on 12 May, in the immediate aftermath of the disastrous Battle of Aubers Ridge. Haig abandoned his previous hopes of a decisive breakthrough to the high ground of Aubers Ridge. He narrowed his ambition to advancing 1,000 yards (less than a kilometre) along the road heading east of Festubert, a limited approach that would become known as 'bite and hold'.[52]

The BEF had continued to expand and now consisted of ten regular divisions, five Territorial divisions, one of which, the 51st (Highland) Division would fight at Festubert, one New Army division, the 9th (Scottish), and the 1st Canadian Division.[53]

The plan for the Battle of Festubert included three significant innovations. The first was that the short 'hurricane' bombardment used at Neuve Chapelle and Aubers Ridge was replaced by a three-day artillery barrage of 5,000 yards (4.5 kilometres) of the German line beginning on 13 May. Field artillery and howitzers conducted three bombardments a day to register the range to their assigned targets. Each bombardment was conducted for two hours and ranged across the full extent of the German positions from the forward barbed-wire entanglements to the rear communication trenches. The second innovation was that the operation would be launched with a night attack on the northern flank followed by a second attack 600 yards to the south, the latter delayed until dawn due to the large number of drainage ditches and other obstructions in the area.

The third was to use Royal Flying Corps (RFC) aircraft equipped with radio to direct artillery fire, though this would be unsuccessful.[54]

Heavy rain on 12 and 13 May resulted in the offensive being postponed to 11.30 pm on 15 May. The day was sunny; this dried the ground, and it was a moonless night. Half an hour before midnight, the 2nd Division's 6th Brigade began its advance. As at Neuve Chapelle and Aubers Ridge, the Germans were not expecting an attack: the British captured the first and second German trenches by midnight.[55]

The stealth which had enabled the success of the 6th Brigade assault was undermined by the British officers of the Lahore Division's Jullundur Brigade who ordered their men to fire at the German positions for periods of five minutes on four occasions between 8.45 pm and 10.30 pm in the misguided belief this would 'mislead the enemy'. Instead, the rifle fire put the Germans on alert and they responded by pouring machine-gun fire on the Indian Army positions.[56]

When the 39th Battalion Garhwal Rifles and the 2nd Leicesters of the Meerut Division attacked at 11.30 pm, the Germans were prepared to face the attack. They turned night into day using flares, star shells and searchlights to reveal the troops and expose them to unremitting fire. After suffering over 300 casualties in 30 minutes, the two battalions retreated to their lines.[57]

Considering that the battle had started before midnight and the German troops were on full alert, the 7th Division's dawn attack at 3.15 am by the 20th and 22nd Brigades was surprisingly successful. The artillery bombardment was effective in supporting the infantry and suppressing the German artillery. A novel but effective innovation was placing six 18-pounder guns in the British trenches so they could fire at short range directly into the German lines. The soldiers captured the first two German trenches by 6.00 am.[58]

As in the previous two battles of Aubers Ridge, it became impossible to continue the advance. General Sir Charles Monro, the I Corps commander, ordered the 2nd and 7th Divisions to attack at 10.00 am, but intense German artillery and machine-gun fire meant that reinforcements and ammunition could not go forward. The 7th Division was soon holding off the inevitable German counter-attacks. As Robert Williams states, this was mostly because the 2nd and Meerut Divisions were unable to maintain their forward movement due to casualties, fatigue and soldiers being separated from their units during the confusion of the night attacks. On the morning of 17 May, when Monro asked the 7th Division commander, Major General Sir Thompson Capper, to attack, he replied that his unit was unable to do so. Haig personally visited the 2nd and 7th divisional headquarters and gained agreement for separate assaults in the early afternoon. Both failed.[59]

Heavy rain returned on the night of 17 May. This delayed the next attack to the afternoon of the following day. The Lahore Division's Sirhind Brigade charged, but the German fire was so intense that half the soldiers had been killed or wounded after advancing only 100 yards. The troops went to ground and began entrenching while still 500 yards from the German front line. When the soldiers' supply of hand grenades became precarious, Lieutenant Smyth of the 15th Ludhiana Sikhs and ten volunteers brought forward 96 grenades in two boxes using turbans as handles. Only Smyth and two Sikh soldiers survived this perilous task.[60]

The 2nd and 7th Divisions were relieved on 20 May after three days of constant combat. Their place was taken by the 1st Canadian and 47th (2nd London) Divisions. These two divisions were brought together in 'a temporary corps', led by Lieutenant General Sir Edwin Alderson, the British officer whom the Canadian government had appointed in 1914 to lead the Canadian Expeditionary Force (CEF), but 'without a corps staff' necessary to devise the detailed plans for a successful operation. The 2nd and 3rd Canadian Brigades were ordered to assault a formidable German fortified position, known as 'K.5', that was surrounded by water obstacles, and barbed wire obstructions, and had clear fields of fire to strike down attacking troops. Major Percy Guthrie, the 10th Canadian Battalion's commander, led the operation. However, Guthrie's vague report of an unsuccessful assault with an undefined number of casualties has led Andrew Iarocci to suggest that the officer and soldiers exercised 'common sense' and did not attempt an attack that would have resulted in the deaths of many Canadian soldiers for no military advantage. Further attempts were made to capture 'K.5', but these failed for several reasons, ranging from design faults in the soldiers' Canadian-made Ross rifles and the lack of artillery ammunition to support the assault. The CEF was relieved on 26 May, and the British began consolidating their new line, ending the Battle of Festubert. German casualties were about 5,000, while total British Empire casualties were more than three times higher.[61]

TABLE 3.3
BRITISH EMPIRE CASUALTIES, FESTUBERT,
15–25 MAY 1915[62]

British	13,113
Canadian	2,107
Indian	1,428
TOTAL	16,648

Soldiers' letters detailed the grim reality of war. On 20 May, Havildar Abdul Rahman of the 59th Scinde Rifles told Naik Rajwali Khan of the 31st Punjabis stationed at Fort Sandeman in Baluchistan:

> For God's sake don't come, don't come, don't come to War in Europe [. . .] and tell my brother Mohammed Yakub Khan for God's sake do not enlist. If you have any relatives, my advice is don't let them enlist.[63]

The local newspaper in Crosby, a coastal town north of Liverpool, published a letter on 29 May from Drummer Alfred Orme of the 1/7th Battalion, King's Liverpool Regiment describing the fighting at Festubert:

> I can tell you it's been awful. You could have got plenty of souvenirs, but the sight of men blown to pieces fed me up, and I do not wish for any souvenirs of that massacre. A better name would be scientific murder. You were walking over dead men all the time, and the smell was suffocating.[64]

The BEF was 'slowly learning its lessons', but, as Jack Sheldon argues, the three battles of Aubers Ridge were 'insignificant events' in the context of the great Western Front campaigns of 1915. The French held most of the line and had the majority of the casualties. The British Empire army at Festubert had suffered 16,500 casualties in ten days, but during the Second Battle of Artois, the French Army lost 100,000 men in six weeks.[65]

Among the innumerable failures and disappointments the BEF experienced during 1915 was a small, unsuccessful dawn attack on 16 June by the 6th Division near Hooge in Belgium. The attack failed, but it would be the stumbling first step towards the tactics and methods that would enable the Allied victory in 1918.

The Hooge operation was important for two reasons. The first was that the field artillery fired first at the German front and support trenches, and then, in a new innovation, lifted their aim to shell the communication trenches. The second was that the bombardment was not designed to wreak wholesale destruction, but rather to temporarily suppress the enemy to enable the infantry to advance. The most likely reason for the attack's failure was that the bombardment was not substantial enough, but the optimum level of shellfire would eventually be found through further experimentation. The person who conceived this technique is unknown. Sanders Marble believes it may have been a French artillery officer, Brigadier W.L.H. Paget, the VI British Corps Artillery Adviser, or G. Humphreys, the 6th Division's chief artillery officer. As Marble points out, this artillery solution 'arrived just three months after Neuve Chapelle had revealed the problem'.[66]

The BEF faced constant shortages of artillery ammunition from the outbreak of war to the end of 1915. In October 1914, 18-pounder guns were allocated only 6 rounds a day during the First Battle of Ypres. The War Office ordered more artillery pieces and shells, but government and private factories were slow to complete contracts. For example, 3,628 18-pounder guns had been ordered by 30 June 1915, but only 802 had been delivered.[67]

The 'shell crisis' entered the British public's consciousness in May 1915 following the Battle of Aubers Ridge and the failure to achieve a quick victory over the Ottoman Empire in the Gallipoli campaign. Charles Repington, the *Times'* military correspondent, sent a letter to the newspaper's editor, Geoffrey Robinson, two days after the battle concluded in which he commented: 'I attribute the failure to want of high explosive [shells].' On 14 May, the *Times* published an editorial stating:

British soldiers died in vain on the Aubers Ridge on Sunday because more shells were needed. The Government, who has so seriously failed to organize adequately our resources, must bear their share of the grave responsibility.[68]

It is true that the British Army had begun the war with a preponderance of shrapnel artillery shells that contained metal projectiles and were designed to kill and maim soldiers on the battlefield, rather than high-explosive ammunition that was filled with TNT or amatol for greater blasting effect. However, it is incorrect to assert that the failure at Aubers Ridge was solely caused by the lack of artillery ammunition and high-explosive shells in particular. The main reason for the defeat was that the German Army in 1915 was better trained, better equipped and more likely to take the initiative than its British Empire counterpart.[69]

Dissatisfaction with how the war was being conducted resulted in two significant political and administrative changes. The first was the formation on 25 May of a coalition government at Westminster. Asquith remained prime minister, but his Cabinet now consisted of 12 Liberals, eight Conservatives, one Labour, and one independent, Lord Kitchener, the War Secretary. The second was the establishment on 9 June of the Ministry of Munitions to increase shell production under the leadership of David Lloyd George. The impact of this government department will be examined more fully in the next chapter.[70]

The BEF would fight one more major battle on the Western Front in 1915. This was at Loos, south of Neuve Chapelle, from 25 September to 13 October 1915, as part of the French Army's double offensive against the Noyon salient with the Second Battle of Champagne (25 September–6 November) and Third Battle of Artois (25 September–4 November). On the day the three operations commenced, Haig wrote in his diary: 'The greatest battle in the world's history begins today. Some 800,000 French and British troops will actually attack to-day.'[71]

Indian infantrymen would not take part in the Battle of Loos. This was not a reflection on their military ability in the lethal Western Front environment. George Morton-Jack points out that Indian soldiers in the trenches had become 'specialists in the most intense kind of regular operations'. In August, the Government of India decided that these divisions should be transferred to fight the Ottomans in Mesopotamia. The last Indian infantry unit departed France in November 1915, but the Indian cavalry regiments would remain on the Western Front until the war ended.[72]

Sir John French continued to be an indecisive leader of the BEF. The British were short of artillery ammunition and particularly high-explosive shells. However, the Field Marshal's proposal following the Battle of Aubers Ridge that he cease all attacks on the German lines until he received more high-explosive shells was a policy that was clearly unacceptable to his French allies. His relationship with Kitchener had not improved. He now held the War Secretary personally responsible for the shell shortage.[73]

Walter Long, Conservative MP and President of the Local Government Board, and his Liberal coalition colleague David Lloyd George, Minister of Munitions, called on Field Marshal Sir John French at his residence at 94 Lancaster Gate, adjacent to both Hyde Park and Kensington Gardens, on the evening of 8 September to discuss the impending offensive at Loos. The strained atmosphere between the military and civilian leadership at this time is suggested by the fact that both Lloyd George and Long felt it necessary to have a transcript made of their discussion with the Field Marshal.

Lloyd George began the interview by asking French: 'You are going to take the offensive very shortly, and I understand that you have plenty of ammunition – indeed, all that you want?' Sir John 'emphatically' replied, 'Most certainly not – I have not all the ammunition I want – certainly not high explosive'. Long and Lloyd George responded, 'But we have been assured that you have stated [. . .] that you have enough for the offensive you are about to undertake.' French stated that there had been 'a misunderstanding'. He continued:

> I have sufficient to justify me in undertaking to support the French in the operation which they are about to commence, and that I shall be able to do my share in ordinary circumstances and provided everything goes exactly as I would wish[.][74]

Sir John asked Lloyd George for more shells, 'as much as you can possibly send me by making *every extra effort* of which your Department is capable'.

He continued: 'I think I have enough ammunition for operations lasting seven days, if nothing unusual occurs.' French then gave examples of the 'unusual' events that occur in a military operation, such as 'instead of lasting seven days it may be prolonged to nine or ten, and I may not have sufficient ammunition'. He then begged Lloyd George 'that every effort shall be made during the time that intervenes between now and the date of the operations, to send me all the ammunition that you can possibly give me'. The Munitions Minister replied that he might be able to 'double the supplies during the next three weeks' and concluded that 'it [was] incumbent upon the Government to do everything in their power to give' Sir John French 'the material, without which success would be improbable and might be impossible.' [75]

The shell shortage led the British Army to use chlorine gas for the first time as part of the opening attack at Loos. This required the placement of 6,500 cylinders into the front line. Each cylinder weighed 150 pounds (68 kilograms) and three men were required to manhandle the cylinder into position. For obvious reasons, the chemical weapon would only be released if the wind was blowing from the British to the German lines. [76]

Haig wrote in his diary that he spent '[a]n anxious night wondering all the time what the wind would be in the morning!' At 5.00 am, Haig determined that the wind was blowing towards the German positions by watching the smoke from the cigarette of Major Alan Fletcher, his aide-de-camp. The chlorine gas was released at 5.50 am, but the vagaries of the wind meant both Germans and British would be affected. [77]

The British made a good initial advance and captured the village of Loos. The battle saw the 9th (Scottish) Division and the 46th (North Midland) Division become the first New Army and Territorial formations to see action. The 9th (Scottish) Division captured a major fortress, the Hohenzollern Redoubt. The Germans counter-attacked and retook the Redoubt on 3 October. The 46th (North Midland) Division made an unsuccessful attack on the fortress on 13 October that resulted in 3,763 casualties. This would be the final action in the Battle of Loos. The 19 days of the battle resulted in approximately 26,000 German casualties and 59,247 British casualties. The intensity of the fighting at Loos is demonstrated by the fact that three British divisional commanders were killed during the battle: Major General Sir Thompson Capper of the

Fig. 3.2 French troops putting on an early version of a gas mask. Chemical
weapons were used by both sides in 1915. Image: UK Ministry of Defence 104053.

7th Division, Major General George Thesiger of the 9th (Scottish) Division
and Major General Frederick Wing of the 12th (Eastern) Division.[78]

The Battle of Loos led to a dispute between French and Haig over the
control of reserve troops that would lead to French's forced resignation.
On the first day of the operation, the initial British success led Haig at
8.45 am to request French to release the British reserves to his control.
The decision was not confirmed until 2.00 pm, by which time it was too
late in the day for the fresh troops to have a decisive effect on the attack.
Edmonds described French's actions as 'ill-considered and tactically out of
date'. Asquith decided on 23 November that the Field Marshal needed to
be replaced. Walter Long telephoned Sir John on 4 December to inform
him that the government required his resignation. Haig was appointed to
command the BEF and would retain this position through controversies,
disasters and failures before gaining eventual victory at the end of the war.[79]

4

Making Munitions

The three battles of Aubers Ridge showed the important role that artillery played in World War I, particularly on the Western Front. It was clear that infantry could not successfully advance on the increasingly lethal battlefield unless they had the protection of the big guns. The public were soon made aware of this new military reality. The *Irish Industrial Journal* declared in June 1915: 'The modern army cannot have enough of ammunition [. . .] Infantry now-a-days seems to be used largely to screen artillery, which really does the fighting under present conditions.' At the beginning of July, the *Times of India* called for an increase in ammunition production to enable 'the much-to-be-desired "curtain of shells" [to] be dropped freely on the Germans, as was the case for a short period at Neuve Chapelle'.[1]

The major European powers, such as Germany and France, had large conscript armies and an established manufacturing base to produce the requisite large numbers of artillery pieces and ammunition. The United Kingdom, India and the other parts of the Empire, with their smaller volunteer armies, lacked this industrial capacity in 1914. During the war, however, artillery ammunition production underwent an unprecedented expansion in Britain, Canada, India and Ireland. This outpouring of guns and shells would enable the British Empire armies to fight industrial warfare and defeat the Central Powers. Making munitions was a practical contribution to the British Empire's war effort, but it was also an emotional commitment that connected civilian workers at home to the soldiers at the front. Shell production also marked the industrialisation of warfare. As David Lloyd George, the first United Kingdom Minister of Munitions, stated in December 1915:

> There has never been a war in which machinery played anything like the part it is playing in this War. The place acquired by machinery in the arts of peace in the nineteenth century has been won by machinery in the grim art of war in the twentieth century.[2]

Canadian corruption: Sam Hughes and the Shell Committee

The United Kingdom government recognised the need to increase the British Army's artillery on the Western Front within three weeks of the outbreak of war. On 24 August 1914, War Secretary Lord Kitchener asked his Canadian counterpart, Colonel Sam Hughes, the Minister for Militia and Defence, to identify United States companies capable of producing 18-pounder shells for Britain. The irrepressible Hughes replied that American imports were unnecessary: Canada could produce all the ammunition the War Office required from North America. The minister met with businessmen and senior military officers in Ottawa on 2 September and gave out initial orders for 2,000 shell cases. This provided much-needed confidence for Canadian manufacturers following the uncertainty resulting from the outbreak of war. In Nova Scotia, both the Dominion Steel Corporation and the Nova Scotia Steel Company closed down parts of their factories, the Lake Superior Corporation in Sault Ste Marie put its workers on half time, and the Grand Forks Smelter in Granby, British Columbia – the largest copper smelter in the British Empire – was entirely shut down. By January 1915, the Shell Committee had received British orders to provide 150,000 complete 18-pounder shells each month from February to July of that year.[3]

Canadian political culture at this time – in both the governing Conservative Party and the opposition Liberal Party – was highly corrupt. Ministers took advantage of being in office to grant lucrative government contracts to their party supporters. For example, Sam Hughes decided in 1913 to replace the existing arsenal in Quebec with several factories to be built across Canada, with the first factory constructed, unsurprisingly, in his hometown of Lindsay, Ontario.[4]

This culture of political patronage was integral to the Shell Committee from its creation. There was no open tender process to gain contracts, and no cabinet oversight. As John Bassett, publisher of the *Montreal Gazette*, confided to one businessman in November 1914:

> Contracts are sent to a great extent to those firms who have political pull [...] The only way to get anything is by coming to Ottawa, securing an interview with the minister and if he thinks it worthwhile, keeping in touch with the contracts branch all the while'.[5]

The Shell Committee had three major shortcomings that would lead to its demise and result in an ignominious end to Sam Hughes' political career. The first was corruption, as exemplified by John Wesley Allison, businessman and Conservative Party crony of Morrisburg, Ontario, who took bribes in exchange for shell contracts. In the worst cases, one individual in northern Ontario received a shell contract who not only did not have a factory, but did not even have the land on which to build a factory, while an Ottawa man who demanded he receive contracts had a workshop with no heating in which the machinery froze solid in winter.[6]

The second was the political pressure to establish ammunition production across the Dominion from the Maritime Provinces to British Columbia, and especially in the Canadian West, in recognition of the large number of volunteers for the CEF from the Prairies. In Moose Jaw, Saskatchewan – 1,800 miles west of Montreal – Ernest Gaskell Sterndale Bennett of the Saskatchewan Bridge and Iron Works gained an initial contract worth 250,000 Canadian dollars to manufacture 50,000 18-pounder shells. This required the hiring of about 150 men, the leasing and transport of ten lathes and seven drilling presses from the east, as well as purchase and shipment of steel from Sydney, Nova Scotia. Production began in the Moose Jaw factory on 19 June 1915. Shell manufacture in British Columbia required first that the steel be transported by rail across the breadth of the nation, and second, once the shells were constructed, being put back on the train for the return journey to eastern Canada: a total journey of 4,000 miles.[7]

The third difficulty for Canadian shell manufacture was the lack of machinery, qualified workers and suitable steel in 1914 and 1915. At the beginning of the war, there were only ten sets of munitions gauges in the country. These were needed to ensure shells conformed to the required specifications and meant that only ten companies could make munitions until more gauges were purchased from Pratt & Whitney in the United States or made locally. When Canada started producing complete shells from April 1915, manufacturers had to source fuses, which had not previously been made in Canada. The Shell Committee contracted American firms to provide 2.5 million fuses, and the Russell Motor Car Company of Toronto to make half a million fuses. Canadian industry could not produce all the complete shells or individual items, such as fuses, that it had promised to provide. Inspectors at Woolwich Arsenal rejected more than half the fuses in the first two batches they received from the Russell Motor Car Company. Almost every company was behind schedule in delivery. By the end of May 1915, Canadian businesses had accepted contracts worth 5.5 million Canadian dollars from the British government, but had completed only 2 per cent of their orders.[8]

There was something very wrong with Canadian munitions production, and the sorry tale of greed, corruption, inexperience and incompetence was soon exposed to public scrutiny. When Parliament resumed in Ottawa in February 1915, both the Liberal Opposition and the Public Accounts Committee began examining Sam Hughes and the Shell Committee. In April, Prime Minister Sir Robert Borden directed his trusted colleague, Albert Edward Kemp, to investigate artillery contracts in order to identify and begin eliminating the most egregious corruption. The following month, he appointed Kemp to chair a War Purchasing Commission that – in contrast to the Shell Committee's practice – held public tenders and awarded contracts to the lowest bidder. Borden increased the external control over the Shell Committee until it was dissolved in November 1915.[9]

On 26 March 1916, George W. Kyte, Liberal MP from Nova Scotia, stood in the Canadian House of Commons and accused both Allison and Hughes of corruption. Borden appointed a Royal Commission to investigate these claims and demanded his Militia Minister, who was in England, to return. Hughes attempted to defend Allison, digging himself 'deeper and deeper', as Canadian historian Tim Cook put it, 'until he made a grave for himself'. In April 1916, Borden resolved that 'Hughes cannot remain in the Government', and on 9 November demanded his resignation. The Canadian attempt to make munitions had been mired in corruption and ended in disaster. A new organisation would need to be devised to enable the effective marshalling of Canada's resources for the British Empire war effort.[10]

The shell crisis

The 'shell crisis' of April–May 1915 combined three separate but related issues. The first was the shortage of artillery ammunition during the three Battles of Aubers Ridge on the Western Front, resulting from the failure to increase munitions production, especially in Canada but also in Britain.[11] This was resolved by the War Office being stripped of responsibility for munitions production and the creation on 9 June of a separate Ministry of Munitions under David Lloyd George. The second was the political dissatisfaction in the United Kingdom with Lord Kitchener as War Secretary and H.H. Asquith as prime minister, leading to the Conservatives joining the Liberals in a coalition government on 25 May.[12] The third was the significant shift in public opinion towards the war across large parts of the British Empire in reaction to four events that occurred in the last two weeks of April and first two weeks of May. As Adrian Gregory points out in *The Last Great War: British Society and the First World War*, there is no evidence for 'mass enthusiasm' for war in the British Empire in 1914. Instead, 'anti-Germanism and popular patriotism' developed in response to the German use of chlorine gas against Algerian, Canadian, French and Moroccan soldiers at the Second Battle of Ypres on 22 April, Zeppelin bombing raids on Ipswich and other English East coast ports from 29 April, German submarine *U.20* sinking the passenger ship *Lusitania* with the deaths of 1,198 people off the south coast of Ireland on 7 May, and the release of the Bryce Report on German war crimes against Belgian civilians on 12 May. The fury unleashed following these events found an immediate outlet in so-called '*Lusitania* riots' that occurred across the Empire from Johannesburg to Vancouver. These saw attacks on German people, on the offices of German-language newspapers, and on businesses and buildings with German-sounding names. This passion then found expression in popular movements, that, in the words of the *Windsor Magazine*, responded to Germany's 'uniquely dreadful' actions by transforming the British Empire 'into an arsenal and divert[ing] every available lathe and wheel, every brain and hand of her peoples, into purposes of war'.[13]

The call to make munitions across the British Empire was a combination of selfless patriotism and self-interested aspiration. As we have seen in the first two chapters, the war had badly affected many individuals' livelihoods in many parts of the Empire. Establishing shell factories was seen, not only as a contribution to the defeat of Germany and its allies, but also as a development of local industry. The *Kalgoorlie Miner* advocated artillery manufacture in Western Australia 'not necessarily with the one sole object of giving immediate help to Britain and her partners in the present strife, but also in order to further her own general development', while the *Indian Patriot* saw shell-making as a way to stem the exodus of Indians overseas: 'Let our emigration depots cease to be, and let ammunition depots rise everywhere.'[14]

Britain: diluting work and drink

In March 1915, a committee of factory inspectors claimed that the shortage of artillery ammunition was due to 'bad time-keeping and drink, shortage of labour, [and] unsatisfactory working of plant'. During a speech at Bangor in Wales on 28 February, David Lloyd George, then Chancellor of the Exchequer, blamed low output on drunken factory workers, asserting: 'Drink is doing more damage in the war than all the German submarines put together.' Lloyd George requested King George V to set an example to the nation and the Empire by announcing he would abstain from alcohol until the conclusion of the war. The King followed the advice of his ministers, but privately described giving up his moderate consumption of a glass of wine or port at dinner as 'a great bore'. In reality, as Robert Duncan argues in his *Pubs and Patriots: The Drink Crisis in Britain during World War One*, the working class was not 'drinking Britain to defeat'. The number of court appearances for drunkenness in 1915 was 20 per cent lower than in 1914. Alcohol was also increasingly watered down as the war continued. A Home Office report on female drinking in May 1916 noted that Beresford Square near Woolwich Arsenal in London was filled with a 'great many smartly dressed Woolwich girls' in the evening consuming port and spirits in the many pubs, but, due to 'the present diluted state' of their drinks, 'they seem little the worse for this kind of amusement'.[15]

In late May 1915, the War Office and the Admiralty recommended:

> A separate Department – the Ammunition Department – to be formed, composed of prominent commercial men representing the various Trades employed in the production of ammunition [. . .] This Department – in cooperation with the Local Armament Committees to be responsible only for the supply of Ammunition to the Admiralty and War Office[.]

This proposal formed the basis for the creation of the Ministry of Munitions, and the formation of local committees, with the 'knowledge', as Lloyd George put it, 'to develop the resources of their district'. At the beginning of November 1915, there were 1346 establishments making munitions in Britain and Ireland. By the end of December, the United Kingdom had 40 local committees organised into 12 munition areas: eight in England and Wales, two in Scotland and two in Ireland.[16]

The Ministry of Munitions would gain more responsibilities and more power as the war continued. It had two roles. The first was to supply munitions – which eventually included explosives, shells, artillery, rifles, rifle ammunition, chemical weapons, aircraft, tanks, trucks and tractors. The second was to control the supply of all raw materials required to make munitions or any other type of war production.[17]

The Liberal government oversaw negotiations between unions and employers that 'diluted' working conditions to increase munitions production. In November 1914, the 'Crayford Agreement' (named for a locality in south-east London) allowed unskilled women to work in factories, as long as skilled male mechanics serviced the machinery. This was followed by the 'Shell and Fuses Agreement' in February 1915 that permitted women to do skilled work, and the 'Treasury Agreement', negotiated between Lloyd George and 33 trade unions in March 1915 that suspended, for the duration of the war, union restrictions that might limit factory production. From 1917, the Ministry of Munitions included in its shell contracts the requirement that at least 80 per cent of employees were female for 6-inch shells and smaller, and 70 per cent for 8-inch shells and larger. These wartime measures were mostly accepted, though some companies refused dilution, and some unions went on strike to oppose female employment.[18]

The 'shell crisis' resulted in many people in the United Kingdom volunteering their free time to work in munitions production. In September 1915, sailors on the Royal Navy's battle cruisers offered to make shell cases when off duty. In 1916 or 1917, Kathleen Scott, sculptor and widow of Antarctic explorer Robert Scott, decided to take her turn as primary carer for her son Peter, so as to allow his nanny to make munitions. On hearing this, J.M. Barrie, the Scottish playwright and creator of *Peter Pan*, wrote to Scott: 'I think that quite splendid of you and one of the kindest things I have ever known of.'[19]

British female munitions workers: 'Tommy's sister'

During World War I, the British soldier – nicknamed 'Tommy' – was joined by the female munitions worker – 'Tommy's sister' – in the popular perception of national mobilisation to defeat Germany. Angela Woollacott, in her classic study, *On Her Their Lives Depend: Munitions Workers in the Great War*, estimates that around one million women worked in a munitions factory of some variety during the war. From July 1914 to July 1918, the number of United Kingdom females in civil employment increased from 3.2 million (23.7 per cent of the workforce) to 4.8 million (37.7 per cent of the workforce).[20] Table 4.1 shows the wartime development of female employment.

TABLE 4.1

UK FEMALE EMPLOYMENT, 1914–18[21]

	July 1914	July 1918
Clerical	452,000	302,000
Commercial	496,000	364,000
Agricultural (permanent)	80,000	33,000
Industrial	2,196,000	3,416,000
TOTAL	3,224,000	4,814,000

Munitions production was carried out across the United Kingdom, but the best-known ammunition factory in the nation was Woolwich Arsenal in south-east London. First established in the 1600s, the Arsenal came under the control of the Ministry of Munitions in August 1915 and expanded during the war to employ 28,000 females, 4,200 men and 6,500 boys in November 1917. By the end of the war, the Arsenal had 31 dining halls and 14 coffee stalls and served between 80,000 and 90,000 meals per day. A further 60,000 females worked in the wider Woolwich area.[22]

Most women who made munitions at Woolwich had an existing connection to the Arsenal. Deborah Thom estimates that a third of female employees gained their position through connection to an existing Arsenal employee, a third were south or south-east London residents who gained employment through the local labour exchange, while the final third were directly recruited by the Arsenal. When women entered employment at the Arsenal in 1915, some male workers verbally abused and physically assaulted the newcomers. Female workers developed their own communities within the Arsenal. Amy May, who worked at Woolwich in March 1917, recalled how women sang as they worked. Shifts of workers organised concerts and sport competitions, and every fortnight, when work hours swapped from the day to the night shift, women without children went out together to the music hall or cinema.[23]

The increasing numbers of workers at Woolwich put pressure on housing and the bus, tram and train systems. London County Council was forced to implement a 60 per cent increase in the number of tram carriages passing Woolwich, raising the passenger capacity from 4,094 to 13,688 people per hour. Accommodation was in short supply and clearly delineated by class status. Working-class women stayed in the Eltham and Well Hall hostels, while 'better-class' ladies were accommodated at the Queen Mary hostel.[24]

Few women worked at Woolwich in the Royal Gun Factory or the Gun Carriage Factory. Only a quarter of the workers in the small arms factory were female. Most women at the Arsenal filled shells. This was a dangerous task as it required workers to work with molten trinitrotoluene (TNT) and often resulted in the women inhaling fumes and developing jaundice. This led to female munitions workers being called 'canary girls'. Those working in the shell filling rooms were regularly checked by doctors: if they showed

Fig. 4.1 Women and men worked long hours in Canadian munitions factories
to make artillery shells. Dorothy Stevens, *Munitions – Heavy Shells*,
etching, *c.*1918. Image: Beaverbrook Collection of War Art,
Canadian War Museum 19710261-0686.

signs of jaundice, they were temporarily transferred to other tasks until the
symptoms receded. In September 1915, Dr Leonard Hill visited the shell
filling rooms at the Arsenal and – with some understatement – described
the work conditions as 'very good [. . . a]part from the poisonous fumes of
T.N.T. in the melting chambers'.[25]

By the end of the war, the United Kingdom had produced a prodigious
218,280,586 artillery shells. This output was only possible because, as
Miss O.E. Monkhouse told the Institution of Mechanical Engineers on
15 May 1918 – when she became the first woman to present a paper to
this body – the war 'made it necessary for the Government to turn to the
largest source of supply of skilled labour, namely, women'. A 1919 Ministry

of Reconstruction report on female employment noted that the conflict had 'afforded an opportunity to women workers to prove their usefulness in many hitherto untried directions'. The Ministry of Munitions, from its inception, identified and trained women to be shop supervisors and forewomen, and by the end of the war, there were female managers in shell, cartridge and filling factories. The report also called 'for equal pay for apparently equal work', not only for the sake of fairness, but also to end 'that old feud between men and women workers which is inspired by the fear of undercutting'. This would not occur. With the end of the war, and the closure of munitions factories, the female labour force shrank. In the 1921 census, the number of women in the labour force was the same as it had been in 1911.[26]

Ireland: forgotten factories

Making munitions is a forgotten part of Ireland's Great War experience. Ulster was the most industrialised Irish province, but the wartime expansion of its existing main industries of shipbuilding and linen production – vital for military aircraft manufacture, as planes in this period were made of wooden frames covered with fabric – meant there was little spare labour or resources for shell factories. For this reason, no government-owned National Factories were established in Ulster. Private companies in Ulster produced 750,000 shells, three million shell components and 66,000 artillery boxes for the Ministry of Munitions during the course of the war, to the value of £939,000. In 1918, only 400 women and 150 men were employed in munitions work. In the provinces of Connaught, Leinster and Munster, five National Factories were established in Dublin, Cork, Galway and Waterford between December 1915 and April 1917, making over 827,000 shells and 382,000 fuses, employing 1,432 female and 737 male workers at the end of the war. The dilution policy was only partially enforced in Ireland, with two thirds of the workforce being female, rather than the required 80 per cent.[27] Table 4.2 details the number of female and male workers in each of these establishments at the end of the war, the factory output and the value of the manufactured items.

TABLE 4.2

IRISH NATIONAL FACTORIES MUNITIONS PRODUCTION,
1915–18[28]

Dublin National Shell Factory (established December 1915)	
Female workers	522
Male workers	294
18-pounder shell high explosive	514,974
9.2-inch shell high explosive	4,917
TOTAL PRODUCTION VALUE	£370,422 15s 1d
Dublin National Fuse Factory (established April 1917)	
Female workers	434
Male workers	116
Fuse No. 101	35,486
Fuse No. 103	196,268
Fuse No. 106	150,697
Aircraft bolts	286,435
TOTAL VALUE	£185,917/15/5
Waterford National Cartridge Factory (December 1916)	
Female workers	266
Male workers	268
18-pounder Mk II cartridge cases	246,640
TOTAL VALUE	£101,834/18/8
Cork National Shell Factory (February 1917)	
Female workers	114
Male workers	35
4.5-inch howitzer shell	30, 041
TOTAL VALUE	£46,904

Galway National Shell Factory (established February 1917)	
Female workers	96
Male workers	24
18-pounder shell high explosive	30,727
TOTAL VALUE	£19,459/9/6
COMBINED TOTAL VALUE	£664,539/5/2

Privately owned Irish factories also manufactured a wide range of war materiel. In Dublin, Sir Howard Grubb's factory made submarine periscopes for the Royal Navy; the Irish Tin Plate Workers Company was created to produce metal linings for ammunition boxes; and T. Dockrell & Sons converted their woodwork factory to make aircraft wings. Companies making shells included the Dublin Dockyard Company with 300 mostly female workers, Pierce's Engineering who employed 200 women in their farm machinery plant in Wexford, and the Cork Shell Factory. These and other firms had produced 290,987 rounds of artillery ammunition by 28 June 1917. Twelve Irish woollen mills across ten counties manufactured blankets for the British Army, and there were uniform factories in Limerick, Dublin and Belfast.[29]

When the 'shell crisis' erupted in May 1915, it did not seem likely that munitions factories would be built in Ireland. Instead, it appeared that the increase in shell production in Britain would see an increase in Irish emigration. As William Townley Macartney-Filgate, Inspector of Industries in the Irish Department of Agriculture and Technical Instruction, recalled, the immediate effect was that 'placards appeared on all the hoardings in Dublin calling on skilled hands in the various trades to cross the Channel'. At war's end, Macartney-Filgate would estimate around 8,000 Irish were working in English munitions and chemical factories. In September 1915, the Waterford *Evening News* reported on three dozen men waiting for the night train to the port of Rosslare, from where they would board the ferry for Fishguard in Wales and then go to work in English munitions factories. The anonymous journalist commented: 'One could not help feeling what a pity it was that instead of sending these men to England we cannot find work for them on this island or ours'.[30]

The impetus to create new munitions factories in Ireland began with the establishment of an Armaments Output Committee in Dublin on 3 June 1915. This sent a delegation to Woolwich Arsenal and received the specifications and drawings required to make ammunition. By September, the Dublin committee had received an 18-pounder shell contract worth £20,000, and selected a site to construct the factory, which began production in December. The *Irish Builder and Engineer* stressed: 'The factory is not intended merely to supply munitions during the war, but will remain as a permanent sphere of industry.'[31]

Waterford had formed a Munitions Committee, and sent William Peare, the committee secretary, and Frank Thompson, of Thomas Thompson & Sons, an engineering firm with workshops in Carlow and Waterford, to Dublin on 13 August to meet Captain R.C. Kelly, the Ministry of Munitions' representative in Ireland. Peare and Thompson returned with the news that the government could not provide Waterford with the equipment to make shells. The Waterford Munitions Committee disbanded in early September, and all seemed lost. Nonetheless, within a week, Thompson & Sons made the decision to commence production. By the end of the year, Frank Thompson was producing 500 shells a week at the Neptune Works in Waterford, and later purchased new machinery produced by the Lee Arrow Company in Cork.[32]

Once an Irish munitions industry had been established, its advocates were keen to develop its manufacturing capacity. In January 1917, E.A. Aston called for the Dublin National Factory to be expanded, arguing that 'a large number of skilled workers' and 'an extensive factory' could 'be rapidly adapted' at the end of the war 'to the manufacture of agricultural machinery, or motor vehicles specially suited to Irish requirements' and encourage economic development.[33]

There were two main reasons, as Edward Riordan of the All-Ireland Munitions and Government Supplies Committee wrote in June 1918, why Ireland 'has not [...] availed itself fully of the opportunities which the war created of extending its existing industries and building up new ones'. The first, as stated in the *History of the Ministry of Munitions*, was that most of Ireland 'was almost entirely non-industrial [...] and [...] skilled labour was very scarce'. The second, as Dr Christopher Addison, the Minister of Munitions, pointed out, was the shipping shortage: 'for in almost all cases, raw materials have to be sent to Ireland to be manufactured and then brought back again'. Making shell boxes in Ireland required the import of over 200,000 tin linings, and the Ministry of Munitions had established a box repair factory at Beddington, south of London, at the end of 1916, in order to reduce the need to make new shell and grenade boxes. Irish companies complained that that they could only tender for box contracts in the Gloucester, Liverpool and Glasgow areas, but the Ministry replied that this restriction would remain because 'these areas can be reached by a short water carriage direct from Irish ports.'[34]

Most Irish munitions workers were women, and few had previous factory experience. Before the Waterford National Cartridge Factory opened, a contingent of female recruits from Waterford were sent for training at the HMV Gramophone factory in Hayes, west of London, which had been converted to a munitions factory. Before 1914, few Irish women were members of trade unions, but from 1917, many female munitions workers joined a British-based organisation, the National Federation of Women Workers (NFWW). Thompson & Sons in Waterford had a dispute with their unionised female workers at the Neptune munitions works and responded by shutting down the factory. In June 1917, Elizabeth Sloan, NFWW Assistant Secretary, chaired a meeting of 300 female munitions workers at the Mansion House in Dublin that discussed the recent 25 per cent pay rises to women workers in England, Scotland and Wales. It was not until April 1918, with the creation of the Special Arbitration Tribunal for Women Employed on Munitions Work, that Irish munitions workers gained pay parity with their British colleagues. In September, a strike and lockout of 595 female and 29 male workers at the Dublin National Factory was resolved with management agreeing to recognise the Shop-Stewards Committee.[35]

It is true, as Niamh Puirséil has written, that 'the low level of munitions output in Ireland' meant that there was 'no industrial transformation of the relatively unindustrialized bulk of the country', and none of the 'dynamic developments, affecting everything from gender relations [. . .] to the power and political clout of organised labour' as seen in Britain. Nonetheless, one should not dismiss the effect that being an Irish female munitions worker had on those individuals in creating a new self-identity and a new community with their fellow workers. It is significant that when the Waterford factory closed following the armistice, the women who were members of the NFWW met in February 1919 and decided to hold monthly meetings 'so as to keep in touch with each other'.[36]

India: shells versus railways

On 11 June 1915, the *Times* published a letter by Abdullah Yusuf Ali, graduate of Bombay and Cambridge Universities, former member of the Indian Civil Service, and barrister of Lincoln's Inn, London, on the 'shell crisis':

> The question of the hour is the supply of munitions of war. Not only shells, but uniforms, bags, and leather goods are in demand. Home industries are working overtime, and orders are flowing to neutral countries. Should not India get the word? With textiles, leather goods, and canvas she is in a position to help immediately. Her industries are waiting for the call of the Empire, as her Armies did at the beginning of the war. 'Khaki,' as the word implies, is an Indian product [. . .] Mr. Lloyd George should certainly give preference to Indian contractors in such matters over contractors in neutral countries. India has given all her resources freely for this year. Financially she has suffered much, as her Budget, just published here as a Bluebook shows. Her business is at a low ebb. She certainly deserves all the support she can get for keeping her industries going. It is both the duty and the interest of Britain to draw upon India's supply before she looks outside the Empire.[37]

India appeared a strong candidate to provide the United Kingdom with munitions. The Government of India had an established infrastructure of state-owned factories that manufactured artillery, rifles, ammunition and other items to equip the Indian Army. The Tata Iron and Steel Company in Bombay was in full production and provided the Indian government annually with 20,000 tons of steel railway tracks. Small shipments of shells from India to Britain had commenced in December 1914. Discussions to expand Indian ammunition production began in May 1915 between the War Office and the India Office in London, and between Government of India railway engineers and private manufacturers in Calcutta, resulting in the creation of the Railway Board Munitions Branch on 6 July.[38]

Attempts to expand munitions production beyond Britain, Ireland, Canada and India would meet with little success. On 12 August 1915, Major General Sir Frederick Robb, Military Secretary to Lord Kitchener, chaired a meeting in London to consider 'how far the resources of India and other Colonies could be developed and made of use' for munitions production. This brought together representatives of the India Office, Ministry of Munitions, Tata Iron and Steel, Australia, New Zealand, South Africa as well as Colonial Office officials representing Ceylon, the Federated Malay States, Nigeria and Singapore. The conference found that India was the strongest candidate to provide the United Kingdom with munitions. The other dominions and colonies – with the exception of Australia – lacked the mineral deposits and capacity to make steel. South Africa did have an industrial centre in the inland Witwatersrand goldfields, but as H.F. Marriott, one of the South African delegates, wondered: 'Was it worth while shipping the steel 5,000 or 6,000 miles by sea and 1,000 by railway, to make it into shell, and then re-ship it?'[39]

Some Indians looked to shell-making as a means to revive the economy. As the Lahore *Tribune* commented on 20 May: 'the effect of the war is acutely felt by the rich and poor alike. Trade has fallen off, industries and manufactures have collapsed, and prices have risen all round.' G.M. Weekley lauded India's industrial potential in a letter to the *Times* in which he praised Indian metal workers for being 'deft in the production of Castings, &c, as they have always been in art metal work and handicraft generally'. The *Hindoo Patriot* stated: 'India will be proud to be of any help to England in the manufacture of munitions an ample supply of which is indispensable to ensure victory.'[40]

In August 1915, Sir Dorabji Tata agreed to consign the entire output of his steel factory to the Government of India. Workshops donated their lathes to set up munitions factories. By September, shells were being made in 16 railway workshops and by nine private companies. Production was concentrated in Calcutta, and included the Albion factory that recruited Chinese fitters and turners from Hong Kong to augment its workforce.

There were also factories in the coal-mining area of Raniganj in West Bengal, the Amristar Public Works Department in Punjab, the Nizam's mint in Hyderabad and the Burmese capital of Rangoon.[41]

By July 1916, India was producing 100,000 shells per month of various calibres. This rate of production, however, was unsustainable, as it was creating a steel shortage in the rest of the economy. In December, the Ministry of Munitions called for Indian ammunition production to continue, arguing that the recently concluded Battle of the Somme demonstrated the need for 'a considerable increase' in shells. Lord Chelmsford, the Viceroy of India, replied to Austen Chamberlain, the Secretary of State for India, in January 1917 that 'steel for shell manufacture is not available'. Despite this assertion, Indian artillery ammunition manufacture did continue, albeit at a reduced rate, into 1918, with a total production of 1.3 million shells.[42]

The German return to unrestricted submarine warfare on 1 February 1917 deepened the British Empire's shipping shortage. This led to the formation – exactly one month later – of the Indian Munitions Board. This organisation was tasked to reduce India's requirement for shipping by reducing imports, encouraging local production, and developing India as a supply centre for the British Empire armies in the Middle East and East Africa.[43]

In December 1916, Brigadier General H.O. Manse suggested to Sir Ernest Moir in the Ministry of Munitions that India should supply railway track to Egypt because the Indian Ocean and the Red Sea had no 'submarine risk', unlike the U-boat-infested waters of the Mediterranean. Early in the new year, the Government of India decided that the bulk of Tata's steel production for the first seven months of 1917, totalling over 30,000 tons, would be allocated to the production of railway track for the War Office and for the Mesopotamian campaign.[44]

The Indian Army's invasion of Mesopotamia – the name given to the three provinces of the Ottoman Empire based on the major centres of Basra, Baghdad and Mosul – had begun on 6 November 1914, when Indian Expeditionary Force D, consisting of the 16th Indian Brigade, captured the port of Fao. This operation was carried out in order to safeguard the nearby Anglo-Persian oil refinery in Abadan, in which the United Kingdom government had a 51 per cent controlling share, and which had gained strategic importance following the 1911 decision to convert the Royal Navy from coal to oil propulsion.[45]

In early 1915, the UK government reinforced the Indian force and directed it to capture Baghdad. The Ottomans blocked the advance south of Baghdad in November, and the Indians withdrew downstream to Kut. After a five-month siege, 13,000 Indian and British troops surrendered on 29 April 1916. Kaushik Roy argues that the defeat at Kut was the result of 'logistical failure'. The British did not provide suitable rations that Hindu and Sikh soldiers could consume, and as the soldiers became weaker, they became unable to conduct offensive operations against the Ottomans.[46]

One of the main reasons the Indian force failed to capture Baghdad in 1915 was an unreliable logistics system. Boats were impeded when river levels were low, and draught animals, ranging from camels to ponies, were in short supply. Railways were faster and more reliable, but the Government of India had refused in 1915 to invest in such infrastructure unless London assured Calcutta that Mesopotamia would remain under British control at the end of the war.[47]

The decision to use Indian steel to make rail tracks for Mesopotamia rather than munitions for the Western Front would have a significant effect on the campaign. The new commander, Lieutenant General Sir Stanley Maude, had spent most of the year rebuilding his force, before beginning his advance in December 1916. Maude's troops captured Kut in February 1917, Baghdad and Fallujah in March, Tikrit in September and Ramadi in November. The rapid advance was made possible due to the provision of Indian-made locomotives (144 in January 1918), rolling stock, and 1,855 miles (just under 3,000 kilometres) of railway track shipped to Mesopotamia, East Africa, Aden and the major Persian port of Bushire (Bushehr).[48]

The steel made by Indian workers, either for shells or railways, had enabled the United Kingdom to retain its hegemony in Egypt and the Suez Canal, and to defeat the Ottoman Empire and seize control of Mesopotamia, Transjordan, and Palestine.

New Zealand: George Birch makes shells in his garage

New Zealand, along with other parts of the Empire, offered to send men to Britain to work in munitions factories. On 18 May 1915, however, Lord

Harcourt, the Colonial Secretary, politely but publicly declined the Kiwi proposal in the House of Lords. A few days after this setback, George Birch told a patriotic meeting in his home town of Blenheim in the Marlborough region in the north of New Zealand's South Island:

> if the Home Country cannot get its workmen to turn out shells and ammunition to meet our pressing demand [...] the New Zealand Government should [...] give me an order and see: that would be the best proof [...] that New Zealand would be leading the way of the Colonies in this urgent need.[49]

George Birch was probably an Englishman called John Birch who changed his first name when he emigrated to New Zealand in 1905. Born in Foleshill, Warwickshire, he completed an apprenticeship in engineering and worked in various manufacturing concerns in Coventry and Sheffield before establishing his own factory in Nuneaton making motorcycles named 'George Eliot' after the famous local author. Birch established the Marlborough Engineering company in Blenheim in 1912 and would construct New Zealand's first locally made motor car.[50]

New Zealanders began a debate on whether they could manufacture munitions. New Zealand had 1,058,312 people in the 1911 census, and the Colonial Ammunition Factory in Auckland had been producing small arms ammunition since 1885. However, the Dominion's economy was concentrated on mining (coal and gold) and agriculture (frozen meat and wool). There was no local steel industry to provide the raw material to make artillery shells.[51]

Charles C. Allen, from the Mechanical Engineering Department at Auckland Technical College, stated: 'The manufacture of shells and ammunition in New Zealand is quite feasible'. The Mayor of Wellington, J.P. Luke, 'an old and experienced ironfounder', told a public meeting that there was 'a large amount of steel [...] at railway and other workshops' that could be turned on lathes to make shells. In contrast, J.B. Laurenson, President of the Canterbury Industrial Association, argued that 'until we are in a position to turn out our own iron and steel it would be useless for us to endeavour to manufacture munitions of war'. Mr Kear of P. & D. Duncan ironmongers in Christchurch bluntly stated:

From a practical point of view it [making munitions] is not to be considered. This is an agricultural and pastoral country and we should set out to feed the Allies. We can do that as well, if not better, than any country in the world.[52]

John Corry, the Mayor of Blenheim, sent a letter to James Allen, the New Zealand Defence Minister, on 25 May asking that Birch be supplied with shells as a template to manufacture his own munitions. Allen, recognising the current public enthusiasm to produce ammunition, instructed Brigadier Alfred Robin, Commandant of the New Zealand Military Forces, to provide Birch with two empty shells. Four weeks later, Birch announced that he had constructed his own 4.5-inch (114-millimetre) shell. He also ambitiously provided Robin with a list of the items necessary to establish a factory capable of producing a thousand 4.5-inch shells per week. The Blenheim Borough Council passed a motion calling for a munitions factory to be established in their town, one councillor noting that Blenheim had a few years previously missed out on becoming the site of Lever Brothers' New Zealand soap factory, and a 'similar mistake could not be made now'.[53]

Birch's shell was tested on 26 June at Mahanga Bay near Wellington. As there was no 4.5-inch howitzer in the entire country, Robin directed that the shell be placed in a pit and detonated by electricity. Lieutenant Robert G.V. Parker of the Royal New Zealand Artillery reported that, although Birch's shell appeared to be well made, when it was fired, 'the body of the shell was much fractured [. . .] denoting an inferior and unsuitable class of steel'. Parker concluded that if Birch's shell had been fired from a gun, it would have exploded within the barrel, with dangerous consequences for the gun crew.[54]

Exactly one month after the 4.5-inch howitzer trial, a second test was carried out at Trentham army camp near Wellington. This time, an 18-pounder gun fired three British-made 18-pounder shells alongside three Birch-made shells. The New Zealand-made shells were successfully fired, however, Birch had used mild rolled steel – rather than harder forged steel – to fabricate his shells. One shell was too soft and scratched the inside of the gun barrel. As Captain W.P. Thring of the Royal New Zealand Artillery stated: 'had even comparatively small number of shells which acted in this manner been fired, it would have meant the gun would have been rendered useless for further service'. With the departure of the NZEF in 1914, only six 18-pounder guns remained in the country. Thring warned the government that 'no more can be obtained' and 'strongly recommend[ed] that no further experiments be carried out with them'. This concern for New Zealand's remaining artillery was justified: from May to August 1917, the German raider *Wolf* laid mines and captured two merchant ships in New Zealand waters. Had the *Wolf*'s captain, Karl Nerger, decided to come inshore and attack coastal cities and towns, these 18-pounders would have been vital for defending coastal cities and towns.[55]

In contrast to the public enthusiasm to make munitions, Allen was coldly practical in his assessment of New Zealand's capacity to manufacture ammunition. When H.B. Burnett, Secretary of the Auckland Harbour Board, offered the government on 23 June 'the use of the whole of its machinery and equipment at Calliope Dock for the manufacture of munitions of war', Allen replied that 'the difficulty' in commencing production was 'not so much machinery as that of suitable material and explosives'. Senator George Pearce, the Australian Defence Minister and Allen's trusted confidante, expressed his doubts of establishing an Australian munitions industry. Allen privately told Professor Robert Scott that if New Zealand attempted to make artillery shells, 'the output would be so small and so costly that it would not be wise for us to attempt it'.[56]

New Zealand soldiers, alongside soldiers of the British and French empires, had been fighting the Ottoman Army since April 1915 to capture the strategically important Dardanelles Straits. Allen's responsibilities for the NZEF greatly increased. To ease his workload, Arthur Myers was appointed in August as minister of a separate Munitions and Supplies Department and took charge of 'the munitions question'.[57]

Myers immediately held a meeting of almost 40 engineers and other experts, including George Birch, on 3 September at the Buckle Street Drill Hall, Wellington. This established a committee, chaired by Professor Robert J. Scott, from the School of Engineering and Technical Science, Canterbury College, University of New Zealand in Christchurch.[58]

Scott's committee promptly presented their report three days later. This stated that making machine guns, rifles or explosives in New Zealand was unviable (a single machine gun had been produced at the Petone railway workshops near Wellington), but that 18-pounder shell cases could be produced if the required materials could be imported from Australia.[59]

The New Zealand government purchased five tons of steel from the Broken Hill Proprietary (BHP) steelworks at Newcastle in New South Wales and 250 copper bands from the Victorian State Munitions Committee that were shipped to the Addington railway workshops in Christchurch for a trial production run in January 1916. However other complex tasks had to be completed before manufacturing could begin: gauges to accurately measure components had to be made from Australian technical drawings, jigs and hydraulic presses had to be constructed, while other machinery had to be modified before it could be used for shell-making. In the end, the effort required outweighed the benefit to be gained. The New Zealand government resolved on 15 February 1916 to halt shell production, before the steel had arrived from Australia to make the base plates and complete the shells. Myers released a statement explaining the decision:

> After full and careful consideration, Cabinet has decided that, having regard to the fact that the supply of shells to the armies of Great Britain and her Allies has now, apparently been placed upon a more satisfactory footing, and the necessary quantities of munitions assured, New Zealand could be of greater service by directing all her energies towards the supply of food for the soldiers, such as butter, cheese, frozen meat, etc, and to take no further action, meanwhile, regarding shell manufacture.

New Zealand never made munitions, but the Munitions and Supply Department began the local manufacture of boots and uniforms for the NZEF and other items including the cord pull-throughs used to clean rifles. New Zealanders would also contribute to the manufacture of artillery ammunition for the British Empire war effort: at least 87 skilled workers travelled to the United Kingdom to work in munitions factories.[60]

On 23 February 1916, George Birch, the most vocal advocate for making shells in New Zealand, wrote to Brigadier Alfred Robin, Commandant of the New Zealand Military Forces, asking for the Defence Department to reimburse his expenses for 'experimental shell-making'. Robin supported Birch receiving some payment, pointing out that his work had 'helped to a great extent to show the New Zealand Engineering Firms the many difficulties confronting the manufacture of shells'. In March 1916, Birch submitted an invoice for £123: in June, Allen approved a payment of only £50. The Marlborough Patriotic Fund wrote to the Defence Minister urging him to pay Birch the full amount. When Allen declined to do so, the Patriotic Fund held a collection and in September 1917 presented Birch with £50.[61]

Australia: building Woolwich on the Murrumbidgee

Like New Zealand, the Commonwealth of Australia had not made artillery shells before the Great War, but unlike its Trans-Tasman neighbour, Australia had a larger industrial infrastructure and was a steel producer. Between 1910 and 1913, Labor Senator George Pearce, had, as Defence Minister, established five state-owned factories – mostly in Melbourne, the temporary federal capital – to provide the Commonwealth Military Forces with uniforms, saddles and accoutrements, cordite, Lee–Enfield rifles and rifle ammunition. When the Labor Party returned to power following the Liberal Party's defeat in the 5 September 1914 national election, Pearce asked the War Office to provide the specifications for both the 18-pounder gun and the ammunition it fired so they could be manufactured in Australia. The reply – which arrived two months later – stated that the ministry was so overwhelmed with work that it was unable to provide this information.[62]

Canberra, the site of the permanent federal capital, had been officially named in March 1913, but the onset of hostilities had stalled the construction of the new city. In March 1915, Pearce's attention was drawn to a proposal in the First General Report of the Parliamentary Standing Committee on Public Works recommending concentrating defence production at an arsenal in Canberra. The senator supported the scheme because the embryonic capital was 100 miles inland and more secure from attack than the existing factories, mostly in coastal cities; establishing the arsenal would provide employment and ensure Canberra would be more than 'a merely political city'; and, as the arsenal would be in Commonwealth territory, the federal government, rather than the state governments, would be responsible for enacting industrial and factory laws and ensure the workers were provided with 'comfortable homes [. . .] at a very reasonable rental'. In October and November 1915, members of the Arsenal Committee visited Indian defence factories to examine their procedures, in order, as the *Times of India* wrote, to introduce 'similarly up-to-date methods in Australia'.[63]

In 1917, the federal government decided that the arsenal would be constructed on the Murrumbidgee River and compulsorily purchased the farm at Tuggeranong to provide the site. Despite Pearce's ambitions, post-war financial stringencies meant that no arsenal would ever rise at Tuggeranong on the Murrumbidgee in emulation of Woolwich on the Thames.[64]

In line with his ideological predilections, Pearce had thought only in terms of making munitions in state-owned factories, and publicly admitted that he had never considered the possibility of converting existing privately owned factories to make shells. Conservative Australians were savage in their criticism of the Labor Defence Minister. James Alexander Smith, a member of the Victorian Institute of Engineers, told Lloyd George that Pearce's proposed arsenal was a worthless bid to establish 'a State labour colony at the, at present, wholly unoccupied site of the Federal Capital City at Canberra'. The Melbourne *Argus* described the Defence Minister's apparent inaction on munitions as a 'humiliating contrast' to his Canadian counterpart, Sam Hughes.[65]

Pearce did not anticipate the Australian people's response to the 'shell crisis' in June 1915. Newspapers ran detailed instructions on how to make shrapnel shells, and examined the potential of using the leaves of the Australian ti-tree for shell-filling. Munitions committees were formed in all six states. In Pearce's home state of Western Australia, Hugh Plaistowe, proprietor of a Perth sweet factory, called for the local production of munitions on 22 June. The Perth Chamber of Commerce, the Ironmasters' Association, the Chamber of Manufactures and the Chemical Society of Western Australia then combined on 28 June to create a Munitions Committee. A delegation was chosen, consisting of Ernest Tomlinson, co-owner of Tomlinson Brothers, Western Australia's largest engineering company, fellow engineer W. Monteith, E.A. Mann, Chief Inspector of Explosives, and E.S. Hume, Chief Mechanical Engineer, Western Australian Government Railways, and travelled to Melbourne by ship (the transcontinental railway linking Western Australia to the rest of the Commonwealth was under construction but not yet completed).[66]

When the West Australians, from the largest, but most sparsely populated and most isolated of all the states, disembarked in Melbourne, Herbert Brooks, President of the Victorian Chamber of Commerce and prominent member of the Victorian Munitions Committee, invited the other state munitions committees to attend a national meeting on 14 July. By coincidence, the West Australians' arrival coincided with the UK government's request for Australia to produce 18-pounder shell cases at an initial price of 22 shillings per item. When Brookes opened the meeting, he invited Pearce to chair the meeting. When the Labor minister rose to speak, he may have been surprised when the assembled businessmen gave him a spontaneous ovation. Pearce instituted a structure where the Federal Munitions Committee provided the state committees with shell specifications, gauges – some from the United Kingdom, but mostly made in Australia – and BHP steel.[67]

Munitions committees began receiving steel in late August 1915. The first workshop to begin ammunition manufacture was the Adelaide engineering company, Murray Aunger Limited, in the second week of November. The Adelaide *Sport* expressed local pride that it was 'a modest but enterprising South Australian firm [that made . . .] the first actual start at turning out shells in quantity'. However, difficulties in establishing and increasing shell production soon emerged. In November 1915, the government of Tasmania, Australia's least populous state, allocated £20,000 on the advice of the state Munitions Committee to build an electric-powered munitions factory. The United Kingdom government refused the export of British machinery and the project was abandoned. The Queensland government won a contract to produce 50,000 shell cases, and converted a section of the Ipswich railway workshops into a munitions factory. By August 1916, only 20 per cent of the shells had been made: almost two thirds of these failed inspection due to defective steel.[68]

In Perth, the War Munitions Supply Company of Western Australia had been formed in early September and received a consignment of 12 tons of steel in October. A shortage of gauges to ensure the shells met the specifications meant production remained at a low tempo. By 21 December 1915, the company had completed only 800 shell cases. Hugh Plaistowe, who had been the leading advocate for shell-making in Western Australia, wrote to Lloyd George for advice, admitting '[w]e are groping in the dark over here so far away from the base of operations'. The Ministry of Munitions passed the letter to the Colonial Office, who responded to Sir Ronald Munro Ferguson, the Australian Governor-General, stating: 'Mr. Lloyd George considers that the energies' of the War Munitions Supply Company of Western Australia 'would be best utilized by furnishing equipment' to AIF recruits.[69]

By the time Australian factories had begun making shells, British production had expanded to such an extent that the Australian output was inconsequential in comparison. As M.M. Henderson, Chief Mechanical Engineer for Commonwealth Railways commented: 'Australia started too late on shell work and the rate of production has been too slow [. . .] the production of Australia is so small as to become an embarrassment instead of an assistance'. On 20 June 1916, Andrew Fisher, the retired prime minister who had become Australian High Commissioner in London, asked Sir Frederick Black, Controller of Munitions Supplies for his 'experienced opinion of the advisableness of continuing shell manufacture in Australia'. Production ceased on 30 June 1916, by which time Australia had produced only 15,000 18-pounder shell-cases. This, however, was not the end of Australian involvement in making munitions. During the war, BHP exported 17,900 tons of steel to the United Kingdom for the Ministry of Munitions. From 1915, British warship and weapons manufacturer Vickers recruited Australians to work in their factories. In May 1916, a group of Australian and New Zealand workers, mostly Vickers employees, founded the Australasian Munitions Workers Association in Barrow-in-Furness, Lancashire. From August 1916, the Australian government selected skilled tradesmen to go to Britain as 'a means of giving effective help to the war, and at the same time prepare a way to enable Australia to build up her own arsenal on sound lines'. By the end of the war, over 6,000 Australian men and some women were engaged in munitions work in British factories.[70]

Canadian competence:
Joseph Flavelle and the Imperial Munitions Board

The failure of the Canadian Shell Committee to produce sufficient artillery shells for the Western Front forced the United Kingdom to become directly involved in the Dominion's ammunition manufacture. The former Welsh Liberal MP David Alfred Thomas (who appeared in Chapter Two with his later title of Lord Rhondda in the role of British Food Controller) disembarked in North America on 5 July 1915. This voyage was less eventful than his previous Atlantic crossing in May, as Thomas had been on the *Lusitania* when it was torpedoed by a German U-boat.[71]

After visiting several Canadian shell factories, Thomas concluded that the Shell Committee needed to be shut down and replaced with a more efficient organisation. With the agreement of the British and Canadian governments, a new body, the Imperial Munitions Board (IMB) was created on 30 November 1915. This was directly responsible to the Ministry of Munitions in London, but would be led by a Canadian. The governments on both sides of the Atlantic agreed that the most qualified person to lead the IMB was the Toronto businessman Joseph Flavelle.[72]

The Board consisted of nine members representing the various Canadian provinces, but Flavelle had demanded and had been granted full executive authority as board chairman, and ran the organisation as 'a one-man show'. Flavelle ensured the Shell Committee's corruption did not infect the IMB. When one board member told Flavelle that he would use his position to look after his 'friends', Flavelle stiffly replied that 'we were all approaching our duties from the standpoint that we had no friends'.[73]

Flavelle began by examining Shell Committee contracts. Ten days into his new job, he told a colleague: 'The waste and extravagance in the securing of supplies for War is appalling and must run into fabulous figures'. He went through unfilled orders and reduced prices or cancelled contracts, saving 4 million Canadian dollars, and tightened the inspection of munitions. In September 1916, for example, 90 per cent of 6-inch shells produced at the Montreal Locomotive Works were rejected.[74]

With this increased scrutiny and accountability, Canadian munitions output greatly expanded, as shown in Table 4.3.

TABLE 4.3

CANADIAN ARTILLERY SHELLS EXPORTS, 1914–18[75]

1914	3,000
1915	5,377,000
1916	19,942,000
1917	23,782,000
1918	16,325,000
TOTAL	65,429,000

During the war, 675 munitions factories were established in 150 different towns in every Canadian province except the smallest, Prince Edward Island. By 1917, this had been rationalised to 466 factories: 381 Canadian factories producing shell components and 24 United States factories making components for 61 Canadian machining and assembly factories. Between 250,000 and 300,000 individuals worked in Canadian munitions factories during the Great War. This included around 35,000 female workers. No woman had worked in a Canadian metalwork factory before October 1916. At the Canada Cement Factory in Montreal, 400 women were solely responsible for every stage of manufacturing large 9.2-inch (234-millimetre) shells from forging to shipping.[76]

Flavelle took the opportunity to purchase extra steel in the middle of 1916, and, due to a US steel shortage, was able to gain extra contracts for the following year. Half of Canada's steel was allocated to munitions, and in 1917 the Dominion produced between a quarter and a third of all the artillery ammunition used by the British Empire armies. Canadian munitions output would decline in 1918. This was because, unlike the United States, Canada did not provide the British with 'financial facilities', and the War Cabinet was forced to reduce ammunition orders in order to purchase food.[77]

Explosions

Munitions, by their very nature, are inherently volatile and potentially lethal for the workers who manufacture, store or transport them. Angela

Woollacott estimates that about a thousand munitions workers were killed in the United Kingdom during the Great War. The following four examples demonstrate both the dangers of working or living in close proximity with explosives, and the courage of the women and men who daily put themselves in peril.[78]

Scottish-born George Kynoch opened an ammunition factory near Birmingham in 1863. The family company expanded and, by the time of World War I, operated factories in South Africa, Ireland and elsewhere. Kynoch Limited's factory at Umbogintwini, south of Durban on the east coast of South Africa experienced explosions on 9 December 1916 and 10 January 1917 that resulted in the deaths of nine workers. The Umbogintwini factory made blasting glycerine and gelignite for the South African mining industry. W.B. Jackson, the Acting Chief Inspector of Explosives could not confirm the cause of either incident as no witnesses survived to recount how the explosions occurred. The December detonation killed Situnzi and Nkibela − adult men described in the racist language of the time as 'first class boys' − and Emile Poilly, Kennedy Leggatt and Sakayedwa Kumalo. Of the first four men, 'only the barest fragments were recovered'. Kumalo was further from the blast and '[t]here was enough of the trunk' to enable his father to identify the body. The January blast killed Beni, Munti, William McMahon and William Thompson. The Works Manager, Ernest Martin, believed this conflagration occurred because McMahon 'was a quick tempered man [...] angry with Thompson for being late' and dropped a box of explosive paste.[79]

Kynoch had established a factory in 1895 in the Irish coastal town of Arklow, County Wicklow, to make cordite, which at this time was replacing gunpowder as the explosive in bullets and artillery shells. During the Great War, the workforce expanded from 600 to 5,000 workers. On 21 September 1917, an explosion during the night shift killed 27 men and injured six others. Initially it was believed that a U-boat had fired on the factory with its deck gun, but this was dismissed. The most likely cause appears to be that the workers had a habit of placing their sweat-sodden handkerchiefs on the steam pipes to dry, and the heat caused them to ignite.[80]

The expansion of munitions production led to the construction in 1916 of a shell filling factory of 'enormous magnitude' on a 185-acre

(75-hectare) site at Chilwell, five miles from the English Midlands city of Nottingham. Employing around 6,000 male and 3,000 female workers, No. 6 National Filling Factory each week produced over 1,000 tons of amatol – a combination of TNT and ammonium nitrate – for filling 60-pounder and larger artillery shells. On the evening of 1 July 1918, over 15 tons of TNT, ammonium nitrate and amatol exploded. The blast obliterated the mixing house, an extension and the TNT mill and killed 134 workers, including every person in the vaporised buildings. This meant there would be 'no direct evidence [...]' as to the cause of the explosion', though the inquiry following the disaster concluded the most likely cause was that 'a large piece of iron' fell into a mixing machine and caused the detonation.[81]

The biggest explosion of World War I – and the largest human-made explosion in history at that time – occurred in the Canadian port of Halifax on 6 December 1917. Halifax had become one of the major ports for Allied and neutral merchant ships crossing the Atlantic. During 1917 2,000 merchant ships carrying 15 million tons transited through the ice-free port. On the morning of 6 December, the French merchant ship *Mont Blanc* prepared to depart carrying 3,000 tons of TNT, gun cotton and picric acid, a volatile form of explosive. The *Mont Blanc*'s deck was stacked with 494 barrels of benzol, a coal-tar product then in short supply in France. As the French ship sailed out of Halifax, the *Imo*, a small Norwegian merchant ship, was coming into the harbour. The *Imo* ignored normal navigation rules and continued to sail straight towards the larger *Mont Blanc*. As the ships closed, both took evasive action at the same time, with the result that the *Imo* hit the *Mont Blanc*. The collision occurred at 8.45 am: some of the benzol barrels on the deck had ruptured and started a fire. The *Mont Blanc*'s captain, Aimé Le Médec, realised his crew was too small to control the encroaching flames and ordered his men to abandon ship. Nineteen minutes after the collision, the *Mont Blanc* exploded. The blast was heard 225 miles away at North Cape Breton at the furthest extremity of Nova Scotia.[82]

The explosion devastated Halifax. In a city of 50,000 people, 1,600 were killed and 9,000 were injured. Vice Admiral Evelyn R. Le Marchant described the city as 'an appalling sight of fallen and burning houses'. Acting Lieutenant Commander F.H.D. Clarke was ordered ashore with a group of officers and sailors to 'report to any Senior Naval Officer met with

Fig. 4.2 Canadian soldiers searching ruins following the Halifax explosion. Image:
Library and Archives Canada/Bibliothèque et Archives Canada PA-000704.

at the scene of the fire, or failing which, to use my own judgement where I
could be of most use'. Clarke found a draper's shop and commandeered a
bale of blankets and rolls of muslin for use as bandages for the injured. He
then divided his sailors into small groups and ordered them to rescue any
survivors, leaving the dead for later.[83]

An Irish factory migrates to Australia

With the end of the war, the Ministry of Munitions announced that the
Waterford Cartridge Factory and the other Irish National Factories would
be shut down and the buildings and their contents would be put up for
sale. The machinery from the Waterford factory would find a second life in
Ireland, Britain – and Australia.[84]

John Jensen, an eager and ambitious 35-year-old public servant from
the Australian Defence Department, had been seconded to the Australian
High Commission in London. He looked to purchase the machinery
from one of the surplus National Factories so the Defence Department

could initiate the manufacture of artillery shells in Australia. The Defence Department Secretary, Thomas Trumble, had estimated in January 1919 that the cost of the requisite factory plant would come to £200,000. Jensen, however, told Senator George Pearce, who had arrived in London in March to oversee the repatriation of the Australian Imperial Force, that there were 'extraordinary bargains being offered' in equipment, and the final cost would be much less.[85]

While Australian Prime Minister William Morris Hughes discussed the acquisition of war surplus machinery with David Lloyd George, and Pearce had similar conversations with Lord Inverforth, the Minister for Munitions, and Lord Milner, the Colonial Secretary, Jensen became a frequent visitor at the Ministry of Munitions' Disposal Office, located in temporary buildings on the Victoria Embankment Gardens by Charing Cross Station. It was here that he learned that the contents of the Waterford National Cartridge Factory would be auctioned on 21 October 1919.[86]

Jensen sent British and Australian experts to Waterford to appraise the quality of the plant, and made a brief journey to Ireland to see the site for himself. The Australian government agreed to the purchase of the factory contents for £20,000. On receiving this approval, Jensen left his desk at the Australian High Commission on the Strand and began walking to the Disposals Office on the Embankment. He did not complete this journey.[87]

As Jensen later wrote: 'And then suddenly another thought flashed into my mind. I had gone about 100 yards, I stopped and turned on my heel and walked back to my office.' He showed the telegram to one of his colleagues named Wrigley and said: 'We are not going to tell the Ministry [of Munitions] about this: we will let it go to auction and buy it then.'[88]

The Waterford sale, conducted by Dublin auctioneers William Montgomery & Son, attracted 600 potential buyers 'from all over Ireland and across [the] Channel'. Jensen and Wrigley arrived on the first morning of the two-day auction. The main interest that day focused on the factory's power plant, eventually purchased by Ford Motor Company representatives for the tractor factory they were constructing in Cork. The two Australians had made no bids that day and tried to be as inconspicuous as possible at dinner that evening at their hotel.[89]

Towards the end of the second day of the auction, a lot was put up consisting of 18 presses for making shell cases with a reserve price of £10,000. After some desultory bids, the auctioneers were about to withdraw the items from sale. Jensen then 'stepped in and offered £10,000 for the lot'. The *Irish Times* reported that the bid 'made the audience gasp'. Messrs Montgomery and Montgomery consulted with a Ministry of Munitions official. Jensen recalled being 'asked in a tense silence to state my credentials'. His reply that he represented the Australian government, created 'a sensation amongst the audience [...] and the offer was accepted'.[90]

Jensen recalled: 'The remaining machines in the cartridge case plant were then put up in lots, and as there was no competition, perhaps I had "frightened off" the dealers and the scrap buyers, I was able to name my own price and purchased them [...] all.' Instead of paying £20,000 for the factory plant, Jensen's tactic meant the Australian government ended up with 18 presses and 25 finishing machines in excellent condition for £10,510. The Waterford auction made over £50,000 in total.[91]

Transporting the machinery from Waterford was more complicated than Jensen anticipated. Transoceanic merchant ships could not dock at Waterford, and the railway to Dublin could not carry the 130 tons of equipment. Instead, the load went by train to Belfast, was shipped to Glasgow and thence to Australia. On arrival in their new home in the southern hemisphere, the machinery was installed in the Maribyrnong defence factories in Melbourne, where they provided the capacity to produce 270,000 shell cases a year.[92]

1916: The East African Campaign

World War I was fought in the age of the great European colonial empires. However, it is often forgotten that many parts of the British Empire had their own 'sub-imperial' agendas. The conflict was seen as providing an opportunity to bring these ambitions – developed without any reference to the indigenous population – into reality. In the Pacific, New Zealand and Australian military chiefs had decided in November 1912 that, in the event of war with Germany, New Zealand would capture Samoa and Australia would take German New Guinea. Following the outbreak of war in 1914, New Zealand troops landed at Apia on 15 August and occupied the German colony without any armed resistance. The Australian Naval and Military Expeditionary Force came ashore at Rabaul on 11 September and fought a short skirmish with German and Melanesian troops to capture the nearby German radio station. When the Indian Army's advance in Mesopotamia was progressing smoothly in May 1915, the Lahore *Desh* predicted:

> its inclusion in the Empire will be of the very greatest benefit of India, as not only will it provide an outlet for the surplus population of India, but it will furnish Indian traders with a new market at not too great a distance. The question for decision is what share India is to have in colonising the new country, and what reward Indians will get for their efforts.

In 1916, Walter Davidson, the Governor of Newfoundland, asked Colonial Secretary Andrew Bonar Law to negotiate a land swap with the French government whereby the nearby French islands of Saint Pierre and Miquelon and their rich fishing grounds would become part of Newfoundland, in exchange for France gaining the Caribbean island of Dominica, or even the entire West African colony of the Gambia. Davidson's proposal would be denied. South Africa held the greatest ambition, which was to gain the port of Lourenço Marques in Portuguese East Africa (now Maputo, Mozambique), as it was the nearest natural harbour for Johannesburg and Pretoria. The South African government saw this expansion as so vital for the nation's future that it created a new army at the end of 1915 to enable it to take the leading role in the East African campaign. As the war was lurching towards its conclusion in August 1918, Walter Long, the British Colonial Secretary commented that, apart from Canadian Prime Minister Sir Robert Borden, 'who is not materially affected and is I can see rather frightened of his big neighbour' the United States, the other Dominion leaders demanded that Germany must be stripped of all its colonies in any peace agreement. South African General Jan Smuts was 'quite clear and emphatic about the African case' and prime ministers Billy Hughes and William Massey 'equally so about the Pacific'. Australia, New Zealand and South Africa would be allocated New Guinea, Samoa and South-West Africa, but the South Africans would never gain Lourenço Marques.[1]

Following the outbreak of war, the British and French decided to seize the Kaiser's four African colonies of Togoland, Kamerun, German South-West Africa and German East Africa. In all these campaigns, the majority of the combatants were African soldiers. The first colony to be invaded was Togoland. This was Berlin's smallest African possession, but the only German colony that generated enough income to cover its budget. Acting Governor Major Hans von Döring had a military force of 152 paramilitary police, 416 civil police and 125 border guards armed with four machine guns and obsolete rifles. On 12 August, two companies of the Gold Coast Regiment marched the thousand yards (roughly a kilometre) from the Gold Coast border to capture the port at Lome, Togoland's capital. A ship disembarked more Gold Coast troops at Lome, and French troops invaded eastern Togoland from Dahomey. Döring retreated inland and bolstered his force by conscripting Africans. German troops rebuffed the British on 22 August where they prevented their foe crossing the Chra river and inflicted 17 per cent casualties. A further northwards withdrawal brought Döring and his men to the Kamina radio station, part of the global network for communicating with colonial authorities and German warships. The acting governor destroyed the radio station to prevent its use by the Allies and surrendered on 25 August 1914. The *Windsor Magazine* described this conquest to its readers in exotic terms, pointing out that while some of the inhabitants of Togoland used coins, for the majority of the population 'cowries, salt and brass or copper rods, constitute the usual currency'.[2]

The British and French then switched their attention to the much larger colony of Kamerun, which was vulnerable as it bordered Nigeria in the west, and various French colonies in the east. On Kamerun's southern border was Rio Muni, a colony of neutral Spain, which would become significant for the Germans during the campaign. The German colonial troops, or *Schutztruppen*, with the inclusion of German reservists and colonial police, consisted of 6,660 Africans and 1,460 Europeans. The *Schutztruppen* had 60 machine guns and several thousand modern Mauser rifles. The French invaded Kamerun on 6 August, and were soon joined by 600 Belgian troops. Nigeria Regiment soldiers entered the colony at the end of the month. The main British strategy was to capture every overseas German radio station so as to blind German cruisers such as the *Emden*. On 26 September, after several weeks of small-scale naval battles, a combined Anglo-French amphibious landing resulted in the capture of the Douala radio mast without a fight.[3]

Brigadier-General Charles Dobell, the Canadian-born officer theoretically in command of the entire Allied force, wanted to defeat the Germans by blockading their supply chain through neutral Rio Muni, but the political ramifications arising from taking such action against a non-belligerent meant the plan was shelved. In May 1915, Dobell despatched two forces – British and French – by different routes to the southern market town of Jaunde (modern Yaoundé), in the mistaken belief that it was the cornerstone of the German defence. The African population stayed mostly loyal to the colonial authorities. The German troops maintained a strong defence and slowed the Allied advance to a crawl. With the onset of the wet season, Dobell halted his operation and withdrew his troops to rest until the rains ended.[4]

From the middle of 1915, the tide began to turn in favour of the Allies. Garua in northern Kamerun, where German troops were conducting cross-border raids into Nigeria, was neutralised when a British 12-pounder gun and a French 3¾-inch (95-millimetre) artillery piece were transported up the Benue River. The French and British attacked Garua on 10 June. The artillery bombardment unnerved the German defenders, many of whom fled, and the Allies occupied the town. By now, the Germans were shifting their forces southwards toward the Spanish colony from where they were receiving their supplies.[5]

In October 1915, French and British forces began converging on Jaunde. Here, the Beti people, who remained pro-German, impeded the Allied advance by abandoning their villages and preventing the soldiers from accessing food or labourers. However, the concentration of troops around Jaunde meant that 125 miles (200 kilometres) of the boundary between Kamerun and Rio Muni formed by the Campo River was left unguarded. Between December 1915 and February 1916, 1,000 Germans, 6,000 African troops and 7,000 family members and followers crossed the river into the neutral sanctuary. The last German garrison, at Mora in the north of the colony, surrendered on 18 February 1916. The Spanish shipped the 14,000 Germans to the nearby Spanish island of Fernando Po where they remained, with their rifles and half a million rounds of ammunition, until the end of the war.[6]

On 14 September 1914, South Africa attacked German South-West Africa with a force of 45,000 white troops, half of which were mounted infantry, supported by 33,000 African, 'coloured' and Indian volunteer auxiliaries who served as drivers, horse grooms, labourers and railway and road workers. A group of 'coloured' men who had spent time in the German colony was covertly formed – in defiance of South African law – into an armed scouting unit. The outnumbered Germans, led by the *Schutztruppen* commander, Victor Franke, had about 2,000 mounted troops and 3,000 reservists called up as infantry. Unlike in Kamerun, few South-West Africans supported the Germans, no doubt due to their genocide of the Herero and Nama from 1904 to 1907. The Germans had three aircraft, while the invaders could call on the recently created South African Aviation Corps. The South Africans attacked on three fronts. A Force attacked the south of the colony from the western Cape, B Force advanced on the eastern frontier, while the Royal Navy landed C Force at the southern port of Lüderitz. The Germans did not stand and fight, but constantly withdrew away from the South Africans, moving northwards and towards the interior.[7]

Louis Botha, South African prime minister and general, left Parliament and arrived in South-West Africa in February 1915 to personally command the advance on Windhoek, the colony's capital. On 20 March, South African mounted troops surrounded and captured around 200 German troops, but forward movement was slow as the South Africans decided to rebuild the narrow-gauge railway to South African standard gauge – a clear indication of sub-imperial ambition. The dry summer meant horses ran short of grass. Mixed race Basters and Rehobothers rebelled against their colonial overlords, and Germans attacked these groups as they tried to flee the conflict. The South Africans continued their advance in April with 12 British armoured cars, whose main advantage was that they required less water than horses. On 12 May, Botha entered Windhoek, capturing one more German radio station.[8]

By now, the South Africans had gained momentum. Botha reinforced his army with mounted troops, artillery and a supply train consisting of 500 wagons, and advanced towards Otavi, in the north of the colony, which had a garrison of 1,000 troops with artillery and machine guns. Major Hermann Ritter, the German commander, was tasked to delay the South Africans to allow Franke to organise a new defensive position 50 kilometres to the east at Tsumeb. The South Africans' swift advance on Otavi on 1 July caught Ritter unprepared. The Germans were forced to retreat once again.[9]

The mounted infantry encircled the remaining German troops, who formally surrendered on 9 July 1915. The casualty rates were surprisingly low for a nine-month campaign: 529 South Africans were killed, wounded or died of illness, while there were 1,188 German casualties of whom only 103 had died. German South-West Africa was now under South African occupation. German civilians returned to their homes and the local civilian administration continued. Lord Buxton, the South African Governor-General, identified the campaign – undertaken by 'a non-professional Defence Department and a non-disciplined "Defence Force"' – as sub-imperialism, pointing out 'South Africans as a whole have always looked with longing eyes to the absorption of this Territory as rounding off their possessions, and as protecting them against the proximity of a Foreign Power.'[10]

The one remaining unoccupied colonial possession was German East Africa. With an area approximately the same as France and Germany combined, the colony had a population of over 7.5 million Africans, 14,000 Indians and 5,300 Europeans. The British Empire effort to capture German East Africa began with a failed attempt by Indian troops to capture the port of Tanga on 3 November 1914, and would continue until 25 November 1918, two weeks after the armistice, when *Generalmajor* Paul von Lettow-Vorbeck finally surrendered at Abercorn in Northern Rhodesia (now Mbala, Zambia). The American historian Francis Parkman's comment on the war between the British and the French in North America in the Seven Years War (1756–63) that the 'question was less how to fight an enemy than how to get at him', applies equally well to the East African Campaign, where logistics, transport and medical support were as important for success as combat operations. The East African campaign is best understood as three separate operations by three different British Empire armies. The first was the Indian Army's amphibious landing at the port of Tanga, 50 miles south of the border with British East Africa (modern Kenya), in November 1914. The second was the white South African campaign commencing in early 1916. The last, from 1917, was the army of East Africans of the King's African Rifles and West Africans of the Gold Coast and Nigeria Regiments with accompanying porters, both volunteer and conscript, who took the campaign to its conclusion in 1918.[11]

It is not surprising that the initial British Empire assault on German East Africa was mounted from India. East Africa, the Middle East and India formed an 'Indian Ocean World' linked by culture, religion, trade and migration. The rupee was the currency of British East Africa and Uganda. Thousands of Indians had gone to East Africa, gaining positions such as clerks and railway stationmasters that may not have been available to them in India.[12]

The Government of India had despatched IEF A to the Western Front, IEF D to Mesopotamia, IEF E and F to occupy Egypt, and IEF C to reinforce British East Africa. IEF B was tasked to invade German East Africa. Commanded by Major General Arthur Aitken, the force consisted

Fig. 5.1 Nigerian troops with ambulance, German East Africa.
Image: Imperial War Museum Q 15614.

of two infantry brigades, a mountain artillery battery and an engineer unit; a total of 8,000 men. Many of the troops were not from the Indian Army, but from the military forces of the Indian princely states, whose training level was more variable, and had to replace their obsolete firearms with modern Short Magazine Lee–Enfield rifles. The force departed Bombay for East Africa on 16 October 1914. In the port of Mombasa in British East Africa, Aitken met with the commander of IEF C, Major General J.M. Stewart, on 31 October. The two generals devised an optimistic plan based on the premise that the Germans would not resist, IEF C would defeat the main enemy force around Mount Kilimanjaro, while IEF B, having taken Tanga, would then be free to sail south and capture Dar es Salaam, the colony's main port and capital.[13]

The British Empire landing at Tanga began on the night of 2 November. The shallowness of the bay meant the troops had to be gradually landed by small lighters. The battle was a series of missed opportunities for the British. Twice the Germans withdrew from the town: either time Aitken could have bloodlessly captured Tanga. Instead, the assault failed. A thousand German troops forced the much larger IEF B to withdraw on 7 November with losses of 360 men killed and 487 wounded. The British left behind at Tanga several hundred rifles, 16 machine guns and 600,000 rounds of ammunition for a grateful enemy. German casualties were 71 killed and 76 wounded. On 3 November, 4,000 Indian soldiers of IEF C from British East Africa had advanced only six miles into German territory to Longido, west of Mount Kilimanjaro, when they were attacked and pushed back by 600 African soldiers and 90 mounted German settlers. These victories made the reputation of the German East African military commander, *Oberstleutnant* Paul von Lettow-Vorbeck, and his African troops, known as askaris, from the Arabic and Swahili word for 'soldier'.[14]

An analysis of the operation, prepared in 1933 by the team writing the British Official History, noted that no planning had been made for the capture of Tanga before 1914. This meant:

> no detailed information as to the topography of the place had been collected; it proved impossible to obtain accurate information after hostilities had commenced; and in the event that lack of information was a prime factor in the disastrous repulse which ensued.'[15]

Aitken wrote an account of the operation which he believed would 'vindicate' his actions. It is true that the general's Indian troops were only partially trained, and suffered 'complete demoralization' when they came under German artillery fire. However, one could argue that the central role of a military commander is to prepare his men for combat. Instead, Aitken attempted to shift the responsibility for the failure at Tanga onto others. He blamed the captain of the escorting warship, the *Fox*, for delaying the landing, and the failure of the attack on his troops, stating that they were from Madras and therefore 'the worst troops in India'.[16]

Following their victory at Tanga, the Germans commenced a raiding campaign on the vulnerable Uganda Railway in British East Africa. This ran 586 miles (943 kilometres) from Mombasa on the coast to Kisumu, also known as Port Florence, on Lake Victoria. The garrison of Indian and British soldiers were stretched in attempting to defend the rail corridor.[17]

As 1914 came to a close, the British Director of Military Operations, Major General Charles Callwell was trying to persuade War Secretary

Lord Kitchener to cooperate with 'Belgians and French and every body we can lay our hands on to help deal with German East Africa'. The Colonial Office opposed Callwell's plan because they wanted 'to prevent the employment of any other troops [. . .] lest we should not get everything at the end of the war'.[18]

In January 1915, the Colonial Office changed its attitude and allowed British generals in East Africa to begin planning coordinated operations with their Belgian counterparts. These included British offensives from Northern Rhodesia and Uganda into German East Africa, and a Belgian attack using Congolese soldiers of the *Force publique* to capture the productive farmland of Ruanda and Urundi (now Rwanda and Burundi).[19]

The German cruiser *Königsberg* had taken shelter in the mangroves of the Rufiji river delta in the south of the colony. The German Admiralty hatched an ingenious plan to send a ship to break the British blockade, rendezvous with the *Königsberg* and unload the coal, ammunition and provisions to enable it to sail back to Germany. A British merchant ship that had been interned in Germany when the war began was disguised as a neutral Danish freighter, evaded the blockade and reached East Africa. The British cruiser *Hyacinth* sank the ship near Tanga, but the cargo in the hold survived. The German troops were able to salvage 2,000 tons of coal, 7,000 rounds of naval ammunition, 1,500 rifles, 4.5 million rounds of ammunition and medical supplies that greatly assisted their ongoing resistance. The British eventually located the *Königsberg* and sent two shallow draft warships up the river where they attacked and destroyed the cruiser on 11 July 1915. This removed the last German warship outside European waters.[20]

The South African election on 20 October 1915 resulted in Louis Botha retaining the prime ministership. With the campaign in South-West Africa having successfully concluded, Botha looked to a second sub-imperial campaign in German East Africa that would allow South Africa to gain the port of Lourenço Marques. As Lord Buxton, the South African Governor-General, had proposed in April 1915:

> if East Africa were conquered and annexed, [. . .] the Northern part might be added to British East Africa, and the Southern and Central part be 'swopped' with the Portuguese for the Southern part of Portuguese East Africa[.][21]

The 'great recruiting campaign' for white volunteers, led by Charles Crewe, brigadier general and Member of the Legislative Assembly for East London in the Eastern Cape, commenced on 23 November 1915, with the aim of raising 2,000 reinforcements for the 1st South African Infantry Brigade that would deploy on the Western Front, and 8,000 infantry recruits and 2,400 mounted troops for East Africa. This dual recruiting demonstrated the divergent priorities of Anglophone and white Afrikaners. As Crewe explained:

> There are in this country two distinct sets of people, i.e. those who insist upon service in Europe mostly home born men with English ties & again another set of men who wish to see service in Africa & nowhere else, to direct either class to the other service will be found most difficult indeed. [22]

The formation of these units resembled the creation of the 'pals' battalions in Britain during 1914 and 1915. The Transvaal Regiment designated the 9th Battalion as a 'Sportsmen's' Battalion, an Irish battalion was proposed to emulate 'the heroism displayed by the 10th Irish Division in the Gallipoli Peninsula', while Australians and New Zealanders living in Johannesburg, probably mostly working in the mining industry, formed a double company of 350 men in the 7th Battalion. Captain Messer stated in Johannesburg's *Illustrated Star*: 'Tell Anzacs [. . .] that they had better roll up soon if they want to go with their old pals. If they don't come along and register quick they'll get left'. The expeditionary force also included 8,000 labourers of the South African Native Labour Corps, and two Indian stretcher-bearer companies formed by the Natal provincial government. In total, 47,521 white South African and about 18,000 black South African soldiers volunteered and served in the East African campaign. [23]

Crewe was optimistic on the prospects of the South African intervention. He wrote:

> I am sure of one thing, that if we have enough men and our military movements are made with all possible rapidity when advancing, the German enemies will soon be dealt with. It is I am sure a big bubble

needing to be pricked, African native troops even when led by whites won't stand.[24]

On 3 February 1916, the United Kingdom government approved the appointment of the South African General Jan Smuts to command the East African theatre. Smuts disembarked at Mombasa on 19 February, and declared his intention to immediately go on the offensive. As he told the Chief of the Imperial General Staff, General Sir William Robertson, on 15 March 1916, Smuts was critical of the 'lamentable slowness' of the previous commanders in this theatre, and argued that his three South African divisions would use their 'mounted forces for rapid turning movements and long marches which the infantry could follow up', that would quickly outmanoeuvre his footslogging foe. The general's decision would have surprised Charles Repington, *The Times*'s military correspondent, who had told his editor on 22 December 1915:

> I don't think we need worry about East Africa just yet. The delay in raising the levies in South Africa until after the late elections has made it too late to undertake important operations before the rains, which, as you know, last from April to June, and make German East Africa practically impassable [. . .] The real campaign will not begin much before July next. [25]

Already, on 12 February, the British Major General Michael Tighe had used his experienced 1st East African Brigade and the newly arrived novice 2nd South African Brigade to attack the Germans on Salaita Hill in British East Africa, south-east of Mount Kilimanjaro. By January 1916, the German force in East Africa had expanded to include 2,712 European soldiers, 11,367 African soldiers and 2,591 auxiliaries. The Germans almost encircled the South African brigade and inflicted many casualties. A rout was prevented only by the steadfast intervention of an experienced Indian battalion.[26]

On 13 March, Smuts ordered a South African mounted brigade and a South African infantry brigade to outflank Salaita Hill, while Tighe's 2nd East African Division carried out a frontal attack. Major General J.M. Stewart's 1st Indian Division marched west of Mount Kilimanjaro towards the rear of the German force. The British Empire force of 40,000 men outnumbered Lettow-Vorbeck's 4,000 askaris, so the Germans withdrew southwards along the high ground. South African mounted troops and infantry attacked the Germans on Taveta Hill. Among these soldiers was Sergeant Jones of the Transvaal Anzac Company who described the battle in a letter to his family in New Zealand as being waged through the day until the summit was finally captured after midnight. The British Empire force advanced into German East Africa, where white South African mounted troops and 'coloured' infantry of the 1st Cape Corps Battalion captured the railhead at Moshi, in the shadow of Mount Kilimanjaro. Smuts believed he could make inroads against Lettow-Vorbeck in early 1916 before – as Repington had anticipated – the wet season began, turning roads into quagmires and bringing the upsurge in insect-borne diseases that affected both men and animals.[27]

The rains did begin, but Lieutenant-General Jacob van Deventer, the South African mounted troops commander, nonetheless led his troops southwards through the incessant downpour in pursuit of the Germans. Their objective was Kondoa Irangi. Here, it would be possible to cut the colony's central railway. In addition, the town was located in a valley surrounded by hills, which should have made it easy to defend. The Mounted Brigade captured the town on 19 April. By now, however, tsetse flies had spread fatal disease among horses, mules and oxen, and mosquitoes brought malaria; German treatment of malaria and other tropical diseases was more effective than that of the British Empire force. The transport shortage meant that tents and other equipment had not been carried during the advance. Soldiers had to sleep in the open in the pouring rain as they marched through mud to Kondoa Irangi, arriving sodden and starving, two weeks after the mounted troops. Reflecting on the campaign in December, Crewe commented:

> Smuts' own mistake was allowing van de Venter to rush off to Kondoa Irangi in the between rains in the early part in the year, he simply formed a salient where he could not be fed & could with difficulty be supported & much of the shortages of supply to our advanced lines dates from this period when in endeavouring to support & feed van de Venter, energies were taxed transport destroyed & all for no real purpose.[28]

Lettow-Vorbeck attacked the South Africans at Kondoa Irangi in May, but was repulsed. He then placed artillery on the hills surrounding the town and began bombarding their positions. As food dwindled, the defenders were placed on half rations. Disease was rife among both men and horses. By June, both armies were exhausted. The Germans withdrew southeast to Turiana on the central railway where they could be supplied. Smuts pursued his foe, but was never able to overtake them.[29]

In April 1916, the Colonial Office told Smuts he was now authorised to occupy all of German East Africa. In September, he captured Dar es Salaam and subsequently occupied the colony's entire coastline. By this stage, however, the South African force was spent. About 12,000 white troops, mostly South African, had been invalided by the end of 1916, due to illness and exhaustion. Nurse Annie Hills, who worked in the British 19th Stationary Hospital at Moshi, noted in her letters to her mother in Tadcaster in Yorkshire that the hospital's capacity had been doubled from 200 to 400 due to the increasing number of cases. Hills started learning Swahili so she could converse with the African staff and villagers. On 13 September, Hills wrote: 'We have such a number of wounded in. I have officers & men, our own, Dutchmen & Germans.' In addition, 53,000 draught animals had died of disease between June and September 1916. As Charles Crewe would tell Long in May 1917:

the initial operations round Kilimanjaro were sound, but the move forward, after Moshi was taken, was a risk which very nearly ended in disaster and led to the huge waste of men & material due to an attempt to move food & supplies in the midst of the rainy season [. . .] It was the incompetent South Africans not the Imperial or Indian people who were to blame for a state of affairs which put out of action hundreds and hundreds of men. The wicked wastage of troops [. . .] was entirely due to lack of organization, whole brigades wasted to next door to nothing, regiments 1100 strong down to 120 & 80, one brigade when all the regiments were put together only numbered 800 fit.[30]

The South Africans were withdrawn, and the campaign entered its final stage where the British Empire army was 'Africanised'. Crewe, writing from East London where he was recovering from malaria he had caught in East Africa, told Long that the Germans would be defeated, 'not with white troops but African troops'. As a member of the British Official History stated in 1933: 'the outstanding lesson' of the East African campaign was 'the value of the African native troops, as compared with troops of any other description, in the peculiar conditions of East African warfare'. While 'troops of almost every other description in the Empire were brought into East Africa', they had all suffered high rates of illness. For example, in the Indian units serving in East Africa, an average of 30 per cent of troops were in hospital. Crewe told Long that 60 per cent of his mostly white South African troops were hospitalised every month, while only 5 per cent of East African troops were admitted for medical treatment each month. East Africans were 'perfectly adapted to local conditions', spoke local languages and could be trained into 'first-class fighting units'. The local military unit, the King's African Rifles, had a peacetime establishment of 3,500 troops organised into three battalions. At the end of 1916, the regiment was expanded to eventually form 22 battalions with a total of 35,000 troops. Table 5.1 demonstrates the Africanisation of the British Empire army in this theatre by the end of the war.[31]

TABLE 5.1
EAST AFRICAN FORCE, NOVEMBER 1918[32]

Western Force	1/1st, 2/1st, 3/1st King's African Rifles
	1/4th, 2/4th King's African Rifles
	Northern Rhodesian Police Battalion
	Rhodesian Native Regiment
Training Battalion	4/1st King's African Rifles
Administrative and Technical Units	South African Engineers
	South African Motor Cyclist Corps
	South African Medical Corps
	Rhodesian Medical Corps
	Mechanical Transport Corps
	South African Supply and Transport Corps

Eastern Corps	1/2nd, 2/2nd, 3/2nd King's African Rifles
	1/3rd, 2/3rd King's African Rifles
	3/4th, 4/4th King's African Rifles
	Howitzer Section, 22nd Derajat Mountain Battery
British East Africa and Northern Frontier	1/5th, 1/6th King's African Rifles
	Intelligence Department Corps of Scouts

In early 1917, Smuts left East Africa to join the Imperial War Cabinet in London. His immediate successor was Major General Arthur Hoskins, but he was replaced in May by Deventer. On Smuts' departure, the British controlled 75 per cent of German East Africa, including all of the colony's major infrastructure. During 1916, the Belgian *Force publique*, which had 719 European and 11,698 African troops in eastern Congo, had sent an expeditionary force commanded by Colonel Frederik Olsen into German East Africa. In May, these troops invaded Ruanda and captured the administrative capital of Kigali and the royal capital of Nyanza. Here, King Yuhi Musinga had raised the Belgian flag to greet the new European colonisers. Olsen then moved south to occupy Urundi, reaching the main centre of Usumbura (modern Bujumbura) in June.[33]

Portugal had entered the war on 9 March 1916, after its government's action – requested by the British – to intern German and Austro-Hungarian merchant ships in Lisbon harbour had resulted in the Germans declaring war on the republic. Portugal aimed to use the war to expand its African colonial empire. In April 1916, it occupied the Kionga Triangle, a small parcel of land between Portuguese and German East Africa. In late October 1916, the Portuguese sent 2,700 troops across the Rovuma River to invade German East Africa. The Portuguese army was poorly trained and poorly led. Defeated by a German force one third the size, within a month the troops had fled back across the Rovuma.[34]

The newly Africanised British force in East Africa continued to pursue Lettow-Vorbeck's *Schutztruppen* in German East Africa. The British gained an advantage in transport and communications, though this was dependent on an often hostile environment. In August 1917, a welcome shipment of trucks arrived, though Major General R.H. Ewart noted the South African drivers were 'pretty raw [. . .] so we had a lot of cars going into the workshops'. During the wet season, 'bridges broke and the wretched porters had to wade waist deep in mud and water'. One five-mile (eight-kilometre) stretch of sticky black soil road would take between two and five hours to traverse. Sapper Frank Rowland of the 41st Airline Section constructed elevated telephone lines in East Africa. Originally they were placed on wooden poles, but termites and the weather destroyed them. Indian-made tubular metal poles provided the solution, though they were sometimes pulled awry by wandering giraffes.[35]

Deventer fought 36 battles in July and August 1917, with the aim of denying the enemy access to water supplies and agricultural areas. On 24 September, Captain A.A. Gardiner of the 2nd Battalion Nigeria Regiment mourned the death of Native Sergeant Major Sambo Buachi, whom he described as 'a splendid soldier' and recipient of the Military Medal who is 'a great loss to the company'.[36]

What would be the last major battle of the East African campaign was fought at Mahiwa from 15 to 18 October 1917. Deventer's plan was to encircle the Germans by sending three Nigerian battalions and the Gambia Company to the enemy's rear, while a second group, known as Linforce, made a frontal attack. Major C.E. Roberts of the 1st Battalion, Nigeria Regiment wrote that during the two-day march to their position, telephone wire was unrolled so that Deventer could communicate with them. The troops reached their objective on 14 October.[37]

The next morning, Germans ambushed a company patrol, but it was able to reach camp with few casualties. On 16 October, the baggage train with 3,000 carriers was ambushed, and, in what Roberts described as 'a horrible nightmare', the Germans attacked the main force for three hours. The Nigerians established a semicircular firing line to prevent flank attacks. The British force suffered 202 casualties in this fight. By the end of the battle, the British had suffered 2,000 casualties and the Germans 600 killed and wounded. The British had lost more soldiers in the battle, but it was the Germans who were running out of men, ammunition and supplies. On 25 November 1917, Lettow-Vorbeck crossed the Rovuma River into Portuguese East Africa, abandoning the sick, the wounded and many of the askaris' wives and children, and taking with him just

300 Europeans and 1,800 Africans. The combined Allied force in East Africa at this time numbered 52,000 troops. Despite the disparity in numbers, Lettow-Vorbeck's act bought him more time. On 4 March 1918, Buxton complained that 'the position in Portuguese East Africa is highly unsatisfactory', noting that when Lettow-Vorbeck left German East Africa:

> he was practically on his last legs, demoralised, very nearly starved, armed mostly with rifles of an old pattern, and with nothing but black powder. Now he is equipped with the best and most modern Portuguese rifle. From all accounts he has never been better off at any time since the campaign opened. [...] He has plenty of food, transport and carriers, and I believe now quinine and medicine.[38]

British Intelligence had not anticipated Lettow-Vorbeck straying into another colony, and had no information on Portuguese East Africa. As the British Official History analysis states, this meant 'the Germans were able to continue the war for another year, the pursuing columns being constantly baffled by lack of information as to the country in which they were working'.[39]

Thanks to his book *My Reminiscences of East Africa*, published in 1919, Lettow-Vorbeck is often portrayed as a gallant leader undefeated in the East African campaign. However, this assessment ignores the cost in African lives of his continued but fruitless resistance. The United Kingdom government estimated that 100,000 British porters had died from overwork, disease and malnutrition. The number of German porters who died is unknown, but is probably similar in scale. At the end, Lettow-Vorbeck was sustaining his force by extorting food and resources from villagers, causing the deaths of unknown numbers of Africans. As Byron Farwell had written, what Lettow-Vorbeck 'did in the end was worse than useless [...] he tore the social fabric of hundreds of communities and wrecked [...] economies' across eastern Africa.[40]

Deventer's strategy in 1918 was to encircle and defeat Lettow-Vorbeck's force. Logistics still remained difficult even at this stage of the war. Nigerian troops were on half rations from 28 March to 1 May and had sent out shooting parties to provide game meat. The askaris were in similar

Fig. 5.2 German askari prisoners of war, Llembule, German East Africa.
Image: Imperial War Museum Q 34474.

difficulties, as the Nigerians captured a group of Germans 'in a semi moribund condition from eating poisonous bush fruit'.[41]

The South African general landed troops along the coast of Portuguese East Africa in July and August, but Lettow-Vorbeck's remaining troops returned to German East Africa at the end of September, and then invaded Northern Rhodesia in search of food and supplies. Lettow-Vorbeck became aware of the armistice on 12 November. He surrendered his troops to Deventer on 25 November at Abercorn in Northern Rhodesia. This town would become the site for one of Sir Edwin Lutyens' last war memorials: 'The Memorial to the Missing' to commemorate 433 Northern Rhodesian carriers with no known grave, unveiled around 1930. South Africa's subimperial ambition to gain Lourenço Marques would not come to fruition. On 27 January 1917, Buxton told Long of his discussion with Smuts on 'the question of a rearrangement of territory with Portugal'. Both men doubted 'that the Portuguese would agree to any swopping [sic] of Delagoa Bay and Beira.'[42]

Dissent

'Dissent' is a useful term as it can encompass the many shades of opposition within the British Empire to World War I. These ranged from armed insurrection in Nyasaland (modern Malawi) to British 'war weariness' in the face of a conflict that it appeared would never end. As Antoinette Burton has written more generally about the British Empire, 'there was a perennial, familiar character to disruption and dissent that made it as common a feature of imperial experience as the flying of the Union Jack'. Wartime industrial action could have broader imperial consequences: a wave of strikes in Australia in 1917 resulted in 444 disputes and the loss of almost 4.6 million working days. This resulted in a pig iron shortage that Governor-General Sir Ronald Munro Ferguson remedied only by requesting Lord Chelmsford, the Viceroy of India, to permit the Bengal Iron and Steel Company in Calcutta to export up to 500 tons to Australia per month. That same year, women in the rural Transkei region of the Cape Province protested against merchants' price fixing by boycotting European goods and demanding cash payment when selling their produce. African clerks in the Gold Coast (modern Ghana) campaigned for a wage rise to take account of the wartime hike in prices and gained a 5 per cent pay increase in May 1918. Conscientious objectors who refused to engage in military combat on religious or moral grounds faced official field punishments and unofficial military beatings. From December 1916 to November 1917, the major powers did seriously consider ending the stalemated conflict with a negotiated peace. Walter Long, the Colonial Secretary, reminded the United Kingdom Prime Minister David Lloyd George on 19 December 1916 that the Dominions must be privately informed of any German peace proposals as it would be disastrous if they first became aware of the decision to conclude the conflict in the newspapers. New Zealand Prime Minister William Massey's concern regarding dissent was focused keenly – if not obsessively – on restricting the free movement of English women in order to prevent Kiwi soldiers catching venereal disease. From 1915, the New Zealand High Commissioner, Sir Thomas Mackenzie, on the Prime Minister's instruction, bombarded the Commissioner of the London Metropolitan Police with a barrage of correspondence on the efficacy of female patrols 'in shielding girls and young women in the vicinity of camps, and elsewhere, from the risks to which their sex and the excitement of the times renders them liable'. When Massey visited London, he warned the War Cabinet: 'Young lads who had left their homes unsullied found themselves exposed to new and incessant temptation. Unfortunately some of them succumbed and were ruined in health.' His solution was to expand the powers of the *Defence of the Realm Act* to make it illegal for a female with a sexually transmitted disease to have intercourse with a soldier. Perhaps focused on more pressing issues in August 1918, the War Cabinet did not enact Massey's proposal.[1]

South African rebels

South Africa's considerable military contribution to the war in Africa, recounted in the previous chapter, could not have been anticipated when the conflict began. Many Afrikaners continued to resent the British conquest of the Orange Free State and the Transvaal in the South African War of 1899–1902 and their loss of independence within the Union of South Africa created in 1910. In August 1914, while Prime Minister Louis Botha and Defence Minister Jan Smuts, both Afrikaners who had fought the British 12 years previously, planned the invasion of German South-West Africa, other Afrikaners hoped to take advantage of the outbreak of war to eject the British and regain autonomy. These included Christian Beyers, Commandant General of the Union Defence Force, who resigned his commission on 15 September. Other Afrikaners joined the revolt, leading Smuts to declare martial law, impose newspaper censorship and ban public meetings. Lieutenant Colonel Manie Maritz refused an order to lead his troops to German South-West Africa, disarmed all his soldiers who remained loyal to the government, and declared South Africa to be an independent republic. The Resident Magistrate in the Orange Free State town of Vrede, about 100 miles (160 kilometres) south-east of Johannesburg, reported that 'almost the whole district is in sympathy with General Christian de Wet', who had been one of the main Afrikaner leaders in the South African War. About 11,500 Afrikaner rebels in the Orange Free State and Transvaal had joined the uprising by the end of October. Buxton informed Lewis Harcourt, the Colonial Secretary that 'it looks as if an armed conflict can hardly be avoided'. In Pretoria, Union Defence Force troops with machine guns guarded the main government buildings.[2]

The United Kingdom government discussed the possibility of diverting the convoy carrying the Australian Imperial Force and the New Zealand Expeditionary Force to Cape Town, but for obvious political reasons, Botha and Smuts preferred 'to rely exclusively on their own forces, if possible'. Cabinet decided that the Prime Minister should

> operate against Beyers himself. General Botha's presence would show publicly [the] importance attached to situation by [the] Government [. . .] and, more important, if General Botha himself went he could count with greater certainty on his commandoes firing on men of their own race and kith and kin.[3]

Botha deployed 32,000 mostly Afrikaner troops to put down the revolt. The rebels lacked coordination, and the General was able to overcome each group one by one. On 12 November, Botha defeated de Wet's column in Orange Free State. De Wet escaped the battle, but was eventually captured in the Northern Cape in December while attempting to reach South-West Africa. Beyers was defeated in Orange Free State, and drowned while trying to swim across the Vaal River in December. Maritz fled to the German colony. The last group to be defeated was Jopie Fourie and his men near Pretoria. Jan Kemp's Transvaal contingent managed to ride

800 miles (1,300 kilometres) across the Kalahari Desert to reach sanctuary in German South-West Africa in December 1914. Theodor Seitz, the German governor, provided both Maritz and Kemp with rations and new equipment with the aim of conducting a joint raid on South Africa. However, Kemp fell out with Maritz and he and his men began riding back to the Transvaal. Maritz's relationship with the Germans was similarly vexed, as their imperialism jarred with his republican values. [4]

The fractured force finally broke on 30 January 1915. Kemp and most of his men surrendered to the South African authorities at Upington in the Northern Cape. Maritz and a few diehards withdrew to South-West Africa as members of the German's miniscule Afrikaner Free Corps. The Union Defence Force suffered 130 killed and 275 wounded, while the rebels lost 190 killed and 400 wounded. Botha sensibly opted for a policy of reconciliation rather than retribution. The only man executed was Jopie Fourie, who had carelessly forgotten to resign his officer's commission before joining the rebellion and was therefore found guilty of committing treason. Otherwise, 239 rebels were convicted, but the majority had their sentences commuted.[5]

John Chilembwe's revolt in Nyasaland

On 23 January 1915, Baptist Minister John Chilembwe met with his followers and called on them to rise up against British rule. He stated:

> You are all patriots [. . .] I do not say you are going to win the war at all. You have no weapons with you and you are not at all trained military men even [. . .] so for love [of] your own country and country men, I now encourage you to go and strike a blow bravely and die.[6]

Chilembwe expected his rebellion to fail, but he knew his failure would provide a model and an inspiration for future African nationalists.

The exact date of John Chilembwe's birth is unknown. He grew up in the southern Shire district of the Nyasaland Protectorate in East Africa. Joseph Booth, a British Baptist missionary, baptised Chilembwe around 1890 and, seeing his potential, brought him to the United States where he studied from 1897 to 1899 at the Negro Baptist Seminary in Lynchburg,

Virginia. During his time as a student, he read Frederick Douglass' auto-biographical *Narrative of the Life of Frederick Douglass, an American Slave* where he learned of John Brown's anti-slavery raid on Harpers Ferry in 1859. This would become the model for his own insurrection. Following his ordination, he returned to Nyasaland in 1900, where he established schools for African children and constructed a solidly built brick church.[7]

According to the census of 31 March 1913, the population of Nyasaland consisted of 1,020,537 Africans, 758 Europeans and 356 Asians, presumably mostly Indians. The main commercial centre was Blantyre, while the administrative capital was at Zomba. The protectorate's main exports were agricultural products such as cotton, tobacco, tea and rubber. Nyasaland had good transport connections. Most of the protectorate's eastern boundary was Lake Nyasa, from which the Shire river flowed southwards to the Zambesi and the Indian Ocean.[8]

Following the outbreak of war, Chilembwe wrote a letter to the *Nyasaland Times* arguing that Africans should not take part in the conflict. He stated:

> It is better to recruit White Planters, Traders, Missionaries and other white settlers in the country, who [. . .] know the cause of the war, and have something to do with it. But not to recruit a black man of this country who has nothing to do with it.

Surprisingly, the letter was published in full on 26 November 1914 in the newspaper's first edition, but these two sentences were swiftly censored from subsequent printings. Chilembwe also wrote to the colonial administrators in nearby German East Africa requesting them to assist the rebellion by invading Nyasaland.[9]

Governor George Smith had been aware of Chilembwe's revolutionary opinions and had been preparing to deport him to the Indian Ocean colony of Mauritius. Before Smith could do this, Chilembwe struck. On 24 January, the day after his rousing speech, Chilembwe led a group of around 200 men, armed mostly with spears, to Magomero Estate, about 20 miles from Zomba. Here, the rebels killed three European men, one of whom they beheaded, and captured three European women and five children, who were later released unharmed. About 70 rebels attacked the African Lakes Store at Blantyre, killed the watchman and took some rifles and 700 rounds of ammunition.[10]

On being informed of the attack at Magomero Estate, Captain L.E.L. Triscott of the King's African Rifles took 105 raw recruits to capture John Chilembwe's village. The initial assault failed as they came under 'very accurate fire' from the well-positioned rebels, killing two soldiers and wounding four. A second attempt succeeded, though Triscott ordered his men to use their bayonets only as the vast majority had not yet been trained to fire their rifle.[11]

The revolt was quashed in early February. On 4 February, Garnet Kaduya and eight police killed John Chilembwe at Mlanje, near the border with Portuguese East Africa, and interred him in an unmarked grave. British retribution now swung into action. Governor Smith instructed Captain H.C. Collins of 1st Battalion King's African Rifles:

> Your object will be to attack and break up any bodies of rebels who may still be banded together, to capture the ringleaders alive if possible, to destroy their villages and those of their adherents, and generally to stamp out the rising and to bring the native population the futility of such attempts and the determination of the Government to exact the severest penalties from those who have taken part in the present movement.[12]

The school and all the houses and huts in Chilembwe's village were destroyed. Razing the brick church proved more difficult: two doses of explosives were required. Hector Duff, the protectorate's Chief Secretary, wished to intimidate the African population in Blantyre by immediately executing four men who 'confessed' to killing the watchman at the African Lakes Store. Duff wanted to hang the men immediately, presumably so the swinging corpses would frighten the rest of the black population. There was no scaffold in the town, so the chief secretary, concerned that 'any failure to execute the sentence [. . .] at the appointed time might be construed by other natives as indicative of weakness and irresolution', had the men shot in the town square.[13]

Indian soldiers mutiny in Singapore

Upon the outbreak of war, British regular battalions on garrison duty across the Empire were redeployed to fight on the Western Front. In Singapore, the 1st Battalion King's Own Yorkshire Light Infantry embarked for Europe on the SS *Monmouthshire* in October 1914. The replacement regiment was the 5th Bengal Light Infantry, a battalion made up of Muslim soldiers. At this time, the radical *Ghadar* (a Punjabi and Urdu word for 'revolution') movement formed by expatriate Indians living on the west coast of the United States and Canada called for an uprising against British rule in India. The revolt was detected in early 1915 and quashed by the Indian authorities. In Singapore, however, it appears that the *Ghadar* activist Kasim Mansur Singh provided the newly arrived sepoys with his organisation's leaflets.[14]

On 3 December 1914, the War Office ordered a local Straits Settlements military unit, the Malay States Guides, to be redeployed to East Africa. This instruction caused much distress before it was rescinded, as these men's terms of enlistment required them to serve only in Malaya. Officer–soldier relations were poor in the 5th Indian Light Infantry. Brigadier General Dudley Ridout, the General Officer Commanding, Straits Settlements, subsequently stated that Lieutenant Colonel E.V. Martin, the battalion commander, 'had an unfortunate personality[, . . .] commanded no respect, and exerted no authority'. On 27 January 1915, Martin told his men that they would be transferred to Hong Kong. On 15 February, the day before the regiment's planned embarkation, Ridout inspected the unit at 7.00 am in the relative cool of the tropical morning. He referred to their departure, but did not state their destination as Hong Kong. This caused dismay among many troops who believed this meant they were being sent to fight fellow Muslims of the Ottoman Army. Sepoys Taj Mohamed Khan and Fazal Ali Khan complained to Ridout regarding the delay in receiving their military discharge. Some soldiers engaged in very unmilitary behaviour by voicing their disapproval on the parade ground.[15]

The 5th Bengal Light Infantry's mutiny began that afternoon around 3.00 pm, when a soldier stacking ammunition in the magazine at the Alexandra Barracks fired at a truck. Two companies, led by Colour Havildar Imtiaz Ali and Havildar Ibrahim took 26,600 rounds of rifle ammunition from the magazine and 1,560 rounds from the truck. They were soon joined by two more companies, meaning half the battalion was in revolt.[16]

One group went to the lines of the Malay States Guides, killed a British officer and persuaded some of the men to join the mutiny. Havildar Ibrahim took 80 men to Tanglin Barracks to liberate the German sailors who had survived the *Emden*'s last battle. As Robert Bradley recalled almost 20 years later, the mutineers entered the barracks 'with shouts of triumph, shaking hands with the prisoners of war and fraternizing with them all they could. But the astonished Germans were not at all keen upon having anything to do with them'. This was not surprising because as the Indian troops arrived, they had accidently shot and killed Ernst Frederick Sethelsen, one of the German prisoners of war. A group of Germans did take advantage of the disorder: four managed to reach the sanctuary of Shanghai in neutral China.[17]

At 6.30 pm, Sir Arthur Young, Straits Settlements Governor, declared martial law. The Chinese New Year festivities had just commenced, and one of the first Emergency Orders banned fireworks – a feature of this holiday period – lest the explosions be mistaken for rifle fire. The mutiny continued for a week, but was eventually put down by a combination of Sikh police, the Johore military forces, led by the Sultan himself, the part-time Singapore Volunteer Corps, armed Europeans, sailors from British, French, Japanese and Russian warships docked in the harbour, and the 1/4th Battalion King's Shropshire Light Infantry which arrived from Rangoon on 20 February. The final casualties were eight British soldiers, three Malay soldiers, 14 British civilians, three Chinese and two Malay civilians and one German prisoner of war. The report on the mutiny noted the difficulty in identifying the soldiers responsible for the killing because, to the white civilians, all Indians looked alike.[18]

The British legal response to the mutiny resulted in a 99.5 per cent conviction rate. Only one sepoy was found not guilty; 47 were executed, including 38 publicly shot in front of the Singapore Central Criminal Prison. The remainder were given punishments that ranged from life sentences of transportation to a penal colony with hard labour to 18 months' imprisonment. The remaining soldiers of the 5th Bengal Light Infantry who had not mutinied were given the 'opportunity of recovering' the regiment's 'good name'. In July they sailed across the Indian Ocean where they would fight in both Kamerun and German East Africa.[19]

Patrick Pearse's Irish Rising

On 24 April 1916 – Easter Monday – about 1,200 armed men and women occupied several buildings in Dublin, including the General Post Office (GPO). Here Patrick Pearse proclaimed the establishment of an Irish Republic that:

> guarantees religious and civil liberty, equal rights and equal opportunity to all its citizens, and declares its resolve to pursue the happiness and prosperity of the whole nation and of all its parts, cherishing all of the children of the nation equally, and oblivious of the differences carefully fostered by an alien Government, which have divided a minority from the majority in the past.

The combatants were members of two paramilitary forces. The first, the Irish Citizen Army, had been established by the Irish Transport and General Workers' Union during the Dublin lockout in 1913. The second was the Irish Volunteers. This had originally been part of the Irish Parliamentary Party's paramilitary force set up in 1914 in opposition to the Ulster Volunteer Force. The Irish Volunteers then split from the broader nationalist movement because it opposed supporting the British war effort. The rising was planned by members of the Irish Republican Brotherhood who had infiltrated the Irish Volunteers. It therefore belonged to the long tradition of radical republican rebellions that included Theobald Wolfe Tone in 1798, Robert Emmet in 1803 and the Fenians of the second half of the nineteenth century.[20]

John Chilembwe's revolt and Patrick Pearse's rising had three similarities. Both had strong links to the United States: Chilembwe was politicised during his time in Virginia, while the proclamation of the Irish Republic specifically mentioned the support of Ireland's 'exiled children in America' that included the New York-born Éamon de Valera. Both Chilembwe and Pearse looked for German military support to achieve autonomy. Most significantly, both insurrections were enacted in the clear knowledge that they were a sacrificial gesture that was unlikely to succeed.[21]

The United Kingdom government knew that a revolt was imminent in April 1916 as Royal Navy intelligence had deciphered telegram messages

Fig. 6.1 Captured Irish Republican with British Army guard in the aftermath of the Easter Rising, April 1916. Image: Imperial War Museum HU 55529.

that German weapons were to be landed in Ireland by a ship named the *Aud* the week before Easter, and that Sir Roger Casement of the Irish Volunteers was being transported by U-boat. Both the arms and the man were captured. Despite this, the rebellion still went ahead. By the time Pearse surrendered on 29 April, 64 rebels, 132 police and soldiers and 230 civilians had been killed. Keith Jeffery argues that the rising 'can *only* be properly understood in the context of the Great War'. Artillery was as important in Dublin as it was on the Western Front, devastating large parts of the city. The office of the *Irish Builder and Engineer* in Lower Abbey Street, about three blocks from the GPO, burnt down. When publication resumed on 13 May, the journal stated 'we shall be pleased to receive from any reader or advertisers, particulars of any new or specialised methods of contraction, or equipment of business premises, likely to be useful in the rebuilding'. Other parts of the city were unaffected by the fighting. The *Farmers' Gazette* reported that the Royal Dublin Society's Spring Show continued during the rising with all classes judged and prizes given, even though it was taking place only three miles from the GPO.[22]

The British response to the rising was inconsistent and ill-considered, mostly because the ministers in the coalition government could not agree on an effective policy for the future governance of Ireland. David Lloyd George, the War Secretary, proposed the immediate granting of Home Rule to Ireland, except for the six Protestant-majority provinces of Ulster. However, Conservatives demanded that Home Rule be deferred until the end of the war, and described Irish Catholics in blatantly pejorative terms. Arthur Balfour, First Lord of the Admiralty, predicted that a parliament of 'Irishmen of the South and West [. . . would] prove conclusively to the world that they are as incapable as Mexicans of carrying out the elementary duties of a civilised State'. R. Hutchinson, a British Army officer on the staff of Headquarters Irish Command in Dublin, told Henry Wilson in July 1916 that Irish nationalists 'are no more fit to make laws than the pigs they grow'.[23]

Fifteen leaders of the rising were executed, as well as Casement. All other participants, including Constance Markievicz of the Irish Citizen Army, and Michael Collins and Éamon de Valera of the Irish Republican Brotherhood, were released by the middle of 1917, and had begun planning for another rebellion before some of them were reimprisoned in 1918. British authorities at the time often referred to the Irish rebels as being members of Sinn Féin, but this was not correct. Sinn Féin was a radical nationalist party established by Arthur Griffith in 1905. It had opposed Irish recruiting for the British Army in 1914, but was not involved in the rising. At the time of its formation, Sinn Féin called for the creation of a dual monarchy of Ireland and Britain, like that of Austria and Hungary, so Ireland could establish protective tariffs to enable the development of its own manufacturing industries. The mistaken British linking of Sinn Féin to republicanism ironically bolstered its membership among Irish nationalists unhappy with the Irish Parliamentary Party. It was not until the party conference of September 1917 that Sinn Féin made the establishment of an Irish republic a central plank of its platform.[24]

Conscientious objectors

The imposition of conscription in Britain in January 1916 meant all males between 18 and 41 (unless exempted for various reasons) in England, Scotland and Wales were liable for military service even if they opposed it on religious, moral or libertarian grounds. The legislation did allow for men to claim an exemption as conscientious objectors (COs), but the number who were successful in their application was only 16,500 out of a male population of approximately 20 million. Research by Cyril Pearce and Helen Durham suggests that the number of British conscientious objectors is considerably underestimated. This was because mining and industrial areas had large numbers of men who were exempted from military service because they were classified as war-essential workers. George Henry Warne, coal miner and pacifist from Northumberland never applied for exemption as a conscientious objector, but because his profession was adjudged vital for the war effort, he was never called for military service. Pearce and Durham persuasively argue that there were many men like Warne who were conscientious objectors, but were '"hidden" within war-essential occupations'.[25]

Howard Marten recalled his experience as a Great War CO in an interview with oral historian Peter Liddle in 1973. Marten was a member of the Society of Friends, the pacifist church commonly called Quakers. When the No Conscription Fellowship was formed in 1915, Marten chaired his local branch in North London. Following the introduction of conscription, he went before the Local Tribunal in Harrow, who rejected his application as a conscientious objector. When he received his call-up papers, Marten was required to resign his bank job. He organised with the local policeman to meet at a nearby railway arch the following day so he could be arrested.[26]

When Marten and the other COs arrived at the army barracks, they refused to pick up their allotted kitbags, 'and that's when the rough handling started. We passed through a line of NCOs kicking at our heels and pushing us but I cannot say we suffered any real violence.' On their train journey to Dover, the military guard left them unguarded at Finsbury Park station, but none of the men attempted to escape. Once in France, the conscientious objectors were subjected to being put in irons and tied up for long periods as part of Field Punishment No. 1. Officers and soldiers regularly threatened the COs with execution while they waited for their courts martial. Marten's first trial was aborted, since an officer who had refused him access to legal representation then appeared in court as the main prosecution witness. In the second trial Marten was sentenced to ten years' imprisonment.[27]

He worked first in Scotland at a quarry near Aberdeen, then at Wakefield and Dartmoor. In 1917, Marten was released. When he returned to the North London bank where he had previously been employed, the bank manager 'did everything possible to humiliate and downgrade' him. This included being demoted to second cashier and being placed under the authority of a man he had originally trained. Marten later moved to Bristol where he took a job with Lever Brothers, and 'never suffered socially for my wartime stance'. His boss respected his beliefs 'because he had a lost a son in the war'.[28]

Strikes: International Association of Machinists in Hamilton

The Ontario city of Hamilton, with a population of 81,959 in the 1911 census, was the fifth-largest city in Canada. As described in Chapter Four, Canada developed a large manufacturing industry making artillery ammunition for Britain. This production was eventually focused in the established industrial areas of Quebec and Ontario. The main trade union representing workers in this calling was the International Association of Machinists (IAM). This organisation had been founded in the United States in the late 1880s, and soon set up branches among Canadian tradesmen working in factories and railway workshops. The boom in munitions production resulted in an increase in union membership: the number of Canadian IAM members increased from 4,654 in 1914 to 7,108 in 1916.[29]

Despite the increasing production and profitability of war industries in the Dominion, and the increasing cost of living, wages remained unchanged. In 1916, James Watters, President of the Trades and Labor Congress of Canada, presented Conservative Prime Minister Sir Robert Borden and businessman James Flavelle, Chairman of the Imperial Munitions Board, with a proposal to establish a Fair Wage Board to set wages and conditions in war industries. Unsurprisingly, the two conservatives rejected the idea.[30]

In December 1915, a machinist shortage in Toronto helped the IAM negotiate with employers to gain better conditions and wages. The union then attempted to spread these improvements to the rest of Ontario. A two-week strike by 400 munitions workers at the Steel Company of Canada in Hamilton in February 1916 failed, and the men had to return

Fig. 6.2 Workers in the blast furnace of the Steel Company of Canada,
Hamilton, Ontario, 1918. Image: Library & Archives Canada/Bibliothèque et
Archives Canada MIKAN 227609 A024645.

to work under the existing conditions. Employers attempted to break the
union, refusing to hire IAM members and sacking existing employees if
they were perceived as being 'strong active Union men'. In April 1916,
the Hamilton branch of the IAM responded by sending copies of the
new terms and conditions, that had been implemented in most Toronto
factories, to all relevant workplaces in the city.[31]

The Canada Foundry Company in Toronto had refused to accept the
new conditions. When the workers went on strike, the plant manager,
Colonel Frederick Nicholls, locked out his employees. IAM members in
Toronto unanimously passed a motion calling for a general strike unless
the conditions were accepted. The government intervened and established
a Royal Commission to examine the conditions of munitions workers in
Toronto and Hamilton. The *Industrial Banner* commented:

> it was only because they were well organized and in a position to
> enforce their demands that the machinists received any consideration
> whatever [. . .] This should be an object lesson to all workers.[32]

The evidence tendered at the Royal Commission revealed that while Hamilton machinists worked ten-hour days, or even longer, their equivalents in Toronto worked nine hours, and machinists in nearby Buffalo, New York were already negotiating for an eight-hour day. The Royal Commission supported the nine-hour day. The Hamilton factory owners did not. The city's munitions workers voted for industrial action. On 8 June, Borden met with Flavelle and Hamilton factory owners regarding the impending strike. Flavelle was a proponent of the nine-hour day, but he backed away from introducing it in Hamilton. On 12 June 1916, between 1,500 and 2,000 IAM workers went on strike in more than 30 factories making munitions in Hamilton, including major firms such as the Dominion Steel Foundry, the Steel Company of Canada and Canadian Westinghouse.[33]

Borden used press censorship to prevent workers across the Dominion becoming aware of the Hamilton strike and walking off the job in sympathy. Ironically, the national shortage in trained machinists weakened the effectiveness of the industrial action. Approximately 600 unionists left Hamilton, mostly travelling the 40 miles (more than 60 kilometres) to find work in Toronto munitions factories. The Hamilton strike ended after a month. The city's factory owners may have defeated the workers, and retained the existing work conditions, but with their workers leaving for better conditions elsewhere, the bosses lacked the men to work their machines.[34]

Peace by negotiation

A negotiated peace became an option that the European powers had to seriously consider after two years of bloodshed and deadlock. However, all these attempts would end in failure because, as Alexander Watson points out, there was always a yawning gap between each government's territorial ambitions and their military capacity to enforce their extensive claims.[35]

The public and private discussions regarding peace negotiations were concentrated in the 12 months between November 1916 and November 1917. Both Chancellor Theobald von Bethmann Hollweg and then-neutral President Woodrow Wilson made public peace offers in December 1916. Karl, the new Austro-Hungarian Emperor who had ascended the throne in November 1916, saw peace as vital for his empire's continued survival. He covertly contacted the Allies through his brother-in-law Prince Sixtus of Bourbon-Parma. Karl was willing to restore Serbian and Belgian independence and return Alsace-Lorraine to France. However, two major obstacles prevented peace. The first was that the French and United Kingdom governments had promised Italy extensive territorial gains at the expense of Austria–Hungary before it joined the war in 1915. The second was that Vienna would not break its ties with Berlin.[36]

In Germany, the civilian politicians were constrained in their negotiations by the grandiose ambitions of the military duopoly: Field Marshal Paul Hindenburg and his assistant, Quartermaster General Erich Ludendorff. A conference of generals and politicians on 23 April 1917 agreed on a plan for German expansion in the Baltic and Poland in the east; and in the west, the annexation of both the main French iron-ore mines in the Longwy–Briey region, south of Luxembourg, and all of Belgium. While Bethmann Hollweg was more moderate in his claims, he still insisted on gaining Longwy–Briey and maintaining some control over Belgium.[37]

The main British war aim was the German withdrawal from France and Belgium and the restoration of the latter as an independent state. The United Kingdom government also wished to retain the German colonies it had captured. A Territorial Changes Committee had been established in 1916 to consider

> how much of the territory already taken from the enemy by Great Britain and her Allies can be used [. . .] for bargaining with Germany in the event of the Allies being unable to impose their own final peace terms upon Germany.

The Committee unsurprisingly concluded that all the colonies the British Empire had occupied should be retained and any overseas territory to be returned to Germany should come at the expense of France.[38]

In July 1917, the German position appeared to be becoming more moderate. On 14 July, Georg Michaelis replaced Bethmann Hollweg as Chancellor, and the Reichstag passed its 'peace resolution' on 19 July. In reality, decision-making remained with Hindenburg and Ludendorff, and the 'peace resolution' was capable of being construed as justifying further eastward and westward expansion.[39]

Pope Benedict XV issued his peace note on 16 August 1917. This called for the guarantee of Belgian independence and the return to 1914 boundaries, including the return of captured German colonies; as this was inconsistent with Hindenburg and Ludendorff's strategy, it made no headway. The final peace proposal came with publication of a letter on 29 November 1917 in the London *Daily Telegraph* by a British politician, the Marquess of Lansdowne. The letter was not defeatist or written in desperation following the end of the costly Third Battle of Ypres. Instead, as Douglas Newton argues, Lansdowne aimed to promote 'clear, moderate and common war aims' in order to encourage 'moderate German opinion' to call for negotiations. This proposal, like its predecessors, foundered on the reefs of ambition. As the year ended, Hindenburg and Ludendorff were preparing the offensive that they believed would give them victory in March 1918.[40]

Australian soldiers and the death penalty

When Lieutenant General Sir William Birdwood took command of Australian troops at Gallipoli in 1915, he did not realise that members of the Australian Imperial Force (AIF) could not be executed. He later commented: 'we might have had men shot illegally, causing endless trouble'. It is true that Australian troops could be sentenced to death, and at least 115 were so sentenced during the Great War. However, under the Australian Defence Act, the Governor-General had to endorse the death penalty before an execution could take place, and the government always denied its approval. As Table 6.1 indicates, 455 British Empire soldiers and labourers were put to death by military authorities during the Great War. None were AIF members.[41]

TABLE 6.1

BRITISH EMPIRE MILITARY EXECUTIONS 1914–22[42]

United Kingdom	396
Canada	25
Chinese, Egyptian & African labourers	19
New Zealand	5
West Indies	4
Gold Coast	3
Nigeria	1
'West African'	1
South Africa	1
Australia	0
TOTAL	455

Australian soldiers were far more likely to be court-martialled than other components of the British Empire army. Table 6.2 shows the percentage of New Zealand, Canadian, British and Australian troops who went before a military court.

TABLE 6.2

COURTS MARTIAL AS A PERCENTAGE OF
TOTAL NUMBER OF TROOPS, 1914–20[43]

Australian Imperial Force	5.5%
British Expeditionary Force	5.3%
Canadian Expeditionary Force	2.0%
New Zealand Expeditionary Force	1.6%

In May and July 1917, each of the five Australian infantry divisions averaged 34.2 courts martial for desertion per month. By comparison, the BEF average was 8.87, and the NZEF average was eight. It was at this time that the two Anzac Corps commanders, Birdwood and Lieutenant General Alexander Godley, asked the Defence Minister, Senator George Pearce, to make Australian soldiers liable for execution. In August, the United Kingdom government made the same request to Australian Prime Minister Billy Hughes.[44]

Hughes and Pearce agreed that the death penalty question was 'too dangerous' to bring to Cabinet because of its political sensitivity. Instead, Hughes' decision to oppose the proposal was based on conversations with two or three trusted senior ministers. Pearce's opposition was not based on issues of morality, but on pragmatic political considerations. He wrote:

> A decision to agree to this penalty if given now would give to our political enemies just that political catch cry they are looking for, and would have a disastrous effect on recruiting.[45]

Long and Munro Ferguson eventually accepted that the political cost of executing Australian soldiers far outweighed any military benefit. However, Haig was still complaining in early March 1918 regarding the number of AIF personnel in prison. He argued that this was 'greatly due to the fact that the Australian government refuses to allow capital punishment to be awarded to any Australian'.[46]

'War weariness' and the National War Aims Committee

A flyer published by Miss F. Melland of Manchester and seized by police in a raid on the No Conscription Fellowship in London on 14 November 1917, put forward the argument for a negotiated peace. It read:

> Three Years of War with millions of men killed, and millions more maimed for life; and treasure enough wasted to have made Europe a Paradise! [. . .] Yet the ruling classes of all nations whose diplomacy brought on the war cannot now stop it; But the peoples can! [. . .] Let

us have NO MORE SECRET DIPLOMACY! But let us think out and discuss NOW a 'GIVE AND TAKE' SETTLEMENT that will be the best for all humanity![47]

'War weariness' included irritation at increasing government interventions. On 15 March 1918, the chair at a meeting of the British Institution of Mechanical Engineers informed the audience that

[f]or some inscrutable reason the Special Intelligence Branch of Munitions, to whom the Papers had to be referred for censorship, had forbidden the reading of Mr. Morgan's Paper[.]

The audience reacted with 'great regret and with some justifiable indignation' at this suppression. It would be logical to think that Ben Morgan's lecture was suppressed because it referred to a new secret invention. This was not the case. The paper was entitled 'The efficient utilization of labour in engineering factories. (With special reference to women's work)'.[48]

Concerned with the state of civilian morale in the context of Tsar Nicholas' abdication and Russia leaving the war, mutinies in the French Army, the rise in British industrial action in April and May, and continued calls for a negotiated peace, the National War Aims Committee (NWAC) was established in July 1917. As David Monger points out, the Committee used 'adversarial patriotism' to promote negative views of Germany and her allies, Bolsheviks, but also of British conscientious objectors, pacifists, advocates of negotiated peace, striking workers and the 'war weary'. At the same time, the Committee encouraged public support for the government and monarchy. It is not surprising that the creation of NWAC coincided with the announcement on 17 July 1917 that the royal family was changing its name from the Germanic Saxe-Coburg-Gotha to the solidly British Windsor.[49]

Initially privately funded and based in the Conservative Party's main offices, NWAC was government-funded from October 1917. Prime Minister David Lloyd George's speech at the organisation's first meeting on 4 August 1917 in the Queen's Hall in Westminster acknowledged the prevailing mood of 'war weariness' in the country:

The strain is great on nations and on individuals, and when men get over-strained tempers get ragged, small grievances are exaggerated, and small misunderstandings and mistakes swell into mountains.[50]

NWAC published and disseminated over 100 million publications. This included over 2.5 million copies of Lloyd George's speech on 5 January 1918 outlining Britain's war aims. Cinema vans showed films in outside venues. For example, in April 1918, films were shown on three consecutive days in Lewisham, Deptford and Rotherhithe in south-east London. The organisation did most of its work in England and Wales. There were some meetings held in Scotland and Ireland, but it appears that the main task of the Irish War Aims Committee, created in the middle of 1918, was to monitor public opinion regarding the imposition of conscription in Ireland. Between August 1917 and December 1918, at least 115 MPs spoke at Committee events, generally open air meetings near factories or in parks, 'with a view to counteracting pacifist propaganda which appears to be growing'.[51]

The National War Aims Committee decided in October 1917 to pay special attention to 'war weariness which is prevalent among women' by providing 'special Meetings for women' chaired by 'leading women in their areas'. Monger points out that this approach was designed to retain a 'gendered distinction between public and private spheres' with the idea that, even in wartime women should be addressed 'on "local" rather than "national" issues'. Despite this view, British women like diarist Ethel Bilsborough did see the war in its wider context. On 4 November, she wrote:

Poor old England is going through dark days just now and one cannot see the faintest prospect of peace in sight . . .[52]

NWAC speakers noted the shift in working class attitudes towards the war following the German offensive on 21 March 1918. In the week following the attack, 2,733 working days were lost in the United Kingdom due to strikes. By the end of the week, however, there were only two cases of industrial action – involving only 155 workers – in the entire country. On 1 May, NWAC member W. Kay Waterson wrote that the weather was 'too bad' in south-east London to hold an open-air meeting, but noted: 'All the people seem firmly determined, and not in need of exhortation'.[53]

Australian Labor and a negotiated peace

The Australian Labor Party had split in 1916 over the issue of overseas conscription and had lost its dominant position in state and federal politics. On 4 April 1918, the first time federal parliament met since the start of the German March offensive, Labor MP William Higgs put forward a motion calling for the war to be ended by peace negotiations. In the House of Representatives, Higgs' motion was defeated by 40 votes to 16. In the Senate, Nationalist Party Senator and Defence Minister George Pearce declared that the harsh terms that the Germans had imposed on the Russians in the Treaty of Brest-Litovsk signed on 3 March meant that any woman or man 'who advocates peace by negotiation with Germany [. . .] is either a madman or a traitor'. Pearce called for a message of 'hope, encouragement and admiration' to be sent 'to those countrymen of ours, to their British cousins, and their gallant French and American Allies' on the Western Front. Albert Gardiner, Senator Labor leader in the upper house, demonstrated the divergent opinions within the Labor Party at this time by seconding Pearce's motion. All senators, Nationalist and Labor, then combined to unanimously pass the motion. Following this, the entire chamber and all visitors in the public gallery stood and sang 'God Save the King'.[54]

In 1918, the party faced the threat of a second split in two years over whether Labor should support a negotiated peace and continued recruiting. In January 1917, the Melbourne Trades Hall Council had forwarded a resolution to party branches and trades unions. This stated

> [t]hat believing the interests of the workers of the world are best advanced during times of peace, and regarding the workers everywhere as the chief sufferers under war, this council considers that the time has arrived in the European war for the consideration of the terms of peace, and this council therefore urges the Federal Government to express this view to the Imperial Government.[55]

In the by-election in the federal seat of Flinders, east of Melbourne, on 11 May 1918, the Labor manifesto stated: 'The Labor Party stands for peace by negotiation'. In late May and early June, the Sydney Trades and Labor Council held a passionate and long-running discussion, attended by hundreds of people and in which 'heated words were used', on whether to endorse the resolutions of Governor-General Sir Ronald Munro Ferguson's April recruiting conference. The debate culminated in the passing of a motion calling on the labour movement to take no further part in AIF recruiting.[56]

The Australian Labor Party Interstate Conference that began in Perth on 17 June voted in support of a negotiated peace and made opposition to overseas conscription part of the party platform. A proposal to ban the departure of further Australian reinforcements to Europe was defeated by only two votes. An immediate party split between moderates and radicals was avoided only by a compromise brokered by an emergency subcommittee. This decided that Labor would continue to support recruiting, but only if the Allies stated their agreement for peace negotiations without annexation of territories or payment of indemnities, and the policy was approved by a majority of party members in a postal ballot.[57]

Counting the ballots began in early November, and the initial numbers were apparently strongly in favour of the motion. By this stage of the war, however, all of Germany's allies had surrendered, the sailors of the High Seas Fleet had mutinied, and workers were in revolt across the country. With the end of the conflict now plainly imminent, the ALP Federal Executive slowed down the counting of votes because what had previously been a popular position now threatened to become a political embarrassment. When news reached Australia on 10 November that Kaiser Wilhelm had abdicated and gone into exile in the Netherlands, the count was stopped altogether. The Labor Party avoided a second schism, and the result of the postal ballot never became public.[58]

1917: The Battle of Messines

The onset of trench warfare on the Western Front at the end of 1914 led to the revival of the medieval military craft of mining. Where in past centuries engineers had dug in darkness to undermine solid stone castle walls, their Great War equivalents in the German and Allied armies now tunnelled and counter-tunnelled beneath their enemy's trench systems – sometimes fighting desperate subterranean skirmishes – to lay explosives to be detonated beneath their foes. British engineers had exploded a mine under the German positions on 9 May 1915 as part of their failed attack at the Battle of Aubers Ridge. This created a crater 10 metres deep and 40 metres in diameter, with the blast burying about 50 German soldiers. *Leutnant* Adolf Meyer of the 16th Bavarian Reserve Infantry Regiment recalled how the artillery bombardment and mine explosion allowed the British to break into the German line and surround Meyer's troops until they withdrew at the end of the engagement. The British Army created specialised tunnelling companies in February 1915. Deep mining operations then commenced during the summer near the German-occupied Belgian town known in Flemish as Mesen and in French as Messines (the British Army used the latter name during the war). Immediately to the east of the town lay Messines Ridge, which dominated the surrounding countryside, including the Second British Army's lines south of Ypres. The German Fourth Army's position on the ridge was a salient surrounded on three sides by the British. This meant it was vulnerable to attack. In January

1916, General Sir Herbert Plumer, the Second Army commander, ordered the excavation of 21 deep mines below or adjacent to Messines Ridge. Some were completed more than a year before the battle took place. The detailed planning for the battle demonstrated how the British Empire force had gained in competence, experience and resources since 1914. Each of the three infantry corps taking part in the operation was trained on terrain similar to the ground on which they would be attacking. Plumer trusted his artillery chief, Major General George Franks, who devised the broad bombardment plan, and left the fine details to be decided through consultation between the corps artillery and infantry division commanders. British Empire munitions production had expanded to the extent that there was an abundance of ammunition and the British had as many artillery pieces as the Germans. During the preliminary 11-day barrage from 26 May to 6 June 1917, 3,561,530 shells were fired. On 7 June at 3.10 am – a time chosen because it had been ascertained there would be enough light for the soldiers to see 100 yards ahead – 19 of the mines below Messines Ridge were detonated. It would hold the record for the largest human-made explosion in history for six months until it was superseded by the Halifax blast described in Chapter Four. The Messines detonation was so loud that it was audible in England. Prime Minister David Lloyd George, who was staying at Walton Heath, south of London, asked to be woken at 3.00 am so he could hear the explosion. Cyril Falls, who was at the Battle of Messines with the 36th (Ulster) Division, described the opening of the attack:

> Then, with one monstrous roar, every British gun upon ten miles of front opened fire. At the same time the great semi-circle of mines exploded, spewing up, as it seemed, the solid earth, of which fragments fell half a mile away, and sending to the skies great towers of crimson flame, that hung a moment ere they were choked by the clouds of dense black smoke which followed them from their caverns. There came first one ghastly flash of light, then a shuddering of earth thus outraged, then the thunder-clap.

Messines was not a faultless operation: the Germans soon recovered and resisted the attack. Nonetheless, Falls justifiably described Messines as the

British Empire army's 'first completely successful single operation' on the Western Front.[1]

At the end of 1915, the Central Powers had maintained their dominant military position in Europe. In the east, Russia had been forced into retreat with great losses in men and equipment. In the Balkans, Bulgaria had joined the war on the side of Berlin and Vienna. Serbia had been defeated. In the west, Germany remained on the defensive, while the armies of the French and British empires had launched attack after attack with little effect but many losses. The French Army's casualties in all theatres – the majority being on the Western Front – from 3 August 1914 to 31 December 1915 numbered 1,961,687, with over half a million killed. The BEF's casualties on the Western Front for 1915 were 284,017.[2]

Joffre convened a conference with Russian, British and Italian representatives at his *Grand Quartier Général* at Chantilly, near Paris, from 8 to 12 December 1915 to discuss the Allied strategy for 1916. Joffre called for simultaneous offensives on the Eastern, Italian and Western Fronts. This aimed to stretch the Central Powers, as they would be unable to shift troops from one theatre to another. The decisions made at this meeting would result in the Russian attack that forced the Austro-Hungarian Army into retreat in Galicia from June to September 1916, instigated by Aleksei Brusilov, Russia's most talented and innovative general; the Italian Army's successful assault on the Austro-Hungarians from 6 to 17 August at the Sixth Battle of the Isonzo, and the offensive at the junction of the British and French lines in the Somme region of northern France from 1 July to 18 November 1916.[3]

Sir John French was still in command of the BEF during the Chantilly conference. Once Haig replaced French, he met Joffre on 14 February 1916 and confirmed that the attack on the Somme would commence on the first day of July on a broad front up to 43 miles (70 kilometre) in length and would involve 39 French divisions and 21 British divisions.[4]

This plan was disrupted when Falkenhayn began to implement his second strategy to achieve German victory. Having failed to gain a negotiated peace with Russia in 1915, he now decided to fight a battle of attrition on the Western Front which would inflict such tremendous losses on the French Army that they would be forced to surrender. Lacking French support, the British would have no choice but to make peace.[5]

Falkenhayn chose Verdun as the site for his attrition strategy since the French would be compelled to fight to defend it because of its symbolic significance for the nation. In 843, the Treaty of Verdun had divided Charlemagne's empire between his three grandsons. During the Franco-Prussian War of 1870–1, Verdun was the only fortress to hold out against the German invaders.[6]

The Battle of Verdun, fought from 21 February to 18 December 1916, was unprecedented in the number of troops committed to combat, the amount of artillery ammunition expended, and the human cost in men killed, wounded or missing. In February 1916, General Hermann von Kuhl, the German Twelfth Army's Chief of Staff, examined the BEF's failed assault at Loos in the previous September to learn lessons for the upcoming offensive. He noted several shortcomings, including keeping reserves too far behind the battle line and not maintaining the momentum of the attack. Kuhl concluded that the Germans could overcome these difficulties: 'with overwhelming artillery and determined infantry it will, despite all the difficulties, be possible to achieve a breakthrough'.[7]

The Fifth German Army, commanded by the Kaiser's son, Crown Prince Wilhelm, began its attack on Verdun at 7.30 am on 21 February with 1,220 German guns firing 2 million shells in an eight-hour bombardment of a segment of the French line just 8 miles (13 kilometres) in length. The Germans broke through the French lines, and advanced further than the French or the British had in any of their 1915 offensives.[8]

Joffre placed General Philippe Pétain in command of the Second French Army at Verdun on 25 February. By the end of the first week, the Germans were halted before they could capture the high ground at Verdun. Elizabeth Greenhalgh argues that Pétain's greatest contribution to the battle was his organisational skills. The two main rail lines into Verdun were unusable because the Germans had captured Saint-Mihiel on the southern line and the western line was within German artillery range. New railway lines were quickly laid to connect to Verdun. As well as this, Pétain established continuous convoys of trucks – travelling at a rate of one vehicle every 14 seconds – that provided general transport for men, rations and ammunition into Verdun. The road became known as *la voie sacrée* (the sacred way).[9]

Pétain maintained his soldiers' morale by rotating divisions through Verdun every two weeks. Over the course of 1916, 70 of the 96 French divisions on the Western Front fought at Verdun. German troops were deployed for longer periods with a commensurately greater chance of becoming casualties: only 46.5 German divisions were deployed to the offensive.[10]

The Battle of Verdun continued until December, but the threat to France had eased long before then. In June, Falkenhayn had been forced to transfer three divisions to the Eastern Front in response to the Russian offensive in Galicia. When the Battle of the Somme began on 1 July, he had to send more men from Verdun north to Picardy. French attacks in October, November and December recovered most of the territory the Germans had captured at the beginning of the battle.[11]

Falkenhayn's attempt to conduct a battle of attrition had failed. The losses at the Battle of Verdun are estimated at 337,000 German and 377,000 French casualties: an almost even ratio of 1 German for every 1.1 French casualty. When Romania, recognising the Central Powers' setbacks on all fronts, entered the war on the Allied side on 27 August, Falkenhayn's demise was inevitable. Within 48 hours he was sacked as Chief of General Staff and sent eastwards to command an improvised force to fight Germany's newest foe. He was replaced by the duo who would control German military strategy, and large parts of the war economy, to the end of the war: Field Marshal Paul von Hindenburg, the new Chief of General Staff, and his assistant, Quartermaster General Erich Ludendorff.[12]

The French casualties suffered during the Battle of Verdun inevitably reduced the number of French troops that could be deployed to the Somme operation. The planned initial deployment of 39 French divisions was cut to 22 divisions, almost equivalent to the British contribution of 19 divisions. Joffre accordingly downgraded the scale of the attack on 21 June, limiting the operation to breaking the German line and advancing about six miles (some ten kilometres) to take the main German logistics and communication link, the road running north–south through Péronne, Bapaume and Cambrai.[13]

On the eve of the battle, Haig confidently wrote to his wife Dorothy 'I feel that everything possible for us to do to achieve success had been done.' The preliminary bombardment on most of the British front was no different to that for the previous year's Battle of Loos: 35 minutes with an 'intense' final five minutes. The Somme offensive began at

7.30 am on 1 July 1916. The French troops had better assault tactics and more effective artillery support than the British. On the first day, they advanced around two and a half miles (four kilometres), captured 6,000 German prisoners and suffered only 1,590 casualties. In the same 24-hour period, the British Empire's army – which included soldiers from Australia, Britain, Canada, India, Ireland, Newfoundland, New Zealand and South Africa – suffered 56,886 casualties, of whom 19,240 were killed. Gary Sheffield points out that 'Haig personally bears a large share of the responsibility for the disaster of 1 July', but he also acknowledges that there were systemic failures at all levels of the BEF in this period. According to Robin Prior and Trevor Wilson, the main reason for this enormous discrepancy between the French and British losses was that the latter's artillery bombardment generally did not destroy the German artillery and machine gun positions. This meant that when the advance began, the Germans had the firepower to turn the forward British trenches and no-man's-land into a killing zone. Prior and Wilson estimate that one third of the British Empire casualties on the first day of the Somme occurred while the men were still in their own lines. [14]

The soldiers generally did not, as is often asserted, walk slowly towards the German lines. Each of the 80 British battalion commanders who took part in the 1 July offensive chose their own mode of assault. Of the 75 battalions for which there is evidence, Prior and Wilson found that 53 battalions advanced into no-man's-land during the pre-assault bombardment and then rushed the German lines, ten attacked from their own front line, and 12 advanced at a steady pace. Some of this latter group of battalions were walking because they were following a creeping artillery barrage. In many cases this protection enabled them to gain their objectives. [15]

A brief survey of five divisions at various stages of the campaign can provide some insight into the British Empire's Somme experience. On 1 July, the 46th (North Midland) Division, which suffered over 3,700 casualties in their failed assault on the Hohenzollern Redoubt on 13 October 1915 during the Battle of Loos, joined with the 56th (1st London) Division for an attack – north of the main battle – on the fortified village of Gommecourt. This was aimed at diverting German troops away from the Somme. The 56th (1st London) Division broke into the enemy lines, but were forced to withdraw as dusk fell. The 46th (North Midland) Division never reached the village as its attack stalled in the face of German machine gun fire. The formation ended the day with 2,455 casualties, the lowest number of losses of all British divisions deployed on 1 July. Haig commented in his diary that the 'right brigade of 46th did not press on' at Gommecourt. Dissatisfied with the division's performance, he sacked the division's commander, Major General Edward Montagu-Stuart-Wortley and sent him home.[16]

Two divisions recruited in Ireland – the 36th (Ulster) Division and the 16th (Irish) Division – had their baptism of fire on the Somme. The 36th (Ulster) Division, recruited as its name implies mostly from Northern Ireland, was staunchly Protestant in religion and strongly Unionist in politics, the latter meaning opposing Ireland gaining Home Rule and supporting remaining part of the United Kingdom. The 16th (Irish) Division was mostly devoutly Catholic and composed of Nationalists who aspired to implement Irish Home Rule and establish a parliament in Dublin.

On 1 July, the 36th (Ulster) Division attacked towards Thiepval on both sides of the Ancre River. The advance on the north bank of the river failed in the face of heavy fire from the Bécourt Redoubt. On the Ancre's south bank, however, the artillery bombardment had successfully cut the barbed wire entanglements and destroyed the German front line. This enabled the Ulstermen to break through the German first position and capture the Schwaben Redoubt. Four of the nine Victoria Crosses awarded on the first day of the Somme went to men of the 36th (Ulster) Division. The troops advanced faster than the 29th Division to their left and the 32nd Division on their right. This meant, as Major General Oliver Nugent, commander of the 36th (Ulster) Division, wrote to his wife Kitty in County Cavan in Ireland, that his formation, who were 'marching far in front over absolutely open ground was shot at from in front and from both sides'. The division suffered 5,100 casualties on 1 July and the surviving soldiers gradually were forced back from the territory they had captured. This loss of life would come to be seen as Ulster's 'blood sacrifice' that could be repaid only by its remaining within the United Kingdom.[17]

Haig continued to stage diversionary attacks away from the Somme to distract the Germans. On 19 July, the XI Corps commander, Brigadier

General Richard Haking, directed Major General Sir James McCay, commanding the 5th Australian Division, and Major General Sir Colin Mackenzie, in charge of the 61st (2nd South Midland) Division, to attack Fromelles in northern France, not far from where the battles of Aubers Ridge had been fought in 1915. Both divisions were inexperienced, and both commanders had failed in earlier operations. Mackenzie had been relieved of command of the 3rd Division on the Western Front in October 1914. McCay had been responsible for a hasty and costly attack at Gallipoli on 6 May 1915 that left over half his brigade as casualties. The attack at Fromelles captured no ground at the cost of 1,547 British and 5,533 Australian casualties. Sheffield describes Haig's reaction to the operation as his 'insensitive worst'. The BEF commander wrote in his diary:

> The reality of the fighting and shelling seems to have been greater than many had expected! So the experience must have been of value to all[.][18]

Lieutenant Edgar McCloughry, who was at Fromelles with the 5th Australian Division engineers and subsequently joined the Royal Air Force, achieving the rank of air vice-marshal, wrote almost 40 years later that this battle

> caused me to be dubious of the High Command which previously I had accepted as highly efficient and able, if not altogether infallible. Certainly I had never imagined that any operation involving certain heavy casualties could ever be launched except for a vital military purpose.[19]

Two Irish divisions were created during the Great War. The 10th (Irish) Division fought at Gallipoli in 1915 and then in Macedonia. The 16th (Irish) Division, commanded by Lieutenant General Sir Lawrence Parsons – who opposed Home Rule, while his wife supported it – arrived in France on 18 December 1915. General Sir Hubert Gough, a staunch Unionist, made clear his prejudice towards his fellow countrymen when he questioned the Irish Nationalists' loyalty and had the division placed under his overall command in I Corps.[20]

Gough's fears would prove to be unfounded. The Irishmen would achieve two significant victories on the right flank of the Allied advance. The 16th (Irish) Division's first battle on 3 September resulted in the 47th Brigade capturing the village of Guillemont and two soldiers being awarded the Victoria Cross. Following the 7th Division's failure to capture Ginchy, about 1,650 yards (1,500 metres) north-east of Guillemont, from 3 to 7 September, the Irishmen were tasked to take the village.[21]

Lieutenant Colonel Rowland Feilding of the 6th Connaught Rangers described his troops as being 'worn out and exhausted by their recent fighting'. Lieutenant Tom Kettle, former Nationalist MP for East Tyrone and Irish Volunteer, now serving in the 9th Royal Dublin Fusiliers, wrote to his brother on 8 September, the day before the attack on Ginchy:

> The bombardment, destruction and bloodshed are beyond all imagination [. . .] Somewhere the Choosers of the Slain are touching, as in our Norse story they used to touch, with invisible wands those who are to die.[22]

The Irishmen endured ten hours of German bombardment and machine-gun fire before they started their assault at 4.45 pm. The 7th Royal Irish Rifles and 7th Royal Irish Fusiliers led the attack, supported by a deafening artillery barrage, and took the German front line. The 8th and 9th Royal Dublin Fusiliers then took over the advance and captured Ginchy. Tom Kettle's premonition of death became an actuality: he died during the battle. In ten days, the 16th (Irish) Division suffered 4,330 casualties, a 40 per cent loss rate.[23]

The next major British attack on the Somme, involving XIV, III and XV Corps, commenced north of Ginchy on 15 September with the aim of breaking into the German positions between the villages of Flers and Courcelette. The battle saw the first use in combat of tanks – the name chosen to indicate they were for water storage so as to disguise their real use as armoured fighting vehicles. Both the French and British developed tanks because their strategy required offensive operations to remove the Germans from France and Belgium. As the Germans were on the defensive on the Western Front and had no need for such vehicles, they were therefore surprised when tanks appeared on the battlefield. British Mark I tanks were slow – they were outpaced by walking infantry – unreliable and vulnerable to artillery fire. Of the 49 tanks deployed at the Battle of Flers–Courcelette, 13 broke down before reaching the start line.[24]

The XV Corps, including the 14th (Light), 47th (1/2nd London), New Zealand and 41st Divisions, made the attack towards Flers. The New Zealand Division was ordered to capture Flers and then push forward to occupy the level ground two miles (approximately three kilometres) west of the village. After a three-day preliminary bombardment, the Kiwis began their initial uphill advance at 6.20 am protected by a creeping barrage. However, they soon came under fire from the flank and took heavy casualties: 46 per cent in the 2nd Auckland Battalion and 68 per cent in the 2nd Otago Battalion.[25]

When the first objective was captured at 7.00 am, the 4th Battalion New Zealand Rifle Brigade took over the downhill advance for about 750 yards, suffering 38 per cent casualties. At 8.00 am the first tank caught up with the infantry. Twenty minutes later, 2nd and 3rd Battalions New Zealand Rifle Brigade continued the assault. By 10.30 am a second tank had joined the fray and assisted the 3rd Battalion New Zealand Rifle Brigade in capturing the Flers trench network. A third tank later arrived. The New Zealand Division's Pioneer Battalion, composed of Maori soldiers, immediately began digging communication trenches. One of the tanks went forward and, as Captain Hugh McKinnon wrote, 'covered the digging parties with his broadsides of Vickers [machine guns] at the same time firing up the road with his forward gun'.[26]

Colonel Hugh Stewart, who commanded the 2nd Canterbury Battalion at Flers, described the brutality of the battle in his history of the New Zealand Division published in 1922:

> In the village of Flers itself a systematic search was made during the course of the afternoon. Many cellars and dugouts still contained Germans. Seven prisoners had been taken when a machine gun party, after surrendering, fired point-blank into the clearing party, of whom 3 were killed and 4 wounded. Thenceforward no prisoners were taken.[27]

Heavy autumn rain began on 17 September, halting the New Zealanders' advance and enabling the Germans to regain their composure. The division was relieved on the evening of 3 October, having suffered 34 per cent casualties in three weeks. As Stewart wrote:

> All had experienced continued privations and repeated perils. There were few that had not seen comrades stricken or blown skywards, or had not themselves been face to face with imminent death in manifold forms of horror [. . .] Their nostrils had not yet banished the stench of putrefying corpses, their eyes the ghastly scenes in entanglements saps and shellholes, their ears the detonations of bursting bombs, the roar of mighty projectiles rushing towards them, and the crash, deafening and soul-shattering, as these exploded all around them.[28]

William Philpott argues that the Battle of the Somme should have been concluded by the end of October. Haig acknowledged on 12 November 'the difficulties of ground and weather' with the onset of winter, but he believed it was necessary 'to run reasonable risks' to assert Allied ascendancy over the German Army. The campaign finally ended on 18 November.[29]

The armies of the British and French empires had been constantly attacking during the Battle of the Somme and therefore suffered more casualties than the defending German Army. Between 1 July and 30 November 1916, the British Empire casualties totalled 419,654. French Empire losses on the Somme from 1 July to 20 November were 202,567. Elizabeth Greenhalgh argues the reason the French casualties on the Somme were less than half that of the British was because

> Foch's more sensible method of making the advance a step at a time, each step prepared by artillery and checked for efficacy, proved better than Joffre's and Haig's intention to break through the German defensive positions and to bring in the cavalry to exploit the breach.

German casualties on the Western Front from 1 July to 31 October are estimated at 597,000. Gary Sheffield concludes that Haig's conduct of the Battle of the Somme was 'sound in principle, but too ambitious in practice given the state of training and inexperience of his army'. The return to open warfare was not achieved in 1916, though hundreds of thousands of men had been killed or maimed in the attempt.[30]

On 20 December 1916, Haig visited the commander of the 36th (Ulster) Division, Major General Oliver Nugent, at Saint-Jans-Cappel in northern France, not far from the Belgian border. As the two men rode through the divisional sector, the BEF commander said to Nugent: 'You did magnificently on the Somme and I always think with regret that we failed to give you all the support we ought to have done.' Nugent thanked Haig for his words and commented, 'Perhaps we had all been rather optimistic as to what it was possible to do'. Haig replied: 'Well, we were all learning.'[31]

General Robert Nivelle replaced Joffre as Commander-in-Chief of the French Army on the Western Front on 13 December 1916. Nivelle had gained rapid promotion and had made his reputation in the last three months of 1916 where he had conducted offensives that had regained much of the territory lost at Verdun. The new French commander asserted that he had developed the strategy to break through the German lines, and devised the plan for a major French offensive in the Chemin des Dames region, north of the River Aisne. In the last week of February 1917, the Germans unexpectedly withdrew to a new defensive line, known in German as the *Siegfriedstellung* (Siegfried Position), and in English as the Hindenburg Line. The new position was shorter and therefore reduced the number of German soldiers required to hold the line.

This withdrawal was part of Hindenburg and Ludendorff's new strategy to win the war – the fourth German attempt to achieve victory – where, as described in Chapter Two, the German Army remained on the defensive on the Western Front, while unrestricted submarine warfare, which commenced on 1 February 1917, was expected to starve the United Kingdom into surrender.[32]

Nivelle's offensive began on 16 April 1917, without complementary attacks on other fronts by Italy, Romania or Russia (where Tsar Nicholas II had abdicated on 15 March and a republic had been formed). Nivelle's expected rapid breakthrough did not occur. He was sacked on 15 May and banished to North Africa. The French casualty rate at Chemin des Dames was similar to the losses in the Artois in 1915 and the Somme in 1916, but this time about half the French Army responded with what Greenhalgh describes as 'collective indiscipline' that would reach its peak in May–June 1917.[33]

The French soldiers did not mutiny. They would defend their lines against German attack, but they would not take part in what they saw as Nivelle's pointless offensives. Pétain became commander-in-chief in May and restored military discipline, rebuilding morale. Of the tens of thousands of soldiers who had refused to follow orders, he had 112 men sentenced to death. Of these, only 25 cases of capital punishment were carried out. Another 345 were convicted on lesser charges, and an unknown number of soldiers were deported to French colonies. Pétain provided the troops with more leave, equipped railway stations to provide soldiers with food and beds when they were in transit and improved field rations. The German Army was aware that discipline had broken down in the French lines, but they did not attack because their strategy was to remain on the defensive while they waited for the U-boat campaign to win the war.[34]

While the French Army slowly recovered, the British Empire Army had to take the main responsibility for fighting Germany on the Western Front for the remainder of 1917. Haig devised a two-stage strategy for offensives in northern France and Belgium. The first stage was to capture the ridges at Vimy and Messines and break into the Hindenburg Line at Cambrai. The second stage, to take place 'some weeks' after the Messines operation, was an ambitious plan to break out of the Ypres salient and advance to the North Sea, capturing the ports of Bruges, Ostend and Zeebrugge along with German airfields, thus removing the threat to Britain of Belgian-based U-boats and bomber aircraft. On 9 April, the attack at Arras in northern France resulted in the 4th and 9th (Scottish) Divisions advancing three and a half miles (some five and a half kilometres), the furthest forward advance on the Western Front since the onset of trench warfare, and the Canadian Corps' four-day battle that captured Vimy Ridge, though at a cost of over 10,500 casualties. Again, the assault lost momentum once the troops moved outside the range of the 18-pounder artillery and were halted by uncut barbed wire and German counter-attacks. In addition, there was a four-week delay in operations as the artillery was transported from Arras about 50 miles northwards to the site of the next attack.[35]

The next British Empire operation was the Battle of Messines. The plan to excavate deep mines beneath the German-held ridge was devised by John Norton Griffiths, former army officer, civil engineer and Conservative MP for the Staffordshire town of Wednesbury. Griffiths had been planning

Fig. 7.1 British Royal Engineers mining and counter-mining beneath Messines. General Sir Herbert Plumer ordered the excavation of 21 deep mines at Messines. Some were completed and filled with explosives more than a year before the battle took place. Image: UK Ministry of Defence 110689.

to move to Australia in 1914, as his company had won a substantial and controversial contract to raise £10 million and construct railways for the New South Wales state government led by Labor Premier William Holman. However, the intervention of the war meant he remained in the United Kingdom and returned to the army. In early 1915, Griffiths pointed out to the War Office that the men he had employed digging drains below Manchester could also dig beneath German trenches. Sir John French approved the idea on 15 February and eight British tunnelling companies were established, soon followed by New Zealand, Canadian and Australian units.[36]

When Major Griffiths first saw the German-held Messines ridge on 12 May 1915, he immediately began developing a proposal to place deep mines beneath the enemy positions. On 6 January 1916, the plan was approved as part of a wider operation to capture the ridge, with Brigadier General Robert Harvey placed in charge of the tunnelling. The digging continued throughout 1916 and into 1917. From November 1916 to the commencement of the battle, the 1st Australian Tunnelling Company fought a tense and vicious underground war with German engineers around the most distant mine beneath Hill 60.[37]

The preparation for the Battle of Messines reflected the British Empire's increasing experience and expertise in Western Front warfare. From the middle of 1916, sound ranging and flash spotting were being used to precisely locate the position of German artillery batteries. Around the new year, the BEF created the Counter-Battery Staff Office to collect information on German artillery from a range of sources, including aerial reconnaissance, in order to make counter-battery fire more effective. The Germans never established a comparable organisation. The main priority of the final three days of the bombardment at Messines was counter-battery fire. During this period, most of the German field artillery was destroyed or withdrawn to safety. British artillery ammunition was now being manufactured with the 106 fuse that detonated the shell when it came in contact with barbed wire or the ground. This made the blast more likely to kill or wound the enemy, and less likely to create craters to impede the advancing infantry. Four pamphlets written in the aftermath of the Somme campaign – 'Instructions for the Training of Divisions for Offensive Action', 'Artillery Notes', 'Preparation for and the Employment of R[oyal] E[ngineers] in Offensive Action' and 'Forward Inter-Communication in Battle' – formed the basis for planning the operation. Colonel Alan Brooke of the Canadian Corps sent his report on the Battle of Arras to X Corps Headquarters so the staff could use it as the model for Messines. In May, Major General Oliver Nugent sent officers from the 36th (Ulster) Division to 'one of the Canadian Divisions who had fought at Arras [. . .] to get the latest tips and information from their experience'. Three corps were deployed to capture the Messines salient: II Anzac Corps, IX Corps and X Corps. Each corps would provide three divisions for the assault along a 17,000-yard frontage (some 15.5 kilometres), supported by 72 Mark IV tanks.[38]

At the Army Commanders' conference at Doullens in northern France on 7 May 1917, General Sir Herbert Plumer, the Second Army

Fig. 7.2 New Zealand troops' rehearsal for the assault on Messines Ridge on 7 June 1917. The success of the attack demonstrated the increasing expertise of British Empire troops with accurate artillery support in capturing German positions. Image: Alexander Turnbull Library, Wellington, New Zealand 1/2-012752-G.

commander, told Haig that he would be ready to attack Messines on 7 June. A million pounds (450 tonnes) of explosives had been placed in 21 mines, but Plumer decided the two southern-most mines were located too far from the main attack and would not be blown. The exact position of these two mines was lost during the German offensive of 1918: one blew up after being hit by lightning in 1955, the other remains unexploded and undiscovered.[39]

The units that would fight at Messines began training for the operation in April 1917. Soldiers were able to view a clay model of Messines Ridge on a quarter-acre (1000-square metre) site that was regularly updated in line with the most recent intelligence. On 26 April, the 49th Brigade of the 16th (Irish) Division rehearsed their attack on a replica of the trench system at Wytschaete. This included an attempt to simulate a creeping barrage using a line of soldiers waving flags with sound effects provided by drummers.[40]

The assault on Messines Ridge can be considered to have begun at 2.00 am on 7 June, when Royal Flying Corps aircraft flew low over the German positions in order to drown out the sound of British tanks moving to their start line. At 3.10, the mines beneath the ridge were detonated, killing about 10,000 German soldiers. The smoke and dust raised by the explosions meant officers had to use compasses to navigate their advance. The British Empire artillery began its creeping bombardment, lifting 100 yards (around 90 metres) every two minutes, behind which the infantry moved forward. Edmonds described the advance as '80,000 men [. . .] moving up the slope' with every man having 'a pre-arranged and carefully rehearsed task'. Each artillery piece was allocated between 15,000 and 20,000 shells per day for the opening two days of the battle.[41]

Nugent, the 36th (Ulster) Division commander, described his reactions to the battle in a series of letters to his wife. Three hours into the attack, he wrote: 'Up to now the reports are all good. We are well into the German lines and our casualties are slight.' At 2.30 pm, the general stated: 'The battle has only begun, but I think there is no doubt that [. . .] it has been the most successful the British Army has had in this war.' On 10 June, Nugent commented:

> What pleases me more than anything is that the 16th Division did equally well and there was nothing to choose between them so neither side can make any capital out of the performance of its own Division in Ireland.[42]

The Nationalist 16th Division and the Unionist 36th Division had advanced side by side at Messines. This shared experience would eventually be officially remembered on 11 November 1998, when Queen Elizabeth II and President of Ireland Mary McAleese opened the Island of Ireland Peace Park, near the site of the battle – now known by its Flemish name Mesen – to remember all the Irish who died in World War I.[43]

The meticulous detail that had gone into the battle plan was rewarded with a rapid advance. The Blue Line, or first objective line, including the southern part of the ridge and Messines village was occupied on schedule at 3.45 am; the Black Line, including the German second position and the far crest of Messines Ridge was achieved at 5.00 am. At this point, the artillery switched to a protective barrage 300 yards beyond the Black Line while the next assault battalions advanced and the troops dug new trenches. At 7.00 am the attack on Messines Ridge commenced. Tanks were to support the infantry attack, but the opening bombardment had cratered the ground to such an extent that it was difficult for them to go forward. The 1st Battalion Royal Munster Fusiliers, with the assistance of one tank, captured Wytschaete village. At 8.00 am the Irish and Ulster divisions met at the Messines–St Eloi road. One hour later, Messines Ridge was occupied. The troops immediately began preparing to defend their gains from the German *Eingreif* divisions, specialist counter-attack units. This would include the artillery of three infantry divisions 'hitherto silent in forward positions' that would announce their existence only when the Germans advanced. When the assault came at 1.35 pm, it was repulsed.[44]

The final British Empire objective at Messines was the Oosttaverne position or Green Line, one mile (around 1.6 kilometres) beyond the ridge. This assault was scheduled for 1.10 pm, but Plumer ordered the attack to be delayed until 3.10 pm because transport was finding it difficult to advance over the broken ground.[45]

The 12th and 13th Brigades of the 4th Australian Division began their advance on the right flank protected by a creeping bombardment and accompanied by three tanks. The water table at Messines was only two or three feet (less than a metre) below the surface and therefore trenches could not be excavated. The Germans had developed reinforced concrete troop shelters called *Mannschafts-Eisenbeton-Unterstände*, in German abbreviated to 'Mebus', and known to British troops as 'pillboxes'.[46]

This was the first time Australian soldiers had encountered pillboxes on the battlefield. Charles Bean described in the Australian Official History the savage nature of this fighting:

> The tension accompanying the struggles around these blockhouses – the murderous fire from a sheltered position, followed by the sudden giving-in of the surrounded garrison – caused this year's fighting in Flanders to be marked by a ferocity that renders the reading of any true narrative peculiarly unpleasant. Where such tension exists in battle, the rules of 'civilised' war are powerless. Most men are temporarily half-mad, their pulses pounding at their ears, their mouths dry. The noblest among them are straining their wills to keep cool heads and even voices; the less self-controlled are for the time being governed by reckless, primitive impulse. With death singing in their ears, they will kill until they grow tired of killing. When they have been racked

by machine-gun fire, the routing out of enemy groups from behind several feet of concrete is almost inevitably the signal for a butchery at least of the first few who emerge, and sometimes the helplessly wounded may not be spared.[47]

In the afternoon, the 37th and 47th Australian Battalions reached their objective: the Oosttaverne Line. Later, other battalions arrived to strengthen the position. The Germans counter-attacked. At the same time, the Australians, who had not followed instructions to fire flares to enable Royal Flying Corps aircraft to identify their position, came under British artillery fire. Most fell back to the Black Line on Messines Ridge.[48]

Despite this setback, the British Empire troops would capture all their objectives except a section of the Comines Canal and 1,000 yards (less than a kilometre) of the Oosttaverne Line. On 14 June, the Germans withdrew from Messines to the River Lys. Edmonds could truthfully write of this battle: 'A great victory had been won'.[49]

The planning for this battle had been impeccable, with one tragic exception. As Table 7.1 shows, the British casualties at Messines had been remarkably light by Western Front standards, except for the losses in II Anzac Corps, which accounted for over half the casualties.

TABLE 7.1

BRITISH EMPIRE CASUALTIES MESSINES, 1–12 JUNE 1917[50]

II Corps	108
VIII Corps	203
IX Corps	5,263
X Corps	6,597
II Anzac	12,391
TOTAL	24,562

Most of these men who were killed or wounded were members of the New Zealand Division who were ordered to spend two days on Messines

Ridge exposed to constant German artillery bombardment. On 9 June, the survivors were withdrawn from the ridge and placed in reserve.[51]

On 2 July, William Holman, the New South Wales Premier, who in 1913 had negotiated a deal with John Norton Griffiths to build railways in his state, visited the Messines battlefield. As will be detailed in the next chapter, the Australian Labor Party split in late 1916 over military conscription. Holman was one of the minority who supported its introduction and was expelled from the party, but he retained power by joining his pro-conscription supporters with the Liberal opposition to form the Nationalist Party. Holman went to the polls on 23 March 1917, and was re-elected. He then sailed to Europe on 6 May, leading to the unusual situation of the state parliament sitting for the first time after an election without the premier. The Sydney *Sun* speculated that the reason for Holman's precipitate departure was that he was going to meet Griffiths to negotiate a release from the pre-war contract. Holman spent time in England, France and Belgium, but it is unclear whether he met Griffiths.[52]

Holman went to Messines to visit the 4th Australian Division, commanded by Major General William Holmes. The general was giving the premier a tour of the sector when a German shell exploded near them. Holman was left bruised, bleeding and bewildered, but otherwise unharmed. Holmes was struck in the chest by a shell fragment and died later that day. Lieutenant General Sir Alexander Godley, the II Anzac Corps commander, describing the incident to his wife, commented: 'Unfortunately, it killed General Holmes and didn't touch the politician. Wasn't it bad luck?'

On 14 June, the Army Commanders Conference at Lillers, about 43 miles (70 kilometres) inland from Calais, decided that the next British attack would be towards the Belgian village of Passchendaele (Passendale). Again, there was a seven-week delay while the artillery was moved into Belgium. The Third Battle of Ypres was fought from 31 July to 10 November 1917. The battle would be remembered as a disaster for three reasons. The first was the geography: the British were attempting to advance uphill out of the Ypres salient under German bombardment from three sides. The second was the weather: heavy autumn rains turned the ground into a quagmire and made it difficult to advance. The third reason was command: Haig appointed General Sir Hubert Gough, Commander of the British Fifth Army to direct the operation. Following a meeting with Gough on 21 August, Nugent wrote:

> no one can talk to him and come away thinking that he is mentally or intellectually fit to command a big Army. He isn't and it is wrong that the lives of thousands of good men should be sacrificed through want of forethought and higher leading.[53]

The Third Battle of Ypres struggled through mud and blood until it concluded with the Canadian capture of Passchendaele on 10 November. It is estimated that the Germans suffered about 200,000 casualties and the British Empire about 275,000.[54]

The final major British battle on the Western Front in 1917 was fought at Cambrai in northern France from 20 November to 7 December. In the lead-up to this operation, France and the United Kingdom had been stunned by events in other theatres of war. In Italy, Germany had joined with Austria–Hungary to inflict a savage defeat on the Italian Army at the Battle of Caporetto from 24 October to 19 November. The Central Powers took 294,000 Italian prisoners, about 15 per cent of the entire army, and captured about half the country's stock of artillery. At the same time, the Bolsheviks had taken power in Russia on 7 November and had begun peace negotiations with the Austrians and Germans.[55]

The assault at Cambrai demonstrated the increasing British expertise in artillery and armour. As will be discussed more fully in Chapter Nine, it was now possible for artillery to accurately bombard enemy batteries or other targets without the need for initial ranging shots. The artillery would combine with a force of 476 tanks. The Germans were shocked by the initial British onslaught, which made a five-mile (eight-kilometre) gap in the line and advanced six miles. The German counter-attack troops soon recaptured most of this ground, at the cost of about 40,000 casualties on each side. Cambrai was not significant for the introduction of a new military technology, but because it demonstrated that the separate combat arms, such as infantry, artillery and tanks, were being more effectively combined and presaging a return to mobile warfare.[56]

During 1917, the BEF had suffered 817,792 casualties on the Western Front – the number including an unknown number of men wounded multiple times. Oliver Nugent ended the year in a pessimistic mood. He wrote on 1 December 1917:

> The Germans are not a beaten enemy. They are stronger now than a year ago because they can draw on all the troops they had in Russia and they have all the guns they took from the Italians. [57]

8

Volunteers and Conscripts

The United Kingdom was the only European power in August 1914 that did not rely on conscription to fill the ranks of its army. The British Army consisted of only 247,432 regular full-time volunteer soldiers and 733,514 territorial part-time soldiers. The government's plan, in the event of a European war with Germany, was to send the highly-trained regulars of the British Expeditionary Force to fight alongside the French Army, to be subsequently supplemented with volunteers from the mostly white Dominions of Canada, Australia and New Zealand. However, as the casualties grew on the Western Front, the British government deployed Indian troops on the Western Front and recruited 2.4 million 'New Army' volunteers − including 200,000 Irishmen. When volunteering dried up at the end of 1915, Prime Minister Asquith introduced conscription in Britain, but − for reasons that will be discussed later in this chapter − not Ireland. On its introduction in January 1916, conscription was applied to single men and childless widows aged 18 to 41 years. Six months later, compulsion was broadened to include all British men in this age range (though appeals were possible, for example in the case of workers in key industries). In April 1918, in the wake of the German spring offensive, the draft was extended to 50-year-olds, with provision to include 56-year-olds and males in Ireland. In total, 2.5 million British men were conscripted.[1]

TABLE 8.1

BRITISH EMPIRE TOTAL ENLISTMENTS, 1914–18[2]

UNITED KINGDOM	5,704,416
INDIA	1,440,437
CANADA	628,864
AUSTRALIA	412,953
WHITE SOUTH AFRICANS	136,070
'COLOURED' SOUTH AFRICAN & COLONIAL TROOPS	134,837
TOTAL	8,586,202

As Table 8.1 shows, over 8.5 million soldiers served in the British Empire Army in World War I. As the conflict continued and the number of casualties climbed, the issues of recruiting and conscription were debated across the British Empire. The Government of India greatly increased the number of 'classes' from which men could be recruited in 1916. When a Bengali infantry unit was established, the Lahore *Panjabee* stated:

> it opens the opportunity of active service to a people who have been burning with zeal and enthusiasm to do and dare, to serve their country and their King; and what is more it removes a disability which Bengal has always keenly resented as being both inconsistent with her loyalty and galling to her self-respect.

British authorities discovered that 'even the supposedly non-martial classes could make fine soldiers, provided they were well-trained and well-led'. In some Dominions and colonies there was formal or informal conscription of some groups, as well as decisions not to conscript other communities, lest their numbers be reduced and this alter the existing political environment. Conscription debates in Canada, Australia and Ireland would be bitter and have long-term political consequences.[3]

Towards the end of the failed Battle of Loos, on 8 October 1915, Andrew Bonar Law, the British Colonial Secretary sent a telegram to every Dominion and colony 'on the possibilities of raising native troops in large numbers in our Colonies + Protectorates for Imperial service'. This confidential request was followed on 25 October by a public call by King George V for 'men of all classes, to come forward voluntarily and take your share in the fight'. In colonies such as the West Indies, the King's appeal was seen as a long-awaited recognition of imperial equality in the war against Germany. Jamaican poet Tom Redcam's 'Gentlemen. The King' proclaimed:

> Listen to the words of the King!
> Listen to the summons they bring!
> Patriots, stand up for the right
> Buckle your armour for fight! [. . .]
> Heedless of race, rank or creed [. . .]
> Mindful of Duty alone.[4]

A thoughtless omission: creating the Canadian Expeditionary Force

The New Zealand, Australian and Canadian governments, as mentioned in the introduction, had all devised mobilisation plans to create expeditionary forces in the event of a war with Germany. When the United Kingdom declared war on 4 August 1914, the New Zealand and Australian defence ministers, James Allen and Senator George Pearce, implemented their existing plans. In contrast, but in keeping with his impulsive personality, Sam Hughes, the Canadian Minister for Militia and Defence, discarded his mobilisation plan in which the Canadian Expeditionary Force would be formed through the existing structure of militia units, and instead ordered volunteers to travel to Valcartier on the St Lawrence river in Quebec. From here, soldiers would be able to embark directly on ocean-going ships to Europe. However, when Hughes made this call, no camp existed at Valcartier.[5]

On this occasion, Hughes' energy and drive resulted in the 'miracle of Valcartier' in which a fully functioning military camp sprouted from the Quebec fields. Men arrived in their thousands by train from across

Canada. As Hughes put it: 'There was really a call to arms like the fiery cross passing through the Highlands of Scotland or the mountains of Ireland in former days.'[6]

Sam Hughes held strong prejudices in favour of the Canadian Conservative Party and the staunchly Protestant Orange Lodge, and equally strong prejudices against Catholics and French Canadians. In 1907, Hughes had described the arrival of some French priests as a 'curse to Canada'. Francophone Canadians responded that Hughes was the 'champion of race hatred'.[7]

Always irrepressible and often irresponsible, Hughes deployed all his biases when choosing officers for the 1st Canadian Division. He denied commissions to officers with whom he had disagreed in the past, were Liberal Party supporters or professional army officers. Most significantly for the future relationship between Francophone and Anglophone Canadians, he refused to appoint the most senior Québécois officer, Major General François-Louis Lessard to command a brigade or even a battalion. As Tim Cook points out: 'With no French-Canadian battalion commanders in the First Contingent, Hughes all but guaranteed that no French Canadians would have the chance to achieve a senior rank in the Canadian Expeditionary Force'. This laid the ground for future disputes on linguistic lines within Canada that would become more bitter as the war continued.[8]

Hughes ignored French Canada, but accepted recruits from another source. In the years leading up to the Great War, large numbers of British migrants had gone to Canada, mostly settling in the Prairie provinces of Manitoba, Saskatchewan and Alberta. In the 12 months to 31 March 1914, 173,250 British people had migrated to Canada. However, the Prairie bubble had burst during 1914: the result being that 65 per cent of the 34,000 recruits in the first Canadian contingent were British-born.[9]

Adding to the predominantly British complexion of the initial Canadian military contribution, Montreal businessman and militia officer, Captain Hamilton Gault offered Sam Hughes 100,000 Canadian dollars to create a battalion recruited from ex-British soldiers resident in the Dominion. The unit, named after the daughter of the Canadian Governor-General, the Duke of Connaught, was titled Princess Patricia's Canadian Light Infantry. On 3 September, Lewis Harcourt, the Colonial Secretary, expressed 'high

Fig. 8.1 The domineering General Sam Hughes arriving in France to visit Canadian troops, 1916. Image: Library and Archives Canada/Bibliothèque et Archives Canada PA-022744.

appreciation' of Gault's 'patriotic conduct' in contributing so large a sum towards the organisation of the force. A week later, as the Battle of the Marne was being fought, Harcourt told the Duke of Connaught:

> There is no limit to the number of men who may ultimately be required in Europe in order to finish this war and I hope, therefore, that you will do what you can, privately, to encourage the gradual formation of a second Canadian contingent.[10]

The Canadian Expeditionary Force and Princess Patricia's Canadian Light Infantry sailed on 1 October and arrived in England 13 days later. Gault's battalion initially served alongside regular British soldiers in the 27th Division, but would later become part of the CEF.[11]

Although the Australian Imperial Force (AIF) was an all-volunteer organisation, the decision to enlist was often made for – and not by – the individual. Reflecting the society and hierarchy of the time, parents, employers, community leaders and ministers of religion were often responsible for putting young men in the ranks, as evidenced by two historians, J.N.I. Dawes and Lloyd Robson, who in 1965 asked Australian Great War veterans to provide anonymous written accounts of how and why they joined up. A junior clerk in a solicitor's office in the rural Victorian town of Ballarat recalled:

> I hardly thought about it. The adults around me all seemed to be of the opinion that enlistment was the right thing for an eligible male to do and I just seemed to conform to that idea without attempting to weigh the pros and cons of the matter.[12]

An Englishwoman who had migrated to Australia told her sons on the outbreak of hostilities: 'Well boys, MY COUNTRY is at War and you know what is expected of you.' Others enlisted to financially assist their families. In June 1915, a 16-year-old boy lied about his age and joined the AIF. Since the age of ten, this youth had been milking cows and delivering newspapers to help support his mother. When he enlisted, he allotted most of his private's pay to his mother, and noted that, now he was in the army, 'mum didn't have to feed and clothe me'.[13]

James Menzies, who had three sons, decided that his eldest two sons, Les and Frank, should join up, but that his youngest son Bob should remain in Australia. This was because Bob had been awarded a scholarship to study law at Melbourne University, and his father believed he would have the financial capacity to provide for his parents in their old age. In rural areas, the senior men of the district calculated how many farm labourers would be required to maintain agricultural production, and then how many men could be spared for the army. In the Woogaree district of north-east Victoria, 14 males enlisted from August 1914 to December 1916. After this, the informal local leadership decided no more men should enlist. Only four men from Woogaree would join up in the last two years of the war.[14]

Britain: conscription and coalitions

Volunteers had swelled the British Army during 1914 and 1915. As Adrian Gregory points out, the highest enlistments were not due to 'war enthusiasm' following the outbreak of war, but on 25 August, when the German victory at Mons was made public. In six days, 174,901 men enlisted, 'at exactly the moment when the war turned serious [. . .] in expectation of a desperate fight for national defence'.[15]

Calls for conscription arose during 1915. The National Service League (NSL) had been formed in 1902 and called for the introduction of compulsory training similar to that instituted in Australia, New Zealand and South Africa. In 1914, the NSL had 270,000 mostly middle- and upper-class members. During the 1911 Morocco Crisis, David Lloyd George, then Chancellor of the Exchequer, had told General Sir Henry Wilson that he would support conscription in the event of major conflict, but would not state this publicly unless a war of this nature occurred. Wilson had argued in January 1913 in a 'Memo for Private Circulation' that the British Army could not be increased in wartime 'without some form of compulsion'.[16]

The creation of the Coalition government under Asquith on 15 May 1915, the passing of the National Registration Bill on 15 August, in which all females and males aged 15 to 64 registered their name and occupation, and the decline in recruiting during the year led to the introduction of conscription in Britain. The formation of the all-party government led to the appointment of a new Cabinet consisting of 12 Liberals, eight Conservative, one Labour and one Independent (the theoretically apolitical War Secretary Lord Kitchener).[17]

In August 1915, in the wake of the series of defeats at Aubers Ridge and at Gallipoli, a majority of members of the all-party War Policy Committee came out in support of conscription. The Labour Party's Arthur Henderson opposed the proposal, arguing introducing compulsion would lead to 'a divided Cabinet, a divided Parliament, and a divided Nation'. A Trades Union Congress meeting in Bristol backed Henderson's stand. Following the defeat at Loos, Kitchener told Cabinet in October that the army would require 35,000 recruits every month until December 1916. This figure was about twice the current enlistment rate.[18]

Asquith decided to introduce the conscription bill to Parliament on 5 January 1916, imposing compulsory military service on unmarried males in Great Britain aged 18 to 41. The Bill did not apply to Ireland, where the Nationalist majority would have opposed compulsion unless it was accompanied by the implementation of Irish Home Rule. As Adams and Poirier argue, the prime minister did this 'in order to ensure a sufficient number of soldiers and to reinforce his hold on the premiership'. With the latter Asquith would be unsuccessful, as Lloyd George would succeed him during the year. Sir John Simon, the Home Secretary was the only Liberal minister to resign in opposition to military compulsion. Kitchener opposed the bill because he refused to concede that his recruiting policy had failed.[19]

Echo in the south: conscription in New Zealand

New Zealand was the second part of the British Empire to introduce conscription, on 1 August 1916. This is not surprising, as New Zealand, though distant from the United Kingdom, felt a strong cultural bond to the Mother Country. New Zealand's wartime prime minister, William Massey, once said 'if it were possible for the point of view of New Zealand and the point of view of the Empire as a whole to come into conflict, I would go for the Empire at once'. On 4 August 1915, New Zealand had followed the United Kingdom in forming a national government, with a Cabinet of seven Reform Party members and six Liberals. The small New Zealand Labour Party was offered one Cabinet position, but rejected the offer. In October–November 1915, New Zealanders once again mimicked Britain by creating a national register. The majority of the population supported the implementation of conscription. The New Zealand Rugby Union banned males aged 20 years or older from playing rugby on the basis that if they were fit enough to play sport they were fit enough to fight in the New Zealand Expeditionary Force. There was some opposition to the Military Service Bill, most notably from the Labour Party and trade unions, Maori *iwi* (tribes) in Taranaki, Waikato and the King Country, and pacifists and conscientious objectors.[20]

Unlike in Britain, conscription was not intended to expand the New Zealand Expeditionary Force. Instead, reflecting the Dominion's small population and the influence of the American Progressive movement, the

New Zealand government used compulsory military service as a means to most efficiently sustain the existing New Zealand Division of three infantry brigades (temporarily augmented by a fourth brigade from March 1916 to February 1917) on the Western Front. Almost 70,000 men volunteered for the NZEF in World War I, but only 32,270 men were conscripted.[21]

New Zealand had four military districts, and each of these was allocated a recruiting quota. Men were conscripted only if insufficient volunteers had come forward to fill the quota. The Dominion's male population between the ages of 20 and 46 were divided into two divisions. The First Division included all unmarried and recently married men; the Second Division comprised all other males in this age range. Reflecting New Zealand views of racial hierarchy, foreign-born non-whites, such as Chinese, Indians and Malays, were exempted from military service and placed on 'indefinite leave'. The first ballot of conscripts did not occur until 16 November 1916. At first, all conscripts came from the First Division. From October 1917, Second Division married men without children, and subsequently married conscripts with one or two children were called up, though few married conscripts had embarked before the conflict concluded.[22]

New Zealand Defence Minister James Allen, who was acting leader while Prime Minister William Massey spent most of the second half of the war in London, used Progressive ideas to create Military Service Boards in 1916 and the National Efficiency Board (NEB) in 1917 to enable effective governance. However, local board members were overwhelmingly pro-conscriptionist and rejected most exemptions. The NEB Report of 1917 pointed out that the overenthusiastic call-up of the First Division had resulted in 'a severe strain upon some of the industries, especially in the country districts'. Allen gave the NEB the power to prevent Military Service Boards conscripting 'the last male worker of a farm' arguing that 'a man working for himself or his family on his own holding was probably of more benefit to the state than he would be in camp or in the firing-line'.[23]

Two aspects of New Zealand's conscription policy remain controversial. These are the treatment of anti-British Maori and conscientious objectors. Maoridom was divided according to how *iwi* had fought during the New Zealand Wars of the 1860s. Some *iwi*, like Te Arawa and Ngati Porou had fought alongside the British Army and settlers. Others, including Waikato and the Maori King Movement, had opposed the British and lost 887,000 acres of land in government land confiscations.[24]

During World War I, the pro-British *iwi* provided only 2,227 volunteers – less than half the recruiting rate of New Zealand as a whole. The New Zealand government did not apply conscription to Maori when it was introduced in 1916. This was a pragmatic political decision. If Maori were to be conscripted, many pro-British Maori would have accepted the ruling, joined the NZEF and suffered Western Front casualty rates. Anti-British Maori would have refused to submit to compulsion, tipping the balance of post-war Maori leadership towards those opposed to the government. It was for this reason that the Maori contingent was converted from infantry to a pioneer battalion (an unskilled engineering unit) when they arrived on the Western Front to ensure, as Ashley Gould puts it, they had 'a less casualty-prone non-combat role'.[25]

In 1918, acting Prime Minister James Allen decided to take action to conscript anti-British Maori. On 11 June, he sent police to Mangatawhiri in the Waikato to arrest 16-year-old Te Rauangaanga Mahuta, brother of the Maori King, and other men. By the time of the armistice, 100 Maori had been detained. Allen had asserted the government's power over this particular group, but he knew his limits. No Maori conscript was sent overseas, and the remaining 11 detainees were quietly set free six months after the war ended.[26]

Conscientious objectors were the other group refusing conscription. The New Zealand Military Service Act allowed those unwilling to engage in military service to be provided with alternative duties. However, when men claiming conscientious objection went before Military Service Boards, as Paul Barker writes, the 'inflexible patriotism of Board members' was met by the 'equally inflexible fundamentalism of most religious appellants'. In all, 273 New Zealand men were imprisoned, mostly for terms ranging from 11 months to two years' hard labour. [27]

In July 1917, Allen ordered that conscientious objectors should be sent – without any military training – to the trenches on the Western Front, and be liable to military discipline (including the death penalty). The Defence Minister demanded this draconian measure because he feared increasing applications for conscientious objection at a time when the war was going badly for the Allies. Fourteen men, apparently chosen at random from Trentham Camp, were shipped to England. After brutal treatment on the voyage and at a British Army camp, some agreed to go to the front, mostly as stretcher bearers. The four remaining conscientious objectors were sent to a British military prison in France, placed on a bread-and-water diet and punished in winter cold with Field Punishment No. 1: being tied to a post for hours at a time, bound so tightly their hands bled. The three remaining men, Lawrence Kirwin, Archibald Baxter and Mark Briggs received the final stage of the New Zealand government's punishment. On 6 March 1918 they were placed 1,000 yards (some 900 metres) behind New Zealand Division's front line and required to walk to the forward position every day, but not to do anything once there. Firm in his beliefs as a conscientious objector, Briggs refused to walk. The first day a group of Kiwi soldiers carried him to the front line. The next day a sadistic New Zealand military policeman tied him in cable wire and dragged him for a mile over rough ground, wooden duckboards and shell holes filled with filthy water, tearing his clothes and lacerating his body. On 28 March, after witnessing Briggs' ordeal, Kirwin submitted and became a stretcher bearer. Around the same time an NZEF captain beat Baxter and refused him food. He was later found wandering on the battlefield by Canadian soldiers, brought to hospital and embarked for New Zealand in August. Briggs refused to be broken. The New Zealand government and military gave up their brutal measures, but kept him in Europe until the war ended. According to Barker, how New Zealand soldiers treated these conscientious objectors can only be described as torture. It is hard to disagree with this assessment.[28]

Caribbean volunteers and conscripts

In his study of Jamaican troops in World War I, Richard Smith argues that one reason men from across the Caribbean volunteered in the ten battalions of the British West Indian Regiment (BWIR) was the belief that 'wartime sacrifice' would lead to post-war 'improved standing'. All these men enlisted to fight. While the battalions sent to Palestine fought as infantry and gained the respect of their fellow British Empire comrades, the other battalions were used as labour troops and given tasks such as unloading merchant ships. Colonel R.E. Willis, who commanded the 9th Battalion British West Indies Regiment (BWIR) at the port of Taranto in Italy, had a record of assaulting his men. On 6 December 1918, they rebelled. Forty-nine men were found guilty of mutiny; Private Arthur Sanches, who led the protest, was given the death penalty, commuted to a 20-year prison sentence.[29]

W.G. Hinchliffe wrote in May 1916: 'the time is now on us when brothers will be compelled to know each other as brothers without thinking of race, nationality, colour, class or complexion', but Jamaican soldiers were denied opportunities due to their complexion. James Slim, a black Jamaican, enlisted in the Coldstream Guards in 1915, but when the War Office became aware of his skin colour, he was immediately discharged.[30]

Jamaica was the next part of the British Empire to bring in conscription. The colony introduced the measure on 1 June 1917, initially for unmarried and childless men aged 18 to 41. Governor Sir William Manning and the Jamaican Legislature appear to have done this in order to place a significant proportion of the male black population under military discipline to prevent unrest at a time of strikes and food shortages. Registration was completed at the end of August, but transporting the conscripts was initially postponed to prevent the men arriving in Europe in the middle of winter. During 1918, however, all available troopships in the Atlantic were devoted to transporting the American Expeditionary Force, so the Jamaican conscripts were discharged in May and returned to their homes.[31]

The hoped-for 'improved standing' for returned soldiers did not materialise. They were permitted to vote in the first post-war election, but thereafter the colony returned to being a white-only electorate. Fearful of armed uprisings, the colonial government encouraged 4,000 BWIR veterans to emigrate to Cuba and other locations. With the return of peace, Jamaica issued a series of new postage stamps. Two featured the departure and return of the BWIR contingents. A third, portraying Jamaican slaves gaining their freedom, was produced by De La Rue & Company in England and sent to the colony in April 1921. The government considered the stamp too controversial and destroyed the entire stock for 'political reasons'.[32]

The people's choice: Australia

The Commonwealth of Australia made concerted attempts to introduce conscription in 1916 and 1917, but would be unsuccessful on both occasions. This failure requires some explanation. The Australian Labor Party (ALP) had dominated federal politics since 1910, and had regained office from the hapless Liberals after a 14-month interregnum in the election of 5 September 1914. By May 1915, the ALP held power in federal government and in each of the six state parliaments, with the exception of Victoria.[33]

Three events led to the demise of Labor dominance. The first was Prime Minister Andrew Fisher's announcement to federal caucus on 30 October 1915 that he would resign and take up the position of Australian High Commissioner in London. Fisher was a pacifist and abhorred the role of a war leader. He was also suffering ill health, resulting from his years as a coal miner, and memory loss presaging the onset of dementia. The Labor caucus unanimously chose the Attorney-General, William Morris (Billy) Hughes, as the new prime minister. Nick Dyrenfurth argues that Hughes and Fisher had made a formidable political team because Fisher could curb Hughes when it was required. With Fisher gone to London, this necessary restraint was removed.[34]

The second was calls within the Labor Party for the 'conscription of wealth' to offset large wartime increases in the cost of living by the imposition of price controls or an excess profits tax. The federal government's war census of manpower and financial resources in 1915 found significant wealth inequality: half the nation's wealth was held by 3 per cent of the population. Labor had put referendum proposals to amend the constitution to grant the federal government the power to set prices in 1911 and 1913, but they had failed to achieve the required majority of votes in a majority of states. Fisher had promised during the 1914 election to put the referendum to the people a third time. Hughes pragmatically abandoned the proposal when he became prime minister because he doubted it would succeed. But in doing so, he alienated the Labor left who demanded intervention to assist workers and their families.[35]

The third event was Hughes' visit to the United Kingdom between January and August 1916. AIF recruiting had declined since the beginning of the year, and the failure of the Somme offensive to break the German line led the prime minister to conclude that Australia needed to follow Britain and New Zealand in introducing conscription. On 24 August, Hughes told the Labor party room that it was necessary to introduce overseas compulsory military service (the Defence Act already authorised compulsory military service within Australia). Caucus agreed, by the narrow margin of 23 votes to 21, to hold a referendum on conscription, on 28 October.[36]

There were three options for Australia to introduce conscription for overseas military service. The first was simply to use a regulation in the War Precautions Act to override the Defence Act's limitation on overseas conscription. When Senator George Pearce, the Defence Minister introduced the Military Service Bill on 21 September, he stated that this method would have destroyed Parliament as an institution. He privately told Fisher that this was an 'altogether distasteful' option that would result in 'turmoil & possibly bloodshed'. The second was to follow Britain and New Zealand and pass legislation through Parliament. However, the Senate would block the legislation as the majority of senators were anti-conscriptionist Labor men. This left the final option of holding a referendum (more correctly a plebiscite). If the majority of Australian voters approved the referendum, Hughes could claim a mandate to introduce conscription. Pearce told Fisher that this was the option that was 'compatible with our principles and platform'.[37]

The Labor Party began to split as soon as the Military Service Bill was introduced in the House of Representatives. On 14 September, Frank Tudor, the Minister for Trade and Customs, resigned over conscription. The following day, the New South Wales branch of the Labor Party expelled any member who supported overseas compulsory military service. This included Billy Hughes, but curiously the federal party room continued to allow him to attend caucus meetings.[38]

Had the 1916 referendum been carried, it would have established a conscription system based on the British system where the army would be enlarged. Senator George Pearce, the Defence Minister had publicly denied this during the referendum campaign. However, General Sir William Birdwood, the Indian Army general commanding the AIF, wrote privately that conscription would result in the creation of another Australian division, bringing the total to six.[39]

AIF soldiers on troopships and in the Middle East, France and Britain were eligible to vote, and Hughes made this 'soldiers' vote', which would occur before the Australian poll, an important part of his strategy to win the referendum. The prime minister expected that the troops would vote overwhelmingly in favour of conscription, and publishing the result would sway the referendum vote in Australia towards the affirmative. Australians in Britain recognised that there would be a substantial 'no' vote. The *British Australasian* – the London-based newspaper for expatriate New Zealanders and Australians – interviewed wounded Australians and found 'few of them expressed themselves in favour of making military service compulsory' and pointed out that 'where one or more of a family had enlisted, the soldier had done so on the understanding that someone was to remain behind and carry on.' Only 55 per cent of the AIF voted in favour of conscription, and Hughes did not release the numbers until 1917.[40]

The referendum on 28 October 1916 was defeated, but by a very narrow margin. The 'no' vote was 51.6 per cent, the 'yes' vote was 48.4 per cent. Three states supported conscription, three states opposed. The Australian people were determined to have their say. The voter turnout was 83.75 per cent: 10 per cent higher than the 1914 election, and 5 per cent higher than the subsequent election in 1917. Sir Ronald Munro Ferguson, the Australian Governor-General sent Walter Long, the British Colonial Secretary a telegram stating: 'Causes of defeat of referendum complex'. That the political campaign coincided with the Somme campaign and the lists of Australian casualties in that battle probably assisted the 'no' vote. Joan Beaumont's statement that Australians 'voted in ways that reflected their class, religion and gender, with class perhaps the dominant variable', is the best assessment that can be made on the available evidence.[41]

The Federal Labor Party caucus met for the first time after the referendum on 14 November and moved a motion of no confidence in Hughes. He responded by calling on his supporters to join him in a walkout: 23 of the 64 Labor MPs and senators followed Hughes, splitting the party. Pearce wrote to Fisher in London in January 1917:

> But I suppose that we cannot wonder that the crisis that is shaking the world has rocked our little boat. It seems to be part of great wars that they bring about great political changes.[42]

Hughes and his supporters held on to government by joining with the Liberals to form the Nationalist Party and called an election for 5 May 1917. Labor believed that their success in the referendum would translate into electoral success. Instead, the Nationalists gained an overwhelming victory with majorities in both the House of Representatives and the Senate. The prime minister had no desire to revisit the conscription issue. However, he was forced to do so due to the decline in Australian volunteering, the increase in casualties during the Third Battle of Ypres, the shock of the Central Powers' victory at Caporetto, and pressure from within his own party. Hughes announced that a second referendum would be held on 20 December 1917.[43]

This time, Hughes proposed a system of conscription based on the New Zealand model. The aim was not to increase the AIF, but to sustain the existing organisation. The monthly recruiting requirement was set at 7,000 men. If volunteers filled the quota then no conscripts were required. If fewer than 7,000 enlisted, the remainder of the quota would be filled by conscripting single men aged 20 to 44, selected from across the entire country.[44]

Despite the proposal being more moderate, the second conscription campaign was more emotionally charged. Frank Tudor, the Labor leader, argued that military compulsion would take so many men out of Australia that women and children would be forced into the workforce and – drawing on long-held racial paranoia – that the country would be flooded with non-white male labourers. Henry Boote was closer to the truth – as shown by his being prosecuted under the War Precautions Act for prejudicing recruiting – when he wrote in the *Australian Worker* on 15 November that Australia conscripting 7,000 men a month would be 'the merest drop of water on a mass of roaring flames'. He continued:

> We have reached that stage in the war when NOTHING that this Government can do with arms will affect the FINAL ISSUE. If we are winning, conscription will not hasten the overthrow of militarism by a single day. If we are losing, as the howls of the jingoes and junkers suggests, conscription would ruin Australia without rendering the smallest material assistance to the Allied nations.'[45]

Fig. 8.2 Australian anti-conscription flyer 1917: 'The Death Ballot. Polling Day, December 20. Vote "No"'. Image: Museums Victoria, https://collections.museumvictoria.com.au/items/1769514.

The labour movement once more led the 'no' campaign and was becoming more radical following the defeat of the 'great strike' earlier in the year. Daniel Mannix, the Irishman who had become Catholic Archbishop of Melbourne in May, became known for his strident opposition of conscription and his anti-English prejudices. On 10 November, Mannix said that 'though the Empire was anxious for conscription, if would not be a good thing for Australia', and told his audience 'to put Australia first and Empire second'.[46]

Australians rejected conscription again on 20 December. The voter turnout of 81.34 per cent was slightly lower than the 1916 poll, but still higher than the number who voted in the 1917 election. The margin was still close: 46.2 per cent voted 'yes' and 53.86 per cent voted 'no'. Only the two least populous states, Tasmania and Western Australia, had a 'yes' majority. The 'soldiers' vote' was 52.5 per cent in favour of conscription, lower than the 1916 poll. The *British Australasian* reported that troops believed conscription would actually be to their disadvantage because 'the more regular the flow of drafts the harder and more remorselessly each unit is worked'.[47]

Australia retained a volunteer army until the end of the war. Recruiting continued to decline and some Australian battalions had been reduced to only 400 personnel. On 5 October 1918, the Australian Corps was withdrawn from the line. Robert Stevenson argues that the corps at this point was a 'spent force' that could not have 'resumed operations at all in 1918'.[48]

In January 1918, the Australian war correspondent Charles Bean suggested to Andrew Fisher that conscription was efficient and logical. Fisher replied:

> I am not blind to the fact that conscription is logical, but men are not logical. It is economical and saves lots of waste – of putting the wrong men in the wrong places – I know that and feel all that as well as you do. But men are not logical and you cannot rule them by logic. I never believed that, if conscription were carried out in Australia, you could enforce it. I think you would have had terrible trouble if the bill had been passed.[49]

Colonial compulsion in South, East and West Africa

The Union of South Africa had captured German South-West Africa in July 1915, and sent troops to the ongoing East African campaign in 1916. The volunteer, mostly white Anglophone, 1st South African Brigade was sent to the Western Front and became part of the British 9th (Scottish) Division, fighting on the Somme in 1916, at the Third Battle of Ypres in 1917, and against the German offensive in 1918. With no new recruits, the brigade shrank to a South African Composite Battalion, but the arrival of a thousand reinforcements in August enabled the brigade to be revived for the final offensive.[50]

The South African Native Labour Corps (SANLC) was also deployed to France, where 21,000 men carried out vital military tasks between September 1916 and January 1918, including road construction and unloading supplies at the Channel ports. On 21 February 1917, the merchant ship *Mendi*, carrying SANLC personnel, collided with another ship in the English Channel. Over 600 South Africans drowned, but the disaster is remembered for the speech said to have been made by the Revd William Isaac Wauchope Dyobha who, as Bill Nasson has written, 'piloted men through a disciplined drill or death dance as the ship slipped beneath the water, so that he and other soldiers drowned in formation, meeting their end with stoic dignity'.[51]

The SANLC was established as a volunteer force. However, two thirds of the corps came from one sparsely populated district in Northern Transvaal. Lord Buxton, the South African Governor-General, admitted to Walter Long in July 1917 that the 'natives' in this region were 'somewhat more under the control of their Chiefs, and the Chiefs there are more under the control of the Government than elsewhere'. He unconvincingly added, 'I do not think [. . .] there has been anything approaching compulsion in the matter'. Nasson counters that the coercive actions of white local magistrates in Northern Transvaal and elsewhere meant that Labour Corps recruiting was 'conscription in all but name'.[52]

When South African recruiting for the East African campaign began, Abdullah Abdurahman, A.H. Gool and other 'coloured' men from Cape Town created the Coloured Cape Corps (sic) – equivalent to an infantry battalion – in December 1915. This unit, with all-white officers, served in

East Africa from February 1916 to December 1917, with 165 men killed. Returning to South Africa, the unit, renamed the Cape Corps Battalion, trained in the desert-like conditions in the Northern Cape in preparation for being deployed to Palestine in April 1918. The battalion joined the 53rd Division and served alongside some British and many Indian troops. At 1.00 am on 19 September, the Cape Corps Battalion attacked the Ottomans at Square Hill as part of the Battle of Megiddo and captured their objective with only one death and one man wounded. The next night they advanced on the next elevated position. This operation failed, due to the difficulty of attacking in darkness and the lack of artillery support. Fifty men were killed and a hundred wounded. As Nasson argues, the capture of Square Hill displayed the Cape men's 'coolness under fire', while the defeat on 20 September showed their willingness to make the 'blood sacrifice' of war.[53]

Buxton recognised the limitations on South Africa's contribution to the war. He told Long on 2 February 1917: 'Compulsory service for external service is absolutely out of the question here.' The Governor-General continued:

> It is just as well that too large a number of British and of 'loyal Dutch' should not be out of the country during the war [. . .] The greater the numbers therefore who go overseas, and meet with casualties or do not return, the worse in the end will be the relative population and electoral position of the British here.[54]

It was for this reason that the recruitment of white men in South Africa in the last two years of the war focused on enlisting pilots for the Royal Flying Corps and its successor, the Royal Air Force (RAF). Major Allister Miller noted that the 'idea of aviation has seized the public imagination and the enthusiasm of the younger men coming of military age is exceptionally keen'. By the time recruiting concluded in May 1918, 1,350 South African men had joined the RAF and had embarked for the United Kingdom or the Middle East. The South African government immediately recognised the coercive potential of aircraft against parts of its own population. On the recommendation of the Union Defence Minister, General Jan Smuts, Miller made flights 'throughout the country [that] have greatly impressed the rebellious elements among the Boer communities as well as among the natives, who have shown open signs of restiveness'.[55]

In East Africa, the colonial government in Kenya ordered the mass conscription in July–August 1917 of males aged 18 to 30 to serve as carriers and labourers as part of the military campaign against the Germans. Two hundred white men were also conscripted as overseers.[56]

The British government considered imposing military compulsion in Nigeria and the Gold Coast in early 1917. Colonel R.A. Haywood estimated that conscription in these colonies would provide an extra 70,000 troops for the East African campaign. Conscription would also improve relations with the French government, as an estimated 150,000 people had crossed the border into British territory in 1916 to avoid conscription. The British proposal was abandoned when colonial governors argued that introducing conscription would result in dissent and even revolt. In May 1918, a West African Field Force Service Brigade of 7,000 Nigerian volunteers was created for service in Palestine. The men were trained in the latest infantry tactics and in the use of Lewis machine guns and Stokes trench mortars. However, many of the soldiers had grievances regarding pay and conditions. Fortunately an influenza outbreak prevented the brigade's departure in September, and the Ottoman surrender the following month meant they were no longer needed.[57]

Canada: conscription's long shadow

CEF recruitment declined in early 1917, and the Conservative Prime Minister Sir Robert Borden announced on 18 May that it was necessary to introduce conscription. He would succeed in his task, but at the cost of bitterly dividing the nation for little military benefit. After Australia's failure to introduce conscription by referendum in 1916, James Allen, the New Zealand Defence Minister told Prime Minister William Massey: 'Thank goodness we have avoided that blunder!' Borden's Conservatives similarly decided they would not allow the people to vote on the issue. The Prime Minister asked Sir Wilfrid Laurier, the French-Canadian Liberal opposition leader, to join him in a 'Union' government. Laurier opposed military compulsion and refused. On the final day of the parliamentary debate on the Military Service Bill, Laurier made a final unsuccessful call for a referendum. The bill became law on 29 August 1917. Borden then delayed the introduction of the draft until a federal election was held on 17 December.[58]

The conscription debate and the 1917 election campaign split Canadians on linguistic lines. Anglophone Canada sent troops and exported wheat and munitions to Britain. In contrast, the war had little impact in Quebec. The province made up 37 per cent of the Canadian population, but Québécois provided perhaps 5 per cent of CEF volunteers. In June 1917, there were 14,100 Francophone Canadians serving overseas. Only 8,200 were from Quebec, the remainder demonstrated the much higher enlistment rates from the much smaller French-speaking communities in the Maritime Provinces, Ontario and the Prairies. In February 1917, Major J.B.E. Malhiot protested against the incorporation of Quebec recruits into his battalion, stating 'my unit is comprised of Western men' and 'such an amalgamation would not be made without friction as a different spirit prevails between the Western and the Eastern French Canadians'. Anglophone Canada had attracted large numbers of migrants from Britain and Central and Eastern Europe. Francophone Canada had few ties to Europe: their ancestors had mostly been in Canada since the 1750s. They had little interest in fighting to defend France, as their agricultural background and devout Catholicism meant they had very little in common with the secular French Republic. The Canadian Governor-General, the Duke of Devonshire, commented in June 1917 that in most Quebec newspapers, 'either intentionally or unintentionally, the war is not brought home to the general public in the same way as elsewhere'.[59]

The 1917 Canadian election was a travesty of democracy. Borden deliberately manipulated the electoral process to his own political advantage. The Military Voters Act gave the vote to all members of the CEF regardless of how long they had resided in the Dominion. The soldiers' ballot papers gave the choice of voting for either 'Government' or 'Opposition' and to provide the name of their constituency. If no constituency was provided, the act enabled the government to count the vote in the electorate of their choice. The War-time Elections Act gave the vote to Canadian women but only if they were the wives, sisters or daughters of living or deceased soldiers. At the same time, it disenfranchised naturalised British subjects from enemy states, conscientious objectors and members of pacifist churches such as the Mennonites.[60]

J.L. Granatstein and J.M. Hitsman argue that the election was 'deliberately conducted [...] on racist grounds'. Anglophone Liberal MPs saw the writing on the wall and joined Borden's new Union Party. Laurier's Liberals won all but three seats in Quebec, and 82 seats in total. Borden used the soldiers' vote to take 14 seats off the Liberals. The Union government dominated the poll and won 153 seats.[61]

During the election campaign Borden had promised that farmers' sons would be exempt from conscription. This commitment had been a significant factor in his victory as 117 of the 153 constituencies won by the Union Party were in rural areas. With the beginning of the German offensive on the Western Front, Borden broke this promise, arguing that more Canadians had to be conscripted to halt the enemy advance. Borden's U-turn caused disquiet in both anglophone and francophone Canada, as it put all other exemptions into question. Anti-conscription riots broke out in Quebec City during Easter from 28 March to 1 April. Rioters fired on the English-speaking troops sent to the province to quash the revolt. The soldiers fired back, killing four and injuring 158.[62]

Beginning in January 1918, Canada called up 124,588 conscripts. Of these, only 24,132 men had departed the Dominion before the war ended. Canadian historian Tim Cook estimates that only a few thousand conscripts ever reached the front line. The minimal role these men played in the Allied victory could not justify the grievous pain conscription caused in Canadian society. It must not be forgotten that Newfoundland also passed a conscription bill on 11 May 1918 and inducted 1,000 men. However, no Newfoundland conscript had departed before the war ended.[63]

Conscription, Quebec and Ireland

A few days after the Quebec riots, Sir Walter Long, the British Colonial Secretary and staunch opponent of Irish nationalism, sent a private telegram to the Duke of Devonshire requesting information on how the Canadian Military Service Act had been applied in Quebec. Long stated: 'Any experience you may have gained may be very valuable as a guide for dealing with analogous situation in Ireland'. The Governor-General replied the next day that 'the passive opposition of almost all the entire population' had made it impossible to enforce the legislation in the province. This meant that in three months only 5,000 Québécois had been conscripted.[64]

At the beginning of the war, John Redmond, leader of the Irish Nationalists had called on Irishmen to 'come together in the trenches and risk their lives together and spill their blood together'. Volunteering in rural Ireland in 1914 and 1915 was comparable to English and Welsh rural enlistment. However, after conscription was imposed in Britain in 1916, Irish volunteering steeply declined among both Nationalists and Unionists. Oliver Nugent, commander of the 36th (Ulster) Division, complained in April 1917 of the 'Ulstermen who have done nothing to keep us up, but brag in the local papers about their glorious Division and how magnificently Ulster has done.'[65]

On 23 March 1918, two days after the start of the German offensive, the British War Cabinet discussed extending the Military Service Act to Ireland. Field Marshal Sir John French, the Lord Lieutenant of Ireland, attended the War Cabinet meeting and expressed his belief that the Irish would accept conscription. David Lloyd George subsequently consulted Henry Duke, Chief Secretary of Ireland, General Sir Bryan Mahon, General Officer Commanding in Ireland, and Sir Joseph Byrne, the Chief of the Royal Irish Constabulary, who all warned the prime minister of the difficulty, if not impossibility, of bringing in military compulsion.[66]

By April 1918, thousands of largely willing American conscripts were being transported across the Atlantic every month, and it could be argued that reinforcement on this scale made the question of conscription from the much smaller population of Ireland irrelevant. Nonetheless, Lloyd George introduced the Military Service Amendment Bill to Parliament on 9 April 1918. When the bill passed its third reading on 16 April, Nationalist Ireland erupted in opposition to conscription. The Irish Trade Union Congress called a general strike on 23 April. Sinn Féin led opposition to conscription, as did the Catholic hierarchy, who followed their congregations in order to continue to lead them. The English Catholic magazine *The Tablet* asserted on 18 May that the Irish bishops' intervention saved Ireland 'from slaughter and ruins, and England from a miscalculated method of getting soldiers here. They did not rise to stop conscription, but to save their flocks and country'. Faced with large-scale opposition, the government backed down.[67]

Long, who had once boasted 'I know Ireland well', stated on 26 April: 'I believe the right policy was to include I[reland] in Conscription and enforce it at all risks.' The next month, Captain Maurice Healy of the Royal Dublin Fusiliers wrote to Long on Ireland and conscription. Healy argued 'Nationalist Ireland is so powerfully organised against the present Government proposals, the latter can only be enforced by something worse than civil war'. The captain suggested Long make contact with the poet George Russell (known by the pseudonym Æ) because he was a friend of Sinn Féin President Éamon de Valera and might enable Long to find 'the minimum constitution Sinn Fein will accept and defend'. Healy concluded by describing the dilemma that he faced as an Irishman, and would, by the end of the year, be faced by most of his countrymen:

> I am the third generation of my family to have professed the political creed of a self-governed Ireland bound in friendship to England; but my loyalty is to Ireland first, and my position at the present moment is one of profound difficulty. I am serving two ideals which should and could be one; but there is every danger of a parting of the ways, and God alone knows what I should then do.[68]

1918: The Battles of Amiens and Megiddo

The British Empire fought two major battles in the second half of 1918 that took place 2,800 miles apart, and in very different environments. Both operations were decisive in the Allied victory over the Central Powers. The first, commencing at 4.20 am on 8 August, was the Battle of Amiens, fought in the lush farmland of northern France. Here, British, Australian and Canadian troops of the Fourth British Army, alongside the First French Army, broke through the German lines on a ten-mile (16-kilometre) front and advanced eight miles in one day. The Germans suffered 27,000 casualties, including 16,000 prisoners of war. Allied casualties were only 9,000. This marked the start of the ongoing offensive in the final hundred days of the war that would end with the German government signing an armistice on 11 November. The second, beginning at 4.30 am on 19 September, was the Battle of Megiddo, conducted in the dry scrubby ridges and valleys of Palestine north of Jerusalem. Here, the Egyptian Expeditionary Force (EEF), consisting mostly of Indian soldiers, but also including West Indian, South African, New Zealand, Irish, British and Australian soldiers, as well as small French and Italian contingents, broke the Ottoman lines on a 12-mile (19-kilometre) front adjoining the Mediterranean Sea. Cavalry poured through the gap made by the artillery and the infantry. By 5.00 pm, the horsemen had reached Tulkeram, which on the morning of the attack had been the headquarters of the Ottoman Eighth Army. By 4 October, British Empire troops had captured

Damascus and Beirut and taken around 75,000 Ottoman prisoners, having suffered only 5,666 casualties. The Ottomans agreed to an armistice on 31 October.

The success in both Western Europe and the Middle East in 1918 demonstrated the increasing proficiency of the British Empire's soldiers in conducting combined arms operations that integrated infantry, artillery, tanks, aircraft, communications and cavalry. Where previously there had been constant failures, lessons drawn from hard-won experience meant there was now the likelihood of battlefield success. For the Battle of Amiens, the four divisions of the Canadian Corps were covertly transported 40 miles (some 64 kilometres) south from Arras with the Germans remaining unaware of both the insertion and its implication. The Canadian Corps would attack alongside the First French Army. The solution for effective liaison between the adjoining Canadian and French forces was found in Brigadier Raymond Brutinel, a bilingual Frenchman who had migrated to Canada in 1905. On the outbreak of war, Brutinel enlisted in the CEF and established the Canadian Motor Machine Gun Brigade. On 8 August, he deployed his armoured trucks, equipped with machine guns and trench mortars, on the boundary between the French and Canadians and liaised with General Deville, commander of the 42nd French Infantry Division.

Increasing expertise was found among the diverse soldiers in the EEF. On 20 and 22 September 1918, soldiers of the 1st and 2nd British West Indies Regiments – described in the Australian Official History as 'British blacks' – displayed their military competence when they captured Ottoman positions in the Jordan Valley in the face of heavy artillery fire. Four Jamaican soldiers were awarded gallantry medals. The *Daily Gleaner* in Kingston published a letter from Major E.G. Orrett of the British West Indies Regiment following the first of these attacks where he noted that veteran Australian or New Zealand soldiers who witnessed the assault 'congratulated and cheered them and would hardly believe that our West Indian men had not been into action before, owing to their steadiness and coolness'.[1]

Following the failure of the German U-boat campaign in 1917 to force the British to surrender, Field Marshal Paul von Hindenburg and Quartermaster General Erich Ludendorff devised the fifth and final

German strategy for winning the war. This was a military offensive on the Western Front in the spring of 1918 that aimed to encircle and defeat the BEF before the United States – which had declared war on Germany on 6 April 1917 – had trained, equipped and shipped sufficient soldiers to France to shift the military balance against the Central Powers.[2]

The German and Austro-Hungarian governments had signed a peace treaty with the Russian Bolsheviks at Brest-Litovsk on 3 March 1918. It might have been expected that Hindenburg and Ludendorff would take advantage of peace in the east and transfer all of their divisions to take part in the Western Front offensive. However, 47 of the 85 German divisions – 1,045,050 troops – remained as occupiers on the Eastern Front to forcibly extract resources, mostly from Ukraine and Romania but even from the Baku oil fields in the Caucasus.[3]

The Treaty of Bucharest signed on 7 May 1918 permitted the wholesale removal of foodstuffs from Romania. German soldiers were able to post ten kilograms (22 pounds) of food to their families, and to take 50 kilograms when they returned on leave. The German Army took almost 2 million tons of grain from Romania between August 1916 and May 1918. At least 400,000 Romanian civilians, or 5 per cent of the population, died of starvation or disease as a result of the German occupation.[4]

German and Austro-Hungarian troops occupied Ukraine, but faced opposition from local nationalists. Only 788,179 tons of Ukrainian grain reached Germany during 1918. On 30 July, Field Marshal Hermann von Eichhorn, the military governor of Ukraine, was assassinated by a Russian Social Revolutionary. In the Caucasus, German and Ottoman soldiers skirmished over oil and other resources.[5]

Between 1 November 1917 and 21 March 1918, 44 divisions – as well as all soldiers under the age of 35 and most horses – were transferred from the east to the Western Front. An indication of the state of soldiers' morale at this stage of the war is provided by the approximately 10 per cent of soldiers who deserted during their train journey across Germany.[6]

Ludendorff deliberately chose generals who had succeeded in recent, increasingly mobile, operations to command the three armies that would spearhead the March offensive. General Otto von Below, who had led the German force at Caporetto in September 1917, took command of the German Seventeenth Army; General Oskar von Hutier, who captured the Baltic port of Riga the same month, was appointed to the Eighteenth Army; while General Georg von der Marwitz, who had fought at Cambrai in November–December 1917, led the Second Army.[7]

The latest developments in artillery tactics would be key to a successful breakthrough. Colonel Georg Bruchmüller, the artillery commander at both Riga and Cambrai, had developed a three-stage process starting with a short surprise bombardment across the full depth of the Allied positions, counter-battery fire to prevent artillery responding, and a focus on specific targets, especially forward trench positions. At Cambrai, Bruchmüller had fired gas shells at all British artillery batteries. Hauptmann Egon von Loebell of the 3rd Foot Guard Regiment wrote:

> the result of the gassing was that all the enemy artillery in our area ceased firing [. . .] Everywhere the infantry was advancing, sometimes in very large formations [. . .] The whole thing was reminiscent of the mobile warfare we all longed for.

In preparation for the offensive, 56 German divisions were put through a three-week intensive training program, based on new training manuals, to inculcate the new doctrine for the offensive. Ludendorff placed an emphasis on elite assault units of stormtroopers. These men were aged between 25 and 35, were issued with better equipment, and – most significantly – received more food than the rest of the army. A quarter of the German divisions on the Western Front were designated as 'attack divisions' who would drive the offensive into enemy territory.[8]

Allied soldiers realised that the German offensive was becoming more likely as the weather improved, but it was not clear when or where the blow would strike. Major General Oliver Nugent, commander of the 36th (Ulster) Division told his wife Kitty on 18 February: 'It is rather an anxious time, this waiting and wondering when the storm will burst. It may come at any moment or not for another month. When and if it does it will be a hurricane'. On 20 March, two soldiers from Alsace – the French region that Germany had annexed in 1871 following its victory in the Franco-Prussian War – deserted to the division's lines and stated that the offensive was imminent. Nugent wrote: 'We expect to be attacked tonight or tomorrow and it is going to be a very big attack.'[9]

The German offensive began at 4.40 am on 21 March with an unprecedented and accurate five-hour artillery bombardment using half their entire artillery resources: 2,435 heavy guns, 4,038 field artillery pieces and 2,532 trench mortars that fired 1.16 million shells. Protected by thick fog and a creeping barrage of high explosive, phosgene and tear gas, 76 divisions began advancing towards the British positions at 9.40 am. The British Fifth Army held 42 miles of front (some 68 kilometres) with 12 infantry divisions and three cavalry divisions (each with the firepower of an infantry brigade), while the British Third Army held 28 miles (45 kilometres) of front with 14 divisions. Of the 26 British divisions in the line, 21 had fought in the Third Battle of Ypres and were still under strength, while the majority of the attacking German divisions had been rested during the previous autumn and winter.[10]

By the end of the day, the German had advanced eight miles (some 13 kilometres) – the largest territorial gain on the Western Front since 1914. Casualties on both sides were roughly similar, in the region of 38,000 to 40,000. General Sir Hubert Gough, the British Fifth Army commander, had no choice but to order his troops to withdraw.[11]

Both the 16th (Irish) and 36th (Ulster) Division were caught up in the German onslaught and the Fifth Army's retreat. On 21 March, the 16th Division was holding the front at Épehy, south of Cambrai. The fog enabled the Germans to manoeuvre and attack the division on the flanks. The unit lost 563 men killed on the first day of the offensive. Timothy Denman writes that it 'ceased in anything but name to be a division', but the troops had to remain in the line for the next two weeks. The Irish Division suffered more than twice the losses of the Ulster Division. Their position at the village of Ollezy, 22 miles (35 kilometres) to the south, was similarly underprepared: barbed wire had to be scavenged from abandoned French Army supply dumps, and most of the trenches were only 18 inches (45 centimetres) deep, and still incomplete when the Germans attacked. Cyril Falls later wrote:

> Hopeless indeed was the position of them in this front system, outnumbered three or four times, taken in rear by parties which came upon them without warning.[12]

Four days into the retreat, Nugent commented: 'This is truly Armageddon. Unless we can finally stop the German attack soon, I fear it will be the end.' Just before midnight on 24 March, the few hundred survivors of the division were placed with the 62nd French Division and began their final three-hour march through the French lines to Sermaize, about 25 miles (40 kilometres) south-west of Saint-Quentin where they were to rest, reorganise and support the French if required. Falls described the last stage of the retreat that ended on 25 March at 2.00 am:

> Men's faces were deeply marked by overwhelming fatigue and lack of sleep. Some moved in a sort of trance, stumbling forward oblivious to their surroundings [. . .] Many company officers, in the last few miles, dispensed with the regulation halts, because they found it almost impossible to get their men on their feet again after them. They lay like logs, and had to be violently shaken before they could be recalled to consciousness.[13]

The German success in the West delighted Kaiser Wilhelm II. On 26 March, he ordered champagne to be served at headquarters, and stated that when the British delegation arrived for peace negotiations, it must first kneel before the German flag, 'for it is a question here of the victory of monarchy over democracy'. However, the Kaiser's vision of imminent victory was premature. As Roger Chickering points out, Ludendorff's troops 'lacked the strength and mobility to fulfil the goals that their leader had set for them'. Hans Delbrück, the German military historian who wrote clear-eyed commentaries on his country's wartime strategic situation, identified at the time that the military offensive needed to be accompanied by a 'political offensive' to achieve victory. After the German defeat, Delbrück would give evidence to the Reichstag commission on the causes of the German collapse, arguing that Ludendorff wrongly attacked the British where they were weak, rather than on the Somme River where he could achieve his strategic goal of splitting the French and British armies and encircling and defeating the BEF. Delbrück concluded that Ludendorff had ignored the great nineteenth-century Prussian strategist Carl von Clausewitz, who wrote that 'no strategical idea can be considered completely without considering the political goal'.[14]

Ludendorff launched five separate offensives between March and July 1918, but as David Zabecki comments, these operations were not 'an integrated campaign' but rather a series of attacks 'that were only loosely connected to each other'. Most significantly, the Germans did not focus on capturing the key railway node at Amiens which would have made it difficult to supply the BEF.

TABLE 9.1
GERMAN OFFENSIVES 1918[15]

Michael	21 March–5 April
Georgette	9–29 April
Blücher	27 May–5 June
Gneisenau	9–15 June
Marneschutz–Reims	15 July–6 August

The Michael offensive of 21 March deployed – from north to south – the German Seventeenth, Second and Eighteenth Armies in the assault. Because the first two of these had not advanced as far as the Eighteenth Army, Ludendorff shifted the focus of his attack to this originally subsidiary operation. A further shift occurred on 26 March, when the Second Army, which was originally planned to attack north of the Somme and capture Amiens, was diverted south of the Somme. That same day, at a conference at Doullens, about 20 miles (30 kilometres) north of Amiens, the British requested the appointment of Marshal Ferdinand Foch as Commander-in-Chief of the Allied Armies on the Western Front in order to ensure unity of command of the American, British and French armies. Foch outlined a simple two-part strategy to his commanders. The first was to prevent the Germans from driving a wedge between the French and British armies. The second was to defend the vital railway node of Amiens. In early 1918, 140 trains travelled through Amiens every day. The majority of trains supplying the BEF ran through the city. If the Germans captured Amiens, all the possible alternative routes could carry only 90 trains per day.[16]

The next attack, commencing on 9 April and codenamed Georgette, saw 23 German divisions attempt to capture the northern French rail centre of Hazebrouck, about 15 miles (25 kilometres) south-west of Ypres. The assault failed after 20 days, but it forced the BEF to withdraw from Passchendaele and Messines in Belgium, the site of major British offensives the previous year.[17]

On 24 April, the German Second Army captured Villers-Bretonneux, 13 miles (21 kilometres) east of Amiens, a battle that included the first tank-on-tank combat in history. The village was higher than the city, dominated the landscape and would enable German artillery to bombard the Longueau railway junction, four miles south-east of Amiens. The strategic significance of the railway network meant that Foch ordered the immediate recapture of Villers-Bretonneux.[18]

A hastily created force, drawing troops from the 4th and 5th Australian Divisions and the 8th and 58th British Divisions, was ordered to carry out an immediate counter-attack. The British began their artillery bombardment at 10.00 pm, which gathered intensity with the addition of heavy guns and aerial bombing that ignited buildings in Villers-Bretonneux and gave the troops the location of their objective.[19]

The Allied troops wore white armbands to enable the identification of friend and foe in the darkness. As the 57th and 60th Australian Battalions advanced around the enemy flank, one of the soldiers made a noise and the troops were suddenly illuminated and exposed by German flares. With few options available in the circumstances, Captain E.M. Young ordered his men to charge. Sergeant Roy Fynch of the 59th Battalion described what happened next:

> With a ferocious roar and the cry of 'Into the bastards, boys,' we were down on them before the Boche realised what had happened. The Boche was at our mercy. They screamed for mercy but there were too many machine-guns about to show them any consideration as we were moving forward.[20]

British and Australian troops would regain Villers-Bretonneux in the early hours of 26 April. Haig, however, recognised that his British Empire force lacked the resources to hold the vital village. At 6.30 pm on 25 April, he had requested Foch to provide French assistance. The following morning, the Division Marocaine and the 131st French Division arrived and attacked. The Moroccan Division made the furthest advance and relieved the exhausted British troops in Hangard Wood. The Germans halted their attack and once more shifted their attention to another part of the front.[21]

After a four-week pause, General Max von Boehn's Seventh Army initiated the Blücher offensive on 27 May in the Chemin des Dames region. As part of the attack, giant German 8¼-inch (210-millimetre) railway guns fired from a range of 60 miles (100 kilometres) on Paris, killing 256 people and increasing the anxiety of both the populace and the government. On 3 June, a representative of Lloyds Bank asked Lord Derby, the British Ambassador to France, to provide a railway wagon to remove bank security notes from the city.[22]

Ludendorff originally intended this operation to be a diversion while a second attack, codenamed Hagen, battered the British in northern France and Belgium. However, Blücher made progress, reaching and crossing the Vesle river by the second day, so the general, drawn like a moth to a lamp, once more changed his focus to this attack. This southward advance made neither strategic nor logistical sense. The railways in this region remained either under French control, or within the range of French artillery attack, and the advance could not be supported beyond the Vauxaillon tunnel which had been demolished by the Germans during their 1917 retreat to the Siegfried Line. The operation ended after eight days.[23]

The Germans attacked again on 9 June with the Gneisenau offensive, to the west of the Blücher attack. On 11 June, General Charles Mangin surprised the Germans by attacking without any preliminary artillery bombardment and pushed them back two and a half miles (four kilometres). In 20 days, however, Blücher and Gneisenau had inflicted 139,160 casualties on the French Army.[24]

The final battle of the German offensives, codenamed Marneschutz, took place on the River Marne, the scene of the climactic struggle of 1914, and would segue into an Allied counter-attack. The Germans had established a toe-hold on the far bank of the Marne on 30 May during the Blücher offensive. The aim of this attack, involving the First, Third and Seventh Armies on the German side, was to capture the French city of Reims and use the railways to support the German advance south of the Marne. Kaiser Wilhelm II's staff made plans to enable him to view the expected victory. However, the German Army was at a disadvantage, as the Allies knew from where the attack would come. Foch's four armies all included troops from France's allies: the Fourth Army had one US and 13 French divisions, the Fifth Army had two Italian and 11 French divisions, the Sixth Army had two US and six French divisions, while the Ninth Army (formerly the *Détachement d'armée du nord* based in Belgium) was held in reserve with four British divisions, eight French infantry and three French cavalry divisions.[25]

The German attack commenced at 12.10 am on 15 July. The French had obtained the details of the time of the attack during a trench raid and started firing on the enemy lines at 11.30 pm. East of Reims, the Fourth French Army held up the assault troops and inflicted heavy casualties. The Germans had more success west of Reims and established a roughly nine-mile (14-kilometre) enclave south of the Marne, but they failed to capture the city they had made their objective. Pétain was able to bring up reinforcements and replied with a decisive counter-attack that began – without a preliminary artillery bombardment – on 18 July at 4.35 am. Eighteen divisions from the French Sixth and Tenth Armies, supported by large numbers of aircraft and accompanied by 321 tanks, advanced behind a protective smokescreen. By the end of the day, the Tenth and Sixth Armies had progressed five and a half and roughly three miles (nine and five kilometres) respectively. Two days later German troops were retreating in large numbers across the Marne. Crown Prince Wilhelm was given the thankless task of informing his father that the offensive had failed. [26]

In Britain, the upper age for conscription had been extended in April to men aged 50. On 22 July, John Galsworthy, the British novelist and playwright, aged 50 years and 343 days, attended his physical examination and was rejected due to poor eyesight. Galsworthy recognised the significance of the battle being fought at the same time in France. He wrote in his diary: 'This day, the turning point of the war, was the day I came nearest to taking fighting part in it.'[27]

The Second Battle of the Marne provided the first evidence that the German Army was falling into a pit of demoralisation. During three days of combat, 17,000 soldiers had surrendered to the French. On 24 July, Foch called his first and only conference of the Allied commanders, Haig, Pétain and Pershing, at Bombon, about 30 miles (50 kilometres) south-east of Paris. Foch outlined his plan to shift the Allied posture to the offensive by securing three key railway corridors and the coalfields in northern France. The Second Battle of the Marne had secured the Paris–Marne line. Foch now requested Pershing to consolidate the Paris–Avricourt line at Saint-Mihiel and for Haig to advance eastwards from Villers-Bretonneux to protect the Paris–Amiens line.[28]

Two minor attacks by Australian troops on 10 June at Morlancourt, ten miles (16 kilometres) north-east of Villers-Bretonneux, and on 4 July at Hamel, some two miles from Villers-Bretonneux, provided a precursor for the upcoming Allied offensive. Combined arms warfare, integrating infantry, artillery, tanks and aircraft had become the norm. Most significant of these was the development of artillery techniques. German guns were located through sound-ranging, flash-spotting and aerial reconnaissance. Trigonometrical surveys accurately located the position of British Empire batteries in order to accurately hit their targets. Consignments of shells were weighed when they arrived at the battery, and the variations were taken into account when calculating range. Artillery units received six meteorological reports each day measuring wind speed and direction, temperature and atmospheric pressure, and these factors were similarly taken into account. The sergeant in charge of each gun team even made adjustments for the muzzle velocity of his individual artillery piece.[29]

At Morlancourt, the four battalions of the 7th Australian Brigade attacked the ridge overlooking the village after sunset at 9.00 pm on 10 June. A creeping barrage provided by nine 18-pounder batteries protected the advance towards the German lines held by the 54th and 24th Saxon Reserve Divisions. Five heavy artillery units conducted effective counter-battery fire on the enemy batteries. By 10.20 pm, the Australians had captured their objective, at the cost of about 350 casualties, and began digging in. A German counter-attack was dissipated by artillery fire, and around 325 prisoners were taken. The most significant aspect of the operation was that 7,000 gunners had enabled the advance of 2,000 infantry with comparatively few losses.[30]

The attack at Hamel can be seen merely as a minor attack by ten Australian battalions and four American companies to straighten a small segment of the line and gain an elevated position from which to observe the Germans in the Somme valley. However, it was also a masterpiece of planning conceived and executed by two talented officers, Brigadier General Anthony Courage, commander of the 5th British Tank Brigade, and General Sir John Monash, General Officer Commanding the Australian Corps.

The commander of the Fourth British Army, General Sir Henry Rawlinson, believed that an attack in the Australian Corps sector supported by the latest Mark V and Whippet tanks would have a strong likelihood of success. He asked Courage to devise a plan, which the brigadier submitted on 20 June. Monash responded with a draft the following day and devised a conference system to develop the complex plan. The final meeting, held on 30 June, was attended by 250 artillery, infantry, air force and tank officers, discussed 133 agenda items, and went for four and a half hours.[31]

The Battle of Hamel began at 3.10 am on 4 July. It concluded at 4.43 am, having achieved its objectives at a cost of around 1,400 Allied casualties. Over 1,600 Germans surrendered. The operation built on existing practice – the creeping barrage bombarded a zone 600 yards deep and aircraft flew above the battlefield before the operation began, so as to drown out the noise of the assembling tanks, as had occurred at the Battle of Messines. There were also many innovations. Four supply tanks each discharged 1,250 rounds of ammunition at sites decided by the infantry commanders. Royal Air Force RE.8 aircraft dropped a further nine tons of supplies by parachute. Australian Flying Corps RE.8s sounded klaxon horns to which soldiers replied by lighting flares. These enabled the pilots to report the extent of the advance. As John Coates, historian and former Chief of the Australian General Staff argues, Hamel was not

a sudden blaze of light, rather like similarly overstated descriptions of the Italian Renaissance of the fourteenth century. Too little credit is given to the painfully collected experiences of 1916 and 1917, which many serious-minded commanders and their staffs had sifted and collated to ensure that such disasters as the Somme battles and Passchendaele would not be repeated. Australians naturally think of the influence of Monash and his methods as impelling sudden and meritorious change, but that grossly simplifies the issue. For a whole series of modifications and improvements were coalescing to make operations, if not bloodless, then certainly more successful in outcome, more predictable throughout their course, and, within limitations, infinitely less wasteful in human terms.[32]

Three days after the battle, Georges Clemenceau visited the 4th Australian Division near Corbie, five miles (eight kilometres) east of Amiens, and made a speech to the Australians in English, which Rawlinson wrote 'pleased them greatly'. The President said:

> We knew that you would fight a real fight, but we did not know that [...] you would astonish the whole continent [...] I shall go back tomorrow and say to my countrymen: 'I have seen the Australians [...] I know that these men [...] will fight alongside us again until the cause for which we are fighting is safe for us and for our children.'[33]

Two months earlier, in the pause between the German Georgette and Blücher offensives, Haig had visited Rawlinson at British Fourth Army Headquarters on 17 May and told him to work with General Marie-Eugène Debeney, First French Army commander, to develop the plan – in line with Foch's strategy – for an Anglo-French offensive driving eastwards from Villers-Bretonneux. This became the basis for the great offensive of 8 August.[34]

Secrecy would be key for the success of the operation. Four corps – III British, Australian, Canadian and XXXI French Corps – would lead the attack. However, this would require the Germans to continue believing that General Arthur Currie's Canadians were in the north and had not been transferred southwards to Amiens. Canadian radio operators remained in Flanders broadcasting messages. Small groups of infantry carried out trench raids in which they deliberately left Canadian equipment in the German trenches. These ruses combined to confirm the enemy's assumption of Canadians' location. Charles Bean, the *Sydney Morning Herald* journalist appointed as official war correspondent, admitted in the Australian Official History that he knew nothing of the impending assault even as it was building around him. On 2 August, the first Canadian artillery units arrived for the operation.[35]

Haig met Rawlinson on 17 July to discuss the developing plan. Following the model for the Battle of Hamel, Rawlinson held a series of six conferences between 21 July and 6 August where he analysed the plan with Debeney, Currie, Monash, III Corps commander Lieutenant General Sir Richard Butler, Tank Corps commander Lieutenant General Sir Hugh Elles, and Cavalry Corps commander Sir Charles Kavanagh, as well as many other officers.[36]

The Battle of Amiens began at 4.20 am, a time chosen so the Allied tanks and troops would break the first German line of defence under cover of darkness and would then have sufficient light to continue their advance in the correct direction. Colonel A.J. Shepherd, Assistant Director of Medical Services in the 2nd Australian Division, described the conditions as: 'Fine morning with a ground mist, most favourable for attack.' The British Empire force at Amiens consisted of 441,588 men and 98,716 horses. The Allies had air dominance with 800 British and 1,104 French aircraft. The entire British Tank Corps of 552 tanks and armoured cars was committed to the battle.

Rawlinson set three stages for the advance. The first advance was protected by a creeping barrage. The second was supported by mobile artillery; the advance to this line was vital as it would remove Amiens from the threat of German artillery. The final advance would have infantry exploiting the breakthrough supported by Mark V* tanks. These were extended vehicles that could carry either 20 soldiers or 15 soldiers and a Lewis or Vickers machine gun and ammunition. The engine fumes within the tanks, however, created an asphyxiating atmosphere for the troops.[37]

In the lead-up to the offensive, the Allies had identified 95 per cent of the enemy artillery batteries. As the battle began, 450 heavy guns opened fire. Bean described the German guns – and their crews – on the Australian Corps front as being 'smothered' by counter-battery fire. Due to the secrecy required in moving the Canadian Corps southwards for the operation, these artillery batteries could not fire their guns for registration purposes. Instead, one gun from three or four separate batteries was assigned to fire on each German battery. Chappelle writes: 'They knew their accuracy would not be perfect, but by blending in several guns with different errors, on average the targets would be hit.' The method worked, and according to the Canadian Corps post-operation report, 'the enemy shelling decreased almost to zero'.[38]

The attacking force did experience some setbacks. III Corps had taken over its part of the line, north of the Australians, on the night of 30–31 July. However, German troops attacked on 6 August and pushed them back, meaning that the British soldiers had to advance across rugged terrain unsuitable for tanks and fight to regain their original start line. Tanks remained vulnerable on the battlefield: 25 per cent were lost on 8 August.[39]

By the middle of the afternoon, the Allied force had advanced up to eight miles (nearly 13 kilometres), had taken 12,000 prisoners and captured over 400 artillery pieces. Most significant was that the normally vulnerable attacking force had suffered only one third of the casualties of the defenders. Rawlinson told General Sir Henry Wilson, Chief of the Imperial General Staff: 'I think we have given the Bosche a pretty good bump this time. The Aust[n] and Can[ns] fought magnificently. Completely surprised the Bosche who thought Cand[n] were at Kemmel.'[40]

The Canadian Corps advanced a further four miles on 9 August, but the rest of the force made less ground, due to what Edmonds identified as the difficulty in making 'the sudden change from trench warfare to open warfare'. Rawlinson sensibly called a halt to the operation on 11 August. The Battle of Amiens revived optimism in senior British Empire commanders. On 16 August, General Sir Alexander Godley, commander of XXII British Corps, visited Monash's headquarters and was shown captured German documents that detailed the decline in German morale. Godley wrote: 'It is worth anything to have regained the initiative and to be again top dog.' Three days later, Haig told General Sir Julian Byng, the Third British Army commander:

> Now is the time to act with boldness, and in full confidence that, if we only hit the Enemy hard enough, and continue to press him, that he will give way and acknowledge that he is beaten.[41]

Foch ordered a new series of offensives in which six British and French armies would advance in sequence from 20 to 26 August on a 75-mile (120-kilometre) front from Soissons to Arras. Byng's troops attacked on 21 August at 4.28 am shrouded by darkness and mist, but soon faced strong

Fig. 9.1 German soldiers killed in the Allied offensive at Amiens,
9–11 August 1918. Image: UK Ministry of Defence 103636.

German resistance and resolute rearguard actions. The New Zealand
Division took eight days to advance seven miles to capture Bapaume on
29 August.[42]

Paul Strong and Sanders Marble describe the BEF's operations in
September as 'day after day of semi-mobile operations'. Infantry divisions
were rotated on the front line every two or three days. A creeping barrage
would be fired in the morning to start the infantry advance, generally along
a recognisable location such as a road. This would result in an average daily
advance of between one and three miles (roughly 1.5 to 5 kilometres), but
also casualty rates of between 20 and 30 per cent.[43]

On 2 September, the continued Allied advance forced the German
Army to withdraw to the *Siegfriedstellung* or Hindenburg Line. Foch
decided on a series of attacks: the Americans in the Meuse–Argonne on
26 September, the First and Third British Armies towards Cambrai on
27 September, an Anglo-Belgian advance in Flanders on 28 September
and the Fourth British Army with United States and French support in
northern France near the Saint-Quentin Canal.[44]

The 46th (North Midland) Division had been an unspectacular British formation. On 13 October 1915, as mentioned in Chapter Three, it had failed to retake the Hohenzollern Redoubt during the Battle of Loos. On 1 July 1916, as mentioned in Chapter Seven, the division had not pressed their assault on the fortified village of Gommecourt. Haig dismissed the divisional commander. However, by September 1918, the level of training and professionalism across the entire British Empire Army had improved to the extent that a previously substandard division would demonstrate its ability to successfully conduct a complex assault on the Hindenburg Line.

On 29 September 1918, the IX British and Australian Corps attacked the Western Front fortification. The 46th Division led the attack across the Saint-Quentin Canal. The bold plan required the troops to descend ladders to reach the canal, cross the water using collapsible boats – wearing life jackets requisitioned from cross-channel ferries – and then scale ladders once more to reach the fortification. The operation was only made possible by heavy artillery support. Fifty-four 18-pounder guns fired rounds every 30 seconds, while 18 4.5-inch (114-millimetre) howitzers fired a round every minute, concentrated on a frontage of only 500 yards. It is perhaps an understatement to state that the German troops were not expecting an attack of this nature. The British soldiers reached all their objectives and captured 7,000 prisoners and 70 guns.[45]

This series of Allied offensives had varying degrees of success. In the Meuse–Argonne, the United States attack stalled by 30 September, due as much to American logistical problems as German resistance. The New Zealand Division reached Cambrai on 29 September, and occupied trenches that had been dug by the 12th British Division during the 1917 battle. However, what the battle-hardened soldiers most appreciated 'was the sight of the smiling country eastwards unscathed by war'.[46]

Stevenson argues that the September offensive was the 'decisive' battle of the war. The breaking of the *Siegfriedstellung* led Ludendorff – with a breathtaking abrogation of personal responsibility from the man who had been largely responsible for German war strategy since 1917 – to inform the Kaiser and the German government on 29 September that the war was lost and that they would need to begin peace negotiations. The military's failure had now become the civilians' responsibility.[47]

Ten days before Ludendorff's admission of defeat, the British Empire had been victorious over its other main enemy, the Ottoman Empire. When the Ottomans entered the war on the side of the Central Powers on 2 November 1914, the United Kingdom perceived this state as weak, yet it would demonstrate surprising resilience in the face of many internal and external threats.[48]

Sultan Mehmed V had lost most of his European territory in the 1912 Balkan War, but Ottoman strategy did not aim to regain this land. Instead, War Minister and de facto leader Enver Pasha sent 150,000 Ottoman troops northwards to fight their old enemy, the Russians, in the Caucasus. In the bitter winter of December 1914–January 1915, the Russian Army attacked at the Battle of Sarikamish, inflicting 60,000 casualties on the Ottomans and forcing them to retreat. The Russian victory confirmed the United Kingdom and French governments' belief that the Ottomans could be easily defeated. The result was the Gallipoli campaign from February 1915 to January 1916. The French and British attempted to capture the Dardanelles, force the Ottomans out of the war and enable the Russians to export wheat and purchase munitions. The Allied operation eventually failed, but the Ottoman leadership's fears of internal revolt following the April landings resulted in the 1915 Armenian genocide.[49]

The military campaigns fought between the British and Ottoman empires in Sinai and Palestine are often seen as being more romantic than the industrial warfare of the Western Front due to the roles of figures like T.E. Lawrence, Hussein, Sharif of Mecca and his sons Abdullah and Faisal. In reality, military success in the Middle East relied – as it did in other theatres – on the effective use of technology and logistics.[50]

In January 1915, the Ottoman Army advanced through the Sinai Desert to attack the Suez Canal with the aim of instigating an Egyptian revolt against British occupation. There was no uprising, but the offensive demonstrated the Ottomans' ability to sustain their troops in a harsh environment.[51]

In January 1916, General Archibald Murray took command of the British Empire garrison, which was renamed the Egyptian Expeditionary Force (EEF). Murray began a slow and steady advance into Sinai, in which the Egyptian Labour Corps played a vital role in constructing the railway and a water pipeline capable of providing half a million tons of filtered water every day. On 26 March 1917, Murray attacked the key town of Gaza. The attempt failed and resulted in 4,000 British Empire casualties. The Second Battle of Gaza on 17 April was even more costly with 6,500 casualties. Murray was sacked at the end of June.[52]

Murray's replacement was General Sir Edmund Allenby, whom Haig had removed from command of the Third British Army after he had grievously mishandled the Battle of Arras (9 April–16 May 1917). On 28 June, Allenby took command of the EEF and seized the opportunity to redeem his military reputation. This began with his planning for the third attempt to take Gaza. As was now the practice on the Western Front, Allenby held planning conferences to develop the operation. In July, Falkenhayn, the former Chief of the German General staff, also arrived in Palestine to command a new German–Ottoman army called the Yıldırım (Thunderbolt) Army Group.[53]

The Ottoman commanders assessed that Allenby was preparing to assault Gaza and noted that, due to his Western Front experience, he would probably make significant use of artillery bombardment. On the night of 27 October, the EEF's guns did indeed begin firing. The next morning, the 60th and 74th British Divisions attacked and captured the Ottoman lines, while on the evening of 31 October, five brigades of Australian light horse and British cavalry attacked from the south, east and north to capture Beersheba and its wells, vital for watering the EEF's thousands of horses. With Beersheba in British hands, the attack on Gaza began on the night of 1 November and continued until the Ottomans abandoned the city six days later. The EEF pursued the retreating Ottoman soldiers, and on 11 December 1917, Allenby formally entered Jerusalem.[54]

As part of this ceremony, the EEF issued a proclamation in Arabic, English, French, Greek, Hebrew, Italian and Russian stating:

> every sacred building, monument, holy spot, shrine, traditional site, endowment, pious bequest or customary place of prayer, of whatever form of the three religions, will be monitored and protected according to the existing customs and beliefs of those to whose faiths they are sacred.[55]

Respecting the beliefs of the many Muslim British Subjects was a long-standing policy. On 20 December 1914, the Armed Merchant Cruiser *Empress of Asia*, which, as mentioned in Chapter One, had taken part in the pursuit of the *Emden*, escorted a ship carrying Muslims undertaking the Hajj from Port Sudan to the port of Jedda in the Ottoman Empire. The ship's captain even had orders to bombard the port if the pilgrims were not allowed to disembark, but this was not required. The Foreign Office generally succeeded in reassuring Muslim opinion in Palestine, India and across the world. As James Kitchen points out, most Indian Muslim soldiers serving in Palestine 'accepted that they were not taking part in a modern crusade and remained loyal to the British Empire'.[56]

As mentioned in Chapter Eight, the United Kingdom made increasing use of non-white troops as the war continued. A key component of this

Fig. 9.2 Indian troops played a significant role in the final stages of the Middle East campaign. Image: Tom Baker Collection, Australian Army History Unit, 11.24.50.

policy was the 'Indianisation' of the EEF, approved in January 1918. By the end of the Middle East campaign, 80 per cent of British Empire divisions included Indian troops. Almost a third of these new troops were Muslim, and when these men took leave, they were, if possible, provided with tours of the Islamic holy sites in Jerusalem. Another significant group of Indian sepoys were Sikhs, and Allenby commented in August how a visit by Sir Bhupinder Singh, the Maharaja of Patiala was 'much appreciated by the Sikhs'. The Ottomans attempted to encourage Indian soldiers to desert, but only 30 did so in 1918.[57]

Allenby initially opposed 'Indianisation' as he believed the soldiers would be influenced either by the prevailing anti-British attitude of the Egyptian population, or by the exhortations of Ottoman Army imams across no-man's-land. He told Sir Henry Wilson that his Indian reinforcements were 'short of training', but this would be overcome with a strict regimen of drills. The Indianised 10th Division – the former 10th (Irish) Division – used field exercises in June and August to introduce the Indian troops to the latest infantry methods based on recent Western Front operations. In addition, the sepoys went on patrols into no-man's-land 'to develop a belief in their own professional military abilities'. This prepared the EEF's soldiers for their final offensive.[58]

On 24 July Allenby reported to Wilson on his planning for his September offensive with the initial objective of Nablus, about 30 miles north of Jerusalem. By this stage of the war, in contrast to the EEF, the Ottoman Army had greatly declined in numbers, as is shown by the number of corps containing only one division in Table 9.2.[59]

TABLE 9.2
OTTOMAN ARMY, SEPTEMBER 1918[60]

THRACE: FIRST ARMY	I CORPS
	42nd Infantry Division
	1st Cavalry Brigade
ANATOLIA: SECOND ARMY	XII Corps (1 Division)
	XV Corps (3 Divisions)
GALLIPOLI: FIFTH ARMY	XIV Corps (1 Division)
	XIX Corps (no divisions)
	XXI Corps (1 Division)
PALESTINE: YILDIRIM ARMY GROUP FOURTH ARMY	II Corps (1 Division, 3 Provisional Divisions)
	Jordan Group (1 Infantry Division, 1 Cavalry Division)
	VIII Corps (1 Division, 1 Provisional Division)
SEVENTH ARMY	III Corps (2 Divisions)
	XX Corps (2 Divisions)
EIGHTH ARMY	XXII Corps (2 Divisions)
	Left Wing Corps (2 Divisions, Asia Corps, 1 Cavalry Division)
CAUCASUS: EASTERN ARMY GROUP THIRD ARMY	(3 Divisions)
NINTH ARMY	(3 Divisions, 1 Cavalry Brigade)
ARMY OF ISLAM	(2 Divisions)
MESOPOTAMIA: SIXTH OTTOMAN ARMY	XIII CORPS (2 Divisions)
	XVIII CORPS (2 Divisions)
ARABIA–YEMEN	VII CORPS (4 Divisions)

TABLE 9.3
EGYPTIAN EXPEDITIONARY FORCE, NOVEMBER 1918[61]

XX Corps	3rd (Lahore) Division
	10th Division
XXI Corps	7th (Meerut) Division
	54th Division
	French Contingent
Desert Mounted Corps	4th Cavalry Division
	5th Cavalry Division
	Australian Mounted Division
	20th Indian Brigade
General Headquarters Troops	53rd Division
	60th Division
	Palestine Brigade, Royal Air Force
	Light Armoured Car Brigade
	Cyprus Detachment
	Khartoum Garrison
Miscellaneous Units	Italian Contingent
	British Detachment Hejaz
Palestine Lines of Communication	Australian and New Zealand Mounted Division
	75th Division

The EEF had deceived the Ottomans at the Third Battle of Gaza in 1917, and would do the same at the Battle of Megiddo. As Allenby told Wilson on 21 August: 'If we can keep our intentions and our dispositions dark, I think the Turk is likely to suffer a severe defeat.' As Erickson writes:

> Allenby's plan was the reverse of the Gaza-Beersheba plan of 1917. Instead of feinting near the sea and then attacking inland at Beersheba, in 1918 Allenby chose to feint near the Jordan River [. . .] and then to smash his way through the Turkish defences on a narrow avenue next to the sea. [62]

On 19 September, the first day of the Battle of Megiddo, the EEF captured 6,000 prisoners and 95 artillery pieces. Three days later, Allenby wrote that 'two [Ottoman] armies, W. of the Jordan, have ceased to exist' and that the number of Ottoman prisoners had risen to 25,000. Despite his initial misgivings about the 'Indianisation' of his infantry divisions, he acknowledged that the 'Indian Battalions did grandly, in spite of their newness & short training'. Edwin Montagu, the Indian Secretary, told Allenby on 25 September:

> At the moment when great successes are being won by British and Dominion troops on the Western Front, I rejoice that Indian Cavalry and Infantry should have had the opportunity of contributing in so large a measure and with characteristic gallantry to magnificent victory in the East.[63]

General Mustafa Kemal, who had taken command of the Ottoman Seventh Army in late August, skilfully led his troops in a fighting withdrawal towards the Jordan. Kemal had achieved fame in April 1915 for his successful defence at Gallipoli, but Erickson argues that his action under such dire circumstances in September 1918 was 'his finest military achievement'.[64]

By 3 October, the number of Ottoman prisoners captured in the two weeks since the opening of the offensive had reached 71,000. Accommodating and feeding such a large number of men at short notice caused difficulties, especially as many of the men were sick from disease or lack of food. The

Fig. 9.3 Canadian soldiers with German prisoners of war, August 1918. By September, the German Army was disintegrating. Image: UK Ministry of Defence 104566

advance now reached Syria: Damascus was occupied on 1 October, and Aleppo on the 25th. The Ottomans attempted to rebuild their army, but they lacked men, equipment and artillery. Allied success on other fronts contributed to the Ottoman decision to end their war. On 15 September, Serbian, French and Greek troops had attacked at Dobro Pole on the Salonika front, broken the Bulgarian Army, and led to Tsar Ferdinand I signing an armistice on 29 October. With Bulgaria out of the war, the Allies could advance through Thrace and capture Istanbul. To prevent this, the Ottoman government sent Major General Charles Townshend, who had been captured at the surrender of Kut in Mesopotamia in 1916, to the town of Mudros on the Greek island of Lemnos in order to inform the Allies that the Ottomans wanted peace. This armistice came into effect on 31 October. Austria–Hungary, following its defeat by the Italians in the Battle of Vittorio Veneto, signed its armistice on 3 November.[65]

The German Army had begun to collapse. A British intelligence report from 10 September stated that German prisoners 'urged our men to go on attacking, and to capture as many Germans as possible so that the war might quickly end'. In the final hundred days of the conflict, 385,000 German soldiers surrendered because, as Alexander Watson asserts, 'they were too physically and mentally exhausted to continue fighting'.[66]

The German government took stumbling steps towards change in the last weeks of the war. On 3 October 1918, the moderate Prince Max of Baden was appointed German chancellor. The next day, he sent a note to Woodrow Wilson requesting an armistice and peace negotiations based on the President's Fourteen Points. At the same time, Ludendorff ensured, despite his central role in controlling war strategy, that the blame for the German defeat would be shifted away from himself to the opposition political parties. The German admirals attempted to put the High Seas Fleet to sea to fight the Royal Navy, but, not surprisingly, the sailors mutinied rather than participate in this suicide mission. From the port of Kiel, revolution spread through the rest of the country. On 9 November, Germany was proclaimed a republic. The following day, Kaiser Wilhelm went into exile in the Netherlands. Finally, on 11 November, the armistice was signed and World War I ended.[67]

When Britain declared war on Germany on 4 August 1914, Sir Edward Grey, the Foreign Secretary, reputedly said that 'the lamps [were] going out all over Europe'. On 11 November 1918, Lord Derby, the British Ambassador in Paris, marked the armistice by having the band of the Royal Regiment of Horse Guards perform at the British Embassy and the Place de la Concorde. Derby had the Embassy illuminated to celebrate the peace, stating that 'it was the only building in Paris that was'. After four years, three months and seven days, the war was over and the lights had come back on.[68]

Farmers and Agriculture

When German troops captured their first Allied trenches in the offensive of 21 March 1918, they were immediately disheartened and disillusioned. Having been told by their political and military masters that the U-boat campaign was successfully strangling the United Kingdom, they realised they had been lied to. The British positions were well stocked with white bread, meat and coffee. One German prisoner of war, interrogated by a British intelligence officer on 22 May 1918, admitted that the main reason he and his comrades had been willing to continue the advance was 'the hope of finding abandoned foodstuffs' in the Allied lines. Agriculture played a key role in the British Empire's victory. In *The First World War: An Agrarian Interpretation*, Avner Offer argues that food production 'decided the war' and that the conflict was 'a war of bread and potatoes' as much as it was 'a war of steel and gold'. Similarly, James Belich contends in *Replenishing the Earth: The Settler Revolution and the Rise of the Anglo-World, 1783–1939* that pre-war improvements in transport and communications had bound the United Kingdom more closely to its Empire and created a system for providing sustenance for the British population that was 'completely reliable, and intimately attuned to demand'. During the German U-boat campaign of 1917, it was Canadian wheat that stopped the British from starving. Less palatable were the frozen rabbits issued on the Western Front as part of a soldier's rations. New Zealand established a Department of Imperial Government

Supplies to export produce to the United Kingdom that included 519,000 frozen rabbits 'eviscerated, fresh and free from disease, with meaty good conditioned carcases'. Sergeant Walter Estabrooks, who served in the 32nd Canadian Field Artillery Battery, noted that the smell was so strong that cooks wore their gas masks, but conceded 'they didn't taste too bad if you held your breath'. In New Zealand, the wartime importance of farming – 'the Country's greatest industry' – was recognised there on 26 July 1917, when Prime Minister William Massey and Governor-General Lord Liverpool laid foundation stones in Wellington for what would become the Dominion Farmers Institute. In South Africa, Louis Botha faced protests from sheep farmers in 1917 because the wool price offered by the United Kingdom government was 20 per cent lower than the return available from Japanese buyers on the open market. In December, Botha – who had survived the Afrikaner revolt in 1914 – took the farmers' grievances so seriously that he considered resigning the premiership. In many cases, as farmers became more prosperous, they became more organised, and more politicised. In Australia, farmers formed state-based political parties that would unite in 1919 to become the Country Party; in Canada, the United Farmers of Ontario had been established in 1913, and the agrarian Progressive Party would gain the second highest number of seats in the 1921 national election. The most successful agrarian party to emerge out of the war was Sinn Féin, who won 73 of the 105 Irish seats in the 1918 United Kingdom election. As Joost Augusteijn points out, the Sinn Féin vote was higher 'the more Catholic, rural, western and less northern an area was'.[1]

Gold Coast: kings of the road

Cocoa was first grown in the West African colony of the Gold Coast (modern Ghana) in 1879. By 1911, the colony had become the world's largest producer. The following year, cocoa exports – three quarters of which went to the United Kingdom – were worth £1,642,733 and comprised almost 40 per cent of the colony's total export income. African farmers grew cocoa, mostly in the three coastal provinces.[2]

Governor Sir Hugh Clifford believed railways were the best form of transport for the colony. However, these required time and money to build, and construction stalled due to the war. In April 1916, the *Gold Coast Leader* stated: 'the cry of the hour is for roads, more roads!' Africans already made roads 'which are kept clear of bush and passable for traders and travellers'. During the war, Gold Coast inhabitants filled the infrastructure gap by constructing 450 miles (over 700 kilometres) of road without any government assistance, and importing 398 motor vehicles to the Gold Coast in 1916 alone. This ensured that farmers and merchants could continue to get their produce to port for export. African farmers even contracted European construction companies to build roads. In one case, a route was made to enable farmers to travel by car to their cocoa fields on the plains during the week, and be able to return home to spend the weekend with their families.[3]

Australia: wearing the wool badge

When the war began, Australia was in the midst of a drought that would not be broken until the first half of 1915. About 180,000 Australian wheat farmers had planted about 10 million acres (40,000 square kilometres) of wheat, but the harvest at the end of 1914 was so poor that no wheat could be exported. On 4 November 1915, the new prime minister, Billy Hughes, met with the six state agriculture ministers and gained their approval to establish the Australian Wheat Board (AWB). This organisation, with representatives from the federal and state governments, farmers and the major wheat-handling companies, paid farmers in advance for their crops, which the Board would then sell on. That first year, wheat farmers received £25 million in payments, but Australian wheat sales were only £6 million. As mentioned in Chapter Two, the United Kingdom government shifted ships away from the Australian route in order to concentrate vessels on the vital North American route. In contrast, sheep graziers saw a 20 per cent rise in the price of the wool, due to increased British demand for blankets, clothing and, especially, military uniforms.[4]

While Hughes was in London in 1916, estimates for the northern hemisphere wheat harvest were reduced due to bad weather and outbreaks of crop disease. Fearing food shortages in the winter of 1916–17, the United Kingdom Wheat Commission purchased the entire 3 million tons of the Australian wheat crop for a cost of £26.6 million. Farmers received their payments, but the 1917 shipping crisis, resulting from the German U-boat campaign, meant the wheat would never reach Britain. Instead, mice and weevils feasted on grain at railway sidings scattered throughout rural Australia. The British demand for wool continued. In November 1916, Hughes and Lord Milner, the former Colonial Secretary, hammered out a deal in which Australia would export wool only to the United Kingdom, in exchange for the British purchasing the entire wool clip of Australia and New Zealand for the duration of the war – at a price 55 per cent above the pre-war average. By July 1918, Australian farmers had been paid £132 million for wheat and wool, much of which the British government would never use.[5]

With the exception of Tasmania, all the Australian states had agrarian political organisations by 1918: the Farmers and Settlers' Association in New South Wales; the Farmers' Parliamentary Union in Queensland; the Victorian Farmers' Union (VFU); the Farmers and Settlers' Association in South Australia and the Country Party in Western Australia. The state farmers' parties had first come together in August 1915 to complain to the federal Labor government regarding the establishment of the AWB. Within a year, the farmers recognised the benefit of centralised marketing. Representatives from Victoria, Western Australia, Queensland and New South Wales met again in Melbourne on 30 September 1916, this time to demand that the AWB be made a permanent organisation. The various organisations combined to establish the Australian Farmers Federal Organisation (AFPO). This would be the precursor of the national Country Party established in 1918.[6]

In the Victorian state election of 15 November 1917, the conservative Nationalist Party won 40 of the 65 seats. However, 27 of these were members of the rural-based 'Economy' faction, which called for cuts to government spending and lower rail costs. Sir John Bowser of the 'Economy' faction became premier and overturned the railway price rises, though he would be forced to resign on 21 March 1918, when the opposition parties united to reject a railway estimates bill.[7]

In June 1918, the federal government used the War Precautions Act to set the price of meat in metropolitan areas following the Interstate Price Commission's finding of price fixing. Farmers were outraged at this decision and descended in large numbers on Melbourne, then the federal capital,

Fig. 10.1 Victorian Farmers Union Conference, Melbourne University Hall, 26 September 1915. By November 1917, the VFU had become a major political force in state politics. Image: Museums Victoria, https://collections. museumvictoria.com.au/items/768315.

on 20 June 1918. Hughes was in Europe, and William Watt, the acting prime minister, met the farmers. These filled Queen's Hall at Parliament House to overflowing, with several hundred spilling onto the steps of the legislature. Many of the demonstrators had a small piece of wool pinned to their jacket as a 'badge'. W.J. M'Lean, the deputation's leader asserted that 'the war had nothing whatever to do with price of meat [. . . which] should be regulated by the law of supply and demand'. The protest did not alter the decision, but it showed the increasing strength of the agrarian political movement.[8]

At this time, federal parliamentary election voting in Australia used the 'first-past-the-post' voting system rather than the preferential system, where voters place numbers against all candidates in order of preference, and, if no candidate receives more than 50 per cent of the vote, preferences are distributed until one candidate achieves a majority. The VFU had decided not to contest the federal election on 5 May 1917, because it did not want to divide the non-Labor vote. J.J. Hall, the VFU General Secretary, wrote to Hughes on 22 January 1918 calling for the introduction of preferential voting in the Federal Parliament's House of Representatives. Hughes left Australia for the United Kingdom on 26 April. The electoral law had not been changed when Sir William Irvine left politics in March to become the Chief Justice of Victoria. Hall announced his intention to contest the ensuing by-election in the Victorian seat of Flinders, but Watt, the acting prime minister, promised to introduce preferential voting in the next parliamentary session. Hall withdrew from the poll, which became a two-horse race between the Labor and Nationalist parties that was easily won on 11 May by the Nationalist candidate, Stanley Melbourne Bruce. The indolent Watt still had not changed the electoral laws when Sir John Forrest – who had accepted a peerage and was on his way to Westminster to sit in the House of Lords – died off Sierra Leone on 2 September. This time, four candidates, independent, Nationalist, Farmers and Settlers' Association, and Labor were on the ballot paper for the by-election. This split the non-Labor vote, and the ALP's E.W. Corboy was elected on 26 October with only 34 per cent of the vote.[9]

Finally, the *Electoral Act* was amended on 25 November to introduce preferential voting. The new act was promptly put into use because the Victorian seat of Corangamite had become vacant due to the death of the Nationalist James Chester Manifold, who had died at sea while returning to Australia from the United States. Five men stood for the seat on 14 December. These were: James Scullin, who had held the seat for Labor from 1910 to 1913, W.G. Gibson, local farmer and founding member of the VFU, and three others who called themselves Nationalist, Independent Nationalist and Returned Soldier Nationalist. Scullin had the highest number of primary votes (42.5 per cent), but when preferences were distributed, Gibson was declared the victor.[10]

Following Gibson's election, the Melbourne *Argus* noted that 'in every state where there had been any organised country or agrarian party', these had split from the Nationalist Party, demonstrating a difference in interests and issues between rural and urban conservatives. The Country Party increased its numbers in the federal election in 13 December 1919, and in the next poll, on 16 December 1922, gained the balance of power in the House of Representatives. Earle Page, the Country Party leader, offered to go into coalition with the Nationalists, but only if Billy Hughes – whom he detested due to his Labor background – was removed as prime minister and replaced by Stanley Bruce. The Nationalists acceded to this Country Party demand, thus ending Hughes' seven climactic years as prime minister.[11]

Canada: prairie progressives

Prime Minister Sir Robert Borden's 1918 decision to renege on his promise not to conscript farmers' sons had caused great distress across rural Canada. This would have political consequences in the immediate post-war period as it resulted in the rapid rise of agrarian political parties.

During the conflict, farmers in both Francophone and English-speaking Canada had stressed the importance of agricultural production to the war effort. In July 1915, *L'Éclaireur* in Beauce, south of Quebec City, asserted that farming should be seen as being as important as making munitions. The Federal Farmers of Ontario made the same point at their annual conference in February 1916, where they passed a resolution stating that farmers would best contribute to the war by staying on their farms. The 1914 wheat harvest had been affected by drought, but the 1915 crop was the biggest on record. A shortage of farm labourers, partly due to the large number of men who had enlisted in the CEF, made it hard to harvest the grain. The 1916 and 1917 harvests were below average, but the British demand for wheat ensured good prices. [12]

On 15 May 1918, about a month after Borden had lifted the exemption on conscripting farmers' sons, the Prime Minister met in Ottawa with 2,000 farmers from the Fermiers unis du Québec and 3,000 agriculturalists from the United Farmers of Ontario. Borden refused to back down and dismissed the farmers' concerns in what was described as an aggressive meeting. The Quebec City *Le Soleil* stated that the farmers left the meeting feeling angry and dissatisfied. When they tried to march on Parliament, a fearful Borden ordered the police to block their passage.[13]

As the Canadian Governor-General, the Duke of Devonshire told Long in December 1917, political opinion in western Canada was less conservative in comparison to those in the east: 'their general line of thought is democratic, with distinctly radical tendencies, but not socialistic'. In 1916, the Canadian Council of Agriculture had devised an agrarian political manifesto and called on farmers to vote for candidates to support the programme. The movement's first electoral success came with Thomas

Crerar, who was elected in the national election of 17 December 1917 as the MP for Marquette in Manitoba. Crerar explicitly described himself as 'the representative of organized farmers'.[14]

From this small beginning the political movement grew quickly. As the brilliant, if erratic, J.J. Morrison, one of the founders of the United Farmers of Ontario stated:

> Men and women of the country are thinking beyond the farms and beyond their own community, and are putting their thoughts into operation. They are acting collectively, and that is what organization makes possible.

On 5 May 1919, the United Farmers of Alberta's Alexander Moore was elected to the provincial legislature in a by-election. In October, Oliver Gould, a Saskatchewan farmer candidate, defeated William Motherwell, the Saskatchewan Agriculture Minister who had held this portfolio for a decade. Then, on 20 October 1919, the Conservatives in Ontario lost power after 14 years of incumbency. A coalition of the United Farmers of Ontario and the Labour Party formed government with Ernest Drury as premier.[15]

The following year, a fall in wheat prices combined with drought increased support for agrarian parties. The success of farmer political organisations put the Liberals into minority government in Manitoba in 1920, while the United Farmers of Alberta won the provincial election in 1921 and retained power for 14 years. The United Farmers of Manitoba would govern for two decades. At the national level, agrarian politicians were known as Progressives. In the federal election on 6 December 1921, the Conservatives were thoroughly defeated, retaining only 49 seats. Progressives came second with 58 seats, and the Liberals, led by William Mackenzie King, formed a minority government with 118 seats. This would be the high-water mark of Canadian rural representation. A nationwide agrarian party including Quebec farmers would never come to fruition. As Alan Bowker concludes: '[o]nce memories of conscription faded [. . . farmers'] traditional political loyalties and individualist philosophy reasserted themselves'.[16]

Fig. 10.2 Canadian farmer parties gained strength in the period
immediately after World War I. Canadian wheat harvest, 20 August 1918.
Image: Library & Archives Canada/Bibliothèque et Archives
Canada MIKAN 3337605, a046043-v8.

Britain: tractors versus U-boats

The British free-trade policy established in the nineteenth century had
resulted in a decline in local agriculture and a reliance on imported food.
However, when the Germans began their submarine campaigns against
merchant ships sailing to the United Kingdom from 1915, English,
Scottish and Welsh farmers were able to rapidly expand production by
returning land to cultivation. In May 1917, the Corn Production Act
provided guaranteed minimum prices for five years to encourage farmers
to increase cultivation. This bill was described by the *Annual Register* as
'the most complete break with the Victorian system of free imports'. The
requirement to plough up pastoral land was, however, opposed by many
landowners, including the Colonial Secretary, Walter Long, who resisted
compulsory ploughing on his Wiltshire estate. In June 1918, Long wrote:

Crops are looking well and if we get good weather I think that, on the whole, the result ought to be satisfactory. Personally I am inclined to the opinion that too much grass land has been ploughed up, some of it unwisely.[17]

As farmers know all too well, weather determines the scale of the harvest. In October 1916, the heavy rains that made life a misery for the BEF on the Somme had a similar debilitating effect on the entire United Kingdom potato harvest, which came in at 19 per cent below average. The small English harvest resulted in price hikes, and despite the traders' complaints, the authorities intervened to set the price of potatoes. In Scotland, the crop was just over half the average harvest. The Minister of Food Control, Lord Devonport, intervened to ensure that almost the entire Scottish potato crop would be diverted to be used as seed potatoes for the next year's crop in Britain and Ireland. English potatoes would be used to feed Scotland, but shortages occurred. The average weekly potato consumption in Glasgow was 2,000 tons, but the city's potato stock on 18 February 1917 was only 300 tons. A week later this had declined to only 30 tons.[18]

Attempts were made to modernise British farming on several fronts. A Seed Testing Station was established in London in 1917 in which women and men worked together to improve the nation's seed stocks. Mechanisation was seen as a way to increase farm production. The Ford tractor factory in Cork was approved in 1916, though the factory would not be completed until after the war. On 18 January 1918, Arthur Amos presented a paper to the Institution of Mechanical Engineers on the 'Utility of motor-tractors for tillage purposes'. He argued that, in appropriate terrain, a tractor travelling at 3.5 miles per hour could till a field in almost half the time taken by a horse-drawn plough walking at 2 miles per hour. After the talk, George Watson, a member of the audience, asserted that 'the use of the agricultural tractor was going to be one of the chief features in defeating the U-boat'.[19]

Ireland: the farmer's vote

On 22 August 1914, an editorial in the Irish *Farmer's Gazette* predicted that the outbreak of war would benefit farmers as it would 'add appreciably to their own and the nation's wealth'. It is fair to say that the Irish agriculturalists generally had a 'good war'. A year into the conflict, the amount of land under cultivation had increased by 85,000 acres (some 340 square kilometres). In some counties, the acreage allocated to crops had increased by 50 per cent. The *Farmer's Gazette* rejoiced:

> prices for all descriptions of farm produce are so favourable for sellers, that even with the increased cost of labour, feeding stuffs, and machinery, farming is for the present in a prosperous condition. Long may it remain so.[20]

The loss of the Belgian and the Russian flax harvests due to the war meant Ulster flax was more in demand. The area under cultivation in that province increased by 3,890 acres (1,574 hectares) in 1915 to a total of 53,143 acres (215 square kilometres).[21]

The 1916 harvest began well. A farmer from Caherconlish in County Limerick reported: 'Hay very good, and saved in such splendid weather. Pasture seldom looked so well at this time.' However, as Table 10.1 indicates, the wet weather at the end of the year affected all major crops. The average potato yield declined from 6.17 tons per acre in 1915 to 5.85 tons per acre in 1916.[22]

TABLE 10.1
IRISH WHEAT, OATS AND POTATO PRODUCTION
IN ACRES, 1914–16[23]

	1914	1915	Increase	1916	Decrease
WHEAT	33,913	86,530	134.4%	76,438	11.7%
OATS	1,028,758	1,088,664	5.9%	1,071,593	1.6%
POTATOES	583,069	586,308	2.0%	586,308	1.4%

The Department of Agriculture and the Royal Dublin Society promoted tractors to Irish farmers. However, one farmer was unimpressed with a demonstration of this emerging technology in County Kildare in early 1917, and reported that the 'general opinion' of those present was 'that three horses and a double farrow plough working on the same land would do more work and do it much better'.[24]

In January 1917, the United Kingdom government introduced compulsory tillage for Irish farmers holding ten or more acres (four or more hectares), as it had in Britain. The *Farmer's Gazette* commented: 'The plough has been at work where it was never seen before.' However, the government's policy led to furious complaints from farmers who argued that they lacked the labourers and machinery to convert pasture to cropping. In August, Mr R. Cooper of Cooper Hill, Clarina in County Limerick chaired a meeting of the Limerick and Clare Farmers' Association which outlined their opposition to the Food Controller Lord Rhondda setting compulsory beef prices. The harvest report from County Armagh in September stated: 'The general prospects of the farmer are good, but the Food Controller's arrangement as regards cattle is causing great dissatisfaction.' Soon afterwards, an Irish deputation met with the Food Controller to state their objections.[25]

Farmers recognised their present prosperity. In June 1917, Ireland was the third-largest exporter of food to England, Scotland and Wales. It provided more cattle and beef, poultry, potatoes, barley and eggs to Britain than any other country, and was the third-largest provider of bacon, ham and oats, and in fourth place for sheep and mutton. Most significantly, Irish farmers looked to continue these beneficial economic conditions when the war ended. The *Farmer's Gazette* wrote in September 1917:

> Farmers are mobilising, the daily papers tell us. Very much so, and about time. There must be few districts in Ireland where farming is engaged in that have not by this time recognised the need for combining and mushroom-like, new farming associations are springing up daily, and mushroom unlike, springing up to stay.[26]

At the same time, farmers railed against the creeping impositions of the Department of Agriculture. For example, two flax farmers in County Armagh were fined 30 shillings each in September 1917 because they had not reserved some of their crop as seed for next year's harvest. On 20 July 1918, the Limerick and Clare Farmers' Association met at Limerick's Royal George Hotel to pass resolutions opposing the Department's new powers 'to restrict, fine, or compulsorily buy out farmers, who, in the opinion of the Department's inspectors, were not farming their land in a proper manner'. In August, the Irish Farmers' Union placed an advertisement in the *Farmer's Gazette* calling on agriculturalists to establish local branches of the organisation 'in order to be able to resist and defeat every attempt BY THE DEPARTMENT to evict our people from the homes of their ancestors'.[27]

The second half of the year would be dominated, not only by the Allied victories in Europe and the Middle East, but also by the United Kingdom general election on 14 December 1918. For the first time in Britain and Ireland, all males over the age of 21, and females over the age of 30 who met a property qualification, were granted the vote. The election result in Ireland was largely predictable due to the political and sectarian divisions in the country at this time. Protestants in Ulster generally voted for Unionist candidates to remain part of the United Kingdom. Catholics, who formed the majority in the rest of the island, outside the six majority-Protestant counties of Ulster, voted mostly for Sinn Féin with the aim of achieving Irish independence. The Royal Irish Constabulary's reports used the phrase 'foregone conclusion' to describe both the high Unionist vote in Ulster and the high Sinn Féin vote in the remainder of the country. The Irish Parliamentary Party, previously the main nationalist party, was reduced to only six seats, the Unionist Party held 22 seats, while Sinn Féin won 73 of the 105 constituencies in Ireland.[28]

Despite the predictable result, the 1918 Irish election demonstrates how Sinn Féin campaigned to win the votes of farmers. Even Lord French, the former general sidelined to become Lord Lieutenant of Ireland, recognised at the end of August that Sinn Féin was placing less emphasis on paramilitary operations in the lead-up to the poll in order to concentrate on 'Franchise work'.[29]

Farmers formed a significant voting bloc in Ireland. The *Northern Standard and Monaghan, Cavan and Tyrone Advertiser* wrote on 28 September 1918: 'Seventy per cent. of the people of Ireland is agricultural, and therefore exceedingly prosperous.' Martin Egan of Loughrea, County Galway, Vice President of the Irish Farmer's Union, argued:

> we, farmers and farm helpers, who can command the majority of votes
> in Ireland over any other class, should take such action immediately

as will secure us necessary representation for the promotion and protection of our business and our political interests after the election.[30]

One of the farmers' largest concerns was that they would be forced to pay more tax. On 17 October, an Irish Farmers' Union meeting in Dublin decried 'proposed excessive taxation'. Closely linked to this was the fear that if Ireland remained part of the United Kingdom, farmers would have to contribute to pay off the British war debt. At an election meeting at Dungarvan, County Waterford in support of Cathal Brugha, the Sinn Féin candidate, Mr Flood of Dublin stated:

> To the farmers present he would like to point out the fact that this year the taxation of the country amounted to 26 millions, and next year it would amount to 40 millions. If they remained tied to England the taxation they would have to pay to defray the cost of the world-war would keep on increasing until they would become bankrupt. If they separated from England it would mean that they would not pay one d--- farthing of this taxation.[31]

Irish women, both Unionist and Nationalist, enthusiastically took part in their first election. The Ulster Women's Unionist Council, which included female Unionists across the entire island of Ireland, had been created in 1911 and attracted a membership of between 115,000 and 200,000 individuals. Sinn Féin's female organisation, Cumann na mBan ('League of Women') was established in 1914 and at the time of the election had a membership of 19,800.[32]

A Cumann na mBan leaflet entitled *The Present Duty of Irishwomen* stated:

> Generations of Irishwomen have longed to possess the weapon which has now been put into your hands. Show that you value it properly, and do your part in publicizing to the world our determination to be free.

Sinn Féin selected three female candidates for the election. Countess Markievicz won in Dublin St Patrick's, but in accordance with the party's policy, did not take her place in the Westminster Parliament. Winifred Carney contested the staunchly Unionist electorate of Belfast Victoria in the city's east and was soundly defeated. Hanna Sheehy Skeffington was also chosen, but decided not to take part in the poll. Kathleen Clarke wanted to be the candidate in her home town of Limerick, but claimed that while she was being held in an English prison, the party nominated Michael Colivet in her place. The Dublin branch of Cumann na mBan wrote to Colivet requesting him to stand aside, but he refused. Colivet was elected to the seat.[33]

The voting age for women in the 1918 election was 30, but Senia Pašeta found that 'some determined women did not let even their age stop them from contributing'. One of these was Máire Comerford, who told the polling station official, whom she knew, that she had 'earned' a vote. The official discussed the matter with his colleagues, and 'the name of a "dead woman" was found' for her, enabling Comerford to make her mark in a historic election.[34]

Crisis of Empire

The United Kingdom and its allies had, at great cost in lives and resources, defeated the Central Powers. The British Empire would reach its greatest extent with German colonies and Ottoman provinces coming under the Crown. However, victory did not mean stability. As Keith Jeffery has written, the British soon found themselves in a 'crisis of Empire' with strikes and protests, uprisings and insurgencies erupting from Ireland to India.[35]

Industrial action became commonplace in Britain from 1918 to 1921 with strikes by police, miners and railway workers. The government responded to a general strike in Glasgow by putting troops and tanks on the streets. Within a week of the end of the war, General Sir Edmund Allenby told General Sir Henry Wilson, the Chief of the Imperial General Staff, that, in spite of the onset of peace, 'there will be a lot of police work to be done in Europe and Asia'. The British Army would be tasked to impose order across the Empire. On 28 January 1919, Cabinet decided to continue conscription. In addition, a large military budget had to be maintained.[36]

In August 1919, Wilson provided Winston Churchill, the War Secretary, with an estimate of the number of troops required 'to keep our four storm centres quiet – Ireland, Egypt, Mesopotamia & India'. Wilson presumed that Canada and Australia would be willing to provide infantry battalions to take part in the occupation of Germany. However, he did not appreciate the ideas of autonomy that had developed in the Dominions during the Great War. As General Jan Smuts had pointed out to Lord Buxton, the South African Governor-General, in October 1916:

> It is clear that the Dominions should no longer remain in their present legal status and that a real attempt should be made to raise them from their present position as subject provinces into co-ordinate states of the Empire.

With combat now concluded, both Borden and Hughes decided their troops should return home.[37]

In 1919 and 1920, the British would be put under pressure in each of the four 'storm centres' Wilson had identified. Following Sinn Féin's electoral victory, the Irish Republican Army (IRA) began attacking police officers of the Royal Irish Constabulary (RIC) from the beginning of 1919 in a conflict that became known as the Irish War of Independence. Sean O'Faolain, an IRA member whose father was in the RIC wrote:

> Men like my father were dragged out [. . .] and shot down as traitors to their country [. . .] they were not traitors. They had their loyalties, and stuck to them.

About 1,400 people were killed in the conflict. The violence was concentrated mostly in Dublin and the south-western province of Munster.[38]

The United Kingdom government responded on 9 August 1920 by passing the Restoration of Order in Ireland Act that continued the wartime powers of the Defence of the Realm Act, deploying British troops, increasing the strength of the RIC, and establishing two new organisations to March and July to support the police. The first were mostly ex-British soldiers recruited as short-term police issued with dark green RIC jackets and khaki army trousers, known as 'Black and Tans'. The second was the Auxiliary Division of the RIC. These paramilitary forces gained a reputation for undisciplined brutality and criminality. They were also ineffective in defeating the Irish insurgency.[39]

General Nevil Macready, the General Officer Commanding Ireland, developed a respect for his IRA enemy. In February 1921, he wrote:

> In country districts these men may be partially educated countrymen and labouring class, but in the towns and cities they are well educated young men, and all are imbued with what, for the want of a better term, I would call 'fanatical patriotism'.[40]

As the IRA gradually gained control of the countryside, British and Irish leaders began negotiating a political settlement. This resulted in the treaty signed on 6 December 1921 that resulted in the partition of Ireland with six Unionist counties remaining part of the United Kingdom as Northern Ireland, and 26 Nationalist counties gaining independence as the Irish Free State. The IRA split over the treaty, resulting in the Irish Civil War which was fought by pro-treaty and anti-treaty factions from 28 June 1922 to 24 May 1923. The campaign ended with the death of 927 individuals and the retention of power by the pro-treaty government.[41]

Major Bernard Montgomery, the future Field Marshal, who served with the 17th Brigade in Cork, supported the negotiated settlement. He wrote in October 1923:

> My own view is that to win a war of this sort you must be ruthless [...] Nowadays public opinion precludes such methods, the nation would never allow it, and the politicians would lose their jobs if they sanctioned it. That being so I consider that Lloyd-George was really right in what he did, if he had gone on we could probably have squashed the rebellion as a temporary measure, but it would have broken out again like an ulcer the moment we removed the troops [...] The only way therefore was to give them some form of self government, let them squash the rebellion themselves, they are the only people who could really stamp it out [.][42]

In acknowledgement of India's war contribution, Edwin Montagu, on becoming India Secretary in July 1917, announced that the United Kingdom would work towards the establishment of responsible government in India. As a first step in this process, Dr Sachchidananda Sinha and the Maharaja of Bikaner were appointed members of the British Empire delegation to the Paris Peace Conference commencing on 18 January 1919.[43]

During 1919, India was wracked with internal and external violence. Early in the year, the Government of India legislated to maintain emergency wartime measures such as internment without trial. These laws were never invoked, but they caused outrage among the population. In this turbulent atmosphere, four Europeans were killed in the Punjabi city of Amritsar on 10 April 1919. Three days later, Colonel Reginald Dyer ordered his Indian troops to fire on a crowd in the enclosed Jallianwala Bagh, killing 379 civilians and wounding many more. The Hunter Committee that examined the massacre in 1920 was divided on ethnic lines. Three Indian members, who were in the minority, condemned Dyer, while the majority British members exonerated him. Conservatives in the United Kingdom lauded Dyer for his willingness to take 'strong measures', and his supporters presented him with a large amount of money raised by public subscription.[44]

Fortunately, both Mohandas Karamchand Gandhi and the Congress Party and Lord Reading, the new viceroy appointed in 1921, stepped back from the abyss of communal violence. Reading stated in a speech in Delhi:

> The shadow of Amritsar has lengthened over the fair face of India. I know how deep is the concern felt by His Majesty the King Emperor at the terrible chapter of events in the Punjab [...] My experience tells me that misunderstandings usually mean mistakes on either side [...] I appeal to you all, British and Indians [...] to work together to realise the hopes that arise from to-day.'[45]

To internal dissension was added external invasion, when Ammanullah, the Amir of Afghanistan, launched the Third Afghan War in May 1919, attacking India via the Khyber Pass. The Indian Army was forced to deploy almost 350,000 troops – the equivalent of eight divisions – and 158,000 animals to the frontier. The Indian Army suffered 250 men killed and 650 wounded in combat, but also 57,000 sick, mostly from cholera, of whom about a thousand died. The Afghan casualties are unknown, but due to a lack of medical services the number was probably twice the British Empire losses. Weapons and technology developed for the Western Front were transferred to the North-West Frontier. The Royal Air Force bombed Kabul, soldiers were equipped with Lewis and Vickers machine guns as well as trucks and armoured cars. The Afghan advance was stopped. However, as a further demonstration of the 'crisis of Empire', the war forced the British to concede full independence to Afghanistan.[46]

During the war, Egypt had become a major supply base for the British Empire in the Middle East. However, after four years of war, food prices had skyrocketed, and the average consumption of cereals per person was 45 per cent lower than what it had been in 1913. Food shortages combined with political grievances to cause the Egyptian rebellion. On 14 November 1918, Saad Zaghlul and other leading Egyptian nationalists met the British High Commissioner, Sir Reginald Wingate, with the request to be allowed to go to the Paris Peace Conference to advocate for Egyptian independence. This illustrated the clash between President Wilson's ideals of national self-determination and the British quest for territorial aggrandisement. The Acting High Commissioner, Sir Milne Cheetham, refused Zaghlul's travel to Versailles and instead had him and his closest supporters deported to Malta.[47]

On 12 March 1919, Egyptians began rioting, and, for two months, the revolt spread across the whole country. The British Empire garrison was used to put down the rising. This force included two divisions of Australian and New Zealand mounted troops who were preparing to return home. Some Australians were sympathetic to the revolt. Colonel A.J. Mills wrote 'the Gyppy had big reasons to kick' against the British authorities. However, most of the Antipodeans looked down on the Arabs, and ruthlessly put down the revolt. On 27 March, the 2nd Australian Light Horse Brigade and a battalion of Gurkhas went in search of a missing Gurkha soldier near Abu Akdar. Major General Sir Granville Ryrie, the force commander, ordered two Australian Aboriginal Lighthorsemen with tracking skills to search for the missing man. When they found that the soldier had been murdered and his body dumped in a canal, Ryrie sent his men into the village. When the local leaders did not surrender the men responsible for the killing, he ordered his troops to set fire to the village, an area of 18 acres

(7 hectares). Another war crime was committed on 13 April following the killing of two Australian soldiers at Saft-el Malouk, probably by Bedouin. The next day, the soldiers – defying their officers – formed a vigilante group, rounded up the adult males of the local villages, and inflicted 20 lashes each to 128 men. The Egyptian revolt was put down, but the British granted the kingdom a form of independence in 1922.[48]

The Mesopotamian rising was the largest of these four insurrections. The campaign to quash this revolt would be the largest British military campaign in the interwar period. The main justification for being in Mesopotamia was to control its oil fields at Basra in the south and Mosul in the north. In early 1920, Arabs and Kurds were dismayed that they would remain under colonial occupation and not gain independence. The rupee had been imposed as the local currency, and locals resented that Indians, rather than Arabs, were gaining administrative positions in the government. The insurgency began in April around Mosul before spreading to the rest of the country. During Ramadan in May and June, peaceful demonstrations in Baghdad united Sunni and Shia. The British Empire force, consisting mostly of Indian troops, was outnumbered. Many of the battalions were understrength. On 26 August, War Secretary Winston Churchill was forced to reinforce Mesopotamia with 19 infantry battalions and two Royal Air Force squadrons from India.[49]

On 19 September, Field Marshal Sir Henry Wilson sent requests to the New Zealand, Canadian and Australian governments to send Dominion troops to Mesopotamia. The New Zealand government had sent troops to the British colony of Fiji in February 1920 to break a strike, and Massey offered Wilson an infantry battalion. The Australian Cabinet did not formally consider Milner's request, so it is likely Hughes, wary of the sensitivities of the issue, discussed the question privately with his senior ministers. Both Canada and Australia refused, and, in the end, no Dominion units were sent to Mesopotamia.[50]

The revolt demonstrated that the British could not maintain Mesopotamia as a subjugated territory. The rebellion ended with 312 British and Indian troops being killed and 1,228 wounded. The search for legitimacy resulted in Faisal, son of Hussein bin Ali, the Grand Sharif of Mecca, becoming King of Iraq in 1921. The kingdom would become an independent state in 1932.[51]

World War I was a shared British Empire experience. The global nature of the conflict brought together individuals from across the world who otherwise would never have met. When Sergeant Ernest Smith sailed through the Panama Canal in 1919 on his return to New Zealand, he discovered that many of the labourers working on the canal were from the British West Indies. He wrote: 'It is rather funny to watch their smiling black faces as they say, "we are of the same nationality as you."' One hopes Smith may have also found it a broadening experience.[52]

The British Empire was an environment of both inclusion and exclusion. In September 1920, the educated elites of Nigeria, Sierra Leone, Gambia and the Gold Coast met to demand change at the first National Congress of British West Africa held in Accra. The nature of the war had given people across the Empire a greater awareness of world affairs and a yearning to end discriminatory practice. The Congress called for Africans to be eligible for election to their legislative councils, the end of racial barriers in civil service appointments, compulsory school education and the establishment of a university in West Africa. Most of these proposals would be enacted. Nigeria, Sierra Leone and Gold Coast would all have partially elected legislatures by 1925; Africans were able to apply for more government positions; and Achimota College was opened in Accra.[53]

World War I was a catalyst for change. The British Empire reached its greatest extent in the early 1920s. However, the demands that equality and self-determination should apply to all people, and not just the privileged white minority, would gain strength and break down the old imperial order. As John Galsworthy wrote of the post-war world in the conclusion of his *Forsyte Saga*:

> The waters of change were foaming in, carrying the promise of new forms only when their destructive flood should have passed its full.[54]

World War I Timeline

1904

8 February–5 September 1905 Japan defeats Russia in Russo-Japanese War in northern China

8 April France and United Kingdom (UK) sign Entente Cordiale that improves relations between the two nations

1905

31 March–31 May 1906 First Moroccan Crisis

1910

3–19 December Liberal Prime Minister H.H. Asquith loses seats in UK election: requires support of Irish Nationalists to form government

1911

26 May UK Foreign Secretary Sir Edward Grey tells Dominion ministers attending Imperial Conference (23 May–20 June) of decline in British relations with Germany

22 June King George V is crowned in Westminster Abbey

1 July–4 November Second Moroccan Crisis

8–12 July King George V and Queen Mary visit Dublin

21 July David Lloyd George gives Mansion House Speech

July Brigadier Henry Wilson, the Director of Military Operations, devises plan for deploying British Expeditionary Force (BEF) to France in event of war with Germany

29 September Italy invades Ottoman Libya: first use of aircraft in warfare

12 December King-Emperor George V and Queen-Empress Mary hold Durbar in Delhi

1912

8 October First Balkan War begins: Bulgaria, Greece, Montenegro and Serbia attack Ottoman Empire and advance to the defensive lines protecting the Ottoman capital of Constantinople

3 December Ottomans sign armistice ending First Balkan War

1913

29 June Second Balkan War begins with Bulgaria attacking Greeks and Serbs in Macedonia

10 August Treaty of Bucharest ends Second Balkan War: Greece, Serbia and Romania gain territory at expense of Bulgaria

1914

JUNE
28 June Archduke Franz Ferdinand, heir to the Austro-Hungarian throne, and his wife Sophie assassinated by Bosnian Gavrilo Princip in Sarajevo

JULY
5 July Kaiser Wilhelm II tells Count Alexander von Hoyos, the civil service head of the Austro-Hungarian Foreign Ministry, that Germany will support Austria–Hungary in any military action it takes against Serbia

20 July Austria–Hungary presents ultimatum to Serbia

28 July Austria–Hungary declares war on Serbia

29 July Austro-Hungarian gunboats in Danube River bombard Belgrade

31 July Italy, a member of the Triple Alliance with Germany and Austria–Hungary, declares neutrality in war against Serbia

AUGUST
1 August Germany declares war on Russia; Montenegro declares war on Austria–Hungary in support of Serbia

2 August Germany invades Luxembourg and demands Belgium allow German troops to pass through its territory as part of General Helmuth von Moltke's strategy to defeat France first before transferring German troops eastward to defeat Russia

3 August Germany declares war on France

4 August Germany invades France; UK presents ultimatum to Germans to respect Belgian neutrality; UK declares war on Germany; UK imposes blockade on Germany that will result in German food shortages and increased mortality rates; Australian Imperial Force (AIF), Canadian Expeditionary Force (CEF) and New Zealand Expeditionary Force (NZEF) established

6 August French African troops invade German West African colony of Kamerun; Australian Naval and Military Expeditionary Force (ANMEF) created to capture German colonies in the Pacific

9 August BEF arrives in France

12 August Austria–Hungary invades Serbia but is pushed back by Serbian army

15 August NZEF captures German colony of Samoa in Pacific Ocean

20 August Russians defeat Germans in Battle of Gumbinnen on Eastern Front

23 August Battle of Mons: Germans force BEF to retreat from Belgium on Western Front; Japan declares war on Germany; forcing German East Asian Squadron to sail southwards towards South America

23 August–11 September Russians defeat Austro-Hungarians in Battle of Lemberg on Eastern Front

25 August British and French African troops from Gold Coast and Dahomey capture German colony of Togoland in West Africa

SEPTEMBER
2 September Sam Hughes, Canadian Militia and Defence Minister, creates Shell Committee to make artillery ammunition for UK

5 September Australian Labor Party led by Andrew Fisher wins national election

5–10 September First Battle of the Marne: French and BEF force Germans to retreat to Aisne River

11 September ANMEF captures German colony of New Guinea

14 September General Helmuth von Moltke sacked as German Chief of Staff following Battle of the Marne: replaced by General Erich von Falkenhayn; South Africa invades German South West Africa with African, 'coloured', Indian and white troops and auxiliaries

15 September White South Africans opposed to joining war revolt against government

22 September German cruiser *Emden* attacks Madras in India; German cruisers *Scharnhorst* and *Gneisenau* bombard Papeete, capital of French Polynesia in South Pacific and sink French gunboat *Zélée*

26 September first Indian troops arrive in France

OCTOBER
14 October first Canadian troops arrive in UK

19 October–24 November First Battle of Ypres in Belgium: French and BEF stop German advance; trench warfare begins on Western Front

20 October *Glitra* first British merchant ship sunk in war by German submarine *U-17*

26 October R.E. Dennett of Nigerian Forestry Department warns of economic crisis in Nigeria unless British create market for palm kernels

26–30 October Battle of Tannenberg on Eastern Front: General Paul von Hindenburg defeats Russians

28 October *Emden* sinks Russian cruiser *Zhemchug* and French destroyer *Mousquet* at Penang in Malaya

29 October Ottoman warships attack Russian fortifications and ships in Black Sea

NOVEMBER
1 November Russia declares war on Ottoman Empire; Battle of Coronel in South Pacific Ocean: German East Asian Squadron defeats Royal Navy's West Indies Squadron; AIF and NZEF convoy departs from Australia

2–7 November Battle of Tanga in German East Africa: Indian Expeditionary Force (IEF) B fails to capture port of Tanga

5 November France and UK declare war on Ottoman Empire

6 November IEF D captures Fao in Mesopotamia

7 November Japanese and British Empire troops capture Tsingtao, main city of German territory of Kiautchou in northern China

8 November *Sydney* defeats *Emden* at Cocos (Keeling) Islands in Indian Ocean

22 November Indian troops capture Basra in Mesopotamia

November Crayford Agreement allows UK women to do unskilled work in munition factories

DECEMBER
3 December AIF and NZEF begin disembarking in Egypt

8 December Battle of the Falkland Islands in South Atlantic Ocean: Royal Navy cruiser squadron defeats German East Asian Squadron

17 December–13 January 1915 French fight First Battle of Artois in a failed attempt to push Germans back from Noyon salient in northern France

20 December–17 March 1915 French fight First Battle of Champagne to push Germans back from Noyon salient

22 December–17 January 1915 Russians defeat Ottomans in Caucasus Mountains in Battle of Sarikamish

December India begins exporting munitions to UK

1915

JANUARY
8 January Japan makes failed attempt to take advantage of major powers being distracted by European war to issue 'Twenty-One Demands', which, if implemented, would have increased Japanese political and economic influence in China

24 January Reverend John Chilembwe leads revolt against British rule in Nyasaland

26 January–4 February Ottoman troops attack British Empire forces in Egypt along Suez Canal

30 January last South African rebels surrender to government forces

FEBRUARY
4 February Chilembwe killed by police: revolt quashed; German government declares sea surrounding Britain and Ireland a war zone where U-boats will attack merchant ships

15 February 5th Bengal Light Infantry mutiny in Singapore; General Sir John French approves the formation of tunnelling companies on the Western Front

25 February British and French begin naval operation to capture Dardanelles from Ottomans

MARCH

3 March New Zealand creates Department of Imperial Government Supplies to export food to UK

5 March 'Shell and Fuses Agreement' allows UK women to be employed as skilled workers in munitions factories

10-12 March Battle of Neuve Chapelle on Western Front: BEF attack fails

17 March 'Treasury Agreement' suspends for the duration of war all UK union restrictions that might limit production

18 March British and French have three battleships sunk and three damaged by Ottoman mines in Dardanelles: naval attempt to capture straits abandoned

22 March Austro-Hungarian fortress of Przemyśl surrenders to Russians after a 133-day siege

30 March King George V pledges to abstain from alcohol for duration of war

APRIL

13 April UK Board of Trade take control of all British Empire refrigerated ships sailing to Australia and New Zealand

22 April–25 May Second Battle of Ypres on Western Front: German attack using chlorine gas fails to defeat African, British, Canadian and French troops

25 April–9 January 1916 British and French Empire forces make failed attempt to use troops to capture Gallipoli peninsula

26 April Italy signs secret Treaty of London with France, Russia and UK that promises Italy territorial expansion in exchange for joining war

29 April German airships begin bombing Ipswich and other English east coast ports

April Ottoman fears of internal revolt in reaction to Russian victory in the Caucasus and Gallipoli landings lead to deportation and killing of Armenians and the deaths of between 600,000 and a million people

MAY

2 May–22 June Battle of Gorlice–Tarnow on Eastern Front: combined

German and Austro-Hungarian army defeat Russians who are forced into the 'great retreat' until September: German peace proposal rejected by Tsar Nicholas II

7 May German submarine sinks *Lusitania* off south coast of Ireland killing 1,198 people

9 May Battle of Aubers Ridge: BEF attack fails as part of the French Army's Second Battle of Artois (9 May–18 June)

12 May UK government release Bryce Report on German war crimes against Belgian civilians

14 May London *Times* editorial states British war effort is failing due to 'shell crisis'

15–25 May Battle of Festubert: BEF attack fails as part of larger French Second Battle of Artois

23 May Italy declares war on Austria–Hungary

25 May UK Liberal government replaced by coalition government with Asquith retaining prime ministership: Winston Churchill is sacked as First Lord of the Admiralty following Dardanelles debacle

JUNE
9 June UK creates Ministry of Munitions

19 June Munitions production begins in Moose Jaw, Saskatchewan

23 June–7 July Italy attacks Austria–Hungary in the Alps with little success in the first of the 12 battles of the Isonzo

JULY
6 July Railway Board Munitions Branch created in India

9 July South African troops capture German South West Africa

11 July British warships destroy the cruiser *Königsberg*, the last surviving German warship outside European waters, in the Rufiji river delta in German East Africa

18 July–3 August Italy attacks Austria–Hungary in the Alps with little success in the Second Battle of the Isonzo

AUGUST
Sir Dorabji Tata agrees to provide the entire output of his steel factory to the Government of India

SEPTEMBER

18 September Admiral Henning von Holtzendorff, German Chief of Naval Staff, orders halt to unrestricted submarine warfare

25 September–13 October Battle of Loos as part of larger French Third Battle of Artois (25 September–4 November): BEF use chemical weapons for first time but make little progress

September First battalion of the British West Indies Regiment created; 1st South African Infantry Brigade formed for service on Western Front

OCTOBER

7 October Austro-Hungarian and German armies invade and occupy Serbia

14 October Bulgaria declares war on Serbia and joins the invasion

18 October–3 November Italy attacks Austria–Hungary in the Alps with little success in the Third Battle of the Isonzo

25 October King George V calls on all men of the British Empire to volunteer for military service

30 October Australian Prime Minister Andrew Fisher resigns and is replaced by William Morris Hughes

NOVEMBER

4 November Australian government creates Australian Wheat Board to sell wheat to UK

10 November–2 December Italy attacks Austria–Hungary in the Alps with little success in the Fourth Battle of the Isonzo

22–25 November Ottoman and Indian Armies fight Battle of Ctesiphon south of Baghdad: Indian troops withdraw down Tigris River to Kut Al Amara

November Indian infantry divisions transferred from Western Front to fight Ottomans in Mesopotamian campaign

DECEMBER

6 December UK government demands General Sir John French resign as Commander-in-Chief BEF; replaced by General Sir Douglas Haig

7 December Ottomans begin siege of Indian force at Kut Al Amara

8–12 December Chantilly Conference near Paris plans Allied strategy for 1916 with offensives on Eastern, Italian and Western Fronts

December Thomas Thompson & Sons begin munitions production in Waterford in Ireland; 'coloured' men from Cape Town create the Cape Corps Battalion which serves in East Africa and Palestine

1916

JANUARY

5 January UK government introduces military conscription bill for single men and childless widowers aged 18 to 41 in Britain but not Ireland

6 January British Empire plan to dig deep mines beneath Messines Ridge approved: tunnelling commences soon afterwards

25 January Montenegro surrenders to Austria–Hungary

27 January United Kingdom creates Shipping Control Committee to make more efficient use of British Empire merchant ships

FEBRUARY

10 February surviving retreating Serbian soldiers reach Adriatic Sea and are transported by ship to Salonika in Greece

18 February British, Belgian and French African troops capture German colony of Kamerun in West Africa

19 February South African General Jan Smuts arrives at Mombasa in British East Africa to take command of the East African campaign

21 February–18 December Germans fight Battle of Verdun in a failed attempt to force France to surrender

MARCH

9 March Germany declares war on Portugal following the internment of German and Austro-Hungarian merchant ships in Lisbon harbour

9–17 March Italy attacks Austria–Hungary in the Alps with the aim to divert German resources away from the Battle of Verdun but with little success in the Fifth Battle of the Isonzo

APRIL

24–29 April Patrick Pearse proclaims Irish Republic in Dublin as part of failed rising against British rule: 15 leaders of revolt executed

29 April British Empire troops at Kut Al Amara surrender to Ottomans after a siege of 147 days

April Gold Coast farmers build roads to increase cocoa exports to UK

MAY

9 May Belgian African troops capture Kigali, administrative capital of Ruanda in German East Africa

25 May British conscription extended to married men aged 18 to 41

31 May–1 June Battle of Jutland in North Sea: largest naval battle of World War I: Germans sink more British warships but Royal Navy retains command of the sea

JUNE

4 June–20 September Russian General Aleksey Brusilov's offensive pushes the Austro-Hungarian Army back on the Eastern Front

12 June Members of International Association of Machinists working in 30 munition factories in Hamilton, Ontario, go on strike for four weeks in a failed attempt to gain better work conditions

17 June Belgian African troops capture Usumbura, main city of Urundi in German East Africa

JULY

1 July–18 November French and British Empire troops attack Germans in Somme Offensive on Western Front

9 July Arab force led by Hussein, Sharif of Mecca, captures Mecca from Ottomans

AUGUST

1 August New Zealand introduces military conscription for white men but not Maori

6–17 August Italy attacks Austria–Hungary in the Alps and successfully advances in the Sixth Battle of the Isonzo

27 August Romania declares war on Austria–Hungary

29 August Falkenhayn sacked as Chief of the German General Staff due to failure at Verdun: replaced by duo of Field Marshal Paul von Hindenburg and Quartermaster General Erich Ludendorff

SEPTEMBER

6 September Falkenhayn takes command of Ninth German Army for the invasion of Romania

14–17 September Italy attacks Austria–Hungary in the Alps without success in the Seventh Battle of the Isonzo

15 September Tanks used for the first time by British at the Battle of Flers–Courcelette on the Somme

September German navy resumes *de facto* unrestricted submarine warfare

OCTOBER
10–12 October Italy attacks Austria–Hungary in the Alps and successfully advances in the Eighth Battle of the Isonzo

28 October Australian referendum to introduce military conscription narrowly defeated by margin of 51.6 per cent 'no' to 48.4 per cent 'yes'

October Portuguese African troops make failed invasion of German East Africa

NOVEMBER
1–4 November Italy attacks Austria–Hungary in the Alps and makes a small advance in the Ninth Battle of the Isonzo

7 November Woodrow Wilson re-elected in US presidential election

14 November Australian Prime Minister William Morris Hughes and other Labor Party pro-conscriptionists leave Labor, joining with Liberal Party to create Nationalist Party

15 November General Robert Nivelle replaces General Joseph Joffre as Commander-in-Chief of the French Army on the Western Front

20 November South African Native Labour Corps (SANLC) created for service on Western Front

21 November Karl becomes Emperor of Austria–Hungary, following the death of his great-uncle Franz Josef: begins secret peace negotiations with France

November UK government agrees to purchase all Australian and New Zealand wool for the rest of the war

DECEMBER
5 December H.H. Asquith resigns as UK Prime Minister: succeeded by David Lloyd George

12 December German Chancellor Theobald von Bethmann Hollweg calls for a negotiated peace: Allies reject proposal

13 December Lieutenant General Sir Frederick Maude begins final British Empire offensive against Ottomans in Mesopotamia

18 December US President Woodrow Wilson issues peace note to no effect

22 December UK government creates Ministry of Shipping

December German potato crop fails: civilians forced to eat turnips as a substitute leading to increased mortality rates during northern hemisphere winter

1917

JANUARY
Most South African troops withdrawn from East African campaign due to illness; King's African Rifles expands because African soldiers best suited to fight in East Africa

FEBRUARY
1 February Germany formally recommences unrestricted submarine warfare

21 February *Mendi* carrying men of the SANLC sinks following collision in the English Channel resulting in deaths of 646 mostly black South Africans

24 February British Empire force recaptures Kut Al Amara in Mesopotamia

MARCH
8 March UK government approves construction of Ford Motor Factory in Cork

11 March British Empire force captures Baghdad in Mesopotamia

12–18 March German U-boats sink four US merchant ships

14 March Germans on Western Front withdraw to the shorter Hindenburg Line which can be held by a smaller number of troops

15 March Tsar Nicholas abdicates: Russia becomes a republic with Prince Lvov leading the provisional government

20 March President Wilson holds cabinet meeting that decides to declare war on Germany

26 March Ottomans defeat British Empire force at First Battle of Gaza

APRIL
6 April United States declares war on Germany

9-12 April Canadian Corps captures Vimy Ridge on Western Front

16 April Nivelle's offensive on Western Front fails: French Army refuse to take part in further attacks; Vladimir Lenin arrives in Russian capital Petrograd, having travelled with German assistance from Switzerland

17 April Ottomans defeat British Empire force at Second Battle of Gaza

23 April German conference agrees that a peace settlement should result in Germany gaining territory on the Baltic and Poland, French iron ore mines and all of Belgium

MAY

5 May Hughes' Nationalist Party retains government with an increased majority in Australian national election

10 May President Woodrow Wilson appoints General John Pershing to command the American Expeditionary Force (AEF) on the Western Front

10 May–8 June Italy attacks Austria–Hungary in the Alps; makes a small advance in the Tenth Battle of the Isonzo

15 May Nivelle is sacked and replaced by General Phillippe Pétain who rebuilds the French Army

18 May US introduces military conscription; Conservative Prime Minister Robert Borden calls for military conscription in Canada

26 May–6 June British Empire expends 3.5 million shells in the preparatory bombardment for the Battle of Messines in Belgium

May UK proposal to impose military conscription in Nigeria and Gold Coast is rejected; UK parliament passes Corn Production Act requiring farmers in Britain to plough grazing land to increase crop production

JUNE

1 June Jamaica introduces military conscription, but shipping shortage means no conscripts go overseas

7–14 June Battle of Messines commences with the detonation of 19 mines resulting in the largest human-made explosion to date

15 June First regular convoy sails from United States to United Kingdom

26 June First US troops arrive in France

28 June Greece declares war on Central Powers; General Sir Archibald Murray is removed as commander of Egyptian Expeditionary Force (EEF) following two defeats at Gaza and replaced by General Edmund Allenby

JULY

1–16 July Russian offensive on Eastern Front has initial success and then breaks down as army disintegrates

6 July Arab force captures Aqaba, the last Red Sea port held by the Ottomans

14 July Georg Michaelis replaces Bethmann Hollweg as German Chancellor; New Zealand government sends 14 conscientious objectors to Western Front and tortures men who refuse to do military service

17 July UK Royal family changes name from Saxe-Coburg-Gotha to Windsor; National War Aims Committee formed to bolster UK morale

19 July German Reichstag passes 'Peace Resolution' but is opposed by Hindenburg and Ludendorff

21 July Alexander Kerensky replaces Prince Lvov as Russian prime minister

31 July–10 November Third Battle of Ypres: British Empire force advances out of Ypres salient but suffers heavy casualties and fails to reach its objectives of capturing German airfields and U-boat bases

July Colonial government in Kenya orders mass conscription of males aged 18 to 30 to serve as carriers and labourers in East African campaign

AUGUST

14 August China declares war on Germany

16 August Pope Benedict XV issues peace note calling for return to 1914 boundaries

18 August–12 September Italy attacks Austria–Hungary in the Alps and makes a small advance in the Eleventh Battle of the Isonzo

August School-children in England, Scotland and Wales tasked to collect horse chestnuts for making explosives

SEPTEMBER

1 September Germans capture Russian port of Riga on Baltic Sea and threaten Russian capital of Petrograd

OCTOBER

15–18 October Battle of Mahiwa in German East Africa: last major battle of East African campaign: British African force loses more men, German African troops retreat into Portuguese East Africa where they capture weapons, rations and medicine from Portuguese troops

24 October–19 November Austro-Hungarian and German troops inflict major defeat on Italian Army in the Twelfth Battle of the Isonzo, also known as the Battle of Caporetto: UK and French send troops to Italy to stabilise line

27–31 October Third Battle of Gaza: EEF captures Beersheba

NOVEMBER
1 November Count Georg von Hertling replaces Georg Michaelis as German Chancellor

1–7 November EEF captures Gaza

6-10 November CEF captures Passchendaele ending the Third Battle of Ypres

7 November Bolsheviks led by Vladimir Lenin take power in Russia

20 November–7 December Battle of Cambrai: British use tanks to break German line, but German counter-attacks retake the lost ground

29 November London *Daily Telegraph* publishes letter by Marquess of Lansdowne calling for a negotiated peace with Germany

DECEMBER
6 December Two merchant ships – one carrying TNT and the other explosives – collide in Halifax harbour in Canada causing largest human-made explosion to date, killing or injuring 1,600 people; Finland declares independence from Russia

9 December Ottomans surrender Jerusalem to EEF

11 December Allenby formally enters Jerusalem

15 December Bolshevik government signs armistice with Austria–Hungary, Bulgaria, Germany and Ottoman Empire

17 December Canadian election supports introduction of conscription; Thomas Crerar of Manitoba Grain Growers' Association elected to parliament

20 December Australians vote second time to oppose introduction of military conscription

1918

JANUARY
8 January President Wilson outlines his 'Fourteen Points' for peace negotiations at a Joint Session of Congress in Washington DC

27 January–15 May Finnish Civil War fought between radical social democrats and conservatives leads to the death of almost 40,000 people: conservatives gain victory but Germans occupy Finland until war ends

FEBRUARY

9 February Austria–Hungary, Bulgaria, Germany and Ottoman Empire sign treaty recognising Ukrainian Republic as an independent state but claiming right to access food

25 February rationing of meat, butter and margarine introduced in London and surrounding region

MARCH

1 March Germans occupy Kiev

3 March German and Austro-Hungarian governments sign peace treaty with Russian government at Brest-Litovsk: Germany and Austria–Hungary aim to extract resources from Eastern Europe to continue war on the west

21 March–5 April 'Michael' offensive on Western Front: Germans break BEF line in northern France and advance eight miles on first day

23 March UK War Cabinet debates extending conscription to Ireland

26 March Marshal Ferdinand Foch appointed Commander-in-Chief of the Allied Armies on the Western Front

28 March Canadian soldiers fire on anti-conscription protesters in Quebec City resulting in four dead and 158 wounded

APRIL

7 April Food rationing imposed in England, Scotland and Wales

9 April British conscription extended to 50-year-old men

9-29 April 'Georgette' offensive on Western Front fails to capture northern French railway centre of Hazebrouck

23 April Irish Trade Union Congress calls general strike in opposition to Irish conscription: UK government abandons policy

24-26 April Germans capture town of Villers-Bretonneux near major railway junction at Amiens; AIF, BEF and French African troops counter-attack and retake town

MAY

7 May Treaty of Bucharest allows Germans and Austro-Hungarians to take food and resources from Romania

11 May Newfoundland introduces military conscription but no conscripts depart before end of war

15 May 5,000 farmers meet Borden in Ottawa to protest against the decision to conscript farmers' sons

27 May–5 June German 'Blücher' offensive in Chemin des Dames region of northern France takes ground but to no military advantage

JUNE

9–15 June Germans begin 'Gneisenau' offensive, west of the failed 'Blücher' offensive

11 June New Zealand government forcibly conscript Maori opposed to conscription

20 June Australian farmers protest in Melbourne at government decision to fix price of meat in metropolitan areas

JULY

4 July AEF, AIF and BEF troops advance in a combined operation using infantry, artillery, tanks and aircraft at Hamel, near Villers-Bretonneux, in northern France

9 July Irish and British schoolchildren called on to collect fruit for jam-making

10 July Ottomans create 'Army of Islam' to take advantage of collapse of Russian Army and invade Caucasus

15 July–6 August 'Marneschutz-Reims' operation: the final attack of the German offensive advances south of Marne river

18-20 July Allied counter-attack pushes Germans north of Marne

24 July Foch calls conference of Western Front commanders – Pétain, Haig and Pershing – to plan next Allied offensive

30 July Field Marshal Hermann von Eichhorn, German military governor of Ukraine, assassinated in Kiev

AUGUST

8 August Battle of Amiens in northern France: African, Australian, British,

Canadian, French and New Zealand troops of Fourth British Army and First French Army break through German lines and advance eight miles in one day: begins final hundred days of war

SEPTEMBER

2 September Germans begin retreat to Hindenburg Line

14 September Ottoman Army of Islam captures Baku oilfields on Caspian Sea

15 September Serbian, French and Greek troops break through Bulgarian lines on Salonika Front in Battle of Dobro Pole

19 September Battle of Megiddo in Palestine: a mostly Indian force, but including Australian, British, French, Irish, Italian, New Zealand, South African and West Indian soldiers, break through Ottoman lines

20–22 September West Indian troops advance in Jordan Valley

29 September British 46th Division break through Hindenburg Line at the Saint-Quentin Canal: Ludendorff tells Kaiser and German government that war is lost

30 September Georg von Hertling resigns as German Chancellor following Ludendorff's assessment of Germany's military position

OCTOBER

1 October EEF captures Damascus in Syria

3 October Prince Max von Baden becomes German chancellor

4 October German government requests an armistice based on President Wilson's Fourteen Points

24 October–3 November Allied Army of mostly Italian troops, but including French, UK and US soldiers, defeats the Austro-Hungarian Army in the Battle of Vittorio Veneto

25 October EEF captures Aleppo in Syria

29 October King Ferdinand I of Bulgaria signs armistice; German sailors refuse to take part in Admiral Rienhard Scheer's plan for the High Seas Fleet to fight final battle with the Royal Navy

31 October Ottoman Empire armistice comes into effect

NOVEMBER

3 November Austria–Hungary signs armistice; protests in German naval base of Kiel spread to rest of Germany

9 November Germany becomes a republic

10 November Kaiser Wilhelm goes into exile in the Netherlands

11 November World War I ends with armistice between Germany and Allies

13 November Emperor and King Karl of Austria–Hungary abdicates

25 November General Paul von Lettow-Vorbeck, on being informed of German armistice, surrenders to British authorities at Abercorn in Northern Rhodesia

DECEMBER
6 December Soldiers of 9th British West Indies Regiment mutiny at Taranto

14 December UK general election: all males over 21 and females over 30 who met a property qualification eligible to vote. Lloyd George's coalition government retains power. Sinn Féin wins 73 of 105 Irish seats; first Australian by-election held under preferential voting results in W.G. Gibson of Victorian Farmers Union winning seat

1919

JANUARY
12 January–28 June Paris Peace Conference

21 January Sinn Féin elected members meet in Mansion House in Dublin to declare Ireland independent and establish the Dáil Éireann (Irish Parliament); Irish War of Independence commences when Irish Republican Army (IRA) kills two Royal Irish Constabulary (RIC) police at Soloheadbeg in County Tipperary

28 January UK Cabinet decides to continue British conscription

MARCH
12 March–25 July Egyptian revolt caused by food shortages and opposition to British occupation results in deaths of 800 civilians

APRIL
13 April Colonel Reginald Dyer orders Indian soldiers to shoot into crowd in Amritsar in Punjab, killing 379 civilians

MAY
5 May Alexander Moore of United Farmers of Alberta elected to provincial legislature in by-election

6 May–8 August Third Afghan War results in British recognising Afghanistan as an independent state

OCTOBER
20 October United Farmers of Ontario and Labour Party form coalition government in Ontario

1920

APRIL
Mesopotamian revolt against British occupation begins

SEPTEMBER
Australian, Canadian and New Zealand governments refuse UK government request to send troops to Mesopotamia; Representatives from Nigeria, Sierra Leone, Gambia and the Gold Coast met in Accra for the first National Congress of British West Africa

OCTOBER
Mesopotamian revolt put down by mostly Indian troops

1921

JULY
18 July United Farmers of Alberta win provincial election and hold power for 14 years

21 July Sinn Féin and UK government agree to ceasefire

AUGUST
23 August Faisal becomes King of Iraq

DECEMBER
6 December Anglo-Irish Treaty divides Ireland into Irish Free State (Saorstát Éireann) and Northern Ireland

1922

22 February UK government grants Egypt partial independence

16 December Country Party gain balance of power in Australian federal election: Hughes forced to resign as prime minister as price for Country Party forming coalition with Nationalist Party

Notes

Introduction
The British Empire and World War I

1   [United Kingdom] War Office, *Statistics of the Military Effort of the British Empire during the Great War 1914–1920*, London, War Office, 1922, rep. Uckfield, East Sussex, Naval & Military Press, 1999, p. 756.

2   Jacqueline Jenkinson, '"All in the same uniform"? The participation of black colonial residents in the British Armed Forces in the First World War', *The Journal of Imperial and Commonwealth History*, Vol. 40, No. 2, June 2012, pp. 207–30; [United Kingdom] War Office, *Statistics of the Military Effort*, p. 756; 'Question of raising native troops for Imperial service', 18 October 1915, The National Archives of the United Kingdom, London (hereafter TNA), CO 537/604; 'Memorandum on steps taken to Increase the Supply of (a) Coloured [sic] Troops, (b) Coloured [sic] Labour, and on the use by the Naval and Military Authorities of Colonial Government Officials', January 1917, TNA, CAB 1/23; Timothy C. Winegard, *Indigenous Peoples of the British Dominions and the First World War*, Cambridge, Cambridge University Press, 2012, pp. 110, 117, 135.

3   Damien Fenton, *New Zealand and the First World War 1914–1919*, Auckland, Penguin, 2013, pp. 38–9.

4   Roger G. Thomas, 'The 1916 Bongo "Riots" and their background: Aspects of colonial administration and African response in Eastern Upper Ghana', *Journal of African History*, No. 24, 1983, pp. 61, 68, 74; John Connor, Peter Stanley & Peter Yule, *The War at Home*: Vol. 4 of Jeffrey Grey (ed.) *The Centenary History of Australia and the Great War*, Melbourne, Oxford University Press, 2015, pp. 70–2; L.L. Robson (ed.),

Australia and the Great War, Melbourne, Macmillan, 1969, pp. 86–7; Bryce Fraser (ed.) *Macquarie Book of Events*, Sydney, Macquarie Library, 1983 p. 263.

5   'Area and Population of the British Empire, by countries, 1911 and 1921', www66.statcan.gc.ca/eng/1922-23/192202200180_p.%20180.pdf, viewed 8 May 2018; A.J. Christopher, 'The quest for a census of the British *Empire c.*1840–1940', *Journal of Historical Geography*, Vol. 34, 2008, pp. 280–1; W.H. Mercer (ed.), *The Colonial Office List for 1914*, London, Waterlow & Sons, p. 200.

6   Ibid., p. 424.

7   Kenneth Rose, *King George V*, London, Phoenix Press, 2000, p. 78, 115; Philip Gibbs, 'The greatest day in the King's life. The Coronation from the King's point of view. An imaginative study', *London Magazine*, Vol. XXVI, No. 9, pp. 622, 626, 628.

8   Mercer, *Colonial List 1914*, pp. 361, 364.

9   [Singapore] *Straits Times*, 19 June 1911.

10 Ibid.

11 Carl Bridge & Kent Fedorowich, 'Mapping the British world', *Journal of Imperial and Commonwealth History*, Vol. 31, No. 2, 2003, pp. 1–15.

12 Committee of Imperial Defence Meeting, 26 May 1911, TNA, CAB 2/2.

13 Annika Mombauer (ed.), *The Origins of the First World War: Diplomatic and Military Documents,* Manchester, Manchester University Press, 2013, p. 44.

14 Mombauer, *Origins of the First World War*, pp. 46, 53.

15 J.S. Connolly (ed.), *The Oxford Companion to Irish History*, Oxford, Oxford University Press, 2007, pp. 257–8; [Dublin] *Irish Times*, 10 July 1911; [London] *Times*, 10 July 1911.

16 Rose, *King George V*, pp. 132–3.

17 James Pope-Hennessy, *Queen Mary, 1867–1953*, London, George Allen & Unwin, 1959, p. 458; Charles W. Nuckolls, 'The Durbar Incident', *Modern Asian Studies*, Vol. 24, No. 3, July 1998, pp. 529–59.

18 G.F. MacMunn, *The Armies of India*, London, Adam & Charles Black, 1911, pp. 14, 129.

19 [London] *Times*, 26 September 1914; Keith Jeffery, *Field Marshal Sir Henry Wilson: A Political Soldier*, Oxford, Oxford University Press, 2006, pp. 111, 129–30; Connolly, *Oxford Companion to Irish History*, pp. 258, 282, 594.

20 Lawrence Sondhaus, *World War One: The Global Revolution*, Cambridge, Cambridge University Press, 2011, pp. 40, 44.

21 Ibid., p. 48; Mombauer, *Origins of the First World War*, p. 193.

22 Sondhaus, *World War One*, pp. 51, 54–5; Mombauer, *Origins of the First World War*, pp. 311–12, 352–6, 404, 482, 522.

23   Sondhaus, *World War One*, pp. 52, 54–5, 57; H.V. Marrot, *The Life and Letters of John Galsworthy*, London, William Heinemann, 1935, p. 396.

1
1914: The *Emden* in the Indian Ocean

1   *Madras Mail Tri-Weekly Supplement*, 24 September 1914; [Bombay] *Times of India*, 24 September 1914; Dan van der Vat, *The Last Corsair: The Story of the* Emden, London, Hodder & Stoughton, 1983, pp. 61–5.

2   *Madras Mail Tri-Weekly Supplement*, 24 September 1914.

3   Van der Vat, *Last Corsair*, p. 61; [Bombay] *Times of India*, 15 October 1914.

4   Van der Vat, *Last Corsair*, p. 66; [London] *Times*, 13 July 1908, 26 December 1910, 24 January 1911, 4 July 1914.

5   [Bombay] *Times of India*, 25 & 29 September, 14 October, 4 November 1914.

6   C. Ernest Fayle, *Seaborne Trade*, Vol. I, *History of the Great War based on Official Documents. By Direction of the Historical Section of the Committee of Imperial Defence*, John Murray, London, 1920, pp. 210, 216; [Bombay] *Times of India*, 29 September, 16 October 1914; *Encyclopaedia Britannica*, 11th edition, Cambridge, Cambridge University Press, 1911, Vol. 22, p. 866.

7   Fayle, *Seaborne Trade*, pp. 199, 210; Omkhar Goswani, 'Collaboration and conflict: Europeans and Indian capitalists and the jute economy of Bengal, 1919–39', *The Indian Economic and Social History*, Vol. XIX, No. 2, 1982, pp. 141–79; Morris D. Morris, 'The growth of large-scale industry to 1947', in Dharma Kumar (ed.), *The Cambridge Economic History of India*, Vol. 2, pp. 568–9; Tara Sethia, 'The rise of the jute manufacturing industry in colonial India: A global perspective', *Journal of World History*, Vol. 7, No. 1, Spring 1996, pp. 71–99.

8   Fayle, *Seaborne Trade*, p. 215; [Narrabri] *North Western Courier*, 19 August 1914; [Calcutta] *Capital* [September 1914] quoted in *Sydney Morning Herald*, 6 October 1914.

9   [Calcutta] *Capital* [October 1914] quoted in [Melbourne] *Argus*, 7 November 1914; [Calcutta] *Capital*, 8 & 15 October 1914; [Sydney] *Daily Commercial and Shipping List*, 4 September 1914.

10   [Bombay] *Times of India*, 24 October 1914; telegram, Lord Hardinge, Indian Viceroy, to Sir Ronald Munro Ferguson, Australian Governor-General, 14 October 1914; letters, W. Freeman Nott, Secretary Melbourne Chamber of Commerce, to S. Mills, Australian Comptroller-General Customs, 29 October 1914; Frederick Winchcombe, President Sydney

Chamber of Commerce, to Mills, 5 November 1914, National Archives of Australia, Canberra (hereafter NAA) A2, 1916/3598 Pt 1.

11　Wm Roger Louis, *Great Britain and Germany's Lost Colonies 1914–1919*, Oxford, Clarendon Press, 1967, pp. 10–14.

12　Vice Admiral Günther von Krosigk, 'Memorandum on the importance of cruiser warfare in the event of war against England', April 1911, 'Most high orders to His Majesty's Ships abroad in case of war', 17 March 1914, in Jürgen Tampke (trans. & ed.), *'Ruthless Warfare': German Military Planning and Surveillance in the Australia–New Zealand Region before the Great War*, Canberra, Southern Highlands Publishers, 1998, pp. 71, 178.

13　Van der Vat, *Last Corsair*, p. 38–42, 48; David Stevens, *In All Respects Ready: Australia's Navy in World War One*, Melbourne, Oxford University Press, 2014, p. 45; Julian S. Corbett, *Naval Operations*, Vol. 1: *To the Battle of the Falkands, December 1914. History of the Great War based on official documents by direction of the Historical Section of the Committee of Imperial Defence*, London, Longmans, Green & Co, 1920, pp. 341–57, 415–36.

14　Corbett, *Naval Operations*, Vol. 1, pp. 283, 289–9; Fayle, *Seaborne Trade*, Vol. 1, p. 331.

15　[London] *Times*, 22 September 1914.

16　Peter Overlack, 'The force of circumstance: Graf Spee's options for the Cruiser Squadron in August 1914', *Journal of Military History*, Vol. 60, No. 4, October 1996, p. 680; Archibald Hurd, *The Merchant Navy*, Vol. 1, *History of the Great War based on official documents. By direction of the Historical Section of the Committee of Imperial Defence*, London, John Murray, 1921, pp. 198–9; Fayle, *Seaborne Trade*, Vol. 1, pp. 116, 213–14.

17　Hurd, *Merchant Navy*, Vol. 1, p. 189.

18　Ibid., pp.190–1; Fayle, *Seaborne Trade*, Vol. 1, p. 205.

19　Hurd, *Merchant Navy*, Vol. 1 pp. 191–2.

20　Fayle, *Seaborne Trade*, Vol. 1, p. 207.

21　Letter, Arthur G. Bray to mother, 20 September 1914, Imperial War Museum, London (hereafter IWM) Documents (hereafter Docs), 6653.

22　Hurd, *Merchant Navy*, Vol. 1, pp. 192–3; Cayzer, Irvine & Co. Weekly Report, 21 August 1914, Cayzer Archives, London, CAY/BS/CLS/4; van der Vat, *Last Corsair*, p. 57.

23　Ibid., p. 58; Hurd, *Merchant Navy*, Vol. 1, p. 193.

24　Letter Bray to mother, 20 September 1914, IWM, Docs.6653.

25　Corbett, *Naval Operations*, Vol. 1, pp. 297–8.

26　Fayle, *Seaborne Trade*, Vol. 1, p. 207; Hurd, *Merchant Navy*, Vol. 1, pp. 194–5; Corbett, *Naval Operations*, Vol. 1, p. 301; van der Vat, *Last Corsair*, pp. 70–1.

27　Letter, Burdick & Cook to Rear Admiral Herbert Savory, Director of Transports, Admiralty, 2 October 1914, TNA, MT 23/319; Hurd, *Merchant Navy*, Vol. 1, p. 196.

28   Hubert Foster, *War and the Empire: The Principles of Imperial Defence*, London, Williams & Norgate, 1914, pp. 77–8; Mercer, *Colonial List 1914*, p. 30.

29   Foster, *War and the Empire*, p. 78; Stevens, *In All Respects Ready*, p, 38; van der Vat, *Last Corsair*, pp. 70–1.

30   Ibid., pp. 72–4; Hurd, *Merchant Navy*, Vol. 1, p. 197; Fayle, *Seaborne Trade*, Vol. 1, p. 333.

31   Mercer, *Colonial Office List*, p. 250; van der Vat, *Last Corsair*, pp. 75–7; Hurd, *Merchant Navy*, Vol. 1, p. 197; Corbett, *Naval Operations*, Vol. 1, p. 333.

32   Van der Vat, *Last Corsair*, p. 76.

33   Ibid., pp. 83–4.

34   Ibid., pp. 51–3.

35   Roger Chickering, *Imperial Germany and the Great War, 1914–1918*, 3rd ed., Cambridge, Cambridge University Press, 2014, p. 41; van der Vat, *Last Corsair*, p. 77.

36   Hurd, *Merchant Navy*, Vol. 1, p. 197; Corbett, *Naval Operations*, Vol. 1, p. 333.

37   Hurd, *Merchant Navy*, Vol. 1, pp. 198–202; Fayle, *Seaborne Trade*, Vol. 1, p. 275; Corbett, *Naval Operations*, Vol. 1, pp. 333–4; [Bombay] *Times of India*, 24 October 1914.

38   Corbett, *Naval Operations*, Vol. 1, pp. 336–7; van der Vat, *Last Corsair*, pp. 85–8; diary, W.M. Meager, 28 October 1914, IWM, Docs.11172.

39   Ibid.

40   Corbett, *Naval Operations*, Vol. I, pp. 337; letter, Arthur Young, Governor Straits Settlements, to Lewis Harcourt, UK Colonial Secretary, 14 January 1915, TNA, CO 273/420.

41   Corbett, *Naval Operations*, Vol. 1, pp. 337; Hurd, *Merchant Navy*, Vol. 1, pp. 202–3; van der Vat, *Last Corsair*, pp. 92–3.

42   Fayle, *Seaborne Trade*, Vol. 1, p. 151; van der Vat, *Last Corsair*, pp. 100–2.

43   Francis Younghusband, 'India' in Charles Lucas (ed.), *The Empire at War*, Vol. 5, London, Oxford University Press, 1926, pp. 179, 180–1, 202; Corbett, *Naval Operations*, Vol. 1, pp. 154–5, 280–1.

44   Corbett, *Naval Operations*, Vol. 1, pp. 288–9, 294–5; Fayle, *Seaborne Trade*, Vol. 1, pp. 140, 214–5; [Bombay] *Times of India*, 16 & 24 October 1914.

45   Letter, Joseph Pope, Canadian External Affairs Under-Secretary, to Maurice Pope, 1 October 1914, Canadian War Museum/Musée Canadien de la Guerre, Ottawa, Maurice Pope papers, 58A 1 177, Folder 13; A. Fortescue Duguid, *Official History of the Canadian Forces in the Great*

War 1914–1919, Ottawa, J.O. Partenaude, 1938, Vol. 1, pp. 105, 108; letter, Harcourt to Duke of Connaught, Canadian Governor-General, 28 October 1914, Bodleian Library, Oxford (hereafter BLO), dep. 476, f. 194.

46 Letter, William Massey, New Zealand Prime Minister, to Andrew Fisher, Australian Prime Minister, 2 October 1914, NAA, A2657, Vol. 2; Corbett, *Naval Operations*, Vol. 1, p. 299; Ian McGibbon (ed.), *The Oxford Companion to New Zealand Military History*, Auckland, Oxford University Press, 2000, p. 92.

47 'Report of the Standing Sub-Committee of the Committee of Imperial Defence appointed to enquire into the question of the Oversea Transport of Reinforcements in Time of War', 16 June 1910, CID Paper 116-B, TNA, CAB 4/3, f. 75; C.E.W. Bean, *The Story of ANZAC from the Outbreak of War to the End of the First Phase of the Gallipoli Campaign, May 4, 1915*, Vol. 1 of C.E.W. Bean (ed.), *The Official History of Australia in the War of 1914–1918* (1st pub. 1921, Sydney, Angus & Robertson, 1942) p. 87; A.W. Jose, *The Royal Australian Navy*, Vol. 9 of Bean (ed.), *Official History of Australia*, pp. 151, 153, 156, 161; memo, Brigadier-General William Bridges GOC AIF to Senator George Pearce, Australian Defence Minister, 26 September 1914, NAA: A2657, Vol. 2; letter, Rear Admiral Sir William Creswell, First Naval Member, Australian Naval Board, to James Allen, New Zealand Defence Minister, 26 October 1914, Archives New Zealand/Te Rua Mahara o te Kāwanatanga, Wellington (hereafter ANZ), Allen Papers, 1/M1/14.

48 Jose, *Royal Australian Navy*, p. 19; Corbett, *Naval Operations*, Vol. 1, pp. 138, 149, 379–80; ship's log, *Empress of Asia*, 4 August 1914, TNA, ADM 53/40798; memo, Admiral Sir Henry Jackson, Chief of Staff, to Winston Churchill, UK First Lord of the Admiralty, 27 October 1914, Churchill Archives Centre, Cambridge (hereafter CAC), CHAR, 13/43/60-63.

49 Diary, Gunner Edgar Mole, 7 & 8 August, 8, 15 & 26 October 1914, IWM, Docs.6881; ship's log, *Empress of Asia*, 16 & 26 October 1914, TNA, ADM 53/40798; Corbett, *Naval Operations*, Vol. 1, p. 333.

50 Stevens, *In All Respects Ready*, pp, 73–7; Corbett, *Naval Operations*, Vol. 1, pp. 382, 384.

51 Corbett, *Naval Operations*, Vol. 1, pp. 380–1; van der Vat, *Last Corsair*, p. 116; Stevens, *In All Respects Ready*, p. 79; diary, Able Seaman Richard Broome, IWM, Docs.7427; diary, Mole, 9 & 16 November 1914, IWM, Docs.6881.

52 Diary, Mole, 1 October 1914, IWM Docs.6881.

53 Van der Vat, *Last Corsair*, pp. 116–17; letter, Lord Stamfordham, Private Secretary to King George V, to Churchill, 10 November 1914, CAC,

CHAR 13/45/158; telegram, Churchill to Vice Admiral Sir Martyn Jerram, Commander-in-Chief China Station, 11 November 1914, CAC, CHAR 13/35/18.

54   [Bombay] *Times of India*, 14 November 1914; Goswani, 'Collaboration and conflict', p. 148.

2
Shipping, Trade and Rationing

1   Hurd, *Merchant Navy*, Vol. 1, p. 85; Ministry of Shipping, 'Memorandum by the Parliamentary Secretary on the Nationalisation of Shipping . . .', p. 11, 26 January 1917, TNA, CAB 1/23; C. Ernest Fayle, *The War and the Shipping Industry*, London, Oxford University Press, 1927, p. 261; Fayle, *Seaborne Trade*, Vol. 1, p. 5.

2   Foster, *War and the Empire*, p. 56.

3   Fayle, *Seaborne Trade*, Vol. 1, p. 3.

4   Source: Ibid.

5   Ibid., pp. 3–4.

6   Fayle, *War and the Shipping Industry*, p. 24; J.A. Salter, *Allied Shipping Control: An Experiment in International Administration*, London, Oxford University Press, 1921, p. 90.

7   Archibald Hurd, *The Merchant Navy* Vol. 2, London, John Murray, 1924, p. vii; Salter, *Allied Shipping Control*, pp. 1, 110; Belinda Davis, 'Food and nutrition (Germany)', 8 October 2014, encyclopedia.1914–1918-online. net/article/food_and_nutrition_germany (accessed 15 May 2018).

8   Mercer, *Colonial Office List*, pp. 419–21; [Singapore] *Straits Times*, 12 August 1914.

9   Charles Lucas (ed.), *The Empire at War*, Vol. 5, London, Oxford University Press, 1926, p. 421; [Singapore] *Straits Times*, 12 August 1914.

10   Letter, J. West Ridgeway, Chairman British North Borneo Court of Directors, to Sir John Anderson, Under-Secretary Colonial Office, 5 August 1914, TNA, CO 531/6; Mercer, *Colonial Office List*, pp. 364, 478.

11   David Blaazer, '"Not only patriotism but self-interest": War, money and finance in British public discourse 1914–1925', *War & Society*, Vol. 23, Special Number, September 2005, pp. 3–6; letter, W.P. Flynn, British North Borneo Court of Directors Assistant Secretary & Accountant, to Anderson, 7 August 1914, TNA, CO 531/6; Lucas, *Empire at War*, Vol. 5, p. 421.

12   Letter, Ralph Paget, Under-Secretary Foreign Office to Anderson, 10 September 1914, TNA, CO 273/415; [Singapore] *Straits Times*, 9 October & 3 November 1914.

13   Mercer, *Colonial Office List*, facing p. 1, pp. 275, 280–1; Margery Perham,

Lugard: The Years of Authority 1898–1945, London, Collins, 1960, p. 579; Akinjide Osuntokun, *Nigeria in the First World War*, London, Longman, 1979, p. 23.

14 Mercer, *Colonial Office List*, p. 280; Peter J. Yearwood, 'The expatriate firms and the colonial economy of Nigeria in the First World War', *Journal of Imperial and Commonwealth History*, Vol. 26, No. 1, January 1998, p. 51; telegram, Alexander Boyle, Nigeria Deputy Governor-General, to Harcourt, 16 August 1914, memo, Alfred J. Harding, Colonial Secretary's Assistant Private Secretary, 10 September 1914, TNA, CO 583/17, ff. 423, 441; Osuntokun, *Nigeria in the First World War*, pp. 23, 26.

15 [London] *Financial Times*, 30 October 1914; Mercer, *Colonial Office List*, p. 290; Osuntokun, *Nigeria in the First World War*, p. 31.

16 Memo, 21 August 1914, TNA, CO 583/17, f. 420; Osuntokun, *Nigeria in the First World War*, pp. 26, 30–1.

17 Memo, 'Palm nut kernel cake and meal', 6 November 1914, London Chamber of Commerce, West African Section; 'The War as affecting West African Trade. Palm Kernels. Report of the Special Committee appointed by the Section on 18th September, 1914, to consider the question of the Palm Kernel Industry as affected by the War', 5 March 1915, p. 2, TNA, AY 4/1211; Osuntokun, *Nigeria in the First World War*, pp. 30–1.

18 Letter, Professor Wyndham Dunstan, Director Imperial Institute, to Sir Sydney Olivier, Board of Agriculture and Fisheries, 30 October 1914; *Coconut Cake and Palmnut Kernel Cake*, Board of Agriculture and Fisheries Special Leaflet No. 20, p. 1; 'The War as affecting West African Trade', pp. 2–3, TNA, AY 4/1211.

19 Letter, Sir Frederick Lugard, Nigerian Governor-General, to Andrew Bonar Law, Colonial Secretary, 4 December 1915, TNA, CO 583/38 ff. 3, 542; Ayodeji Olukoju, 'Elder Dempster and the shipping trade of Nigeria during the First World War', *Journal of African History*, Vol. 33, No. 2, 1992, pp. 257–9; Osuntokun, *Nigeria in the First World War*, p. 61; Yearwood, 'Expatriate firms and the colonial economy', pp. 52–3.

20 Memo, Edward Harding, Assistant Private Secretary to Colonial Secretary, to Charles Strachey, Principal Clerk, Colonial Office, 1 January 1916, TNA, CO 583/38, f. 537.

21 Olukoju, 'Elder Dempster and the shipping trade', pp. 264–6; Yearwood, 'Expatriate firms and the colonial economy', pp. 52–3.

22 Olukoju, 'Elder Dempster and the shipping trade', pp. 259, 263.

23 Olukoju, 'Elder Dempster and the shipping trade', pp. 260–1.

24 Osuntokun, *Nigeria in the First World War*, pp. 28–29, 37, 44; memo, Harding, 17 May 1916, TNA CO 583/45, f. 590; Olukoju, 'Elder Dempster and the shipping trade', pp. 270–1.

25 Donald R, Pearce, *The Senate Speeches of W.B. Yeats*, London, Faber & Faber, 1961, pp. 80–1.

26 Marguerite Helmers, *Harry Clarke's War: Illustrations for Ireland's Memorial Records 1914–1918*, Sallins, Co. Kildare, Irish Academic Press, 2016, pp. 47; [Dublin] *Irish Times*, 12 February, 23, 24 & 27 June 1916; *Irish Builder and Engineer*, 26 February 1916, p. 77.

27 Shirley Anne Brown, 'Wilhelmina Geddes' Ottawa window', *Irish Arts Review*, Vol. 10, 1994, pp. 181–8; [Dublin] *Irish Times*, 9 November 1917.

28 Fayle, *War and the Shipping Industry*, pp. 35–6; Fayle, *Seaborne Trade*, Vol. 1, p. 9; Argentine Cargo Line, Application for a Certificate of Incorporation, 21 February 1908, TNA, BT 31/96942.

29 Fayle, *Seaborne Trade*, Vol. 1, p. 9; letter, Gordon Campbell, Weddel & Co, to Brigadier-General Long, Director of Supplies, 11 November 1914, NAA, BT 13/60; Argentine Cargo Line, Board Meeting Minutes, 7 October 1914, 6 October 1915, National Maritime Museum, London (hereafter NMM), FWS/C/1/4, ff. 76–8, 83; [Sydney] *Daily Commercial News and Shipping List*, 23 September, 1 October, 30 November 1914, 23 February & 10 August 1915; [Melbourne] *Leader*, 3 October 1914.

30 C. Ernest Fayle, *Seaborne Trade*, Vol. 2, London, John Murray, 1923, pp. 79–81; Fayle, *War and the Shipping Industry*, pp. 114, 139; Mercer, *Colonial List*, p. 630; [Brisbane] *Telegraph*, 23 November 1914; 'Argentine Meat Trade. Conference – August 26th, 1914', 'Supply of Refrigerated Meat. Distribution of Refrigerated Tonnage. Board of Trade, 9th December, 1914', 10 December 1914, TNA, BT 13/60.

31 Fayle, *War and the Shipping Industry*, p. 143; Argentine Cargo Line, Board Meeting Minutes, 19 May 1915 & 11 October 1916, NMM, FWS/C/1/4, ff. 79–80, 98; Fayle, *Seaborne Trade*, Vol. 2, p. 86.

32 Ibid., Vol. 2, pp. 180–5; Fayle, *War and the Shipping Industry*, pp. 114–15, 133–4, 157.

33 Fayle, *Seaborne Trade*, Vol. 2, pp. 227–9; communiqué, F.P. Robinson, Requisitioning (Carriage of Foodstuffs) Committee, to Walter Runciman, President Board of Trade, 27 January 1916, TNA, CO 323/709.

34 Fayle, *Seaborne Trade*, Vol. 2, pp. 258, 342, 368.

35 John Connor, Peter Stanley & Peter Yule, *The War at Home*: Vol. 4 of Jeffrey Grey (ed.) *The Centenary History of Australia and the Great War*, Melbourne, Oxford University Press, 2015, pp. 45–6.

36 Paul G. Halpern, *A Naval History of World War I*, Annapolis, Maryland, Naval Institute Press, 1994, pp. 291, 300.

37 Ibid., pp. 293–7.

38 Ibid., pp. 299, 302.

39 Ibid., pp. 304–5, 308.

40 Ibid., pp. 226–8.
41 Fayle, *Seaborne Trade*, Vol. 2, p. 373; Fayle, *War and the Shipping Industry*, pp. 193–4, 203–5; letter, Sir Hubert Llewellyn Smith, Secretary Board of Trade, to Sutherland, 7 December 1916, TNA, MT 9/1620.
42 'Controller of Shipping', 11 December 1916, TNA, ADM 116/1520.
43 C. Ernest Fayle, *Seaborne Trade*, Vol. 3, London, John Murray, 1924, p. 17.
44 Ibid., pp. 122–3, 282–3; Fayle, *War and the Shipping Industry*, p. 231.
45 Algernon Aspinall, 'The war effort of the British West Indies' and T.E. Fell & A. Somers Cox, 'Barbados', in Charles Lucas (ed.), *The Empire at War*, Vol. 2, London, Oxford University Press, 1923, pp. 328, 355, 369–70.
46 [Sydney] *Farmer and Settler*, 6 June 1917; letter, Colonel G. Sanders, Purchasing Officer, Indian Army Supplies, Sydney to Reginald Brade, Permanent Under-Secretary War Office, 14 June 1918, TNA, MUN 4/5296.
47 Telegram, T. Ryan, Secretary Indian Munitions Board, to George Steward, Australian Governor-General Private Secretary, 20 July 1917, NAA: A11803, 1917/89/881; letter, Malcolm Shepherd, Secretary Prime Minister's Department, to Steward, 19 July 1918, NAA: A11803, 1918/89/663.
48 Mercer, *Colonial List*, pp. 298–300.
49 J. Louis Devaux, 'Report on the effects of the war on the colony of Seychelles and of the special organisations brought into being and legislation enacted on account of the war', 24 October 1919, pp. 4–7, 9, TNA, CAB11/165.
50 David Stevenson, *1914–1918: The History of the First World War*, London, Allen Lane, 2004, pp. 260–2.
51 Halpern, *Naval History*, pp. 338–9; Fayle, *War and the Shipping Industry*, p. 245; Salter, *Allied Shipping Control*, pp. 69, 80, 122.
52 Source: Fayle, *War and the Shipping Industry*, p. 417.
53 Halpern, *Naval History*, pp. 341–2.
54 Hurd, *Merchant Navy*, Vol. 3, pp. 8–9, 11–13.
55 Ibid., pp. 269–70.
56 Hurd, *Merchant Navy*, Vol. 2, p. 259; [London] *Financial Times*, 27 May 1916; Argentine Cargo Line, Board Meeting Minutes, 11 October 1916, p. 94, NMM, FWS/C/1/4.
57 [Dundee] *Courier and Argus*, 5 December 1917; [Hull] *Daily Mail*, 5 December 1917; Argentine Cargo Line, Board Meeting Minutes, 27 February 1918, p. 106, NMM FWS/C/1/4.
58 Letter, R. Smiles, Master *La Blanca* to Naval Control Officer, Dartmouth, 24 November 1917, John Clark, 'Re the Late s.s. "La Blanca"' [November 1917], 'SS "La Blanca" Enquiry into loss of' [December 1917], TNA, ADM 137/3285, [Hull] *Daily Mail*, 5 December 1917.

59 Argentine Cargo Line, Special resolution, 14 March 1918, TNA, BT 31/96942.

60 Hurd, *Merchant Navy*, Vol. 2, pp. 234, 237–8; Vol. 3, pp. 109, 130–1, 136.

61 Halpern, *Naval History*, p. 354; Fayle, *War and the Shipping Industry*, pp. 286–7; Hurd, *Merchant Navy*, Vol. 3, p. 88; Salter, *Allied Shipping Control*, pp. 125–6, 128.

62 Fayle, *War and the Shipping Industry*, p. 325; *The Elder Dempster Fleet in the War*, Liverpool, Elder Dempster & Co Ltd, 1921, p. 8.

63 War Cabinet Meeting 297, 13 December 1917, Ministry of Food, 'Report by Departmental Committee on Rationing and Distribution as to Scale of Rations', January 1918, pp. 11, 16, TNA, MAF 60/108; Ministry of Food, 'History of Rationing', TNA, MAF 60/109; Wilson, *Myriad Faces of War*, pp. 513, 530, 534.

64 War Cabinet meeting 285, 28 November 1917; Ministry of Food, 'Report by Departmental Committee on Rationing and Distribution as to Scale of Rations', January 1918, p. 2; Lord Rhondda, 'Compulsory Rationing. Further Memorandum by the Food Controller', 24 January 1918; UK War Cabinet Minute 334, 30 January 1918, TNA, MAF 60/108; Wilson, *Myriad Faces of War*, p. 649.

65 Circular letter 1009, L.A. Selby-Bigge, Board of Education, 15 August 1917, letters Board of Education to W.P.H. Vaughan, Roscrea, Co. Tipperary, 24 August 1917, James C. Young to A.R. Ainsworth, Board of Education, 22 August 1918, TNA, ED 10/74; [London] *Times*, 18 August 1917.

66 R.H. Carr, Ministry of Food Control, to H.A.L. Fisher, Secretary Board of Education, 20 July 1918, TNA, ED 10/73.

67 Letter, R.S. Wood, Board of Education, to Tracy Higgins, Hanslope Central School, near Stony Stratford, Buckinghamshire, 24 August 1917, TNA, ED 10/74; [Dublin] *Irish Times*, 13 October 1917, 12 August, 28 September 1918; [London] *Times*, 27 July, 9 September 1918.

68 [Dublin] *Irish Times*, 12 & 26 August, 28 September 1918; [London] *Times*, 12 September 1918; [Chelmsford] *Essex County Chronicle*, 12 July & 16 August 1918.

3
1915: The Three Battles of Aubers Ridge, France

1 Diary, Lieutenant Colonel J.W. Barnett, Regimental Medical Officer, 34th Sikh Pioneers, 10 March 1915, quoted in George Morton-Jack, *The Indian Army on the Western Front: India's Expeditionary Force to France and Belgium in the First World War*, Cambridge, Cambridge University Press, 2014, pp. 230–2; Jack Sheldon, *The German Army on the Western Front*

1915, Barnsley, Pen & Sword, 2012, p. 45; J.E. Edmonds & G.C. Wynne, *Military Operations, France and Belgium, 1915*, Vol. 1, London, Macmillan & Co, 1927, pp. 69–70, 84, 91–96, 114; Sanders Marble, *British Artillery on the Western Front in the First World War*, Farnham, Ashgate, 2013, p. 83; Spencer Jones, '"To make war as we must, and not as we should like": The British Army and the problem of the Western Front, 1915', in Spencer Jones (ed.), *Courage Without Glory: The British Army on the Western Front 1915*, Solihull, Helion, 2015, p. 45; J.P. Harris, *Douglas Haig and the First World War*, Cambridge, Cambridge University Press, 2008, p. 112; Gary Sheffield, *The Chief: Douglas Haig and the British Army*, London, Aurum Press, 2011, p. 104.

2   Edmonds & Wynne, *1915*, Vol. 1, pp. vi, 3; J.E. Edmonds, *Military Operations France and Belgium, 1915*, Vol. 2, London, Macmillan & Co, 1928, p. 393.

3   Letter, Field Marshal Sir John French to Brigadier-General Hubert Gough, 23 March 1914, 'Circular announcing the resignation of Field Marshal Sir John French . . .', 30 March 1914, in Ian F.W. Beckett (ed.), *The Army and the Curragh Incident, 1914*, London, The Bodley Head, 1986, pp. 218–9, 234–5; Roy A. Prete, *Strategy and Command: The Anglo-French Coalition on the Western Front, 1914*, Montreal & Kingston, McGill-Queen's University Press, 2009, pp. 33, 81–2; Holger H. Herwig, *The Marne, 1914: The Opening of World War I and the Battle That Changed the World*, New York, Random House, 2009, pp. 78, 85.

4   Prete, *Strategy and Command*, pp. 97, 101–4; Herwig, *Marne*, pp. 152–4, 182–3.

5   Prete, *Strategy and Command*, pp. 105, 108–9; Herwig, *Marne*, pp. 105, 193; John Spencer, 'Friends disunited: Johnnie French, Wully Robertson and "K of K" in 1915', in Jones (ed.), *Courage Without Glory*, p. 80.

6   Herwig, *Marne*, pp. 156, 198, 219–21.

7   Ibid., pp. 226, 231; Prete, *Strategy and Command*, p. 111.

8   Ibid., p. 107; Herwig, *Marne*, p. 222.

9   Prete, *Strategy and Command*, pp. 113–15; E.L. Spears, *Liaison, 1914: A Narrative of the Great Retreat*, London, William Heinemann, 1930, p. 417.

10   Herwig, *Marne*, pp. 240–4, 277; Prete, *Strategy and Command*, pp. 114–15, 118; Ian F.W. Beckett, *Ypres: The First Battle 1914*, Harlow, Pearson Education, 2004, p. 12.

11   Beckett, *Ypres*, pp. 5, 15–16.

12   Ibid., pp. 24–5, 34–5.

13   Ibid., pp. 5, 24–5, 47, 68; Morton-Jack, *Indian Army*, pp. 135–6, 139, 142; Graham Winton, 'British-Indian Army cavalry: From mobilisation to the Western Front 1915' in Jones (ed.), *Courage Without Glory*, pp. 147–8.

14   Letter, Major-General Charles Callwell, Director of Military Operations,

to Major-General Henry Wilson, Sub-Chief of Staff, BEF, 3 September 1914, IWM, Wilson Papers, HHW 2/75/4; Morton-Jack, *Indian Army*, pp. 135–6, 142, 144–5.

15 Beckett, *Ypres*, pp. 36–7, 64, 78.

16 Beckett, *Ypres*, pp 4, 47, 176.

17 Robert T. Foley, 'East or West? General Erich von Falkenhayn and German Strategy, 1914–15', in Matthew Hughes & Matthew Seligmann (eds), *Leadership in Conflict 1914–1918*, Barnsley, Leo Cooper, 2000, p. 122.

18 Foley, 'East or West?', pp. 120–21; Edmonds & Wynne, *1915*, Vol. 1, p. 13.

19 Jones, 'To make war as we must', pp. 32, 38; Edmonds, *1915*, Vol. 2, p. viii.

20 Morton-Jack, *Indian Army*, p. 222.

21 Jones, 'To make war as we must', and Watt, 'Douglas Haig and the planning of the Battle of Neuve Chapelle' in Jones (ed.), *Courage Without Glory*, pp. 43, 183–4; Andrew Iarocci, *Shoestring Soldiers: The 1st Canadian Division at War, 1914–1915*, Toronto, University of Toronto Press, 2008, pp. 57, 288; C.E.W. Bean, *The A.I.F. in France: 1916*, in Bean (ed.), *The Official History of Australia in the War of 1914–1918*, Sydney, Angus & Robertson, 1942, Vol. 3, p 115.

22 Spencer, 'Friends disunited', p. 87.

23 Letter, Callwell to Wilson, 19 December 1914, IWM, Wilson Papers, HHW 2/75/29.

24 Elizabeth Greenhalgh, *The French Army and the First World War*, Cambridge, Cambridge University Press, 2014, pp. 71, 85, 89.

25 Watt, 'Haig and Neuve Chapelle', pp. 184; Timothy Bowman & Mark Connelly, *The Edwardian Army: Recruiting, Training, and Deploying the British Army 1902–1914*, Oxford, Oxford University Press, 2012, p. 85.

26 Watt, 'Haig and Neuve Chapelle', pp. 184–5, 187; Lieutenant-General Sir Charles Anderson, Commanding Officer, Meerut Division, 'Operation Order No. 21', 9 March 1915, quoted in Edmonds & Wynne, *1915*, Vol.1, pp. 80, 384; Sheffield, *The Chief*, p. 105.

27 Harris, *Haig and the First World War*, p. 114; Sheldon, *German Army 1915*, p. 45.

28 Marble, *British Artillery*, p. 75.

29 John Baynes, *Morale: A Study of Men and Courage. The Second Scottish Rifles at the Battle of Neuve Chapelle 1915*, London, Cassell, 1967, p. 61; Paul Strong & Sanders Marble, *Artillery in the Great War*, Barnsley, Pen & Sword, 2011, p. 46; Marble, *British Artillery*, p. 72; Watt, 'Haig and Neuve Chapelle', p. 188; Edmonds & Wynne, *1915*, Vol. 1, pp. 85–6, 92.

30 Baynes, *Morale*, p. 66.

31 Ibid., p. 68.

32 Ibid., pp. 74, 82, 84; Peter Liddle, *Captured Memories 1900–1918: Across the Threshold of War*, Barnsley, Pen & Sword, 2010, p. 81.
33 Liddle, *Captured Memories*, pp. 265–71; Edmonds & Wynne, *1915*, Vol. 1, pp. 88, 105.
34 Ibid., p. 95, 102–3, 105; Sheldon, *German Army 1915*, pp. 49, 53.
35 Edmonds & Wynne, *1915*, Vol. 1, p. 116; Jones, 'To make war as we must', p. 53.
36 Edmonds & Wynne, *1915*, Vol. 1, p. 117; Sheldon, *German Army 1915*, pp. 54, 57, 68.
37 Edmonds & Wynne, *1915*, Vol. 1, pp. 123–6.
38 Ibid., pp. 85, 149.
39 Edmonds & Wynne, *1915*, Vol. 1, p. 119–50; Baynes, *Morale*, p. 79; Strong & Marble, *Artillery in the Great War*, pp. 46–7.
40 Edmonds & Wynne, *1915*, Vol. 1, p. 151; Sheldon, *German Army 1915*, pp. 77–8; Niall Barr, 'Command in the transition from mobile to static warfare, August 1914 to March 1915', in Gary Sheffield & Dan Todman (eds), *Command and Control on the Western Front: The British Army's Experience 1914–1918*, Staplehurst, Spellmount, 2004, p. 32; letter, Haig to Edmonds, 6 August 1925, Liddell Hart Centre for Military Archives, King's College London (hereafter LHCMA), Edmonds Papers, II/4/39.
41 Edmonds & Wynne, *1915*, Vol. 1, p. 151.
42 Stevenson, *1914–1918*, pp. 154–5.
43 Stevenson, *1914–1918*, pp. 155–6.
44 Greenhalgh, *French Army*, pp. 92–5.
45 Edmonds, *1915*, Vol. 2, pp. 6–7, 13–14.
46 Ibid., pp. 17, 19, 33; Marble, *British Artillery*, p. 88; Sheldon, *German Army 1915*, p. 141.
47 Edmonds, *1915*, Vol. 2, pp. 19–21, 24–5, 28; Marble, *British Artillery*, p. 47.
48 Sheldon, *German Army 1915*, pp. 136–7.
49 Ibid., pp. 139–40; Edmonds, *1915*, Vol. 2, p. 39.
50 Edmonds, *1915*, Vol. 2, pp. 35, 37, 39–40.
51 Robert Williams, 'The Battle of Festubert' in Jones (ed), *Courage without Glory*, p. 259.
52 Edmonds, *1915*, Vol. 2, pp. 9–10, 45–50; Jones, 'To make war as we must', pp. 51–2; Williams, 'Battle of Festubert', p. 261.
53 Ibid., p. 259.
54 Edmonds, *1915*, Vol. 2, pp. 52–4; Williams, 'Battle of Festubert', pp. 261–2.
55 Edmonds, *1915*, Vol. 2, pp. 55–7; Williams, 'Battle of Festubert', p. 263.
56 Edmonds, *1915*, Vol. 2, p. 57.
57 Williams, 'Battle of Festubert', p. 267.
58 Ibid., p. 269.

59 Edmonds, *1915*, Vol. 2, pp. 63, 67, 69; Williams, 'Battle of Festubert', p. 271.

60 Edmonds, *1915*, Vol. 2, pp. 71–3; Morton-Jack, *Indian Army*, pp. 237–8.

61 A. Fortescue Duguid, *Official History of the Canadian Forces in The Great War 1914–1919*, Ottawa, J.O. Patenaude, 1938, Vol. 1, pp. 119, 480; Edmonds & Wynne, *1915*, Vol. 1, p. 37; Edmonds, *1915*, Vol. 2, pp. 72–3, 76; Iarocci, *Shoestring Soldiers*, p. 208; Ronald G. Haycock, 'Early Canadian weapons acquisition: "– That damned Ross rifle"', *Canadian Defence Quarterly*, Vol. 14, No. 3, 1984–5, pp. 48–57.

62 Edmonds, *1915*, Vol. 2, p. 76.

63 Letter, Havildar Abdul Rahman, 59th Scinde Rifles, to Naik Rajwali Khan, 31st Punjabis, 20 May 1915, quoted in Gajendra Singh, *The Anatomy of Dissent in the Military of Colonial India During the First and Second World Wars*, Edinburgh Papers in South Asian Studies, No. 20, 2006, p. 12.

64 Adrian Gregson, '"Seven days in Hell": The 1/7th Battalion King's Liverpool Regiment at the Battle of Festubert, May 1915' in Jones (ed.), *Courage Without Glory*, p. 302.

65 Williams, 'Battle of Festubert', p. 280; Jack Sheldon, *The German Army on Vimy Ridge 1914–1917*, Barnsley, Pen & Sword Military, 2008, p. 122; Wilson, *Myriad Faces of War*, p. 144.

66 Marble, *British Artillery*, pp. 88–9.

67 Beckett, *Ypres*, p. 87; John Mason Sneddon, 'The supply of munitions to the Army, 1915' in Jones (ed.), *Courage Without Glory*, pp. 61, 63.

68 Letter, Charles Repington, [London] *Times* military correspondent, to Geoffrey Robinson, [London] *Times* editor, 11 May 1915, in A.J.A. Morris (ed.), *The Letters of Lieutenant-Colonel Charles à Court Repington CMG: Military Correspondent of The Times, 1903–1918*, Stroud, Sutton Publishing, 1999, pp. 229–30; [London] *Times*, 14 May 1915.

69 Sneddon, 'Supply of munitions to the Army', pp. 63–4; Edmonds, *1915*, Vol. 2, p. 41.

70 R.J.Q. Adams & Philip P. Poirier, *The Conscription Controversy in Great Britain, 1900–18*, Basingstoke, Macmillan, 1987, pp. 80–1.

71 Greenhalgh, *French Army*, pp. 111–17; Brian Curragh, '"A great victory all but gained": The Battle of Loos, 1915' in Jones (ed.), *Courage Without Glory*, p. 377.

72 Morton-Jack, *Indian Army*, pp. 7, 24, 154, 228, 402–3.

73 Marble, *British Artillery*, p. 107; Spencer, 'Friends disunited', pp. 85–6, 91.

74 'Interview between F.M. Sir John French and Mr. Lloyd George and Mr. Long at Lancaster Gate – September 8th', TNA, MUN 9/27, p. 1.

75 Ibid., pp. 1–3.

76 Curragh, 'A great victory all but gained', pp. 367–8, 377–8.

77 Ibid., pp. 367–8, 377.

78   Ibid., pp. 383–5; Michael Woods, 'Gas, grenades and grievances: The attack on the Hohenzollern Redoubt by 46th (North Midland) Division, 13 October 1915' in Jones (ed.), *Courage Without Glory*, pp. 426–30; Edmonds, *1915*, Vol. 2, pp. 392–3.

79   Curragh, 'A great victory all but gained', pp. 382–3; Edmonds, *1915*, Vol. 2, p. 397; Richard Holmes, *The Little Field Marshal: Sir John French*, London, Jonathan Cape, 1981, p. 312.

4
Making Munitions

1   *Irish Industrial Journal*, 19 June 1915, Vol. X, p. 289; [Bombay] *Times of India*, 2 July 1915.

2   [UK] *Parliamentary Debates*, 20 December 1915, Vol. 77, col. 95.

3   Letter, J.C. Campbell Davidson, Colonial Secretary Private Secretary, to H.J. Creedy, War Office, 12 October 1914, United Kingdom Parliamentary Archives, London [hereafter UKPA], Davidson Papers, DAV/11; [London] *Canadian Gazette*, 17 September 1914, p. 825; David Carnegie, *The History of Munitions Supply in Canada*, London, Longmans, Green & Co., 1925, pp. 2–3, 6; Shell Committee Minutes, 2 & 7 September, 31 October 1914, 6 January 1915, Library and Archives Canada/Bibliothèque et Archives Canada, Ottawa [hereafter LAC], MG 27 II D 23, Vol. 3, File 6.

4   Ronald G. Haycock, *Sam Hughes: The Public Career of a Controversial Canadian, 1885–1916*, Wilfrid Laurier University Press in collaboration with Canadian War Museum, Canadian Museum of Civilization, National Museums of Canada, 1986, p. 2; Ronald Haycock, '"Done in our own country": The politics of Canadian munitioning' in B.D. Hunt & R.G. Haycock (eds), *Canada's Defence: Perspectives on Policy in the Twentieth Century*, Toronto, Copp Clark Pitman, 1993, p. 59.

5   Letter, John Bassett to Smeaton White, 25 November 1914, quoted in Haycock, *Sam Hughes*, p. 227.

6   Haycock, *Sam Hughes*, pp. 228–9; Michael Bliss, *A Canadian Millionaire: The Life and Business of Sir Joseph Flavelle, Bart., 1858–1939*, University of Toronto Press, Toronto, 1992, p. 263.

7   Ibid., pp. 239–41, 251–2, 265; [Moose Jaw] *Morning News*, 21 & 28 May, 19 & 25 June 1915; Carnegie, *Munitions Supply in Canada*, pp. 15–16, 87; Tim Cook, *The Madman and the Butcher: The Sensational Wars of Sam Hughes and General Arthur Currie*, Toronto, Allen Lane, 2010, p. 164.

8   Carnegie, *Munitions Supply in Canada*, p. 14; Bliss, *Canadian Millionaire*, pp. 240, 245, 280.

9   Haycock, *Sam Hughes*, p. 229–33; Shell Committee Minutes, 17 May,

31 July, 6 September & 4–5 October 1915, LAC, MG 27 II D 23, Vol. 3, File 6.

10   Haycock, *Sam Hughes*, pp. 242–3, 309; Cook, *Madman and the Butcher*, pp. 107, 166, 176.

11   Bliss, *Canadian Millionaire*, p. 245.

12   J.M. Bourne, *Britain and the Great War 1914–1918*, London, Edward Arnold, 1989, pp. 107–14, 185–90; Wilson, *Myriad Faces of War*, pp. 215–38.

13   Adrian Gregory, *The Last Great War: British Society and the First World War*, Cambridge, Cambridge University Press, 2008, pp. 11, 39, 46; Bill Nasson, *Springboks on the Somme: South Africa in the Great War 1914–1918*, Johannesburg, Penguin, 2007, p. 29; [Moose Jaw] *Morning News*, 10 May 1915; W.G. Fitzgerald, 'The workshops of war', *Windsor Magazine*, Vol. 42, June–November 1915, p. 350.

14   *Kalgoorlie Miner*, 16 August 1915; *Indian Patriot*, quoted in [Bombay] *Times of India*, 15 July 1915.

15   R.E. Grace, Deputy Chief of Inspector of Factories, & Gerald Bellhouse, Superintending Inspector of Factories, 'Output of Munitions of War', 24 March 1915, p. 1, TNA, MUN 5/6; Robert Duncan, *Pubs and Patriots: The Drink Crisis in Britain during World War One*, Liverpool, Liverpool University Press, 2013, pp. 8, 68, 118; pp. 161–2; Kenneth Rose, *King George V*, London, Phoenix Press, 1983, p. 178.

16   'These notes were made several days ago by the head of affirm on the W.O. & Admiralty List', pp. 1, 26 May 1915, TNA, MUN 5/6; [UK] *Parliamentary Debates*, 17 & 23 June, 3 November, 20 December 1915, Vol. 72, cols. 769, 1188, Vol. 75, col. 643, Vol. 77, col. 106.

17   Stephen Broadberry & Peter Howlett, 'The United Kingdom during World War I: Business as usual', in Stephen Broadberry & Mark Harrison (eds), *The Economics of World War I*, Cambridge, Cambridge University Press, 2005, pp. 213–14, 223; Salter, *Allied Shipping Control*, pp. 94–5.

18   Ben H. Morgan, 'The efficient utilization of labour in engineering factories (with special reference to women's work)', *The Institution of Mechanical Engineers Proceedings*, Vol. 94, No. 1, January–May 1918, pp. 240–1, 248–50, 266.

19   'Conference Report', 24 September 1915, TNA, MUN 4/519; Viola Meynell (ed.), *Letters of J.M. Barrie*, London, Peter Davies, 1942, p. 48.

20   Angela Woollacott, *On Her Their Lives Depend: Munitions Workers in the Great War*, Berkeley & Los Angeles, University of California Press, 1994, p. 2; Broadberry & Howlett, 'United Kingdom during World War I', p. 207.

21   Ministry of Reconstruction, *Report of the Women's Employment Committee*, London, His Majesty's Stationery Office, 1919, p. 8, TNA, MUN 4/6361.

22 [UK] *Parliamentary Debates*, Vol. LXXV, 3 November 1915, col. 643; Woollacott, *On Her Their Lives Depend*, p. 29; Deborah Thom, 'Tommy's sister: Women at Woolwich in World War One', in Raphael Samuel (ed.), *Patriotism: The Making and Unmaking of British National Identity*, Vol. 2, London, Routledge, 1989, p. 144.
23 Ibid., pp. 147–8, 150–1.
24 Woollacott, *On Her Their Lives Depend*, pp. 47, 53.
25 Thom, 'Tommy's sister', pp. 145–6; Woollacott, *On Her Their Lives Depend*, p. 81; 'Report by Dr. Leonard Hill on a visit to Woolwich Arsenal on 24 September 1915', Circulated Paper No. 17, Health of Munition Workers Committee, p 1, TNA, SUPP 5/1051.
26 Ernest Scott, *Australia during the War*, Vol. 11 of C.E.W. Bean (ed.) *Official History of Australia in the War of 1914–1918*, Sydney, Angus & Robertson, 7th ed., 1941, p. 247; O.E. Monkhouse, 'The employment of women in munition factories', *The Institution of Mechanical Engineers Proceedings*, Vol. 94, No. 1, January–May 1918, p. 213; Ministry of Reconstruction, *Report of the Women's Employment Committee*, London, His Majesty's Stationery Office, 1919, pp. 10–11, 23, TNA, MUN 4/6361; Broadberry & Howlett, 'United Kingdom during World War I', pp. 207–8.
27 'Values of Goods etc., Supplied from Ireland to the order of the Ministry of Munitions' [1918], TNA MUN 4/6726; 'Short note on the general position of the manufacture of munitions in Dublin and the South of Ireland' [1917?], TNA, MUN 4/413; Ministry of Munitions, *History of the Ministry of Munitions*, London, His Majesty's Stationery Office, 1923, Vol. 2, Pt II, pp. 148–50; 'Committee on Reconstruction Report', 28 November 1918, p. 2, Wiltshire and Swindon History Centre, Chippenham (hereafter WSHC), Walter Long Papers, 947/230.
28 'Description, quantity and value, based on standard prices of goods, which passed inspection produced in the Irish National Factories', 8 July 1919, TNA, MUN 4/6726; 'Ireland Reconstruction and Development' [1918], pp. 2–4, WSHC, Long Papers, 947/230.
29 'Ireland Reconstruction and Development' [1918], pp. 4–5, WSHC, Long Papers, 947/230; 'Deliveries to date of H.E. shell by contractors and National Factories in Ireland' 28 June 1917, TNA, MUN 4/413; Theresa Moriarty, 'Work, warfare and wages: industrial controls and Irish trade unionism in the First World War' in Adrian Gregory & Senia Pašeta (eds), *Ireland and the Great War: 'A War to Unite Us All?'*, Manchester, Manchester University Press, 2002, p. 78.
30 W.T. Macartney-Filgate, 'Ireland – An Industrial Survey – Past and Present with Possible Suggestions for the Future' [1917], p. 21, WSHC, Long Papers, 947/298; [Waterford] *Evening News*, 30 September 1915.
31 [UK] *Parliamentary Debates*, 1 July 1915, Vol. 72, col. 1945; *Irish Builder and Engineer*, 25 September 1915, p. 420.

32 [Dublin] *Irish Times*, 16 April 1915; [Waterford] *Evening News*, 18 August, 8 & 13 September 1915; 'Ireland Reconstruction and Development' [1918], p. 6, WSHC, Long Papers, 947/230; Thomas P. Dooley, *Irishmen or English Soldiers? The Times and World of a Southern Catholic Irish Man (1876–1916) Enlisting in the British Army during the First World War*, Liverpool, Liverpool University Press, 1995, p. 122.

33 E.A. Aston, 'Dublin C.B. Relief Employment. Suggested Extension of National Shell Factory', 6 January 1917, TNA, MUN 4/109.

34 E.J. Riordan, 'Four years of Irish economies, 1914–1918. II. – Restraint of industry', *Studies: An Irish Quarterly Review*, Vol. 7, No. 6, June 1918, p. 307; Ministry of Munitions, *History*, Vol. 2, Pt II, p. 103; Doctor Christopher Addison, UK Minister of Munitions, to E.H. Duke, Chief Secretary, Dublin, 29 January 1917, 'Special Report by the All-Ireland Munitions and Government Supplies Committee', 7 November 1916, letter, Ministry of Munitions to E.J. Riordan, All-Ireland Munitions & Government Supplies Committee, 28 November 1916, TNA, MUN 4/109; Gary Sheffield, 'Haig and the British Expeditionary Force in 1917' in Peter Dennis & Jeffrey Grey (eds), *1917: Tactics, Training and Technology. The 2007 Chief of Army History Conference*, Sydney, Australian Military History Publications, 2007, p. 13; 'Committee on Reconstruction Report', 28 November 1918, p. 3, WSHC, Long Papers, 947/230.

35 Memo to Sir Laming Worthington-Evans, UK Parliamentary Secretary for Munitions, 5 January 1917, TNA, MUN 4/109; 'Ireland Reconstruction and Development' [1918], p. 6, WSHC, Long Papers, 947/230; Theresa Moriarty, 'Work, warfare and wages', pp. 86–7; [Dublin] *Irish Times*, 2 June 1917.

36 Niamh Puirséil, 'War, work and labour' in John Horne (ed.), *Our War: Ireland and the Great War. The 2008 Thomas David Lecture Series*, Dublin, Royal Irish Academy, 2008, pp. 185, 192–3; Moriarty, 'Work, warfare and wages', p. 88.

37 [London] *Times*, 11 June 1915; C. Hayavadana Rao, *The Indian Biographical Dictionary 1915*, Madras, Pillar & Co. Publishers & Booksellers, 1915, p. 3.

38 Kaushik Roy, 'Equipping Leviathan: Ordnance factories in British India, 1859–1913', *War in History*, Vol. 10, No. 4, October 2003, pp. 398–423; [Bombay] *Times of India*, 1 July 1915; T.L. Matthews, 'The Manufacture of Munitions of War in India', 5 September 1917, pp. 14–15, British Library, London (hereafter BL), IOR/L/MIL/7/18978; Government of India, *India's Contribution to the Great War*, Calcutta, Superintendent Government Printing, 1923, pp. 128–9; Ministry of Munitions, *History*, Vol. 2, Pt V, pp. 5–7; [Calcutta] *Hindoo Patriot*, 11 October 1915.

39 Letter, U.F. Wintour, War Office, to W. Carter, Ministry of Munitions, 16 July 1915, TNA, MUN 4/42; 'Minutes of Proceedings of the Indian &

Colonial Conference. Held at Armament Buildings, on Thursday August 12th, 1915', pp. 1–6, TNA, MUN 5/176/1144/1.

40 [Lahore] *Tribune*, 20 May 1915, quoted in Andrew Tait Jarboe (ed.), *War News in India: The Punjabi Press During World War I*, London, I.B.Tauris, 2016, p. 78; [London] *Times*, 14 June 1915; [Calcutta] *Hindoo Patriot*, 28 June 1915; letter, Haig to Edmonds, 6 August 1923, Liddell Hart Centre for Military Archives, Edmonds Papers, II/4/39

41 Ibid., 5 July 1915; [Bombay] *Times of India*, 18 November 1915; Government of India, *India's Contribution*, pp. 104, 128–9; Matthews, 'Manufacture of Munitions of War in India', 5 September 1917, p. 18, BL, IOR/L/MIL/7/18978; Ministry of Munitions, *History*, Vol. 2, Pt V, pp. 10–11.

42 Telegram, Lord Hardinge, Indian Viceroy, to David Lloyd George, UK War Secretary, 11 July 1916, letter, Edmund Phipps, Ministry of Munitions, to Director-General of Stores, India Office, telegram, Lord Chelmsford, Indian Viceroy, to Austen Chamberlain, India Secretary, 8 January 1917, TNA, MUN 4/2307; Government of India, *India's Contribution*, p. 112; Ministry of Munitions, *History*, Vol. 2, Pt V, p. 3.

43 Government of India, *India's Contribution*, p. 105.

44 Letter, Brigadier-General H.O. Manse to Sir Ernest Moir, Ministry of Munitions, 30 December 1916, TNA, MUN 4/512; telegram, Chelmsford to Chamberlain, TNA, MUN 4/2307.

45 Peter Sluggett, *Britain in Iraq: Contriving King and Country*, 1st pub. 1976, rep. London, I.B.Tauris, 2007, pp. 67–8; James Goldrick, 'The battleship fleet: The test of war, 1895–1919' in J.R. Hill (ed.), *Oxford Illustrated History of the Royal Navy*, Oxford, Oxford University Press, 1995, p. 291; F.J. Moberly, *The Campaign in Mesopotamia, 1914–1918*, London, His Majesty's Stationery Office, 1923, Vol. 1, pp. 106–17.

46 Kaushik Roy, 'The Army in India in Mesopotamia from 1916 to 1918: Tactics, technology and logistics reconsidered' in Ian F.W. Beckett (ed.), *1917: Beyond the Western Front*, Leiden, Brill, 2009, p. 148.

47 Moberly, *Mesopotamia*, Vol. 3, pp. 64; N.S. Nash, *Betrayal of an Army: Mesopotamia 1914–16*, Barnsley, Pen & Sword, 2016, p. 50.

48 Ministry of Munitions, *History*, Vol. 2, Pt V, p. 14; Roy, 'Army in India in Mesopotamia', pp. 154–5.

49 Telegrams, Lord Liverpool, New Zealand Governor-General, to Lord Harcourt, Colonial Secretary, 17 April 1915, Harcourt to Liverpool, 16 May 1915, Archives New Zealand, Te Rua Mahara o te Kāwanatanga, Wellington (hereafter ANZ) AD1/700, 6/111; [UK] *Parliamentary Debates*, 18 May 1915, Vol. 71, col. 2158; [Wellington] *Evening News*, 19 May 1915; *Marlborough Express*, 21 May 1915.

50 'John Birch (engineer)', en.wikipedia.org, viewed 26 October 2016; *Manuwatu Times*, 28 April 1920.

51 Mercer, *Colonial Office List 1914*, pp. 262–3; McGibbon, *Oxford Companion*, p. 239.

52 [Auckland] *New Zealand Herald*, 14 June 1915; [Wellington] *Evening Post*, 17 & 22 June 1915; *Auckland Star*, 17 June 1915.

53 Letters, John Corry, Mayor Blenheim Borough Council, to James Allen, New Zealand Defence Minister, 25 May, 1915, Major J. O'Sullivan, to Corry, 2 June 1915, Birch to Brigadier Alfred Robin, Commandant New Zealand Military Forces, 22 June 1915, ANZ, AD1/700, 6/114; *Marlborough Express,* 26 June 1915; 'Mayor of Blenheim', en.wikipedia. org, viewed 12 December 2016.

54 Lieutenant Robert G.V. Parker, 'Report on Locally-made 4.5" Q.F. Howitzer Shrapnel Shell', 28 June 1915, memo Robin to Allen, 4 August 1915, ANZ, AD1/700, 6/114.

55 Memo, Captain W.P. Thring, Royal New Zealand Artillery, to Allen, 28 July 1915, letter, Birch to Robin, 18 August 1915, ANZ, AD1/700, 6/114; *Marlborough Express*, 18 August 1915; Peter Dennerly, 'New Zealand and the naval war' in John Crawford & Ian McGibbon (eds), *New Zealand's Great War: New Zealand, the Allies and the First World War*, Auckland, Exisle Publishing, 2007, pp. 320–1.

56 Letters, H.B. Burnett, Secretary, Auckland Harbour Board, to Allen, 23 June 1915, Allen to Burnett, 30 June 1915, telegram, Senator George Pearce, Australian Defence Minister, to Allen, 6 September 1915, ANZ, AD1/700, 6/111; letter, Allen to Professor Robert Scott, School of Engineering and Technical Science, Canterbury College, University of New Zealand, Christchurch, 23 August 1915, ANZ, AD1/700, 6/114.

57 H.T.B. Drew, *The War Effort of New Zealand: A Popular History of (a) Minor Campaigns in which New Zealanders Took Part; (b) Services Not Fully Dealt with in the Campaign Volumes; (c) The Work at the Bases*, Auckland, Whitcombe & Tombs, 1923, p. xxi; McGibbon, *Oxford Companion*, pp. 239–40; letter, Allen to Professor Robert Scott, School of Engineering and Technical Science, Canterbury College, University of New Zealand, Christchurch, 3 September 1915, ANZ, AD1/700, 6/114.

58 'Munitions' [1916], ANZ, AD1/700, 6/111; [Wellington] *Evening Post*, 3 September 1915.

59 [Wellington] *Evening Post*, 3 September 1915; *Manuwatu Standard*, 7 September 1915; telegram, Allen to Pearce, 9 September 1915; Professor Thomas Easterfield, Victoria College, University of New Zealand, Wellington, 'Report to the Hon. Minister in Charge of Munitions re the manufacture of Explosives in New Zealand' [October 1915], pp. 1–2, ANZ, AD1/700, 6/114.

60 Letter, A.J.C. Bult, Secretary, Victorian State Munitions Committee, to
    Myers, 7 December 1915, memo, Robin to Myers, 26 January 1916, Scott,
    'Report on the Manufacture of Projectiles in New Zealand', pp. 1–2,
    31 January 1916, letter, E.H. Hiley, General Manager, New Zealand
    Railways, to Myers, 2 March 1916, ANZ, AD1/700, 6/114; Drew,
    War Effort of New Zealand, p. xxxi; *Auckland Star*, 3 December 1915;
    [Wellington] *Dominion*, 16 February 1916; telegram, Andrew Bonar Law,
    UK Colonial Secretary, to Liverpool, 27 November 1916, ANZ, AD1/700,
    6/111; Roy MacLeod, '"The industrial invasion of Britain": Mobilising
    Australian munitions workers, 1916–1919', *Journal of the Australian War
    Memorial*, No. 27, 1995, pp. 37–46.

61 Letter, Birch to Robin, 23 February 1916, invoice, Birch to New Zealand
    Defence Department, 21 March 1916, memo, Robin to Allen, 26 May
    1916, letters, Robin to Birch, 6 June 1916, A.J. Maclaine, Secretary
    Marlborough Patriotic Fund, to Allen, 13 July 1916, ANZ, AD1/700,
    6/114; *Marlborough Express*, 3 September 1917.

62 'Typescript of Jensen's "Defence Production in Australia" and supporting
    evidence', NAA, MP598/30, 7, pp. 223–5, 228, 236–7, 247–8; Scott,
    Australia during the War, pp. 239–40.

63 *Commonwealth Parliamentary Debates*, 17 June 1915, Vol. 76, p. 4067; 18
    & 20 August 1915, Vol. 78, pp. 5811–16, 6001; letter, Malcolm Shepherd,
    Prime Minister's Department Secretary to George Steward, Governor-
    General's Secretary, 16 October 1915, telegram, Hardinge to Munro
    Ferguson, 20 October 1915, NAA, A11803, 1914/89/79; [Bombay] *Times
    of India*, 1 December 1915.

64 Eric Andrews, *The Department of Defence*, Melbourne, Oxford University
    Press, 2001, p. 49.

65 *Commonwealth Parliamentary Debates*, 17 June 1915, Vol. 77, p. 4068;
    letter, James Alexander Smith to Lloyd George, UK Munitions Minister,
    30 August 1915, NAA, A11803, 1914/89/79; [Melbourne] *Argus*, 24 June
    1915.

66 [Perth] *West Australian*, 30 June & 3 July 1915.

67 [E.A. Mann], 'Report of the Delegation Sent by the W.A. Munitions
    Committee to Melbourne' [July 1915], J.S. Battye Library of West
    Australian History, MN300, ACC1688A, 112; [Melbourne] *Argus*,
    14 & 15 July 1915; telegram, Andrew Bonar Law, UK Colonial Secretary,
    to Munro Ferguson, 9 July 1915, NAA, A11803, 1914/89/79; Ministry of
    Munitions, *History*, Vol. 2, Pt IV, p. 10.

68 [Melbourne] *Argus*, 30 August 1915; [Adelaide] *Sport*, 12 November 1915;
    letter, Sir William Ellison-Macartney, Tasmanian Governor, to Bonar
    Law, 22 November 1915, NAA, A11803, 1914/89/79; [Launceston]
    Telegraph, 17 November & 15 December 1915; Connor, Stanley & Yule,

War at Home: Vol. 4 of Jeffrey Grey (ed.), *The Centenary History of Australia and the Great War*, Melbourne, Oxford University Press, 2015, pp. 23–4.

69   [Perth] *West Australian*, 9 October & 22 December 1915; letter, Hugh Plaistowe to Lloyd George, 5 October 1915, Bonar Law to Munro Ferguson, 16 December 1915, NAA, A11803, 1914/89/79.

70   Letter, M.M. Henderson, Chief Mechanical Engineer, Commonwealth Railways to Pearce, 'Manufacture of munitions. Special report on the American, Canadian and British practice compared with the Australian', 23 August 1916, p. 15, NAA, A2023, B11/18/903; letter, Andrew Fisher, Australian High Commissioner, London, to Sir Frederick Black, Controller Munitions Supplies, Ministry of Munitions, 20 June 1916, TNA, MUN 4/2905; Scott, *Australia during the War*, pp. 246, 248, 266; [London] *British Australasian*, 18 May 1916, p. 13; letter, William Morris Hughes, Australian Attorney-General, to Munro Ferguson, 23 November 1915, telegram, Munro Ferguson to Bonar Law, 16 May 1916, NAA, A11803, 1914/89/79; Macleod, 'Industrial invasion of Britain', pp. 43, 45.

71   [London] *Times*, 8 May 1915; [Toronto] *Globe*, 6 & 28 July 1915.

72   Bliss, *Canadian Millionaire*, pp. 248, 251, 255–6.

73   Ibid., pp. 257–8.

74   Ibid., pp. 259, 262–4, 287; Carnegie, *History of Munitions Supply in Canada*, p. 273.

75   Source: Ibid., p. 294.

76   Ibid., pp. xix, 26, 47, 136, 254–5, 271.

77   Ibid., pp. 133, 136; Bliss, *Canadian Millionaire*, p. 289; [London] *Canadian Gazette*, 11 January 1917, p. 373; 'Extract from War Cabinet 167', 16 July 1917, TNA, WO 32/5159.

78   Angela Woollacott, *On Her Their Lives Depend*, p. 9.

79   D.H.L. Black, 'Kynoch, George (1834–1891), *Oxford Dictionary of National Biography*, www.oxforddnb.com/view/article/48741, viewed 22 February 2017; W.B. Jackson, Acting South African Chief Inspector of Explosives, 'Report on the circumstances attending two explosions which occurred in the mixing houses of the factory of Messrs Kynoch Ltd., Umbogintwini, Durban, Natal, on December, 9th, 1916 and January, 10th, 1917', pp. 1, 3–6, 13, TNA, SUPP 5/333.

80   Anthony Cannon, 'Arklow's explosive history: Kynoch, 1895–1918', *History Ireland*, January/February 2006, historyireland.com, viewed 26 January 2017.

81   Memo, DDG(C) to Director-General Munition Supplies, 'Chilwell Filling Factory', 15 March 1916, TNA, MUN 4/463; 'Explosion of amatol at No. 6 National Filling Factory, Chilwell. Report of the Committee appointed by the Right Honourable the Secretary of State for the Home Department to enquire into the cause of the explosion which occurred

on July 1st, 1918, at No. 6 National Filling Factory, Chilwell, near Nottingham', pp. 1–10, 17, TNA, HO 45/10896/364648.

82 John Griffith Armstrong, *The Halifax Explosion and the Royal Canadian Navy: Inquiry and Intrigue*, Vancouver, UBC Press, 2002, pp. 3, 10, 23, 40–2.

83 Ibid., pp. 3, 41–2; letters, Vice Admiral Evelyn R. Le Marchant, HMS *Knight Templar*, to Admiralty Secretary, 9 December 1917, Acting Lieutenant Commander F.H.D. Clarke RNR to Commanding Officer HMS *Changuinola*, 7 December 1917, TNA, ADM 1/8507/273.

84 [Dublin] *Irish Times*, 14 January 1920.

85 'Jensen's Defence Production in Australia', NAA, MP598/30, Item 10, pp. 40, 47.

86 Letter, Lord Inverforth, Minister for Munitions, to Lord Milner, Colonial Secretary, 2 September 1919, TNA, MUN 4/5959; 'Jensen's Defence Production in Australia', NAA, MP598/30, Item 10, pp. 49, 52–3, 57.

87 Ibid., pp. 57–9.

88 Ibid., p. 59.

89 [Dublin] *Irish Times*, 25 October 1919; 'Jensen's Defence Production in Australia', NAA, MP598/30, Item 10, pp. 59–61.

90 Ibid.

91 [Dublin] *Irish Times*, 6 November 1919; 'Jensen's Defence Production in Australia', NAA, MP598/30, Item 10, pp. 59–61.

92 Ibid., pp. 61–2, 90.

5
1916: The East African Campaign

1 'Proceedings of the conference between Major-General A.J. Godley, CB, Commanding New Zealand Military Forces, and Brigadier-General J.M. Gordon, CB, Chief of the General Staff, CM Forces', 18 November 1912, NAA, MP84/1, 1856/1/33, pp. 1–2, 4; S.J. Smith, 'The seizure and occupation of Samoa' in H.T.B. Drew (ed.), *The War Effort of New Zealand*, Auckland, Whitcombe & Tombs, 1923, pp. 25, 33–35; John Connor, 'The capture of German New Guinea' in Craig Stockings & John Connor (eds), *Before the Anzac Dawn: A Military History of Australia*, Sydney, NewSouth Publishing, 2013, pp. 291–6; [Lahore] *Desh*, 22 May 1915, quoted in Jarboe, *War News in India*, pp. 71–2; letter, Sir Walter Davidson, Newfoundland Governor, to Andrew Bonar Law, UK Colonial Secretary, 28 March 1916, UKPA, Davidson Papers, DAV 20; Ronald Hyam, *The Failure of South African Expansion 1908–1948*, London, Macmillan, 1972, p. 24; letter, Walter Long, UK Colonial Secretary, to Lord Buxton, South African Governor-General, 27 August 1918, WSHC, Long Papers, 947/601.

2 Timothy J. Stapleton, *A Military History of Africa*. Vol. 2, *The Colonial*

Period: From the Scramble for Africa to the Algerian Independence War, Santa Barbara, California, Praeger, 2013, pp. 143–4; David Killingray, 'The war in Africa' in John Horne (ed.), *A Companion to World War I*, Chichester, Blackwell Publishing, 2012, pp. 115–16; C.L. McCluer Stevens, 'Togoland: The German colony taken by the Allies after the declaration of war', *Windsor Magazine*, September 1914, p. 513.

3   Stapleton, *Military History of Africa*, pp. 144–6.

4   Ibid., p. 147.

5   Ibid., p. 148.

6   Ibid., p. 149; Killingray, 'War in Africa', pp. 116–18.

7   Bill Nasson, *Springboks on the Somme: South Africa in the Great War 1914–1918*, Johannesburg, Penguin Books, 2007, pp. 63, 65; Stapleton, *Military History of Africa*, p. 154.

8   Nasson, *Springboks on the Somme*, pp. 73–4; Stapleton, *Military History of Africa*, pp. 155–6.

9   Ibid., pp. 156–7

10   Ibid., p. 158; Nasson, *Springboks on the Somme*, pp. 75–7; Killingray, 'War in Africa', p. 120; memo, Buxton 'Peace Proposals. The Future of German South West [Africa] (now called the S.W. Protectorate)' [December 1916], WSHC, Long Papers, 947/601.

11   Ross Anderson, *The Forgotten Front 1914–1918: The East African Campaign*, Stroud, Tempus, 2007, p. 13; Killingray, 'War in Africa', pp. 120–1, 123; Francis Parkman, *Montcalm and Wolfe*, London, Macmillan & Co., 1884, Vol. 2, p. 395.

12   Mercer, *Colonial Office List 1914*, p.173; Charles Turner, IWM, Docs.7754, 'Reminiscences' [1915], pp. 29–30; letter, Nurse Annie Hills, British 19th Stationary Hospital, German East Africa, to mother, 18 July 1916, IWM, 99/76/1.

13   Anderson, *Forgotten Front*, pp. 49–52; Stapleton, *Military History of Africa*, p. 158; Brigadier General A.E. Aitken, IWM, Docs.4678, 'Account of the Indian Expeditionary Force to German East Africa by Brig-General A.E. Aitken' [December 1915], p. 4.

14   Anderson, *Forgotten Front*, pp. 54–5; Stapleton, *Military History of Africa*, pp. 158–9.

15   'Memorandum' [on the East Africa Campaign] [1933] p. 9, TNA, CAB45, 27.

16   Aitken, IWM, Docs.4678, 'Account of the Indian Expeditionary Force to German East Africa', pp. 2, 8, 11.

17   Mercer, *Colonial List 1914*, p. 173; Turner, 'Reminiscences', 17 June 1915, p. 11, IWM, Docs.7754; Stapleton, *Military History of Africa*, p. 159; Anderson, *Forgotten Front*, pp. 68, 71, 76, 111; Nasson, *Springboks on the Somme*, p. 99; letter, Repington to Robinson, 22 December 1915 in Morris (ed.), *Letters*, p. 248

18   Letter, Major-General Sir Charles Callwell, Director of Military Operations, to Wilson, 12 December 1914, IWM, Wilson Papers, HHW 2/75/23.

19   Anderson, *Forgotten Front*, pp. 66–7.

20   Ibid., pp. 65–7, 74–5, 91–3.

21   Ian van der Waag, *A Military History of Modern South Africa*, Jeppestown, Jonathan Ball Publishers, 2015, p. 106; letter, Buxton to Harcourt, 28 April 1915, quoted in Hyam, *Failure of South African Expansion*, p. 28.

22   Letter, Brigadier-General Charles Crewe to Long, 17 November 1915, WSRC, Long Papers, 947/469.

23   [Johannesburg] *Illustrated Star*, 27 November 1915, 18 December 1915, 12 & 26 February 1916; [Perth] *Daily News*, 22 November 1915; van der Waag, *Military History*, p. 112, Nasson, *Springboks on the Somme*, p. 96.

24   Letter, Crewe to Long, 17 November 1915, WSHC, Long Papers, 947/545.

25   Mercer, *Colonial List 1914*, p. 173; Turner, 'Reminiscences', 17 June 1915, p. 11, IWM, Docs.7754; Anderson, *Forgotten Front*, pp. 68, 71, 76, 111; Nasson, *Springboks on the Somme*, p. 99; letter, General Jan Smuts to General Sir William Robertson, Chief of the Imperial General Staff, 15 March 1916, TNA, WO141, 62; letter, Repington to Robinson, 22 December 1915 in Morris (ed.), *Letters*, p. 248.

26   Anderson, *Forgotten Front*, pp. 112–13; Stapleton, *Military History of Africa*, p. 161.

27   [Wellington] *Dominion*, 6 June 1916; Stapleton, *Military History of Africa*, pp. 161–2; Nasson, *Springboks on the Somme*, pp. 91, 100, 157.

28   Ibid., pp. 100–2; Anderson, *Forgotten Front*, pp. 117–19; letter, Crewe to Long, 3 December 1916, WSRC, Long Papers, 947/545.

29   Stapleton, *Military History of Africa*, pp, 162–3; Nasson, *Springboks on the Somme*, pp. 103–7.

30   Nasson, *Springboks on the Somme*, pp. 105–7; letters, Annie Hills to mother, 1 & 21 May, 13 September 1916, 23 January 1917, diary, Hills, 6 June, 1916, IWM, 99/76/1; letter, Crewe to Long, 15 May 1917, WSRC, Long Papers, 947/545.

31   Letter, Crewe to Long, 3 December 1916, WSRC, Long Papers, 947/545; 'Memorandum' [1933], pp. 1–2, TNA, CAB45, 27; Killingray, 'War in Africa', p. 123.

32   [United Kingdom] War Office, *Statistics of the Military Effort of the British Empire during the Great War 1914–1920*, 1st pub. 1922, rep. Uckfield, Naval & Military Press, 1999, p. 23.

33   Telegram, Buxton to Long, 2 January 1917, WSRC, Long Papers, 947/601; Killingray, 'War in Africa', p. 123.

34   Stapleton, *Military History of Africa*, p. 165.

35   Letter, Major-General R.H. Ewart, East Africa GHQ to Major-General
       Richard Crofton-Atkins, Director-General Supply and Transport, 28 March
       & 9 August 1917, TNA, WO107, 46; F.D. Rowland, 'Young Contemptible:
       A Signaller in Kitchener's Army', p. 64 [1973], IWM, 74/98/1.
36   Captain A.A. Gardiner, 'A record of the doings of the overseas contingent
       Nigeria Regiment, during the campaign in German East Africa. December
       1916–December 1917', IWM, 67/39/1.
37   Stapleton, *Military History of Africa*, pp. 167; letter, Major C.E. Roberts,
       1st Battalion, Nigeria Regiment, to G.G. Waters, 31 October 1917, IWM,
       Docs.13583.
38   Letter, Buxton to Long, 4 March 1918, WSRC, Long Papers, 947/603.
39   Stapleton, *Military History of Africa*, p. 167; Killingray, 'War in
       Africa', p. 124; letter, Roberts to Waters, 31 October 1917, IWM,
       Documents.13583; 'Memorandum' [1933], p. 9, TNA, CAB45, 27.
40   Bruce Vandervort, 'New light on the East African Theater of the Great
       War: A review of English-Language Sources' in Stephen M. Miller (ed.),
       Soldiers and Settlers in Africa, 1850–1918, Leiden, Brill, 2009, pp. 288–9,
       293; Stapleton, *Military History of Africa*, pp. 166–7.
41   E. St C. Stobart, 'A record of the doings of the overseas contingent, Nigeria
       Regiment, during the campaign in German East Africa. December 1916–
       December 1917', p. 8, TNA, CO445, 47.
42   Stapleton, *Military History of Africa*, p. 167; Tim Skelton & Gerald
       Gliddon, *Lutyens and the Great War*, London, Frances Lincoln, 2008,
       pp. 102–3; letter, Buxton to Long, 27 January 1917, WSRC, Long Papers
       947/601.

6
Dissent

1   Antoinette Burton, *The Trouble with Empire: Challenges to Modern British
       Imperialism*, Oxford, Oxford University Press, 2015, pp. 9–10, 104; Connor,
       Stanley & Yule, *War at Home*, p. 69; telegrams, Munro Ferguson to Lord
       Chelmsford, Indian Viceroy, 27 October 1917, Chelmsford to Munro
       Ferguson, 28 November 1917, NAA, A11803, 1918/89/935; Elizabeth
       Wrangham, 'The Gold Coast and the First World War. "Carrying on":
       The service under strain', in John Smith (ed.), *Administering Empire: The
       British Colonial Service in Retrospect*, London, University of London Press,
       1999, p. 171; letter, Walter Long, President UK Local Government Board,
       to David Lloyd George, UK War Secretary, 19 December 1916, UKPA,
       Lloyd George Papers, F/32/4/4; letter, Sir Edward Henry, Commissioner
       of Police of the Metropolis, to Sir Thomas Mackenzie, New Zealand
       High Commissioner, 29 June 1916, TNA, MEPO2, 1684; 'War Cabinet,

Defence of the Realm Regulation 40 D. Memorandum by the Deputy Secretary of State for War', 25 August 1918, TNA, CO537, 1121.

2 Telegrams, Buxton to Lewis Harcourt, UK Colonial Secretary, 21 September, 24, 25 & 26 October 1914, UKPA, Davidson Papers, DAV/11; Timothy J. Stapleton, *A Military History of South Africa: From the Dutch–Khoi Wars to the End of Apartheid*, Santa Barbara, California, Praeger, 2010, pp. 150–1.

3 Telegrams, Harcourt to Buxton, 23 October 1914, Buxton to Harcourt, 24 & 27 October 1914, UKPA, Davidson Papers, DAV/11.

4 Telegrams, Harcourt to Buxton, 23 October 1914, Buxton to Harcourt, 24 October 1914, UKPA, Davidson Papers, DAV/11; Stapleton, *Military History of South Africa*, pp. 150–2.

5 Ibid., p. 153.

6 George Simeon Mwase, *Strike a Blow and Die: The Story of the Chilembwe Rising*, Cambridge, Massachusetts, Harvard University Press, 1975, pp. 48–9.

7 Ibid., pp. xx–xxi, xxiv, 20–3.

8 Mercer, *Colonial List 1914*, pp. 293–4.

9 Mwase, *Strike a Blow and Die*, pp. 34, 51.

10 Letter, George Smith, Nyasaland Protectorate Governor, to Harcourt, 3 February 1915; 'Report on the operations of the Troops under Captain L.E.L. Triscott extending from Sunday January 24th, 1915 to February 1st, 1915'; Hector Duff, Nyasaland Chief Secretary, to Smith, 'Summary of Events at and near Blantyre January 24th–30th', all in TNA, DO119, 905.

11 Letter, A.M.D. Turnbull, Political Officer, to Smith [February 1915], TNA, DO119, 905.

12 Duff, 'Summary of Events at and near Blantyre January 24th–30th [1915]'; letter, Smith to Harcourt, 20 Feb 1915, Smith, 'Instructions to Captain H.C. Collins, 1st Battalion King's African Rifles, Commanding Punitive Force against John Chilembwe and his rebels', 31 January 1915; letter, Colin Grant, Resident Magistrate, Mlange to Duff, 12 February 1915, all in TNA, DO119, 905; Mwase, *Strike a Blow and Die*, p. 52.

13 Letter, Turnbull to Smith [February 1915]; Duff, 'Summary of Events at and near Blantyre January 24th–30th', TNA, DO119, 905.

14 Malcolm M. Murfett, John N. Miksic, Brian P. Farrell & Chiang Ming Shun, *Between Two Oceans: A Military History of Singapore from 1275 to 1971*, 2nd ed., Singapore, Marshall Cavendish International, 2011, p. 129; Burton, *The Trouble with Empire*, pp. 193–4; *Report in Connection with Mutiny of 5th Light Infantry at Singapore 1915*, Simla, Government Central Branch Press, 1915, BL, IOR/L/MIL/17/19/48, pp. 8–9; Sunit

Singh, 'Ghadar Conspiracy', 1914–1918-online.net, 29 October 2015, accessed 23 May 2018.

15 Murfett, Miksic, Farrell & Ming, *Between Two Oceans*, pp. 129–31; 'Report by Brigadier-General Ridout, General Officer Commanding, Singapore, with remarks on Proceedings of Court of Enquiry' [1915], pp. 423, 431 TNA, WO141, 7; *Mutiny of 5th Light Infantry*, p. 3, BL, IOR/L/MIL/17/19/48.

16 Ibid., pp. 3–4.

17 Ibid., pp. 4, 132–3; Letter, Robert C.D. Bradley to George McMunn, 9 June 1933, UNSW Canberra Library (hereafter UNSWCL), George McMunn Papers, MS21, Box 5, Folder 35.

18 Ibid.; Murfett, Miksic, Farrell & Ming, *Between Two Oceans*, pp. 135, 138; *Mutiny of 5th Light Infantry*, p. 5, BL, IOR/L/MIL/17/19/48; telegram, Brigadier-General Dudley Ridout, GOC Straits Settlements to Lord Kitchener, Secretary UK War Office, 27 February 1915, TNA, WO32, 9559.

19 *Mutiny of 5th Light Infantry*, p. 2, BL, IOR/L/MIL/17/19/48; letter, Bradley to McMunn, 9 June 1933, UNSWCL, McMunn Papers, MS21, Box 5, Folder 35; telegram, Kitchener to Ridout, 28 May 1915, TNA, WO106, 1412.

20 Richard Aldous & Niamh Puirséil (eds), *We Declare: Landmark Documents in Ireland's History*, London, Quercus Publishing, 2008, p. 115; S.J. Connolly, *Oxford Companion to Irish History*, 2nd ed., Oxford, Oxford University Press, 2002, pp. 272–3, 180, 514; Brian Lalor (gen. ed.), *Encyclopaedia of Ireland*, Dublin, Gill & Macmillan, 2003, pp. 352, 897, 932, 1055.

21 Aldous & Puirséil, *We Declare*, p. 114.

22 Keith Jeffery, *1916: A Global History*, London, Bloomsbury, 2015, pp. 101–4; *Irish Builder and Engineer*, 13 May 1916, pp. 196, 198; *Farmers' Gazette*, 13 May 1916, p. 371.

23 Arthur Balfour, UK First Lord of the Admiralty, 'Ulster and the Irish Crisis', p. 2, 24 June 1916, Walter Long, 'The Proposed Irish Settlement', p. 1, 21 June 1916, TNA, CAB1, 17; letter, R. Hutchinson, HQ Irish Command Dublin, to General Henry Wilson, General Officer Commanding IV Corps, 7 July 1916, IWM, Wilson Papers, HHW, 2/83/65.

24 Connolly, *Oxford Companion to Irish History*, pp. 542–4.

25 Ian F.W. Beckett, *The Great War*, 2nd ed., Harlow, Pearson, 2007, p. 295; Cyril Pearce & Helen Durham, 'Patterns of dissent in Britain during the First World War', *War & Society*, Vol. 34, No. 2, May 2015, p. 158.

26 Peter Liddle, *Captured Memories 1900–1918: Across the Threshold of War*, Barnsley, Pen & Sword, 2010, pp. 279–81.

27 Ibid., pp. 282–4.
28 Ibid., pp. 285–7.
29 Mercer, *Colonial Office List 1914*, p. 122; Myer Siemiatycki, 'Munitions and labour militancy: The 1916 Hamilton machinists' strike', *Labour/Le Travail*, Vol. 3, 1978, p. 133.
30 Ibid., pp. 134, 136.
31 Letter, Bowes Jamieson Ltd to Flavelle, 6 March 1916, quoted in Siemiatycki, 'Munitions and labour militancy', p. 139.
32 [Toronto] *Industrial Banner*, 28 April 1916, quoted in Siemiatycki, 'Munitions and Labour Militancy', p. 141.
33 Siemiatycki, 'Munitions and Labour Militancy', p. 145.
34 Ibid., pp. 148–9.
35 Alexander Watson, *Ring of Steel: Germany and Austria–Hungary at War, 1914–1918*, London, Penguin, 2015, p. 466.
36 Roger Chickering, *Imperial Germany and the Great War, 1914–1918*, 3rd ed., Cambridge, Cambridge University Press, 2014, p. 191; David Stevenson, 'The failure of peace by negotiation in 1917', *The Historical Journal*, Vol. 34, No. 1, 1991, pp. 67–9.
37 Chickering, *Imperial Germany*, pp. 72–4; Stevenson, 'Failure of peace', pp. 70–2.
38 Wm. Roger Louis, *Great Britain and Germany's Lost Colonies, 1914–1919*, Oxford, Clarendon Press, 1967, pp. 70–1.
39 Stevenson, 'Failure of peace', pp. 72–3.
40 Stevenson, 'Failure of peace', p. 78; Douglas Newton, 'The Lansdowne "Peace Letter" of 1917 and the prospect of peace with Germany', *Australian Journal of Politics and History*, Vol. 48, No. 1, 2002, pp. 18–19.
41 Letter, Lieutenant-General Sir William Birdwood, General Officer Commanding, Australian Imperial Force, to Sir Ronald Munro Ferguson, 4 April 1917, Australian War Memorial, Canberra (hereafter AWM), 3DRL/2222; Robert Stevenson, *The War with Germany*: Vol. 3 of Jeffrey Grey (ed.), *The Centenary History of Australia and the Great War*, Melbourne, Oxford University Press, 2015, p. 122; John Connor, *Anzac and Empire: George Foster Pearce and the Foundations of Australian Defence*, Melbourne, Cambridge University Press, 2011, p. 106.
42 Source: Stevenson, *War with Germany*, p. 122.
43 Source: Ibid., p. 118.
44 Ibid., p. 120; letters, Lieutenant-General Sir William Birdwood, GOC I Anzac Corps, to Senator George Pearce, Australian Defence Minister, 22 May 1917, AWM, AWM38, 3DRL/6673/67; Lieutenant-General Alexander Godley, GOC II Anzac Corps, to Pearce, 8 July 1917, AWM, 3DRL/2222; Walter Long, UK Colonial Secretary, to Ronald Munro-

Ferguson, Australian Governor-General, 22 August 1917, WSRC, Long Papers, 947/624.

45 Pearce, 'The Minister for Defence in war time', 31 August 1939, National Library of Australia, Canberra, MS1927, ff. 2369–71; letters, Pearce to Birdwood, 20 September 1917, AWM, AWM38, 3DRL/6673/67; Munro Ferguson to Long, 27 July & 29 August 1917, Long to Munro Ferguson, 1 November 1917, WSRC, Long Papers, 947/624.

46 Diary, Haig, 3 March 1918, in Gary Sheffield & John Bourne (eds), *Douglas Haig: War Diaries and Letters*, London, Weidenfeld & Nicolson, p. 386.

47 Miss F. Melland, 'Three Years of War' [1917], TNA, PRO 10/802.

48 Ben H. Morgan, 'The efficient utilization of labour in engineering factories. (With special reference to women's work)', *The Institution of Mechanical Engineers Proceedings*, Vol. 94, No. 1, January–May 1918, pp. 248–50, 266.

49 David Monger, *Patriotism and Propaganda in First World War Britain: The National War Aims Committee and Civilian Morale*, Liverpool, Liverpool University Press, 2012, pp. 1, 91–2.

50 Ibid., p. 17.

51 Ibid., pp. 42, 58, 110; 'National War Aims Committee. Meetings Department Report, 25th September, 1917', p. 1, 'National War Aims Committee. Minutes of Meeting held at 54, Victoria Street, S.W. 1, 4th April 1918', p. 3, TNA, T102, 16; letter, W. Kay Waterson, National Unionist Association, to T. Cox, 11 April 1918, National War Aims Committee, TNA, PRO10, 801.

52 'National War Aims Committee. Meetings Department Report, 10th October 1917', p. 1, TNA, T102, 16; Monger, *Patriotism and Propaganda*, pp. 78–9; Adrian Gregory, *The Last Great War: British Society and the First World War*, Cambridge, Cambridge University Press, 2008, p. 217.

53 Ibid., p. 205; letter, Waterson, to S.P.C. Vesey, National War Aims Committee, 1 May 1918, TNA, PRO10, 801.

54 *Commonwealth Parliamentary Debates* (hereafter *CPD*), Vol. LXXXIV, pp. 3585–6, 3595–646, 4244; [Perth] *West Australian*, 5 April 1918.

55 *Newcastle* [New South Wales] *Morning Herald and Miners' Advocate*, 10 January 1917.

56 Ibid., 17 May 1918; Connor, Stanley & Yule, *War at Home*, p. 135; Ian Turner, *Industrial Labour and Politics: The Dynamics of the Labour Movement in Eastern Australia, 1900–1921*, Cambridge, Cambridge University Press, 1965, pp. 171–2, 175–6.

57 [Perth] *West Australian*, 18 June 1918; Connor, Stanley & Yule, *War at Home*, p. 135; *Newcastle Morning Herald and Miners' Advocate*, 2 May 1918.

58   Federal Caucus Meeting, 17 September 1918 in Patrick Weller (ed.), *Caucus Minutes, 1901–1949: Minutes of the Meetings of the Federal Parliamentary Labor Party*, Vol. 2, Melbourne, Melbourne University Press, 1975, p. 69; Turner, *Industrial Labour and Politics*, pp. 176–8; [Melbourne] *Argus*, 7 & 12 November 1918; *Kalgoorlie Miner*, 11 November 1918.

7

1917: The Battle of Messines

1   James E. Edmonds, *Military Operations France and Belgium, 1915*, Vol. 2, London, Macmillan & Co, 1928, pp. 3, 351; Jack Sheldon, *The German Army on the Western Front 1915*, Barnsley, Pen & Sword, 2012, pp. 138, 142–3; James E. Edmonds, *Military Operations France and Belgium, 1917*, Vol. 2, London, His Majesty's Stationery Office, 1948, pp. 34–5, 43, 49; C.E.W. Bean, *The A.I.F. in France: 1917*: Vol. 4 of C.E.W. Bean (ed.), *The Official History of Australia in the War of 1914–1918*, Sydney, Angus & Robertson, 1943, p. 574; Sanders Marble, *British Artillery on the Western Front in the First World War*, Farnham, Ashgate, 2013, pp. 184–5; Alexander Barrie, *War Underground: The Tunnellers of the Great War*, 1st pub. 1961, rep. London, Tom Donovan Publishing, 1990, pp. 192, 247; *Aberdeen Journal*, 8 June 1917; Cyril Falls, *The History of the 36th (Ulster) Division*, 1st pub. 1922, rep. London, Constable & Co, 1996, pp. 82, 91–2.

2   Elizabeth Greenhalgh, *The French Army and the First World War*, Cambridge, Cambridge University Press, 2014, p. 126; UK War Office, *Statistics of the Military Effort of the British Empire during the Great War 1914–1920*, 1st pub. 1922, rep. Uckfield, Naval & Military Press, 1999, pp. 254–6.

3   Greenhalgh, *French Army*, p. 128; Stevenson, *1914–1918*, pp. 161, 166.

4   Gary Sheffield, *The Chief: Douglas Haig and the British Army*, London, Aurum Press, pp. 159–60; Greenhalgh, *French Army*, p. 129.

5   Chickering, *Imperial Germany*, pp. 62–3.

6   Norman Davies, *Europe: A History*, London, Book Club Associates, 1996, p. 306; Greenhalgh, *French Army*, pp. 129–32.

7   Sheldon, *German Army 1915*, pp. 243–4.

8   Stevenson, *1914–1918*, pp. 162–4; Greenhalgh, *French Army*, p. 141.

9   Ibid., pp. 137, 141–2; Stevenson, *1914–1918*, p. 164.

10   Ibid., p. 164.

11   Ibid., pp. 101, 165; Greenhalgh, *French Army*, pp. 146–7.

12   Stevenson, *1914–1918*, pp. 133, 162; Chickering, *Imperial Germany*, pp. 72–4.

13   Stevenson, *1914–1918*, p. 169; Greenhalgh, *French Army*, pp. 150–1.

14   Letter, Sir Douglas Haig to Lady Haig, 30 June 1916 quoted in Gary

Sheffield & John Bourne (eds), *Douglas Haig: War Diaries and Letters*, London, Weidenfeld & Nicolson, 2005, p. 195; Marble, *British Artillery*, p. 139; William Philpott, *Bloody Victory: The Sacrifice on the Somme*, London, Abacus, 2010, pp. 10, 207; Sheffield, *The Chief*, p. 369; Robin Prior & Trevor Wilson, *The Somme*, 2nd ed., Sydney, NewSouth Publishing, 2016, pp. 115–16.

15   Ibid., pp. 112, 114–15.

16   Philpott, *Bloody Victory*, pp. 194, 201; diary, Douglas Haig, 1 July 1916 in Sheffield & Bourne, *Haig Diaries*, p. 196; 'Edward Montagu-Stuart-Wortley', en.wikipedia.org, accessed 9 August 2017.

17   Letter, Major-General Oliver Nugent, General Officer Commanding 36th (Ulster) Division, to Kitty Nugent, 3 July 1916 in Nicholas Perry (ed.), *Major General Oliver Nugent and the Ulster Division 1915–1918*, Stroud, Sutton Publishing, 2007, pp. 28, 81; Richard S. Grayson, *Belfast Boys: How Unionists and Nationalists Fought and Died Together in the First World War*, London, Continuum, 2009, p. 83; Prior & Wilson, *Somme*, pp. 85–7, 89; Philpott, *Bloody Victory*, pp. 194–5.

18   'Colin John Mackenzie', en.wikipedia.org, accessed 11 August 2017; Christopher Wray, *Sir James Whiteside MacCay: A Turbulent Life*, Melbourne, Oxford University Press, 2002, pp. 135–40; C.E.W. Bean, *The A.I.F. in France: 1916*: Vol. 3 of C.E.W. Bean (ed.), *The Official History of Australia in the War of 1914–1918*, Sydney, Angus & Robertson, 1st pub. 1929, 12th ed. 1941, pp. 442–4; Sheffield, *The Chief*, p. 178; diary, Haig, 20 July 1916 in Sheffield & Bourne, *Haig Diaries*, p. 208.

19   E.J. Kingston-McCloughry, *The Direction of War: A Critique of the Political Direction and High Command in War*, London, Jonathan Cape, 1955, p. 55; NAA, B2455, 'McCloughry E.J.'.

20   Terence Denman, *Ireland's Unknown Soldiers: The 16th (Irish) Division in the Great War, 1914–1918*, Dublin, Irish Academic Press, 1992, pp. 38–9, 62, 68.

21   Philpott, *Bloody Victory*, pp. 251, 348; Denman, *Ireland's Unknown Soldiers*, pp. 80–3.

22   Denman, *Ireland's Unknown Soldiers*, pp. 95, 97.

23   Ibid., pp. 96, 98–101.

24   Stevenson, *1914–1918*, pp. 188–90.

25   Macdonald, 'Awkward salient', pp. 228–31.

26   Stevenson, *1914–1918*, pp. 188–90; Macdonald, 'Awkward salient', pp. 232–3.

27   Hugh Stewart, *The New Zealand Division 1916–1919. A Popular History Based on Official Records*, Auckland, Whitcombe & Tombs Ltd, 1921, p. 83.

28   Ibid., pp. 117–18.
29   Philpott, *Bloody Victory*, p. 408; diary, Douglas Haig, 12 November 1916 in Sheffield & Bourne, *Haig Diaries*, p. 254.
30   Philpott, *Bloody Victory*, pp. 600–3; Greenhalgh, *French Army*, p. 163; James McRandle & James Quirk, 'The Blood test revisited: A new look at German casualty counts in World War I', *Journal of Military History*, Vol. 70, No. 3, June 2006, pp. 692; Sheffield, *The Chief*, pp. 174, 194.
31   Letter, Nugent to Kitty Nugent, 20 December 1916 in Perry, *Nugent*, p. 126.
32   Greenhalgh, *French Army*, pp. 169–70, 181; Stevenson, *1914–1918*, p. 175.
33   Greenhalgh, *French Army*, pp. 196–7.
34   Ibid., pp. 209–15.
35   Gary Sheffield, 'Haig and the British Expeditionary Force in 1917' in Peter Dennis & Jeffrey Grey (eds), *1917: Tactics, Training and Technology. The 2007 Chief of Army History Conference*, Sydney, Australian Military History Publications, 2007, pp. 6–7; Tim Cook, *Shock Troops: Canadians Fighting the Great War, 1917–1918*, Toronto, Viking Canada, 2008, pp. 142–3; Edmonds, *France and Belgium*, Vol. 2, pp. 24–5; Marble, *British Artillery*, p. 183.
36   [Sydney] *Sun*, 30 May 1913; [Sydney] *Daily Telegraph*, 22 August 1913; Barrie, *War Underground*, pp. 24–5.
37   Ibid., pp. 118, 131, 135, 140–1, 247; Bean, *AIF in France 1917*, Vol. 4, pp. 957–9.
38   Marble, *British Artillery*, pp. 119, 133, 183; Albert P. Palazzo, 'The British Army's counter-battery staff office and control of the enemy in World War I', *Journal of Military History*, Vol. 63, No. 1, January 1999, pp. 57–61; Edmonds, *France & Belgium*, Vol. 2, pp. 32, 35, 174; letter, Nugent to Kitty Nugent, 21 May 1917 in Perry, *Nugent*, p. 146.
39   Barrie, *War Underground*, pp. 246–7; Edmonds, *France & Belgium*, Vol. 2, pp. 24–5.
40   Denman, *Ireland's Unknown Soldiers*, p. 110.
41   Edmonds, *France & Belgium 1917*, Vol. 2, pp. 48, 54, 61; Marble, *British Artillery*, p. 185.
42   Letters, Nugent to Kitty Nugent, 7 & 10 June 1917 in Perry, *Nugent*, pp. 153–5, 157.
43   'Island of Ireland Peace Park', en.wikipedia.org, accessed 23 August 2017.
44   Edmonds, *France & Belgium 1917*, Vol. 2, pp. 43–4, 63, 66–9, 71–3.
45   Ibid., pp. 75–6; Bean, *AIF in France 1917*, Vol. 4, p. 620.
46   Edmonds, *France & Belgium, 1917*, Vol. 2, pp. 45, 75–6.
47   Bean, *AIF in France 1917*, Vol. 4, p. 624.
48   Ibid., pp. 623, 628, 637–9.
49   Edmonds, *France & Belgium, 1917*, Vol. 2, pp. 81–2, 87.

50 Ibid., p. 87.

51 Glyn Harper, 'Masterpiece or massacre: The New Zealand Division and the Canadian Corps in 1917' in Peter Dennis & Jeffrey Grey (eds), *1917: Tactics, Training and Technology. The 2007 Chief of Army History Conference*, Sydney, Australian Military History Publications, 2007, p. 65; Bean, *AIF in France 1917*, Vol. 4, p. 664.

52 [Sydney] *Sun*, 18 April 1917; H.V. Evatt, *Australian Labour Leader: The Story of W.A. Holman and the Labour Movement*, Sydney, Angus & Robertson, 1942, p. 436.

53 Stevenson, *1914–1918*, pp. 334–6; Marble, *British Artillery*, p. 195; letter, Nugent to Kitty Nugent, 21 August 1917 in Perry, *Nugent*, pp. 168–9.

54 Stevenson, *1914–1918*, p. 336.

55 Ibid., pp. 337, 379.

56 Ibid., p. 337–8; Jack Horsfall & Nigel Cave, *Cambrai: The Right Hook*, Barnsley, Leo Cooper, 1999, pp. 24–5; Jack Sheldon, *The German Army at Cambrai*, Barnsley, Pen & Sword, 2009, pp. 230–6, 273–4, 312.

57 UK War Office, *Statistics*, pp. 260–5; letter, Nugent to Kitty Nugent, 1 December 1917 in Perry, *Nugent*, p. 190.

8
Volunteers and Conscripts

1 Ian F.W. Beckett, *The Great War*, 2nd ed., Harlow, Pearson Longman, 2007, p. 55–6, 289, 294; Philip Orr, '200,000 volunteer soldiers' in John Horne (ed.), *Our War: Ireland and the Great War*, Dublin, Royal Irish Academy, 2010, pp. 63–77.

2 Source: War Office, *Military Effort of the British Empire*, p. 756.

3 [Lahore] *Panjabee*, 9 August 1916, quoted in Jarboe, *War News in India*, p. 133; David Omissi, '"Martial races": Ethnicity and security in colonial India 1858–1939', *War & Society*, Vol. 9, No. 1, May 1991, p. 21.

4 Timothy C. Winegard, *Indigenous Peoples of the British Dominions and the First World War*, Cambridge, Cambridge University Press, 2012, p. 98; [London] *Times*, 25 October 1915; Richard Smith, *Jamaican Volunteers in the First World War: Race, Masculinity and the Development of National Consciousness*, Manchester, Manchester University Press, 2004, pp. 55–6.

5 Tim Cook, *The Madman and the Butcher: The Sensational Wars of Sam Hughes and General Arthur Currie*, Allen Lane, Toronto, 2010, p. 59.

6 Ibid., p. 59.

7 Ronald Haycock, *Sam Hughes: The Public Career of a Controversial Canadian, 1885–1916*, Wilfrid Laurier University Press in collaboration with Canadian War Museum *et al*, 1986, p. 115.

8 Cook, *Madman and the Butcher*, pp. 66–7.

9   Charles Lucas, 'Canada and the war' in Charles Lucas (ed.), *The Empire at War*, Vol. 2, London, Oxford University Press, 1923, p. 31; Desmond Morton, *A Peculiar Kind of Politics: Canada's Overseas Ministry in the First World War*, Toronto, University of Toronto Press, 1982, p. 21.

10   Letters, Rodolphe Boudreau, Clerk of the Canadian Privy Council, to Duke of Connaught, Canadian Governor-General, 14 August 1914; Lewis Harcourt, UK Colonial Secretary, to Duke of Connaught, 3 September 1914, TNA, WO32, 5137; letter, Harcourt to Duke of Connaught, 10 September 1914, Bodleian Library, Oxford (hereafter BLO), Harcourt Papers, dep. 476, f. 170.

11   Lucas, 'Canada and the war', pp. 3, 9.

12   J.N.I. Dawes & L.L. Robson, *Citizen to Soldier: Australia before the Great War: Recollections of Members of the First A.I.F.*, Melbourne, Melbourne University Press, 1977, p. 130.

13   Ibid., pp. 112, 155–8.

14   A.W. Martin, *Robert Menzies: A Life*, 2nd ed., Melbourne, Melbourne University Press, Vol. 1, pp. 310–12; John McQuilton, *Rural Australia and the Great War: From Tarrawingee to Tangambalanga*, Melbourne, Melbourne University Press, 2001, pp. 175–6.

15   Gregory, *Last Great War*, pp. 31–2.

16   R.J.Q. Adams & Philip P. Poirier, *The Conscription Controversy in Great Britain, 1900–18*, Basingstoke, Macmillan, 1987, pp. 7, 10, 17; IWM, Wilson Papers, HHW, Wilson Diary, 12 September 1911; IWM, Wilson Papers, HHW, HHW3/7/1 'Policy and the Army', 1 January 1913, p. 106.

17   Adams & Poirier, *Conscription Controversy*, pp. 80–1, 94–5.

18   Ibid., pp. 203–5.

19   Ibid., pp. 205–7; David Gilmour, *Curzon*, London, John Murray, 1994, pp. 444–5.

20   Paul Baker, *King and Country Call: New Zealanders, Conscription and the Great War*, Auckland, Auckland University Press, 1988, pp. 26, 42, 90; McGibbon, *Oxford Companion*, pp. 110, 118, 313.

21   John Crawford, '"New Zealand is being bled to death": The formation, operations and disbandment of the Fourth Brigade' in Crawford & McGibbon, *New Zealand's Great War*, pp. 260–5.

22   Letter, James Allen, New Zealand Defence Minister, to William Massey, New Zealand Prime Minister, 20 January 1917, ANZ/Te Rua Mahara o te Kāwanatanga, Wellington, Allen Papers, Miscellaneous files and papers – Correspondence between J Allen and WF Massey, 1 September 1916–1 August 1919; McGibbon (ed.), *New Zealand Military History*, p. 118; John E. Martin, 'Blueprint for the future? "National efficiency" and the First World War' in Crawford & McGibbon, *New Zealand's Great War*, pp. 519–20.

23   McGibbon (ed.), *New Zealand Military History*, p. 118; letter, James
      Allen, New Zealand Defence Minister, to William Massey, New Zealand
      Prime Minister, 17 March 1917, ANZ, Allen Papers, 1/9; New Zealand
      Parliamentary Paper H–43, 'National Efficiency Board (Report Of)'
      [1917], pp. 4, 6, 9, ANZ, NEB1, 22.
24   Barker, *King and Country*, pp. 210–13.
25   McGibbon (ed.), *New Zealand Military History*, p. 297.
26   Letter, Allen to Massey, 11 June 1918, ANZ, Allen Papers, 1/9; McGibbon,
      New Zealand Military History, p. 298; Barker, *King and Country*, pp. 210–
      20.
27   Ibid., pp. 173, 175.
28   Barker, *King and Country*, pp. 179, 183–7, 189.
29   Smith, *Jamaican Volunteers*, pp. 5, 127, 130–1.
30   Ibid., pp. 56, 63.
31   Charles Lucas, 'Jamaica' in Lucas (ed.) *Empire at War*, Vol. 2, pp. 349–50;
      Smith, *Jamaican Volunteers*, p. 140.
32   Smith, *Jamaican Volunteers*, pp. 163, 165; Stanley Gibbons Ltd, *Stanley
      Gibbons' Postage Stamp Catalogue 1952*, Part 1: *British Empire (Complete)*,
      London, Stanley Gibbons, 1952, p. 320.
33   John Connor, Peter Stanley & Peter Yule, *The War at Home*: Vol. 4 of
      Jeffrey Grey (ed.) *The Centenary History of Australia and the Great War*,
      Melbourne, Oxford University Press, 2015, pp. 94–5.
34   Nick Dyrenfurth, *Heroes and Villians: The Rise and Fall of the Early
      Australian Labor Party*, Sydney, Fourth Estate, 2008, p. 185; Connor,
      Stanley & Yule, *War at Home*, p. 97.
35   Ibid., pp. 93–4, 103.
36   Connor, Stanley & Yule, *War at Home*, p. 106.
37   *Commonwealth Parliamentary Debates* (hereafter *CPD*), Vol. 80,
      21 September 1916, pp. 8799–800; letter, Pearce to Fisher, National
      Library of Australia, Canberra (hereafter NLA), Fisher Papers, MS2919,
      1/265; David Day, *Andrew Fisher: Prime Minister of Australia*, Sydney,
      Fourth Estate, 2008, p. 294.
38   ALP Federal Caucus Meeting, 14 September 1916 in Patrick Weller (ed.),
      *Caucus Minutes: Minutes of the Meetings of the Federal Parliamentary Labor
      Party*, Melbourne, Melbourne University Press, 1975, Vol. 1, pp. 436–7.
39   John Connor, *Anzac and Empire: George Foster Pearce and the Foundations
      of Australian Defence*, Melbourne, Cambridge University Press, 2011,
      pp. 101–3.
40   Letter, General Sir William Birdwood, GOC AIF, to Colonel R. Rintoul,
      Clifton College, 12 November 1916, IWM, Birdwood Papers, WRB/1,
      9; [London] *British Australasian*, 7 September 1916; Ross McMullin,
      'Australian perceptions of the Great War: The soldiers' vote in the

conscription referenda, 1916 & 1917', paper, Australian War Memorial History Conference, 1981, pp. 4–6.

41   Ernest Scott, *Australia during the War*, Vol. 11 of C.E.W. Bean (ed.) *Official History of Australia in the War of 1914–1918*, 7th ed., Sydney, Angus & Robertson, 1941, p. 352; Australian Electoral Commission www.aec.gov.au/Elections/Australian_Electoral_History/Voter_Turnout. htm, accessed 10 October 2017; telegram, Munro Ferguson to Long, 3 January 1917, WSRO, Long Papers, 947/6241; Joan Beaumont, *Broken Nation: Australia in the Great War*, Sydney, Allen & Unwin, 2013, p. 224.

42   Connor, Stanley & Yule, *War at Home*, p. 115; letter, Pearce to Fisher, 25 January 1917, NLA, MS2919, 1/301.

43   Connor, Stanley & Yule, *War at Home*, p. 116–23.

44   Ibid., p. 123.

45   [Sydney] *Australian Worker*, 15 November 1917; Connor, Stanley & Yule, *War at Home*, p. 124.

46   Ibid., pp. 70–7; [Melbourne] *Argus*, 12 November 1917.

47   Connor, Stanley & Yule, *War at Home*, p. 127; McMullin, 'Australian perceptions', pp. 7–8; [London] *British Australasian*, 24 January 1918.

48   Robert Stevenson, *The War with Germany*, Vol. 3 of Jeffrey Grey (ed.), *The Centenary History of Australia and the Great War*, Melbourne, Oxford University Press, 2015, pp. 198–9.

49   Scott, *Australia during the War*, p. 299.

50   Nasson, *Springboks on the Somme*, pp. 125–54; John Buchan, *The History of the South African Forces in France*, Cape Town, T. Maskew Miller, 1921, p. 224.

51   Nasson, *Springboks on the Somme*, pp. 161–6, 168–9.

52   Letter, Lord Buxton, South African Governor-General, to Long, WSRO, Long Papers, 947/602; Nasson, *Springboks on the Somme*, p. 164; *The Annual Register. A Review of Public Events at Home and Abroad. For the Year 1917*, London, Longman, Green & Co., 1918, p. 305.

53   Nasson, *Springboks on the Somme*, pp. 96, 157–9; TNA, CAB1, 23, 'Memorandum on steps taken to Increase the Supply of (a) Coloured [sic] Troops, (b) Coloured [sic] Labour, and on the use by the Naval and Military Authorities of Colonial Government Officials' [January 1917]; 1st Battalion, Cape Corps, War Diary, 19 & 20 September, 1918, WO95, 4632.

54   Letter, Buxton to Long, 2 February 1917, WSRO, Long Papers, 947/601.

55   Letters, Major J.Y.A. Leipoldt, Union of South Africa General Staff Intelligence, to Major Allister Miller, Royal Flying Corps [1917], Miller to Director-General, UK Air Ministry, 7 August 1918, TNA, AIR2, 197

56   Beckett, *Great War*, p. 95; *Annual Register 1917*, p. 305.

57   Colonel R.A. Haywood, Nigeria Regiment, 'Recruiting in West Africa', 2 May 1917, TNA, CO445, 42; memo, C.H. Harper, Assistant Colonial Secretary, Gold Coast, 31 May 1917, TNA, CO445, 39; Beckett, *Great War*, pp. 96–7; Osuntokun, *Nigeria in the First World War*, pp. 247–8, 258–61.

58   Letter, Allen to Massey, 29 October 1916, ANZ, Allen Papers, 9/9a; J.L. Granatstein & J.M. Hitsman, *Broken Promises: A History of Conscription in Canada*, Toronto, Oxford University Press, 1978, pp. 66, 68, 81, 86; James Wood, *Militia Myths: Ideas of the Canadian Citizen Soldier, 1896–1921*, Vancouver, University of British Columbia Press, 2010, pp. 237–8.

59   Letter, Major J.B.E. Malhiot, OC 233rd Battalion, to CSC, NB Troops, 22 February 1917, LAC, RG 24, Vol. 4576, 3-35-1; J.L. Granatstein & Dean F. Olivier (eds), *The Oxford Companion to Canadian Military History*, Toronto, Oxford University Press, 2011, pp. 67–8, 352–3; Granatstein & Hitsman, *Broken Promises*, p. 73; letter, Duke of Devonshire to Long, 20 June 1918, WSHC, Long Papers, 947/609.

60   Wood, *Militia Myths*, p. 239.

61   Granatstein & Hitsman, *Broken Promises*, pp. 67–8, 71–2.

62   Granatstein & Olivier, *Canadian Military History*, p. 123; Martin F. Auger, 'On the brink of civil war: The Canadian government and the suppression of the 1918 Quebec Easter Riots', *Canadian Historical Review*, Vol. 89, No. 4, December 2008, pp. 503–40.

63   Wood, *Militia Myths*, p. 248; Granatstein & Olivier, *Canadian Military History*, pp. 289–90; Tim Cook, *Shock Troops: Canadians Fighting the Great War, 1917–1918*, Toronto, Viking Canada, 2008, p. 504.

64   Telegrams, Long to Devonshire, 5 April 1918, Devonshire to Long, 6 April 1918, WSHC, Long Papers, 947/610.

65   J. Finnan, ' "Let Irishmen come together in the trenches": John Redmond and Irish party policy in the Great War, 1914–1918', *Irish Sword*, Vol. 22, No. 88, Winter 2000, p. 183; Gregory, *Last Great War,* p. 81; Royal Irish Constabulary (hereafter RIC), Belfast City Confidential Reports, January 1916 to October 1918, TNA, CO904, 99 to CO904, 107.

66   Adams & Poirier, *Conscription Controversy*, pp. 229–32.

67   Ibid., pp. 232, 237; Michael Laffan, *The Resurrection of Ireland: The Sinn Féin Party 1916–1922*, Cambridge, Cambridge University Press, 1999, pp. 138–40; [London] *Tablet*, 18 May 1918.

68   Letters, Long to Herbert Asquith [May 1916], Long Papers, WSHC, 947/144; Long to Sir George Cave, 26 April 1918, Long Papers, WSHC, 947/177; Captain Maurice Healy, 29th Division, to Long, 18 May 1918, Long Papers, WSHC, 947/253.

9
1918: The Battles of Amiens and Megiddo

1   Stevenson, *War with Germany*: Vol. 3 of Jeffrey Grey (ed.), *The Centenary History of Australia and the Great War*, Melbourne, Oxford University Press, 2015, pp. 190–1, 198; Cameron Pulsifer, 'Canada's First Armoured Unit: Raymond Brutinel and the Canadian motor machine gun brigades of the First World War', *Canadian Military History*, Vol. 10, No. 1, Winter 2001, pp. 45–7, 50–1; Greenhalgh, *French Army*, p. 326; Jeffrey Grey, *The War with the Ottoman Empire*: Vol. 2 of Grey (ed.), *Centenary History*, Oxford University Press, Melbourne, 2014, pp. 168, 177–8; Stevenson, *1914–1918*, p. 437; H.S. Gullett, *The Australian Imperial Force in Sinai and Palestine 1914–1918*, Vol. 7 of C.E.W. Bean (ed.), *The Official History of Australia in the War of 1914–1918*, Sydney, Angus & Robertson, 1944, p. 719; Smith, *Jamaican Volunteers*, p. 90; G.W. Rhys Jenkins, 'The fighting in Egypt, Sinai, and Palestine' in Charles Lucas (ed.), *The Empire at War*, Vol. 5, London, Oxford University Press, 1926, pp. 127–8; [Kingston] *Daily Gleaner*, 14 November 1918.

2   Chickering, *Imperial Germany*, p. 202.

3   Stevenson, *1914–1918*, pp. 297, 398–9.

4   David Hamlin, 'The fruits of occupation: food and Germany's occupation of Romania in the First World War', *First World War Studies*, Vol. 4, No. 1, January 2013, pp. 83, 87, 91.

5   Wolfram Dornik & Peter Lieb, 'Misconceived *realpolitik* in a failing state: the political and economical fiasco of the Central Powers in the Ukraine, 1918', *First World War Studies*, Vol 1, No. 4, January 2013, pp. 114–15, 117; Chickering, *Imperial Germany*, p. 196.

6   Stevenson, *1914–1918*, p. 399; Chickering, *Imperial Germany*, p. 208.

7   Stevenson, *1914–1918*, pp. 399–400.

8   Ibid., pp. 400; Jack Sheldon, *The German Army at Cambrai*, Barnsley, Pen & Sword, 2009, pp. 208, 229.

9   Letter, Nugent to Kitty Nugent, 18 February & 20 March 1918 in Perry, *Nugent*, pp. 204, 210.

10   Stevenson, *1914–1918*, p. 408; Elizabeth Greenhalgh, *Victory through Coalition: Britain and France during the First World War*, Cambridge, Cambridge University Press, 2005, p. 189.

11   Stevenson, *1914–1918*, p. 409.

12   Denman, *Ireland's Unknown Soldiers*, pp. 156, 160, 167; Falls, *36th (Ulster) Division*, pp. 184–5, 195.

13   Letter, Nugent to Kitty Nugent, 25 March 1918 in Perry, *Nugent*, p. 215; Falls, *36th (Ulster) Division*, p. 217.

14   Matthew Stibbe, 'Kaiser Wilhelm II: The Hohenzollerns at war' in Matthew Hughes & Matthew Seligmann (eds), *Leadership in Conflict*

1914–1918, Barnsley, Leo Cooper, 2000, p. 278; Chickering, *Imperial Germany*, p. 204; Gordon A. Craig, 'Delbrück: The military historian' in Peter Paret (ed.), *Makers of Modern Strategy from Machiavelli to the Modern Age*, Princeton, New Jersey, Princeton University Press, 1986, pp. 349–52.

15 David Zabecki, 'Railroads and the operational level of war in the German 1918 offensives', in Jennifer D. Keene & Michael S. Neiberg, *Finding Common Ground: New Directions in First World War Studies*, Leiden, Brill, 2011, p. 166.

16 Ibid., pp. 170, 173; Greenhalgh, *Victory through Coalition*, pp. 193–4, 198.

17 Zabecki, 'Railroads', pp. 176–7; Greenhalgh, *Victory through Coalition*, p. 207.

18 C.E.W. Bean, *The A.I.F. in France: December 1917–May 1918*: Vo. 5 of Bean (ed.), *Official History*, Sydney, Angus & Robertson, 1943, pp. 564, 568, 600.

19 Ibid., pp. 581, 587.

20 Ibid.; 'Fynch Roy Andrew', NAA, B2455.

21 Bean, *December 1917–May 1918*, pp. 612–13, 618.

22 Diary, Lord Derby, 27 & 30 May, 3 June 1918 in David Dutton (ed.), *Paris 1918: The War Diary of the British Ambassador, the 17th Earl of Derby*, Liverpool, Liverpool University Press, 2001, pp. 18, 32; Michael S. Neiberg, *The Second Battle of the Marne*, Bloomington & Indianapolis, Indiana University Press, 2008, p. 6; Zabecki, 'Railroads', pp. 179–80; Greenhalgh, *Victory through Coalition*, pp. 213, Greenhalgh, *French Army*, p. 298.

23 Zabecki, 'Railroads', pp. 179–80; Greenhalgh, *Victory through Coalition*, pp. 213; Greenhalgh, *French Army*, p. 298.

24 Zabecki, 'Railroads', p. 181; Greenhalgh, *French Army*, pp. 298, 301–4.

25 Neiberg, *Second Battle of the Marne*, p. 90; Greenhalgh, *French Army*, pp. 296, 306–8.

26 Ibid., pp. 296, 306–9, 317–20; Neiberg, *Second Battle of the Marne*, p. 115.

27 H.V. Marrot, *The Life and Letters of John Galsworthy*, London, William Heinemann, 1935, p. 443.

28 Greenhalgh, *Victory through Coalition*, pp. 247–8.

29 John Coates, *An Atlas of Australian Wars*: Vol. 7 of Peter Dennis & John Coates (eds), *The Australian Centenary History of Defence*, 2nd ed., Melbourne, Oxford University Press, 2006, p. 78; Strong & Marble, *Artillery in the Great War*, p. 147.

30 Coates, *Atlas of Australian Wars*, pp. 78–9; C.E.W. Bean, *The A.I.F. in France: May 1918–the Armistice*, Vol. 6 of Bean (ed.), *Official History*, Sydney, Angus & Robertson, 1942, pp. 227–40.

31 Ibid., p. 247; Coates, *Atlas of Australian Wars*, p. 80.

32 Bean, *May 1918–the Armistice*, pp. 282, 284, 326–7; Coates, *Atlas of Australian Wars*, pp. 78, 80–81.

33 Letter, General Sir Henry Rawlinson, GOC Fourth British Army, to General Sir Henry Wilson, Chief of the Imperial General Staff, 8 July 1918, IWM, Wilson Papers, HHW 2/13A/23; Bean, *May 1918–the Armistice*, p. 335.
34 Diary, Douglas Haig, 17 May 1918 in Sheffield & Bourne, *Haig Diaries*, p. 413.
35 Bean, *May 1918–the Armistice*, p. 511.
36 Ibid., p. 504.
37 James Edmonds, *Military Operations France and Belgium 1918*, Vol. 4, London, His Majesty's Stationery Office, 1947, pp. 22, 41; War Diary, Assistant Director Medical Services, 2nd Australian Division, August 1918, AWM, AWM4, 26/19/32, Pt 1; Stevenson, *1914–1918*, p. 426; Dean Chappelle, 'The Canadian attack at Amiens, 8–11 August 1918', *Canadian Military History*, Vol. 2, Issue 2, 1993, p. 94; Bean, *May 1918–the Armistice*, pp. 497, 501.
38 Edmonds, *France & Belgium 1918*, p. 299; Marble, *British Artillery*, p. 236; Bean, *May 1918–the Armistice*, pp. 499, 544; Chappelle, 'Canadian attack at Amiens', p. 97; Strong & Marble, *Artillery in the Great War*, p. 184.
39 Edmonds, *France & Belgium 1918*, pp. 11, 74, 87, 154, 298, 495, 519.
40 Stevenson, *1914–1918*, p. 426; letter, Rawlinson to Wilson, 9 August 1918, IWM, Wilson Papers, 2/13A/25a.
41 Letter, Sir Alexander Godley, GOC XXII British Corps to Sir Ian Hamilton, 16 August 1918, LCHMA, Hamilton Papers, 8/1/29; diary, Haig, 19 August 1918 in Sheffield & Bourne, *Haig Diaries*, p. 447.
42 Jonathan Boff, *Winning and Losing on the Western Front: The British Third Army and the Defeat of Germany in 1918*, Cambridge, Cambridge University Press, 2012, pp. 26–8; Stewart, *New Zealand Division*, p. 428.
43 Strong & Marble, *Artillery in the Great War*, pp. 187–8; Boff, *Winning and Losing*, pp. 28–9.
44 Stevenson, *1914–1918*, pp. 428–9.
45 Strong & Marble, *Artillery in the Great War*, pp. 190–1; Stevenson, *War with Germany*, pp. 197, 201.
46 Stevenson, *1914–1918*, p. 430; Stewart, *New Zealand Division*, p. 500.
47 Stevenson, *1914–1918*, p. 429.
48 Edward J. Erickson, *Ordered to Die: A History of the Ottoman Army in the First World War*, Westport, Connecticut, Greenwood Press, 2001, pp. 1–3, 19, 36.
49 Mesut Uyar, *The Ottoman Defence against the Anzac Landings 25 April 1915. Australian Army Campaigns Series 16*, Sydney, Big Sky Publishing, 2015, p. 73; Edward J. Erickson, *Gallipoli and the Middle East 1914–1918: From the Dardanelles to Mesopotamia*, London, Amber Books, 2008, p. 17;

Erickson, *Ordered to Die*, pp. 125, 135, 214, 217–18; Stevenson, *1914–1918*, pp. 116–17.

50 James E. Kitchen, *The British Imperial Army in the Middle East: Morale and Military Identity in the Sinai and Palestine Campaigns, 1916–18*, London, Bloomsbury, 2014, pp. 19–20.

51 Erickson, *Gallipoli and the Middle East*, p. 42; Stevenson, *1914–1918*, p. 122; Kitchen, *British Imperial Army*, p. 16.

52 Ibid., pp. 16–17; Grey, *War with the Ottoman Empire*, pp. 103, 116–23.

53 Sheffield, *The Chief*, pp. 217, 221; Grey, *War with the Ottoman Empire*, p. 130, Erickson, *Ordered to Die*, p. 169.

54 Sheffield, *The Chief*, pp. 217, 221; Grey, *War with the Ottoman Empire*, pp. 130, 139–45; Erickson, *Ordered to Die*, p. 174; Kitchen, *British Imperial Army*, p. 61.

55 Ibid., p. 74.

56 Diary, Mole, 20 & 21 November 1914, IWM, Docs.6881 *Empress of Asia*; Kitchen, *British Imperial Army*, p. 74.

57 Letter, General Sir Edmund Allenby, General Officer Commanding Egyptian Expeditionary Force, to Wilson, 21 August 1918, IWM, Wilson papers, HHW, 2/33A/20; James E. Kitchen, 'The Indianization of the Egyptian Expeditionary Force: Palestine 1918' in Kaushik Roy (ed.), The *Indian Army in the Two World Wars*, Leiden, Brill, 2011, pp. 166, 169, 176–7.

58 Letters, Allenby to Wilson, 5 & 22 June 1918, IWM, Wilson Papers, HHW, 2/33A/4, 2/33A/12; Kitchen, 'Indianization of the EEF', pp. 180, 182.

59 Letter, Allenby to Wilson, 24 July 1918, IWM, Wilson Papers, HHW, 2/33A/4.

60 Source: Erickson, *Ordered to Die*, p. 197.

61 Source: War Office, *Military Effort of the British Empire*, p. 17.

62 Letter, Allenby to Wilson, 21 August 1918, IWM, Wilson Papers, HHW, 2/33A/20; Erickson, *Ordered to Die*, pp. 196–8.

63 Letter, Allenby to Wilson, 23 September 1918, IWM, Wilson Papers, HHW, 2/33A/23; telegram, Wilson to Allenby, 25 September 1918, IWM, Wilson Papers, HHW, 2/67/6.

64 Erickson, *Gallipoli and the Middle East*, p. 220.

65 Erickson, *Ordered to Die*, p. 173; Grey, *War with the Ottoman Empire*, pp. 171, 173; Stevenson, *1914–1918*, p. 468.

66 Alexander Watson, *Enduring the Great War: Combat, Morale and Collapse in the German and British Armies, 1914–1918*, Cambridge, Cambridge University Press, 2014, pp. 198, 209, 235.

67 Stevenson, *1914–1918*, pp. 470–3, 493–4, 497–8.

68   T.G. Otte, '"Postponing the evil day": Sir Edward Grey and British
      foreign policy', *The International History Review*, Vol. 38, No. 2, March
      2016, p. 250; diary, Lord Derby, 11 November 1918 in Dutton, *Paris 1918*,
      pp. 336–7.

10
Farmers and Agriculture

1   Jim Beach, *Haig's Intelligence: GHQ and the German Army, 1916–1918*,
      Cambridge, Cambridge University Press, 2013, p. 297; Watson, *Enduring
      the Great War*, p. 196; Avner Offer, *The First World War: An Agrarian
      Interpretation*, Oxford, Clarendon Press, 1989, p. 1; James Belich,
      *Replenishing the Earth: The Settler Revolution and the Rise of the Anglo-
      World, 1783–1939*, Oxford, Oxford University Press, 2011, pp. 208, 468;
      'Purchase of frozen rabbits on behalf of the Imperial Government', 15
      February 1918, letter, Secretary New Zealand Department of Imperial
      Government Supplies to Secretary New Zealand Department of
      Agriculture, 1 March 1918, ANZ, W1708, 412 14 Ag. 11/130/4; Hal A.
      Skaarup, 'Whiz bangs and woolly bears: Walter Estabrooks and the Great
      War, compiled from his diary and letters', *Canadian Military History*, Vol.
      4, No. 2, Spring 1995, p.64; [Wellington] *Evening Post*, 26 July 1917;
      letters, Buxton to Long [October 1917]; Botha to Long, 21 December
      1917, WSRC, Long Papers, 947/603; Connor, Stanley & Yule, *War
      at Home*, pp. 91–2, 143; Alan Bowker, *A Time Such as There Never Was
      Before: Canada After the Great War*, Toronto, Dundurn, 2014, pp. 222, 232;
      Connolly, *Oxford Companion to Irish History*, p. 543.
2   Mercer, *Colonial Office List 1914*, p. 200.
3   Elizabeth Wrangham, 'An African road revolution: The Gold Coast in the
      period of the Great War', *Journal of Imperial and Commonwealth History*,
      Vol. 32, No. 1, January 2004, pp. 5–6, 11–14; Mercer, *Colonial Office List
      1914*, p. 198.
4   Connor, Stanley & Yule, *War at Home*, pp. 35–6, 39, 40, 42.
5   Ibid., pp. 47–9.
6   Bryce Fraser (ed.), *The Macquarie Book of Events*, Sydney, Macquarie
      Library, 1983, pp. 286, 304, 315, 326, 336; B.D. Graham, *The Formation
      of the Australian Country Parties*, Canberra, Australian National University
      Press, 1966, p. 100; [Melbourne] *Argus*, 2 October 1916.
7   Connor, Stanley & Yule, *War at Home*, p. 137; Fraser, *Macquarie Book of
      Events*, p. 315.
8   Graham, *Formation of Australian Country Parties*, p. 118; [Melbourne] *Age*,
      21 June 1918; *Colac Herald*, 24 June 1918.
9   Connor, Stanley & Yule, *War at Home*, p. 137.

10 Ibid., pp. 137–8; 'Corangamite by-election, 1918', en.wikipedia.org, accessed 26 May 2018.

11 [Melbourne] *Argus*, 24 December 1918; Connor, Stanley & Yule, *War at Home*, pp. 142–3.

12 Mourad Djebabla, '"Fight or farm": Canadian farmers and the dilemma of the war effort in World War I (1914–1918)', *Canadian Military Journal*, Vol. 13, No. 2, Spring 2013, p. 60; Charles Lucas, 'Canada and the War' in Lucas, *The Empire at War*, Vol. 2, London, Oxford University Press, 1923, pp. 21–2, 32, 54.

13 Djebabla, 'Fight or farm', pp. 65–6; Bowker, *Time Such as There Never Was Before*, p. 234.

14 Letter, Devonshire to Long, 19 December 1917, WSRC, Long Papers, 947/610; Bowker, *Time Such as There Never Was Before*, pp. 233–4.

15 Ibid., pp. 239–40.

16 Ibid., pp. 241–2, 245, 247.

17 Stephen Broadberry & Mark Harrison, 'The economics of World War I: An overview' and Stephen Broadberry & Peter Howlett, 'The United Kingdom during World War I: Business as usual' in Stephen Broadberry & Mark Harrison (eds), *The Economics of World War I*, Cambridge, Cambridge University Press, 2005, pp. 18, 211–13; *Annual Register 1917*, Pt 1, p. 107; Keith Grieves, 'War comes to the fields: Sacrifice, localism and ploughing up the English countryside in 1917' in Ian F.W. Beckett (ed.), *1917: Beyond the Western Front*, Leiden, Brill, 2009, p. 169; letter, Long to Buxton, 7 June 1918, WSRC, Long Papers, 947/604.

18 [Dublin] *Farmers' Gazette*, 23 December 1916 p. 1059; 'Note on the potato crop of 1916, with reference to the fixing of prices', 7 February 1917; 'Memorandum by the Secretary for Scotland as to the potato problem in Scotland', 5 March 1917, [UK] Parliamentary Archives, DAV, 54.

19 Dominic Berry, 'Agricultural modernity as a product of the Great War: The founding of the Official Seed Testing Station for England and Wales, 1917–1921', *War & Society*, Vol. 34, No. 2, May 2015, pp. 121–39; 'Proposed Ford Factory in Ireland for Manufacture of Agricultural Tractors' [1916], [UK] Parliamentary Archives, DAV, 31; Arthur Amos, 'Utility of motor-tractors for tillage purposes', *The Institution of Mechanical Engineers Proceedings*, Vol. 94, No. 1, June 1918, pp. 47–54, 159.

20 [Dublin] *Farmers' Gazette*, 22 August 1914, p. 809, 28 August 1914, p. 749, 4 September 1915, p. 778, 11 September 1915, p. 800.

21 Ibid., 16 January 1915, p. 43, 25 September 1915, p. 815.

22 Ibid., 2 September 1916, p. 701.

23 Ibid., 16 September 1916, p. 739.

24 Ibid., 20 January 1917, p. 49, 10 February 1917, p. 109.

25 Ibid., 17 March 1917, p. 219, 25 August 1917, p. 687, 1 September 1917, pp. 703, 729.

26 Ibid., 16 June 1917, p. 483, 1 September 1917, p. 704.

27 Ibid., 1 September 1917, p. 724, 27 July 1918, p. 636, 10 August 1918, p. 666.

28 '[Royal Irish Constabulary] Inspector General's Monthly Report for December, 1918' '[Royal Irish Constabulary County Antrim] Confidential Report for December 1918', 19 January 1919, TNA, CO904, 105.

29 Lord French, Lord Lieutenant of Ireland, 'Report on the State of Ireland', 30 August 1918, WSRC, Long Papers, 947/230.

30 *Northern Standard and Monaghan, Cavan and Tyrone Advertiser*, 28 September 1918; [Dublin] *Farmers' Gazette*, 24 August 1918 p. 720.

31 *Northern Standard and Monaghan, Cavan and Tyrone Advertiser*, 28 September 1918; *Limerick Leader*, 21 October 1918; [Waterford] *Evening News*, 5 & 21 November 1918.

32 Senia Pašeta, *Irish Nationalist Women, 1900–1918*, Cambridge, Cambridge University Press, 2013, pp. 221, 250–2.

33 Ibid., pp. 257, 260–1; *Limerick Leader*, 4 December 1918; *Sligo Independent*, 14 December 1918.

34 Pašeta, *Irish Nationalist Women*, p. 265.

35 Keith Jeffery, *The British Army and the Crisis of Empire 1918–22*, Manchester, Manchester University Press, 1984, pp. 1, 10.

36 Ibid., pp. 14–15, 24–5, 27–30; letter, Allenby to Wilson, 16 November 1918, IWM, Wilson Papers, HHW2/33A/30.

37 Keith Jeffery, *Field Marshal Sir Henry Wilson: A Political Soldier*, Oxford, Oxford University Press, 2006, p. 244; letter, Smuts to Buxton, 20 October 1916, WSRC, Long Papers, 947/601; letters, Wilson to Hughes, 11 November 1918, Hughes to Wilson, 13 November 1918, IWM, Wilson Papers, HHW2/39/12–13; Jeffery, *Crisis of Empire*, p. 32.

38 Sean O'Faolain, *Vive Moi! An Autobiography*, London, Hart-Davis, 1965, p. 39; David Fitzpatrick, 'Militarism in Ireland, 1900–1922' in Thomas Bartlett & Keith Jeffery (eds), *A Military History of Ireland*, Cambridge, Cambridge University Press, 1996, p. 405; Peter Hart, *The I.R.A. at War 1916–1923*, Oxford, Oxford University Press, 2005, pp. 34–41.

39 Connolly, *Oxford Companion to Irish History*, pp.16–17, 34, 49–50.

40 Peter Hart, *The I.R.A. and its Enemies: Violence and Community in Cork, 1916–1923*, p. 140.

41 Connolly, *Oxford Companion to Irish History*, p. 277.

42 Letter, Major Bernard Montgomery to General Arthur Percival, 14 October 1923 in William Sheehan (ed.), *British Voices from the Irish*

War of Independence 1918–1921: The words of British servicemen who were there, Wilton, Co. Cork, Collins Press, 2005, pp. 151–2.

43   'Draft Letter from Lord Islington to the Prime Minister' [1917], WSRC, Long Papers, 947/560.

44   Jeffery, *Crisis of Empire*, pp. 99–102.

45   Ibid., pp. 104–5; Sir Verney Lovett, *India*, London, Waverley Book Company [1923], p. 222.

46   Brian Robson, *Crisis on the Frontier: The Third Afghan War and the Campaign in Waziristan 1919–1920*, Stroud, Spellmount, 2007, pp. 43–4, 139–42.

47   Suzanne Brugger, *Australians and Egypt 1914–1919*, Melbourne, Melbourne University Press, 1980, pp. 84, 87, 93; Kristian Coates Ulrichsen, *The Logistics and Politics of the British Campaigns in the Middle East, 1914–22*, London, Palgrave Macmillan, 2010, pp. 175–6, 179–80; Jeffery, *Crisis of Empire*, p. 111.

48   Brugger, *Australians and Egypt*, pp. 91, 96, 134, 136–8; Jeffery, *Crisis of Empire*, pp. 111–12; Ellis Goldberg, 'Peasants in revolt – Egypt 1919', *International Journal of Middle East Studies*, Vol. 24, No. 2, May 1992, p. 262.

49   Ulrichsen, *Logistics and Politics*, pp. 185, 190; Mark Jacobsen, '"Only by the sword": British counter-insurgency in Iraq, 1920', *Small Wars & Insurgencies*, Vol. 2, No. 2, August 1991, pp. 323, 332, 338, 351.

50   Telegram, Lord Milner, War Secretary, to Munro Ferguson, 19 September 1920, NLA, MS1538, 16/2234–5; Carl Bridge, 'Australia's refusal to send troops to Mesopotamia, September 1920: A note', *Journal of Australian Studies*, Vol. 9, November 1981, pp. 71–6; Connor, *Anzac and Empire*, pp. 138–9.

51   Ulrichsen, *Logistics and Politics*, pp. 183–4, 186, 192, 195; Jacobsen, 'Only by the sword', p. 358.

52   *A Souvenir of the Return Voyage to Maoriland to Members of the N.Z.E.F. on the First Voyage of H.M.T. Kigoma*, Wellington, Fleet Printing Works, 1919, p. 11.

53   G.I.C. Eluwa, 'The National Congress of British West Africa: A study in African nationalism', *Présence Africaine*, Nouvelle Série, No, 77, 1971, pp. 131–49.

54   John Galsworthy, *The Forsyte Saga*, London, William Heinemann, 1950, p. 821.

SELECT BIBLIOGRAPHY

ARCHIVAL MATERIAL

Archives New Zealand/Te Rua Mahara o te Kāwanatanga, Wellington
James Allen Papers
Army Department, AD 1/700
Department of Imperial Government Supplies, W1708, 412 14 Ag. 11/130/4
National Efficiency Board, NEB 1/22

Australian War Memorial, Canberra
War Diary, Assistant Director Medical Services, 2nd Australian Division,
August 1918, AWM4, 26/19/32, Pt 1
George Pearce Papers, AWM38, 3DRL/6673/67 and 3DRL/2222

Bodleian Library, Oxford
Lewis Harcourt Papers

British Library, London
India Office Papers
IOR/L/MIL/7/18978
IOR/L/MIL/17/19/48

Canadian War Museum/Musée Canadien de la Guerre, Ottawa
Maurice Pope Papers, 58A 1 177, Folder 13

Cayzer Archives, London
Cayzer, Irvine & Co Weekly Report, CAY/BS/CLS/4

Churchill Archives Centre, Cambridge
CHAR 13/35/18
CHAR 13/43/60-63
CHAR 13/45/158

Imperial War Museum, London
Aitken, A.E., IWM.Docs.4678
Birdwood, William, WRB 1/9
Bray, Arthur G., IWM.Docs.653
Broome, R.H., IWM.Docs.7427
Gardiner, A.A., IWM.Docs.67/39/1
Hills, Annie, IWM.Docs.99/76/1
Meager, W.M., IWM.Docs.11172
Mole, Edgar, IWM.Docs.6881
Rowland, F.D., IWM.Docs.74/98/1
Turner, Charles, IWM.Docs.7754
Waters, G.G., IWM.Docs.13583
Wilson, Henry, HHW

J.S. Battye Library of West Australian History, Perth
Western Australian Branch Australian Labor Party Papers, AMN300,
ACC1688A

Library and Archives Canada/Bibliothèque et Archives Canada, Ottawa
Shell Committee Minutes, MG 27 II D 23, Vol. 3, File 6
233rd Battalion, RG 24, Vol. 4576, 3-35-1

Liddell Hart Centre for Military Archives, King's College, London
James Edmonds Papers, II/4/39
Ian Hamilton Papers, 8/1/29

National Archives of Australia, Canberra
A2, 1916/3598 Pt 1
A2023, B11/18/903
A2657, Vol. 2
A11803, 1914/89/79
A11803, 1917/89/881
A11803, 1918/89/663
A11803, 1918/89/935
B2455
MP84/1, 1856/1/33
MP598, 30

National Library of Australia, Canberra
Andrew Fisher Papers, MS2919
William Morris Hughes Papers, MS1538
George Pearce Papers, MS1927

National Maritime Museum, London
Argentine Cargo Line, FWS/C/1/4

The National Archives [of the United Kingdom], London

ADM 1/8507/273	MUN 4/42
ADM 53/40798	MUN 4/109
ADM 116/1520	MUN 4/413
ADM 137/3285	MUN 4/463
AIR 2/197	MUN 4/512
AY 4/1211	MUN 4/519
BT 13/60	MUN 4/636
BT 31/96942	MUN 4/2307
CAB 1/17	MUN 4/2905
CAB 1/23	MUN 4/5296
CAB 4/3	MUN 4/6726
CAB 45/27	MUN 5/6
CAB 11/165	MUN 5/176/1144/1
CO 273/415	MUN 9/27
CO 273/420	PRO 10/801
CO 323/709	PRO 10/802
CO 445/39	SUPP 5/333
CO 445/42	SUPP 5/1051
CO 445/47	T 102/16
CO 531/6	WO 32/5137
CO 537/1121	WO 32/5159
CO 583/17	WO 32/9559
CO 583/38	WO 95/4632
CO 583/45	WO 106/1412
CO 904/105	WO 107/46
DO 119/905	WO 141/7
ED 10/74	WO 141/62
HO 45/10896/364648	
MAF 60/108	
MAF 60/109	
MEPO 2/1684	
MT 9/1620	
MT 23/319	

[United Kingdom] Parliamentary Archives, London
J.C. Campbell Davidson Papers
David Lloyd George Papers

University of New South Wales Canberra Library
George McMunn Papers, MS21, Box 5, Folder 35

Wiltshire and Swindon History Centre, Chippenham
Walter Long Papers

NEWSPAPERS AND PERIODICALS

Aberdeen Journal
[Adelaide] *Sport*
[Auckland] *New Zealand Herald*
Auckland Star
[Bombay] *Times of India*
[Brisbane] *Telegraph*
[Calcutta] *Capital*
[Calcutta] *Hindoo Patriot*
[Chelmsford] *Essex County Chronicle*
Colac Herald
[Dublin] *Farmers' Gazette*
[Dublin] *Irish Builder and Engineer*
[Dublin] *Irish Industrial Journal*
[Dublin] *Irish Times*
[Dundee] *Courier and Argus*
[Hull] *Daily Mail*
[Johannesburg] *Illustrated Star*
Kalgoorlie Miner
[Kingston] *Daily Gleaner*
[Launceston] *Telegraph*
Limerick Leader
[London] *British Australasian*
[London] *Canadian Gazette*
[London] *Financial Times*
[London] *Tablet*
[London] *The Annual Register for 1917*
[London] *Times*
[London] *Windsor Magazine*
Madras Mail Tri-Weekly Supplement

Manuwatu Standard
Manuwatu Times
Marlborough Express
[Melbourne] *Argus*
[Melbourne] *Leader*
[Moose Jaw] *Morning News*
[Narrabri] *North Western Courier*
Newcastle [New South Wales] *Morning Herald and Miners' Advocate*
Northern Standard and Monaghan, Cavan and Tyrone Advertiser
[Perth] *Daily News*
[Perth] *West Australian*
[Singapore] *Straits Times*
Sligo Independent
[Sydney] *Australian Worker*
[Sydney] *Daily Commercial and Shipping List*
Sydney Morning Herald
[Toronto] *Globe*
[Waterford] *Evening News*
[Wellington] *Dominion*
[Wellington] *Evening Post*

PARLIAMENTARY DOCUMENTS AND PAPERS

[Australian] *Commonwealth Parliamentary Debates*

New Zealand Parliamentary Paper H-43, 'National Efficiency Board (Report Of)' [1917]

[United Kingdom] *Parliamentary Debates*

BOOKS

Adams, R.J.Q., & Poirier, Philip P., *The Conscription Controversy in Great Britain, 1900–18*, Basingstoke, Macmillan, 1987.
Aldous, Richard, & Puirséil, Niamh, (eds), *We Declare: Landmark Documents in Ireland's History*, London, Quercus Publishing, 2008.
Anderson, Ross, *The Forgotten Front 1914–1918: The East African Campaign*, Stroud, Tempus, 2007.
Andrews, Eric, *The Department of Defence*: Vol. 3 of John Coates & Peter Dennis (eds), *The Australian Centenary History of Defence*, Melbourne, Oxford University Press, 2001.

[Anonymous] *A Souvenir of the Return Voyage to Maoriland of Members of the N.Z.E.F. on the First Voyage of H.M.T. Kigoma*, Wellington, Fleet Printing Works, 1919.

Armstrong, John Griffith, *The Halifax Explosion and the Royal Canadian Navy: Inquiry and Intrigue*, Vancouver, UBC Press, 2002.

Baker, Paul, *King and Country Call: New Zealanders, Conscription and the Great War*, Auckland, Auckland University Press, 1988.

Barrie, Alexander, *War Underground: The Tunnellers of the Great War*, 1st pub. 1961, rep. London, Tom Donovan Publishing, 1990.

Bartlett, Thomas & Keith Jeffery (eds), *A Military History of Ireland*, Cambridge, Cambridge University Press, 1996.

Baynes, John, *Morale: A Study of Men and Courage. The Second Scottish Rifles at the Battle of Neuve Chapelle 1915*, London, Cassell, 1967.

Beach, Jim, *Haig's Intelligence: GHQ and the German Army, 1916–1918*, Cambridge, Cambridge University Press, 2013.

Bean, C.E.W., *The Story of ANZAC from the Outbreak of War to the End of the First Phase of the Gallipoli Campaign, May 4, 1915*, Vol. 1 of C.E.W. Bean (ed.), *The Official History of Australia in the War of 1914–1918*, Sydney, Angus & Robertson, 1st pub. 1921, 11th ed. 1941.

——, *The A.I.F. in France: 1916*, Vol. 3 of C.E.W. Bean (ed.), *The Official History of Australia in the War of 1914–1918*, Sydney, Angus & Robertson, 1st pub. 1929, 12th ed. 1941.

——, *The A.I.F. in France: 1917*, Vol. 4 of C.E.W. Bean (ed.), *The Official History of Australia in the War of 1914–1918*, Sydney, Angus & Robertson, 1st pub. 1933, 11th ed. 1941.

——, *The A.I.F. in France: December 1917–May 1918*, Vol. 5 of C.E.W. Bean (ed.), *The Official History of Australia in the War of 1914–1918*, Sydney, Angus & Robertson, 1st pub. 1937, 8th ed. 1941.

——, *The A.I.F. in France: May 1918–the Armistice*, Vol. 6 of C.E.W. Bean (ed.), *The Official History of Australia in the War of 1914–1918*, Sydney, Angus & Robertson, 1942.

Beaumont, Joan, *Broken Nation: Australia in the Great War*, Sydney, Allen & Unwin, 2013.

Beckett, Ian F.W. (ed.), *The Army and the Curragh Incident, 1914*, London, The Bodley Head, 1986.

——, *Ypres: The First Battle, 1914*, Harlow, Pearson Education, 2004.

——, *The Great War*, 2nd ed., Harlow, Pearson Longman, 2007.

—— (ed.), *1917: Beyond the Western Front*, Leiden, Brill, 2009.

Belich, James, *Replenishing the Earth: The Settler Revolution and the Rise of the Anglo-World, 1783–1939*, Oxford, Oxford University Press, 2011.

Bliss, Michael, *A Canadian Millionaire: The Life and Business of Sir Joseph Flavelle, Bart., 1858–1939*, Toronto, University of Toronto Press, 1992.

Boff, Jonathan, *Winning and Losing on the Western Front: The British Third Army and the Defeat of Germany in 1918*, Cambridge, Cambridge University Press, 2012.

Bourne, J.M., *Britain and the Great War 1914–1918*, London, Edward Arnold, 1989.

Bowker, Alan, *A Time Such as There Never Was Before: Canada After the Great War*, Toronto, Dundurn, 2014.

Bowman, Timothy, & Mark Connelly, *The Edwardian Army: Recruiting, Training, and Deploying the British Army 1902–1914*, Oxford, Oxford University Press, 2012.

Brugger, Suzanne, *Australians and Egypt 1914–1919*, Melbourne, Melbourne University Press, 1980.

Buchan, John, *The History of the South African Forces in France*, Cape Town, T. Maskew Miller, 1921.

Burton, Antoinette, *The Trouble with Empire: Challenges to Modern British Imperialism*, Oxford, Oxford University Press, 2015.

Carnegie, David, *The History of Munitions Supply in Canada*, London, Longmans, Green & Co., 1925.

Chickering, Roger, *Imperial Germany and the Great War, 1914–1918*, 3rd ed., Cambridge, Cambridge University Press, 2014.

Coates, John, *An Atlas of Australian Wars*: Vol. 7 of Peter Dennis & John Coates (eds), *The Australian Centenary History of Defence*, 2nd ed., Melbourne, Oxford University Press, 2006.

Connolly, S.J., *Oxford Companion to Irish History*, 2nd ed., Oxford, Oxford University Press, 2002.

Connor, John, *Anzac and Empire: George Foster Pearce and the Foundations of Australian Defence*, Melbourne, Cambridge University Press, 2011.

Connor, John, Stanley, Peter & Yule, Peter, *The War at Home*, Vol. 4 of Jeffrey Grey (ed.), *The Centenary History of Australia and the Great War*, Melbourne, Oxford University Press, 2015.

Cook, Tim, *Shock Troops: Canadians Fighting the Great War, 1917–1918*, Toronto, Viking Canada, 2008.

———, *The Madman and the Butcher: The Sensational Wars of Sam Hughes and General Arthur Currie*, Toronto, Allen Lane, 2010.

Corbett, Julian S., *Naval Operations*, Vol. 1: *To the Battle of the Falkands, December 1914. History of the Great War based on official documents by direction of the Historical Section of the Committee of Imperial Defence*, London, Longmans, Green & Co., 1920.

Davies, Norman, *Europe: A History*, London, Book Club Associates, 1996.

Dawes, J.N.I., & L.L. Robson, *Citizen to Soldier: Australia before the Great War: Recollections of Members of the First A.I.F.*, Melbourne, Melbourne University Press, 1977.

Day, David, *Andrew Fisher: Prime Minister of Australia*, Sydney, Fourth Estate, 2008.

Denman, Terence, *Ireland's Unknown Soldiers: The 16th (Irish) Division in the Great War, 1914–1918*, Dublin, Irish Academic Press, 1992.

Dooley, Thomas P., *Irishmen or English Soldiers? The Times and World of a Southern Catholic Irish Man (1876–1916) Enlisting in the British Army during the First World War*, Liverpool, Liverpool University Press, 1995.

Drew, H.T.B., *The War Effort of New Zealand: A Popular History of (a) Minor Campaigns in which New Zealanders Took Part; (b) Services Not Fully Dealt with in the Campaign Volumes; (c) The Work at the Bases*, Auckland, Whitcombe & Tombs, 1923.

Duguid, A. Fortescue, *Official History of the Canadian Forces in the Great War 1914–1919*, Vol. 1, Ottawa, J.O. Patenaude, Printer to the King's Most Excellent Majesty, 1938.

Duncan, Robert, *Pubs and Patriots: The Drink Crisis in Britain during World War One*, Liverpool, Liverpool University Press, 2013.

Dutton, David (ed.), *Paris 1918: The War Diary of the British Ambassador, the 17th Earl of Derby*, Liverpool, Liverpool University Press, 2001.

Dyrenfurth, Nick, *Heroes and Villians: The Rise and Fall of the Early Australian Labor Party*, Sydney, Fourth Estate, 2008.

Edmonds, James E., *Military Operations France and Belgium, 1915*, Vol. 2, London, Macmillan & Co, 1928

———, *Military Operations France and Belgium, 1918*, Vol. 4, London, His Majesty's Stationery Office, 1947.

———, *Military Operations France and Belgium, 1917*, Vol. 2, London, His Majesty's Stationery Office, 1948.

Edmonds, James E., & Wynne, G.C., *Military Operations, France and Belgium, 1915*, Vol. 1, London, Macmillan & Co, 1927.

The Elder Dempster Fleet in the War, Liverpool, Elder Dempster & Co Ltd, 1921.

Encyclopaedia Britannica, 11th edition, Cambridge, Cambridge University Press, 1911.

Erickson, Edward J., *Ordered to Die: A History of the Ottoman Army in the First World War*, Westport, Connecticut, Greenwood Press, 2001.

———, *Gallipoli and the Middle East 1914–1918: From the Dardanelles to Mesopotamia*, London, Amber Books, 2008.

Evatt, H.V., *Australian Labour Leader: The Story of W.A. Holman and the Labour Movement*, Sydney, Angus & Robertson, 1942.

Falls, Cyril, *The History of the 36th (Ulster) Division*, 1st pub. 1922, rep. London, Constable & Co, 1996.

Fayle, C. Ernest, *Seaborne Trade*: *History of the Great War based on official documents. By direction of the Historical Section of the Committee of Imperial*

Defence, Vol. 1, London, John Murray, 1920; Vol. 2, London, John Murray, 1923; Vol. 3, London, John Murray, 1924.

————, *The War and the Shipping Industry*, London, Oxford University Press, 1927.

Foster, Hubert, *War and the Empire: The Principles of Imperial Defence*, London, Williams & Norgate, 1914.

Fraser, Bryce (ed.), *The Macquarie Book of Events*, Sydney, Macquarie Library, 1983.

Galsworthy, John, *The Forsyte Saga*, London, William Heinemann, 1950.

Gilmour, David, *Curzon*, London, John Murray, 1994.

Government of India, *India's Contribution to the Great War*, Calcutta, Superintendent of Government Printing, 1923.

Graham, B.D., *The Formation of the Australian Country Parties*, Canberra, Australian National University Press, 1966.

Granatstein, J.L., & Hitsman, J.M., *Broken Promises: A History of Conscription in Canada*, Toronto, Oxford University Press, 1978.

Granatstein, J.L., & Olivier, Dean F. (eds), *The Oxford Companion to Canadian Military History*, Toronto, Oxford University Press, 2011.

Grayson, Richard S., *Belfast Boys: How Unionists and Nationalists Fought and Died Together in the First World War*, London, Continuum, 2009.

Greenhalgh, Elizabeth, *Victory through Coalition: Britain and France during the First World War*, Cambridge, Cambridge University Press, 2005.

————, *The French Army and the First World War*, Cambridge, Cambridge University Press, 2014.

Gregory, Adrian, *The Last Great War: British Society and the First World War*, Cambridge, Cambridge University Press, 2008.

Grey, Jeffrey, *The War with the Ottoman Empire*: Vol. 2. of Jeffrey Grey (ed.), *The Centenary History of Australia and the Great War*, Melbourne, Oxford University Press, 2014.

Gullett, H.S., *The Australian Imperial Force in Sinai and Palestine 1914–1918*, Vol. 7 of C.E.W. Bean (ed.), *The Official History of Australia in the War of 1914–1918*, 1st pub. 1923, 11th ed. Sydney, Angus & Robertson, 1941.

Halpern, Paul G., *A Naval History of World War I*, Annapolis, Maryland, Naval Institute Press, 1994.

Harris, J.P., *Douglas Haig and the First World War*, Cambridge, Cambridge University Press, 2008.

Hart, Peter, *The I.R.A. and its Enemies: Violence and Community in Cork, 1916–1923*, Oxford, Oxford University Press, 1999.

————, *The I.R.A. at War 1916–1923*, Oxford, Oxford University Press, 2005.

Haycock, Ronald G., *Sam Hughes: The Public Career of a Controversial Canadian, 1885–1916*, Wilfrid Laurier University Press in collaboration with Canadian War Museum, Canadian Museum of Civilization, National Museums of Canada, 1986.

Helmers, Marguerite, *Harry Clarke's War: Illustrations for Ireland's Memorial Records 1914–1918*, Sallins, Co. Kildare, Irish Academic Press, 2016.

Herwig, Holger H., *The Marne, 1914: The Opening of World War I and the Battle That Changed the World*, New York, Random House, 2009.

Holmes, Richard, *The Little Field Marshal: Sir John French*, London, Jonathan Cape, 1981.

Horsfall, Jack, & Cave, Nigel, *Cambrai: The Right Hook*, Barnsley, Leo Cooper, 1999.

Hurd, Archibald, *The Merchant Navy: History of the Great War based on official documents. By direction of the Historical Section of the Committee of Imperial Defence*, 3 Vols, London, John Murray, 1921–9.

Hyam, Ronald, *The Failure of South African Expansion 1908–1948*, London, Macmillan, 1972.

Iarocci, Andrew, *Shoestring Soldiers: The 1st Canadian Division at War, 1914–1915*, Toronto, University of Toronto Press, 2008.

Jarboe, Andrew Tait (ed.), *War News in India: The Punjabi Press During World War I*, London, I.B.Tauris, 2016.

Jeffery, Keith, *The British Army and the Crisis of Empire 1918–22*, Manchester, Manchester University Press, 1984.

———, *Field Marshal Sir Henry Wilson: A Political Soldier*, Oxford, Oxford University Press, 2006.

———, *1916: A Global History*, London, Bloomsbury, 2015.

Jones, Spencer (ed.), *Courage Without Glory: The British Army on the Western Front 1915*, Solihull, Helion, 2015.

Jose, A.W., *The Royal Australian Navy*, Vol. 9 of C.E.W. Bean (ed.), *The Official History of Australia in the War of 1914–1918*, Sydney, Angus & Robertson, 1st pub. 1928, 9th ed. 1941.

Kingston-McCloughry, E.J., *The Direction of War: A Critique of the Political Direction and High Command in War*, London, Jonathan Cape, 1955.

Kitchen, James E., *The British Imperial Army in the Middle East: Morale and Military Identity in the Sinai and Palestine Campaigns, 1916–18*, London, Bloomsbury, 2014.

Laffan, Michael, *The Resurrection of Ireland: The Sinn Féin Party 1916–1922*, Cambridge, Cambridge University Press, 1999.

Lalor, Brian (gen. ed.), *Encyclopaedia of Ireland*, Dublin, Gill & Macmillan, 2003.

Liddle, Peter, *Captured Memories 1900–1918: Across the Threshold of War*, Barnsley, Pen & Sword, 2010.

Louis, Wm. Roger, *Great Britain and Germany's Lost Colonies 1914–1919*, Oxford, Clarendon Press, 1967.

Lovett, Sir Verney, *India*, London, Waverley Book Company [1923].

Lucas, Charles (ed.), *The Empire at War*, 5 Vols, London, Oxford University Press, 1921–6.

McGibbon, Ian (ed.), *The Oxford Companion to New Zealand Military History*, Auckland, Oxford University Press, 2000.

McQuilton, John, *Rural Australia and the Great War: From Tarrawingee to Tangambalanga*, Melbourne, Melbourne University Press, 2001.

Marble, Sanders, *British Artillery on the Western Front in the First World War*, Farnham, Ashgate, 2013.

Marrot, H.V., *The Life and Letters of John Galsworthy*, London, William Heinemann, 1935.

Martin, A.W., *Robert Menzies: A Life*, Vol. 1, 2nd ed., Melbourne, Melbourne University Press, 1996.

Mercer, W.H., *Colonial Office List for 1914*, London, Waterlow & Sons, 1914.

Meynell, Viola (ed.), *Letters of J.M. Barrie*, London, Peter Davies, 1942.

Moberly, F.J., *The Campaign in Mesopotamia, 1914–1918*, London, His Majesty's Stationery Office, Vol. 1, 1923; Vol. 3, 1927.

Monger, David, *Patriotism and Propaganda in the First World War Britain: The National War Aims Committee and Civilian Morale*, Liverpool, Liverpool University Press, 2012.

Morris, A.J.A. (ed.), *The Letters of Lieutenant-Colonel Charles à Court Repington CMG: Military Correspondent of The Times, 1903–1918*, Stroud, Sutton Publishing, 1999.

Morton, Desmond, *A Peculiar Kind of Politics: Canada's Overseas Ministry in the First World War*, Toronto, University of Toronto Press, 1982.

Morton-Jack, George, *The Indian Army on the Western Front: India's Expeditionary Force to France and Belgium in the First World War*, Cambridge, Cambridge University Press, 2014.

Murfett, Malcolm M., Miksic, John N., Farrell, Brian P., & Chiang Ming Shun, *Between Two Oceans: A Military History of Singapore from 1275 to 1971*, 2nd ed., Singapore, Marshall Cavendish International, 2011.

Mwase, George Simeon, *Strike a Blow and Die: The Story of the Chilembwe Rising*, Cambridge, Massachusetts, Harvard University Press, 1975.

Nash, N.S., *Betrayal of an Army: Mesopotamia 1914–16*, Barnsley, Pen & Sword, 2016.

Nasson, Bill, *Springboks on the Somme: South Africa in the Great War 1914–1918*, Johannesburg, Penguin, 2007.

Neiberg, Michael S., *The Second Battle of the Marne*, Bloomington & Indianapolis, Indiana University Press, 2008.

O'Faolain, Sean, *Vive Moi! An Autobiography*, London, Hart-Davis, 1965.

Offer, Avner, *The First World War: An Agrarian Interpretation*, Oxford, Clarendon Press, 1989.

Osuntokun, Akinjide, *Nigeria in the First World War*, London, Longman, 1979.

Overlack, Peter, 'The force of circumstance: Graf Spee's options for the Cruiser Squadron in August 1914', *Journal of Military History*, Vol. 60, No. 4, October 1996, pp. 657–82

Parkman, Francis, *Montcalm and Wolfe*, Vol. 2, London, Macmillan & Co., 1884.

Pašeta, Senia, *Irish Nationalist Women, 1900–1918*, Cambridge, Cambridge University Press, 2013.

Pearce, Donald R., *The Senate Speeches of W.B. Yeats*, London, Faber & Faber, 1961.

Perham, Margery, *Lugard: The Years of Authority 1898–1945*, London, Collins, 1960.

Perry, Nicholas (ed.), *Major General Oliver Nugent and the Ulster Division 1915–1918*, Stroud, Sutton Publishing, 2007.

Philpott, William, *Bloody Victory: The Sacrifice on the Somme*, London, Abacus, 2010.

Pope-Hennessy, James, *Queen Mary, 1867–1953*, London, George Allen & Unwin, 1959.

Prete, Roy A., *Strategy and Command: The Anglo-French Coalition on the Western Front, 1914*, Montreal & Kingston, McGill-Queen's University Press, 2009.

Prior, Robin, & Wilson, Trevor, *The Somme*, 2nd ed., Sydney, NewSouth Publishing, 2016.

Rao, C. Hayavadana, *The Indian Biographical Dictionary 1915*, Madras, Pillar & Co. Publishers & Booksellers, 1915.

Robson, Brian, *Crisis on the Frontier: The Third Afghan War and the Campaign in Waziristan 1919–1920*, Stroud, Spellmount, 2007.

Rose, Kenneth, *King George V*, London, Phoenix Press, 1983.

Salter, J.A., *Allied Shipping Control: An Experiment in International Administration*, London, Oxford University Press, 1921.

Scott, Ernest, *Australia during the War*, Vol. 11 of C.E.W. Bean (ed.) *Official History of Australia in the War of 1914–1918*, first pub. 1936, Sydney, Angus & Robertson, 7th ed., 1941.

Sheehan, William (ed.), *British Voices from the Irish War of Independence 1918–1921: The Words of British Servicemen who were There*, Wilton, Co. Cork, Collins Press, 2005.

Sheffield, Gary, & Bourne, John (eds), *Douglas Haig: War Diaries and Letters*, London, Weidenfeld & Nicolson, 2005.

———, *The Chief: Douglas Haig and the British Army*, London, Aurum Press, 2011.

Sheldon, Jack, *The German Army on Vimy Ridge 1914–1917*, Barnsley, Pen & Sword Military, 2008.

———, *The German Army at Cambrai*, Barnsley, Pen & Sword, 2009.

———, *The German Army on the Western Front 1915*, Barnsley, Pen & Sword, 2012.

Singh, Gajendra, *The Anatomy of Dissent in the Military of Colonial India During the First and Second World Wars*, Edinburgh Papers in South Asian Studies, No. 20, 2006, pp. 1–45.

Skelton, Tim, & Gerald Gliddon, *Lutyens and the Great War*, London, Frances Lincoln, 2008.

Sluggett, Peter, *Britain in Iraq: Contriving King and Country*, 1st pub. 1976, rep. London, I.B. Tauris, 2007.

Smith, Richard, *Jamaican Volunteers in the First World War: Race, Masculinity and the Development of National Consciousness*, Manchester, Manchester University Press, 2004.

Spears, E.L., *Liaison, 1914: A Narrative of the Great Retreat*, London, William Heinemann, 1930.

Stanley Gibbons Ltd, *Stanley Gibbons' Postage Stamp Catalogue 1952*, Part 1: *British Empire (Complete)*, London, Stanley Gibbons, 1952.

Stapleton, Timothy J., *A Military History of South Africa: From the Dutch–Khoi Wars to the End of Apartheid*, Santa Barbara, California, Praeger, 2010.

———, *A Military History of Africa*. Vol. 2, *The Colonial Period: From the Scramble for Africa to the Algerian Independence War*, Santa Barbara, California, Praeger, 2013.

Stevens, David, *In All Respects Ready: Australia's Navy in World War One*, Melbourne, Oxford University Press, 2014.

Stevenson, David, *1914–1918: The History of the First World War*, London, Allen Lane, 2004.

Stevenson, Robert, *The War with Germany*: Vol. 3 of Jeffrey Grey (ed.), *The Centenary History of Australia and the Great War*, Melbourne, Oxford University Press, 2015.

Stewart, Hugh, *The New Zealand Division 1916–1919: A Popular History Based on Official Records*, Auckland, Whitcombe & Tombs Ltd, 1921.

Strong, Paul, & Marble, Sanders, *Artillery in the Great War*, Barnsley, Pen & Sword, 2011.

Tampke, Jürgen (trans. & ed.), *'Ruthless Warfare': German Military Planning and Surveillance in the Australia–New Zealand Region before the Great War*, Canberra, Southern Highlands Publishers, 1998.

Turner, Ian, *Industrial Labour and Politics: The Dynamics of the Labour Movement in Eastern Australia, 1900–1921*, Cambridge, Cambridge University Press, 1965.

Ulrichsen, Kristian Coates, *The Logistics and Politics of the British Campaigns in the Middle East, 1914–22*, London, Palgrave Macmillan, 2010.

[United Kingdom] Ministry of Munitions, *History of the Ministry of Munitions*, London, His Majesty's Stationery Office, 12 vols, 1918–22.

[United Kingdom] War Office, *Statistics of the Military Effort of the British Empire during the Great War 1914–1920*, 1st pub. 1922, rep. Uckfield, Naval & Military Press, 1999.

Uyar, Mesut, *The Ottoman Defence against the Anzac Landings 25 April 1915. Australian Army Campaigns Series 16*, Sydney, Big Sky Publishing, 2015.

van der Vat, Dan, *The Last Corsair: The Story of the* Emden, London, Hodder & Stoughton, 1983.

van der Waag, Ian, *A Military History of Modern South Africa*, Jeppestown, Jonathan Ball Publishers, 2015.

Watson, Alexander, *Enduring the Great War: Combat, Morale and Collapse in the German and British Armies, 1914–1918*, Cambridge, Cambridge University Press, 2014.

———, *Ring of Steel: Germany and Austria–Hungary at War, 1914–1918*, London, Penguin, 2015.

Weller, Patrick (ed.), *Caucus Minutes, 1901–1949: Minutes of the Meetings of the Federal Parliamentary Labor Party*, Vol. 1, Melbourne, Melbourne University Press, 1975.

Wilson, Trevor, *The Myriad Faces of War*, Cambridge, Polity Press, 1986.

Winegard, Timothy C., *Indigenous Peoples of the British Dominions and the First World War*, Cambridge, Cambridge University Press, 2012.

Wood, James, *Militia Myths: Ideas of the Canadian Citizen Soldier, 1896–1921*, Vancouver, University of British Columbia Press, 2010.

Woollacott, Angela, *On Her Their Lives Depend: Munitions Workers in the Great War*, Berkeley & Los Angeles, University of California Press, 1994.

Wray, Christopher, *Sir James Whiteside MacCay: A Turbulent Life*, Melbourne, Oxford University Press, 2002.

INDEX

Achimota College, Accra, 247
Afghan War 1919, 244–5
agrarian political parties, 228, 230, 233–4
agriculture, importance of, 227–8
  horses & tractors, 236–7
  UK 1916 potato harvest, 236
  UK Corn Production Act, 235
Ah Yee, 47
alcohol, 84–6
Amiens, Battle of, 201–15
Amritsar massacre, 244
An Túr Gloine, 37
Anderson, Sir John, 32
Argentine Cargo Line, 38
Arklow explosion, 108
Arras, Battle of, 166
artillery
  British, 65, 74, 168, 214
  French, 210
  German, 57, 203–4
Ascension Island, 3
Asquith, Herbert, 7, 41, 75
Association of Native Merchants (Nigeria), 36

Aubers Ridge, Battle of, 67–9
Australia, 2
  Australian Wheat Board, 229–30
  drought, 229
  preferential voting, 231–3
  UK buys entire wheat crop, 229
  UK buys entire wool clip, 230
Australian Imperial Force (AIF), 25, 60, 181
  Australian Corps, 212
  Divisions
    4th Division, 208
    5th Division, 161, 208
  Battalions
    57th Battalion, 208
    60th Battalion, 208
  death penalty not imposed, 147–9
Australian Labor Party
  1916 referendum, 190
  1917 referendum, 191–3
  1918 negotiated peace, 152–3
  splits over conscription, 152, 189
Austria–Hungary, 7–8, 225

Baroda, Gaekwar of, 6

Barrie, J.M., 86
Bean, Charles, 213
Below, General Otto von, 203
Bethmann Hollweg, Theobold von, 59
Bilsborough, Ethel, 151
Birch, George, 97–102
blockade, 31, 45–9
Bombay (Mumbai), 15
Bonar Law, Andrew, 1, 35, 41, 43, 178
Bongo revolt, Gold Coast (Ghana) 1916, 2
Borden, Robert, 24, 82, 233
Botha, Louis, 132, 228
Bray, Arthur, 17–18
Brest-Litovsk, Treaty of, 203
Britain
    blockade on Germany, 31
    coalition government, 75
    declares war on Germany, 8
    popular mobilisation, 1915, 83–4
    rationing, 49–52
    relies on imported food, 29–30
    strikes, 241–2
British Army, 53–78
    Armies
        First Army, 60
        Second Army, 60
        Third Army, 215
    Corps
        I Corps, 67, 71
        II Corps, 55
        III Corps, 213–215
        IV Corps, 65, 67
        XXII Corps, 215
        Tank Corps, 214
    Divisions
        2nd Division, 71–2
        7th Division, 64–5, 71–2, 77–8
        8th Division, 53, 64–5
        9th (Scottish) Division, 60, 77–8

10th (Irish) Division, 161
12th (Eastern) Division, 78
14th (Light) Division, 163
16th (Irish) Division, 162, 169, 205–6
17th (Northern) Division, 60
36th (Ulster) Division, 155, 160, 205–6
46th (North Midland) Division, 60, 77, 159, 217
47th (1/2nd London) Division, 163
51st (Highland) Division, 70
56th (1st London) Division, 159
    Brigades
        23rd Brigade, 53
        25th Brigade, 53
        5th Tank Brigade, 212
    Battalions
        2nd Battalion, Cameronians, 63–4
        1/7th Battalion, King's Liverpool Regiment, 73
        2nd Battalion, Rifle Brigade, 69
        1st Battalion, Royal Dublin Fusiliers, 9
        1st Battalion, Royal Irish Rifles, 69
        1/13th London Regiment (Kensington Battalion), 69
British Empire
    casualties, 1, 66
    enlistment, 177
    population 1911, 1
    recruiting non-white troops, 1, 177
British merchant navy, 29
British North Borneo, 31–2
British West Indies Regiment, 186–7, 202
Bruchmüller, Colonel Georg, 204
Brusilov, General Aleksei, 156

Bucharest, Treaty of, 203
Bulgaria, 156, 225
Butler, Lieutenant General Sir
    Richard, 214
Byng, General Sir Julian, 215

Calcutta (Kolkata), 12
Callwell, Charles, 60–1
Cambrai, Battle of, 174–5, 204
Canada
    economic slowdown 1914, 80
    munitions production, 106–7
    political corruption, 80–2
    strikes, 143–5
Canadian Expeditionary Force
    (CEF), 24
    Hughes refuses to appoint senior
    French Canadian officers, 179
    Canadian Corps, 202
    Divisions
        1st Canadian Division, 60, 72
    Battalions
        Princess Patricia's Canadian
        Light Infantry, 179–80
Caporetto, Battle of, 203
Capper, Major General Sir
    Thompson, 77–8
Carney, Winifred, 241
Casement, Sir Roger, 140–1
censorship, 150
Ceylon (Sri Lanka), 11
children
    collecting horse chestnuts, 50–1
    picking fruit, 51–2
Chilembwe, John, 134–6
Chilwell explosion, 109
Chinese sailors, 21, 26, 29
Chinese workers, 31
chlorine gas, 60, 77
Churchill, Winston, 5, 25, 28, 242
Clark, Harry, 37
Clarke, Kathleen, 241

Clemenceau, President Georges,
    212
Cocos Islands, 26
Collins, Michael, 141
Comerford, Máire, 241
Commonwealth Shipping Line, 41
Congress Party, 244
Connaught, Duke of, 37
Conrad von Hötzendorf, General
    Franz, 7
conscription
    Australia opposes, 188–93
    Britain, 176, 182–3
    Canada, 196–9, 233
    Ireland opposes, 198–9
    Jamaica, 187
    New Zealand, 183–5
    New Zealand tortures
    conscientious objectors, 186
    Nigeria opposes, 196
    South African Native Labour
    Corps coerced to enlist, 194
conscientious objectors, 141–3,
    184–6
convoys, 24–7, 48–9
Cook Islands, 3
Country Party (Australia), 228
Courage, Brigadier General
    Anthony, 212–13
Crewe, Charles, 125
'crisis of Empire' 1918–1921, 241–7
Currie, General Arthur, 214

Damascus, 225
Das, Hemchandra Kanungo, 11
Debeney, General Marie-Eugene,
    213
Delbrück, Hans, 206
Dennett, R.E., 33–5
Derby, Lord, 226
De Valera, Éamon, 141
Deventer, General Jacob van, 127

Devonport, Lord, 49, 236
Devonshire, Duke of, 198
De Wet, General Christian, 133–4
Diego Garcia, 19–21, 26
Dissent, 131–53
Dobro Pole, Battle of, 225
Dominions, 4
Dondra Head, Ceylon (Sri Lanka), 16
Du Cane, General Sir John, 61
Durbar 1911, 6
Dyer, Colonel Reginald, 244

East African campaign, 113–30
Easter Rising, 139–41
Edmonds, James, 66
Egyptian Expeditionary Force, 218
    Indianisation, 221
Egyptian Labour Corps, 218–19
Egyptian Revolt, 245–66
El Argentino, 47
Elder Dempster, 35–6, 49
Elles, General Sir Hugh, 214
Emden, SMS
    affects British prestige, 11, 15
    attacks Cocos Islands, 22–3
    attacks Madras (Chennai), 9
    attacks Penang, 21
    captures ships, 16–23
    economic effects, 11–12, 23
    employs Chinese sailors, 21
    HMAS *Sydney* battle, 26–7
    living conditions, 20
Empress of Asia, 24, 26, 220
Estabrooks, Sergeant Walter, 228
explosions, 107–10

Falkenhayn, General Erich von, 57, 59,
    sacked 1916, 158
    commands Yildirim Army Group 1918, 219

Falklands Islands, Battle of, 15
farmer protests
    Australia, 231
    Canada, 233
female munition workers, 86–9, 93–4
Festubert, Battle of, 70–3
Flavelle, Joseph, 106, 143
Fletcher, Major Alan, 77
Foch, Marshal Ferdinand, 207–9, 211
Food Control, Ministry of, 49–52, 236
food shortages, 31–2, 44–5, 49–52, 187, 229–30, 236, 245
Foster, Colonel Hubert, 19
Franz Ferdinand assassinated 1914, 7
French, Field Marshal Sir John, 55–7, 76–8
French Army
    African troops, 60
    'collective indiscipline', 165
    Armies
        First Army, 213
        Fourth Army, 210
        Fifth Army, 210
        Sixth Army, 57, 210
        Ninth Army, 210
        Tenth Army, 210
    Corps
        XXXI Corps, 213
    Divisions
        45th Algerian Division, 56
        Division Morocaine, 209
Fynch, Sergeant Roy, 208

Galsworthy, John, 8, 210, 247
Gandhi, Mohandas Karamchand, 244
Gaza, Battles of, 219
Geddes, Wilhelmina, 37
George V, King, 2, 6, 28
    abstains from alcohol, 84

changes name to Windsor, 150
call for volunteers, 178
German Army
Armies
First Army, 55–7, 209
Second Army, 57, 207–8
Third Army, 209
Fourth Army, 58
Fifth Army, 157
Sixth Army, 58
Seventh Army, 209
Seventeenth Army, 203
Eighteenth Army, 204
Corps
IX Corps, 44
German colonies, 113–30
German East Africa, 118–30
Belgians invade Ruanda (Rwanda), 127
East and West Africans' campaign, 125–30
Indian landing at Tanga, 118–21
South African campaign, 121–5
German Navy, 13–14, 41–2
Germany
British relations with, 4–5
colonies, 13
five German strategies:
Falkenhayn Russia, 1915, 67
Falkenhayn Verdun 1916, 156–8
Hindenburg & Ludendorff, U-boats 1917, 45–9
Hindenburg & Ludendorff, March offensive 1918, 205–10
Moltke France 1914, 55–7
Gibbs, Philip, 4
Godley, General Sir Alexander, 173, 215
Gold Coast (Ghana), 2, 131
roads for cocoa export, 228–9
Gorlice–Tarnow, Battle of, 67
Gough, General Sir Hubert, 161

Grant, Captain Henry, 23
Grey, Sir Edward, 4–5, 32, 226
Griffiths, John Norton, 166–8
Gumbinnen, Battle of, 56

Haig, General Sir Douglas, 60, 66, 78, 213
Halifax, Nova Scotia, explosion, 109–10
Hamel, Battle of, 211–13
Hamilton, Ontario strike, 143–5
Harcourt, Lord, Colonial Secretary, 32, 179
Hardinge, Lord, Viceroy of India, 13
Healy, Captain Maurice, 200
Hills, Nurse Annie, 125
Hindenburg, Field Marshal Paul von, 158
Hindenburg Line, 165, 216–17
Holmes, Major General William, 173
Hoyos, Alexander, 7
Hughes, Colonel Sam, 80–3
Hughes, William Morris, 188–93
Hussein, Sharif of Mecca, 218
Hutier, General Oskar von, 203

Imperial Conference 1911, 4
Imperial Munitions Board (Canada), 106–7
India, 2, 11–13
Indian Army, 6, 44, 75–6, 177
Indian Corps, 65, 67
Divisions
Lahore, 58, 72
Meerut, 53, 68, 71
Brigades
Garwhal, 53
Jullundur, 71
Secunderabad, 58
Sirhind, 72

Battalions
  15th Ludhiana Sikhs, 64, 72
  39th Garhwal Rifles, 71
Indian Munitions Board, 96
Ireland, 7, 89–94, 108
  agriculture, 236–40
  Cumann na mBan, 240–1
  Irish Citizen Army, 139–41
  Irish Civil War, 243
  Irish Free State, 243
  Irish Republican Army, 242–3
  Irish Republican Brotherhood,
    139
  Irish Volunteers, 139
  Irish War of Independence, 242–3
  Island of Ireland Peace Park,
    Mesen, 170
  1918 election, 239–41
  Royal Irish Constabulary, 242–3
  Ulster Women's Unionist Council,
    240
Islington, Lord, Colonial Under-
  Secretary, 33
Italian Army, 191, 210

Jamaica encourages returned soldiers
  to leave island, 187
Jeffery, Keith, 7
Jensen, John, 110–12
Jerusalem, 219–20
Joffre, General Joseph, 156
Jute, 12–13, 28

Kamerun, 115–16
Kavanagh, General Sir Charles, 214
Kemal, General Mustafa, 224
Kettle, Lieutenant Tom, 162
King's African Rifles, 126–30
Kitchener, Field Marshal Lord, 55,
  80
Königsberg, SMS, 23, 121

La Blanca, 47–8
Lanrezac, General Charles, 55
Lettow-Vorbeck, General Paul von,
  127–9
Lewisham, south-east London, 151
Lindsay, Ontario, 80–1
Liverpool, Lord, 228
Lloyd George, David, 5, 31, 80, 155
Long, Walter, 76–8, 114, 198–200,
  236
Loos, Battle of, 75
Lorenço Marques (Maputo), 130
Ludendorff, Quartermaster General
  Erich, 158, 203–4
Lusitania, 83
'*Lusitania* riots', 1915, 83–4

Maclay, Sir Joseph, 43
MacMunn, George, 7
Madras (Chennai), 9–11
Mangin, General Charles, 209
Mannix, Archbishop Daniel, 6
Markievicz, Constance, 141, 241
Markomannia, 14, 16, 19
Marne, First Battle of, 57
Marne, Second Battle of, 210
'martial race theory', 7
Marwanis, 11–12
Massey, William, 228
McCay, Major General Sir James, 161
McCloughry, Lieutenant Edgar, 161
Meager, W.M., 21–2
Megiddo, Battle of, 201–2, 224
Melland, Miss F., 149–50
Mendi, 194
Mesopotamia campaign, 96–7
Mesopotamia revolt, 246
Messines (Mesen), Battle of, 154–6,
  166–73
mines, 155, 169
Minikoi (Minicoy) Island, 16

Ministry of Shipping, 42–4
Mole, Gunner Edgar, 26–7
Moltke, General Helmuth von, 56–7
Monash, General Sir John, 212, 214
Monro, Lieutenant General Sir
    Charles, 61, 71
Mons, Battle of, 55–6
Montagu, Edwin, 224, 244
Montagu-Stuart-Wortley, Major
    General Edward, 160
Montgomery, Major Bernard, 243
Moose Jaw, 81
Morlancourt, Battle of, 211
Morocco crises, 5
Mousquet, 22
Müller, Captain Karl von, 9–10
munition production, 79–80
    Australia, 84, 102–5
    Britain, 86–9
    Canada, 80–3, 106–7
    India, 84, 94–7
    Ireland, 89–94
    New Zealand, 97–102
Munitions, Ministry of, 83, 85–6
Murray, General Archibald, 218
mutinies
    Singapore, 137–8
    Taranto, 187

National Congress of British West
    Africa, 247
National War Aims Committee,
    150–2
negotiated peace proposals 1917,
    132, 145–7
Neuve Chapelle, Battle of, 61–6
New Zealand, 97–102
    Imperial Government Supplies,
        Department of, 227–8
New Zealand Expeditionary Force
    (NZEF), 24, 163, 184–6
    2nd Auckland Battalion, 163

2nd Otago Battalion, 163
2nd, 3rd & 4th Battalions, New
    Zealand Rifle Brigade, 163
New Zealand Division, 163
Nigeria, 33–6, 196
Nigeria Regiment, 128–9
Niue, 2
Nivelle, General Robert, 165
Norddeutscher Lloyd, 31
Nugent, Major General Oliver
    expects German attack, 204
    meets Haig on Somme, 165
Nürnberg, SMS, 23

Orme, Drummer Alfred, 73
Ottoman Empire, 202, 218
    Armenian genocide, 218
    attacks Suez Canal, 218
    Gallipoli campaign, 218

palm kernels, 33–6
Paris bombarded by German long-
    range artillery, 209
Parsons, Lieutenant General Sir
    Lawrence, 161
Patiala, Maharaja of, 221
Pearce, Senator George, 102–5
Pearse, Patrick, 139–41
Pershing, 211
Pétain, General Phillipe, 157–8
Plumer, General Sir Herbert, 155,
    169
Poincaré, President Raymond, 8
Pope, Joseph, 24
Progressive Party (Canada), 228
Purser, Sarah, 37

rabbits, 228
Rahman, Havildar Abdul, 73
Rangoon (Yangon), 11
rationing
    Britain, 49–52

British North Borneo, 31–2
Jamaica, 44
Rawlinson, General Sir Henry, 61,
    214
revolts
    Gold Coast (Ghana), 2
    Ireland,
    Nyasaland, 134–6
    South Africa, 132–4
Rhondda, Lord, 50
Riga, Battle of, 204
Robinson, Sir Thomas, 38–9
Romania, 158, 203
Royal Australian Navy
    escorting troopships 1914, 25
Royal Navy
    escorting troopships 1914, 15
Russell, George (Æ), 200
Russia, 156

Sabang, 22
Savarkar, Vinayak Damodar, 11
Schlieffen Plan 1914, 8
Scott, Kathleen, 86
Serbia, 8, 67
Seychelles, 44–5
'shell crisis', 74–5, 83–4
shipping, 31–52
Shipping, Ministry of, 42–4
Singapore, 3–4
Singapore mutiny, 137–8
Sinn Féin, 141, 228
Smith, Sergeant Ernest, 247
Smith-Dorrien, General Sir Horace,
    60
Smuts, General Jan, 123–5, 127, 242
Somme, Battle of,
    Flers-Courcelette, 162–3
    French advance further than
        British, 159
    Fromelles, 161
    Ginchy, 162

Gommencourt, Battle of, 159–60
    Thiepval, 160
South Africa, 108, 194–5
    fails to gain Lorenço Marques,
        130
South Wales coal, 18–21
South West Africa, 116–18
Spee, Admiral Maximilian von,
    13–15
stained glass, 36–7
Straits Settlements, 3
strikes, 2, 131, 143–5, 151, 199
sugar, 30
sub-imperialism, 113–14
    Australia, 113
    India, 113
    Newfoundland, 114
    New Zealand, 113
    South Africa, 114
Sydney, HMAS, 26–8

tanks, 162–3, 174–5, 212, 214–15
Tata, Sir Dorabji, 95
Thesiger, Major General George, 78
Togoland, 114–15
Transkei women boycott 1917, 131
trenches, 59,

U-boats, 41–2, 45–9
Umbogintwini, Natal explosions, 108
United Farmers of Canada, 228
United States Army, 210
Urdu language school, Marseilles, 60

venereal disease, 132
Verdun, Battle of, 157–8
Villers-Bretonneux, Battle of, 208–9

'war weariness', 149–52
Waterford National Cartridge
    Factory, 90, 110–12

Wilhelm II, Kaiser, 7
  Germany abolishes monarchy, 226
  orders champagne in expectation
    of victory 1918, 206
Wilhelm, Crown Prince, 157, 211
Willcocks, General Sir James, 61
Wilson, Field Marshal Sir Henry,
  5, 55
Wing, Major General Frederick, 78
Woermann Linie, 35
Woolwich, south-east London, 84–5

Yarmouth, HMS, 19
Yeats, William Butler, 36–7

Ypres, First Battle of (1914), 57–9
Ypres, Second Battle of (1915), 60
Ypres, Third Battle of (1917), 166,
  173–4

Zaghlul, Saad, 245
Zhemchug, 21